John Lancaster Spalding

The life of the Most Rev. M.J. Spalding, D.D., archbishop of Baltimore

John Lancaster Spalding

The life of the Most Rev. M.J. Spalding, D.D., archbishop of Baltimore

ISBN/EAN: 9783741139871

Manufactured in Europe, USA, Canada, Australia, Japa

Cover: Foto ©Thomas Meinert / pixelio.de

Manufactured and distributed by brebook publishing software (www.brebook.com)

John Lancaster Spalding

The life of the Most Rev. M.J. Spalding, D.D., archbishop of Baltimore

THE LIFE

OF THE

MOST REV. M. J. SPALDING, D.D.

ARCHBISHOP OF BALTIMORE.

BY

J. L. SPALDING, S.T.L.

"Romæ nutriri mihi contigit atque doceri."
                                              HORACE.

NEW YORK:
THE CATHOLIC PUBLICATION SOCIETY,
No. 9 WARREN STREET.
BALTIMORE: JOHN MURPHY & CO.

1873.

PREFACE.

ARCHBISHOP SPALDING left his papers and letters to the Very Rev. I. T. Hecker, that he might make whatever use of them he should think proper.

Those to whom the task of writing this life might have been entrusted, with the confident hope that it would be well performed, were not at leisure; and I was chosen, less from the conviction that I was fitted for the work than from the belief that what I lacked in ability might in some measure be supplied by zeal and industry.

Though to others this choice may be matter for regret, in my mind it will ever remain associated with the pleasant memories of the happy days which I spent in the society of the Fathers of the Congregation of St. Paul, whilst engaged in this work.

Even to have failed is, possibly, not wholly without honor.

Success in biographical writing, under the most favorable circumstances, is rare.

The difficulty is increased when the subject of biography is but recently dead.

Time, the approver, which destroys false and factitious reputations, is alone able to bring out in all their worth and loveliness those which are founded in merit.

Then, the surroundings of a man's life are like the frame to the picture and the light in which it is seen.

Only time can give this setting and mellow down the light.

No life with which we are perfectly familiar can be wholly beautiful.

Omne ignotum pro magnifico est, is the phrase of the Roman historian.

It is this unknown that is wanting in biography which deals with the lives of men whom we have seen face to face and touched with our hands.

The life of a priest, too, in ordinary times, is necessarily uneventful.

There are no "battles, sieges, fortunes"; "disastrous chances, moving accidents by flood and field, hair-breadth 'scapes i' th' imminent, deadly breach," to be told of; and though

> "The drying up a single tear has more
> Of honest fame than shedding seas of gore,"

men now, as in ages past, will make heroes of the successful butchers of the race, whilst its benefactors are forgotten.

"The inventor of a spinning-jenny," says Carlyle, "is pretty sure of his reward in his own day; but the writer of a true poem, like the apostle of a true religion, is nearly as sure of the contrary."

On the other hand, there are persons who will find matter for wholesome thought in the history of a man whose record is without stain, whose purposes were benevolent, and all of whose aims were to strengthen faith in those doctrines without which human nature has but a material and animal value, and life no sacredness. The sympathy which I could not but feel with the subject of my work I cannot look upon as an obstacle to its right performance. As sympathy is one of the chief agencies in developing the nobler and better qualities of human nature, it also gives the truest insight into character.

What my partiality may have caused me to see in a light too favorable will receive a more correct coloring from the calmer judgment of my readers—*At mihi nunc narraturo vitam defuncti hominis, venia opus fuit.*

CONTENTS.

	PAGE
CHAPTER I.	
ANCESTRY—PARENTAGE—BIRTH—EARLY EDUCATION,	11
CHAPTER II.	
PROFESSOR AT ST. MARY'S COLLEGE—ENTERS THE SEMINARY AT BARDSTOWN—IS SENT TO ROME,	23
CHAPTER III.	
STUDENT LIFE IN ROME,	36
CHAPTER IV.	
LAST YEAR IN ROME—PUBLIC DEFENCE OF THESES FOR THE DOCTOR'S CAP,	48
CHAPTER V.	
ORDAINED PRIEST—RETURNS HOME—IS MADE PASTOR OF THE CATHEDRAL IN BARDSTOWN—PROFESSOR IN THE SEMINARY—THE "MINERVA,"	61
CHAPTER VI.	
THE "CATHOLIC ADVOCATE"—RELIGIOUS JOURNALISM—EFFORTS TO EXTEND ITS INFLUENCE,	71
CHAPTER VII.	
PRESIDENT OF ST. JOSEPH'S COLLEGE—PASTOR OF ST. PETER'S CHURCH, IN LEXINGTON—DIOCESE OF NASHVILLE,	83
CHAPTER VIII.	
DR. SPALDING IS APPOINTED VICAR-GENERAL — THE LOUISVILLE "LEAGUE"—HIS LABORS AS A LECTURER AND PREACHER,	95
CHAPTER IX.	
POPULAR OBJECTIONS TO THE CHURCH—DR. SPALDING'S MANNER OF ANSWERING THEM,	106

CHAPTER X.

APPOINTED BISHOP OF LENGONE, IN PART. INFID., AND COADJUTOR OF BISHOP FLAGET—DEATH OF BISHOP FLAGET—STATE OF THE DIOCESE AT THE TIME OF DR. SPALDING'S CONSECRATION, . . . 118

CHAPTER XI.

STATE OF THE DIOCESE, CONTINUED—BISHOP SPALDING'S FIRST VISITATION—THE EARLY CATHOLICS OF KENTUCKY, ... 131

CHAPTER XII.

RETREAT OF THE CLERGY—BUILDING OF THE CATHEDRAL IN LOUISVILLE—DIVISION OF THE DIOCESE—THE FIRST PLENARY COUNCIL OF BALTIMORE—DESIRE TO SECURE THE SERVICES OF A TEACHING BROTHERHOOD, ... 144

CHAPTER XIII.

VISIT TO EUROPE—THE XAVERIAN BROTHERS—THE AMERICAN COLLEGE AT LOUVAIN, ... 158

CHAPTER XIV.

RELIGION AND NATIONALISM—THE KNOW-NOTHING CONSPIRACY—"BLOODY MONDAY," 174

CHAPTER XV.

THE "MISCELLANEA"—CONTROVERSY WITH PROFESSOR MORSE, . . 188

CHAPTER XVI.

THE PROVINCIAL COUNCILS OF CINCINNATI—THE COMMON-SCHOOL SYSTEM, ... 200

CHAPTER XVII.

DIOCESAN AFFAIRS—TRAITS OF CHARACTER—CORRESPONDENCE WITH ARCHBISHOP KENRICK, ... 216

CHAPTER XVIII.

HISTORY OF THE REFORMATION—VIEWS ON THE DUTIES OF ECCLESIASTICS IN THEIR RELATIONS WITH THE STATE—EPISCOPAL LABORS, 230

CHAPTER XIX.

THE CIVIL WAR AND THE CHURCH IN KENTUCKY—STATE OF THE DIOCESE OF LOUISVILLE—BISHOP SPALDING IS APPOINTED TO THE SEE OF BALTIMORE, ... 244

Contents.

CHAPTER XX.

ARCHBISHOP SPALDING TAKES POSSESSION OF HIS NEW CHARGE—SUMMARY OF IMPORTANT FACTS IN THE HISTORY OF THE ARCHDIOCESE OF BALTIMORE, ... 257

CHAPTER XXI.

ARCHBISHOP SPALDING'S FIRST WORKS IN THE DIOCESE OF BALTIMORE—THE SYLLABUS—THE SIXTH SYNOD OF BALTIMORE—CORRESPONDENCE ON VARIOUS SUBJECTS, ... 269.

CHAPTER XXII.

THE SUFFERING PEOPLE OF THE SOUTH—THE DIOCESE OF CHARLESTON—THE CATHOLIC PROTECTORY—SERMON AT THE UNIVERSITY OF NOTRE DAME, ... 285

CHAPTER XXIII.

THE SECOND PLENARY COUNCIL OF BALTIMORE, ... 298

CHAPTER XXIV.

SECOND PLENARY COUNCIL OF BALTIMORE, CONTINUED—APPOINTMENT OF BISHOPS—PAROCHIAL RIGHTS—CATHOLIC UNIVERSITY, . . 310

CHAPTER XXV.

THE PAST, THE PRESENT, AND THE FUTURE, ... 321

CHAPTER XXVI.

THE EMANCIPATED SLAVES—THE CATHOLIC PUBLICATION SOCIETY—THE CENTENARY OF THE MARTYRDOM OF ST. PETER, . . . 337

CHAPTER XXVII.

TRAVELS IN EUROPE—IRELAND—PROGRESS OF THE CHURCH IN THE ARCHDIOCESE OF BALTIMORE—THE AMERICAN COLLEGE IN ROME, 350,

CHAPTER XXVIII.

THE DANGERS THAT THREATEN THE DESTRUCTION OF OUR FREE INSTITUTIONS—THE REMEDY—THE CRAVING FOR SENSUOUS INDULGENCE, ... 362

CHAPTER XXIX.

DEATH OF THE VERY REV. B. J. SPALDING—VISITATION OF THE DIOCESE—THE LITTLE SISTERS OF THE POOR—THE VATICAN COUNCIL, 374

CHAPTER XXX.

The Vatican Council—The Postulatum of Archbishop Spalding—Letter to Bishop Dupanloup, ... 387

CHAPTER XXXI.

The Definition of Papal Infallibility not only Opportune, but Necessary—Devotion of the American Church to the Holy See, ... 404

CHAPTER XXXII.

The Manner in which the Discussions of the Vatican Council were Conducted—The Infallibility of the Pope—Liberty and Liberalism—Tour in Switzerland, ... 416

CHAPTER XXXIII.

The Sacrilegious Invasion of Rome—Archbishop Spalding Returns Home—His Reception in Baltimore and Washington City—A Retrospect, ... 430

CHAPTER XXXIV.

Last Illness and Death of Archbishop Spalding, ... 449

Index, ... 461

LIFE OF ARCHBISHOP SPALDING.

CHAPTER I.

ANCESTRY.—PARENTAGE.—BIRTH.—EARLY EDUCATION.

HE ancestors of Martin John Spalding belonged to the band of Catholic Pilgrims who, fleeing from religious persecution in England, founded the Maryland Colony in 1634, fourteen years after the landing of the Puritans at Plymouth.

If the Spaldings were not among the two hundred families who came over with Lord Baltimore in 1634, they certainly arrived in Maryland very soon after the first settlement had been made. In a letter on this subject, written in 1871, Archbishop Spalding says:

"It is certain that the Spaldings of Maryland were fully established in St. Mary's County before the year 1650; for deeds and other papers of that date in their name are still found in Leonardtown; though, if I mistake not, an accident of fire destroyed some of the documents. I incline to think that they came some years before this date, probably in the early commencement of the colony, very shortly after the arrival of the first ship of emigrants. . . . I believe that the headquarters of the family in England was Lincolnshire, where one of them at a very early period founded and gave his name to the great Abbey of Spalding, one of the thirteen great abbeys of England spared by Henry VIII., but confiscated under his son, Edward VI. I think, from my researches, and from whatever knowledge I may have in such matters, that the town of Spalding grew up around and under the fostering influence of this abbey."*

Archbishop Spalding's ancestors were not all of English origin; for through his great-grandmother, Ellen O'Brian, he received a tinge of Celtic blood, to which he was very fond of alluding.

Ellen O'Brian was a woman of strong character and of more than ordinary intelligence. She married Samuel

---

* The town of Spalding existed already in the reign of Ethelbald, A.D. 716–757; for in Ethelbald's foundation-charter for the Monastery of Crowland, its lands are said to extend in one direction "*usque ædificid* Spaldeling." The name is most probably of Anglo-Saxon origin.

As a patronymic, the name has existed from an early period in English history, as the following citations will show:

"Henry de Walpol sold lands by deed, *sans* date, to John de Spalding (Burgess of Lenn), in Tyrington, and sealed, as by his deed appears, with a Fesse between two Chevrons, about 51 Henry III." (A.D. 1267).—*Collins' Peerage*, vol. v. p. 32.

"West Hall Manor, Denver, Norfolk. In ninth of Edward II. (A.D. 1316), Peter de Spalding was Lord, and presented to the Meediety of St. Michael's of Denver as Lord of this Manor."—*Blomfield's History of the County of Norfolk, England*, vol. vii. p. 316.

Blomfield also says: "Peter Spalding sold his part or Manor (having enfranchised several villeins) to Sir John Howard, the elder," vol. ix. p. 87.

In 1318, Sir Pierce Spalding commanded Berwick Castle, and delivered it up to the Earl of Murray. In Blomfield's *History of the County of Norfolk*, town of Brockdish, there is a description of the church: "In 1518, Henry Bakenham was buried in this church, as were many of the Spaldings, Withes, Howards, Grices, Tendrings, and Lawrences, families of distinction in this town." The Maryland Spaldings were related to at least one branch of the Fenwicks, an old English Catholic family which came over with Lord Baltimore, and has given to the church in this country two bishops and several zealous priests. Mother Catherine Spalding, first mother of the Sisters of Charity of Nazareth, Ky., and foundress of the orphan asylum in Louisville, and Mother Hardey, Assistant-General of the Order of the Sacred Heart, whose mother was a Spalding, both belong to the Maryland branch of the family.

Abell, a Protestant, who was high-sheriff of St. Mary's County at a time when a Catholic could not hold office without taking the test oath, which was equivalent to renouncing his faith. He allowed his wife to bring up her daughters in her own faith, but strongly protested against any attempt to make Catholics of his sons. The Assembly had, in 1704, passed a new law, entitled "An act to prevent the increase of Popery in the province," which forbade bishops and priests to say Mass or exercise any of the functions of their ministry, and thus suppressed all public Catholic worship. Samuel Abell, therefore, had little opportunity to know whether or not his sons held the faith of their mother. He, of course, took it for granted that they would be too wise to unite themselves with a church which was persecuted and despised. When his oldest son, Philip, had grown to manhood, he took him to Leonardtown, to have him sworn in as deputy sheriff. What was his surprise when Philip refused downright to take the oath, saying publicly before the whole court that it would choke him. However, there was no remedy. The blood of Ellen O'Brian was strong in the boy, and the father, finding that neither threats nor persuasion would move him from his set purpose, finally consented to let him have his way; and he himself gradually lost his prejudices, and on his death-bed sent for a priest, and died in communion with the church.

Robert, another son of Samuel Abell, moved to Kentucky in 1788, and was a delegate to the convention which framed the State constitution, and the only Catholic in that body. As in those days log-cabins were the best hotels the commonwealth could provide, Robert Abell, during the sessions of the convention, occupied the same room with Felix Grundy, a well-known lawyer of Kentucky, and another delegate who had been a Presbyterian preacher.

Each member had the right to present to the convention a draught of the constitution which he wished to see adopted, and those provisions which should meet with the approval of a majority of the members were to become a part of the law of the land. One day, the ex-preacher read to his two companions a clause which he had inserted in his draught, which ran as follows: "And be it further provided, that no Papist or Roman Catholic shall hold any office of profit or trust in this commonwealth." Felix Grundy at once took his pen, and placed the following clause in the draught which he proposed to present to the convention: "And be it also provided, that no broken-down Presbyterian preacher shall be eligible to any office in this commonwealth." The preacher was converted, and the constitution of Kentucky placed no restriction upon religious liberty.*

Alethia Abell, the sister of Robert, and the daughter of Ellen O'Brian, was the grandmother of Martin Spalding.

His grandfather, Benedict Spalding, brought out a colony of Catholics from St. Mary's County in Maryland, in 1790, and settled in Central Kentucky, in the valley of a small river called the Rolling Fork. No Catholics are known to have emigrated to Kentucky before 1775. In that year, William Coomes, with his family and Dr. Hart, both Catholics, settled in Harrod's Station, which was then, with the exception of one or two small forts, the only place in the "Dark and Bloody Ground" where a white man could call his scalp his own. The first Catholic colony which came out to Kentucky was that which accompanied the Haydons and Lancasters in 1785. This colony settled in and around Bardstown, which then became and for many years remained the centre of Catholicity in the State. The chief

---

* This incident was related to a son of Robert Abell by Felix Grundy himself.

causes which determined the Catholics of Maryland to seek what was then the "far West" were the hope of finding a more healthy climate and a soil which would better remunerate them for their toil. The report made by the pioneer colony awakened a greater desire in those who remained behind to emigrate, and other colonies came out in 1786, 1787, and 1788. The Archbishop's grandfather, as I have stated, removed to Kentucky in 1790. He had married Alethia Abell in Maryland. God blessed them with six sons and six daughters, all of whom grew up to be men and women, married, and, with a single exception, lived to be quite old. Their descendants constitute to-day one of the most numerous families in Kentucky.

Richard Spalding, the eldest son of Benedict, was the father of the Archbishop. He was born in St. Mary's County, Maryland, and came to Kentucky with his father. He was thrice married, and by these unions became the father of twenty-one children. He was a man of fine sense, of great industry and perseverance, and, in spite of his numerous family, to which he gave the best education it was possible to obtain in Kentucky in that day, he became wealthy.

The Archbishop's mother was Henrietta Hamilton, who was also born in Maryland, having come out to Kentucky with her father, Leonard Hamilton, in 1791, when still a mere child.

When Father Badin arrived, in 1794, he estimated the Catholic population of the State at three hundred families. Among the first stations which he attended for the purpose of saying Mass and administering the sacrament was the one on the Rolling Fork, near where Archbishop Spalding's grandfather and father were then living. A little later, in 1797, Father Fournier, another French priest, who had come to the assistance of Father Badin, bought a hundred acres of ground in this neighborhood, and built there a log-cabin, of which he took possession in 1798. Holy Mary's Convent of Lorettine Nuns now stands on this spot.

Kentucky was in that day covered with dense forests and tangled woods. There was scarcely a place in its whole territory that might be dignified with the name of village, and the only roads were the almost untrodden paths of the forest, on either side of which lines of blazed trees showed the traveller the route from point to point.

The forests were filled with a luxuriant undergrowth, thickly interspersed with cane and briers, which the intertwining wild pea-vine wove into an almost impenetrable net-work; so that, in certain parts, the only way of getting from place to place was to follow the paths worn by the migrating buffalo and other wild beasts. The Indian still hunted on the "Dark and Bloody Ground," or prowled about the new settlements, ready to attack them whenever an opportunity was offered. It has been stated on good authority that, from 1783 to 1790, fifteen hundred persons were killed or made captive by the Indians in Kentucky, or in migrating thither.*

In 1794, the Indians appeared on the Rolling Fork, and killed a Catholic by the name of Buckman. This produced a panic in the little settlement which caused many Catholics to move for a time to Bardstown, where the population was more dense. But Benedict Spalding remained at home, and the Indians disappeared without committing further outrage.

The early emigrants to Kentucky had to endure all the hardships incident to pioneer life. Even the ordinary comforts were not to be had in the wilderness in which they had taken up their abode, and they not unfrequently suffered the want of the most indispensable necessaries. To

* Judge Jones, of Kentucky, states this in a letter written to Secretary Knox, July 7, 1790.

obtain salt, they had to go to the *Licks*, travelling often many miles through a country infested by savages. They dwelt in rudely constructed log-cabins, the windows of which were without glass, whilst the floors were of dirt, or, in the better sort of dwellings, of rough-hewn boards. After the clothing which they had brought from Virginia and Maryland became unfit for use, the men, for the most part, wore buckskin and the women homespun gowns. The furniture of the cabins was of an equally simple kind. Stools did the office of chairs, the tables were made of rough boards, whilst wooden vessels served instead of plates and china-ware. A tin cup was an article of luxury. The chase supplied abundance of food. All kinds of game abounded, and, when the hunter had his rifle and a goodly supply of ammunition, he was rich as a prince. This was the school in which was trained the Kentucky rifleman, whose aim on the battle-field was certain death. The game was plainly dressed and served up on wooden platters, and, with corn-bread and hominy, it made a feast which the keen appetite of honest labor and free-heartedness thought good enough for kings.

> "Vivitur parvo bene, cui paternum
> Splendet in mensa tenui salinum
> Nec leves somnos timor aut cupido
> Sordidus aufert."

"Such was the simple manner of life," said Archbishop Spalding, "of *our* 'Pilgrim Fathers.' They had fewer luxuries, but were, withal, perhaps happier than their more fastidious descendants. Hospitality was not then an empty name. Every log-cabin was freely thrown open to all who chose to share in the best cheer its inmates could afford. The early settlers of Kentucky were bound together by the strong ties of common hardships and dangers, to say nothing of other bonds of union, and they clung together with great tenacity. On the slightest alarm of Indian invasion, they made common cause, and flew to the rescue. There was less selfishness and more generous chivalry, less bickering and more cordial charity, then than now, notwithstanding all our boasted refinement."*

Old men love to praise the bygone age, when they were boys, by a sweet reversion to childhood, forgetting the evil and remembering only the good of the morning of life: and all find a certain pleasure in carping at the present by contrasting it with the seeming more perfect past. But making allowance for this proneness of our nature, there was doubtless in the society of those early days in Kentucky rare beauty and goodness. The men were brave and honest, the women were pure and gentle; and these virtues sat so naturally upon them that they seemed unconscious of them, as not contemplating a contrary state. They sometimes lent money without note or witness, and this implicit trust to what is best in human nature was rarely ever betrayed. They were truly hospitable, they were kind-hearted, and they loved liberty in the highest sense of the word.

This state of primitive republican society had not yet disappeared at the time of the birth of Martin John Spalding, which took place on the 23d of May, 1810. He was born on the Rolling Fork, in sight of the farm on which his grandfather had settled upon his arrival in Kentucky twenty years before this date. He was baptized by Father Nerincks, of whose apostolical life and labors he was destined to become the historian. He was a frail, delicate child, and so subject to frequent attacks of sickness that it was not thought he could long survive. His mother, who

* *Sketches of Kentucky*, p. 33.

was noted for the purity and gentleness of her character, and whom he very much resembled, both in feature and disposition, manifested, probably on account of his weak and suffering condition, greater tenderness for him than for her other children. She always called him her little bishop. He had the great misfortune to lose her when but five or six years old. After her death, he was confided to the care of his oldest sister, who was still a mere girl. She was assisted in the performance of her responsible duties by the wise counsel of her grandmother, Alethia Spalding, the daughter of Samuel Abell and Ellen O'Brian.

Alethia Spalding was remarkable both for great beauty and for great holiness. Even Protestants thought her a saint; and Father Badin, who knew her well, used to say, after her death, that she was certainly in heaven.

In those days, when Mass was said at the different stations only once a month, or at most once in two weeks, she was in the habit, whenever the priest was absent from Holy Mary's, of going on horseback a distance of six or eight miles to Lebanon, to assist at the holy sacrifice there. On these occasions, she always took one of her grandchildren, frequently Martin, behind her on her little gray mare; and she never failed to sanctify the journey by reciting the rosary with her little travelling companion.

Of the seven children of Richard Spalding who had the example of her virtues so constantly before their eyes, two became priests, and two took the veil in the Convent of Loretto.

Bishop Carroll wrote of the early Catholic colonists of Kentucky that they were in general good, and that some of them were eminent in virtue.

Their religious character was certainly earnest and profound. They were not puritanical, which Catholics, I believe, never are; but their faith was strong and healthful, and their attachment to Catholic truth unwavering. As an instance of this, I may state that, towards the close of the last century, when it seemed impossible to get priests to remain in Kentucky, many of the Catholic colonists determined to remove to Missouri, induced by the offer of the Spanish governor to secure them the opportunity of complying with their religious obligations. A committee had been appointed, and had gone to St. Louis to confer with the governor, when Bishop Carroll finally succeeded in sending a priest to Kentucky, which led to the abandonment of the project of removing the colony to Missouri. Their solicitude to preserve the faith of their children was equally great, evidences of which may be seen in the Catholic schools and colleges which they founded and supported, and in the care with which they avoided mixed marriages. Of the twelve children of Benedict Spalding, all of whom married, not one, in the first instance, married a Protestant.

Their opposition to intermarrying with Protestant families led them not unfrequently to approve of the marriage of blood relations, as the lesser of two evils. Their objection to mixed marriages did not proceed from any unfriendly feeling towards Protestants, which did not exist, but from the conviction that difference of faith in the father and mother could not but have a bad effect upon the religious character of the children.

Martin Spalding was sent to school, when about eight years old, to a Mr. Merrywether, whose college was a log-cabin in the backwoods near the Rolling Fork.

His earliest intellectual feat was learning the multiplication-table in a single day when but eight years old. He was even then as remarkable for the sweetness of his disposition as for the quickness of his mind. He made his first communion when only ten years old, which is worthy of remark when we consider that he had never been to a

Catholic school, and had but on rare occasions received instruction from a priest.

The year in which he made his first communion, 1820, was the one in which the first Catholic college was founded in Kentucky. This was St. Joseph's College, at Bardstown.

The year following, the Rev. William Byrne opened St. Mary's College, near Lebanon, and among the very first students who entered that institution were Martin Spalding and his two older brothers. The founding of St. Mary's College is an instance of what energy and zeal may enable God's priest to accomplish. When the project first presented itself to Father Byrne's mind, he had neither men nor money, and without these it was not thought possible to establish a college. But he was a man to whom nothing that was right seemed impossible. "Viam aut inveniam aut faciam," was his motto, and his faith in God and in the power of labor gave him strength to triumph over difficulties which would have appalled weaker and less believing men. He bought a farm, on which stood an old stone distillery. To pay for this, he asked contributions from the Catholics of the country, and since they had but little money, he took produce or whatever they were able to give, which, with great delay and difficulty, he converted into cash.

The next step was to transform the old distillery into an academy of learning. He himself put his hand to the work, and became carpenter or mason as circumstances demanded. When everything was in readiness, he offered to furnish education in return for wheat, corn, and bacon. This plan, which was perfectly adapted to the wants of the community, could not fail of success. When at length, in the early spring of 1821, the anxiously expected day for the opening of St. Mary's Seminary arrived, it was filled to overflowing.

Father Byrne was president, disciplinarian, prefect, treasurer, and professor.

The seminary soon became known for its strict discipline and the moral and literary advancement of its pupils, and, in consequence, it grew in public favor.

Father Byrne had paid his debts, and had nearly completed another building for the accommodation of a greater number of students, when, during his absence in Louisville, the college was consumed by fire.

"We well remember," says Archbishop Spalding, in his *Sketches of Kentucky*, "the sadness which sat upon his brow when the next day he rode into the enclosure and beheld the smouldering ruins of what had cost him years of anxious toil. Yet the suddenness of the shock did not unnerve him—it gave him new energy. In a few short months, St. Mary's Seminary rose from its ashes fresher and more beautiful than before."

A second time St. Mary's was burned to the ground, and again Father Byrne rebuilt it, and finally succeeded in placing it on a firm and enduring foundation. In his difficulties, Father Byrne found a warm friend in Richard Spalding, the father of the Archbishop, who was very desirous of procuring for his children a good education. He offered to give Father Byrne one hundred acres of ground, and otherwise to assist him, if he would remove the college to Holy Mary's; but Bishop Flaget did not think it advisable to change the location.

CHAPTER II.

PROFESSOR AT ST. MARY'S COLLEGE—ENTERS THE SEMINARY AT BARDSTOWN—IS SENT TO ROME.

MARTIN SPALDING was Father Byrne's favorite pupil. When the college was destroyed by fire, Martin did not return home with his brothers, but continued his studies with Father Byrne, and, upon the reopening of the school, he was made professor of mathematics, though he was but fourteen years old. He was at this time a slender, delicate boy, soft and gentle as a girl, and to a remarkably bright and quick mind added a disposition so sweet that no one could help loving him. He soon became quite famous as professor of mathematics, and Father Byrne was persuaded that no problem could be proposed to him which he would not be able to solve. He made this boast to the county surveyor, who, in reply, said that he thought he could give Martin a question in surveying which would puzzle him. Father Byrne desired that the proficiency of his youthful professor should be put to the test, and the problem was accordingly proposed. Martin asked for time to consider it, and in a short while returned with the answer.

A certain Mr. Dougherty, who was at this time professor of mathematics in St. Joseph's College, had great contempt for the reputation of the boy-professor of St. Mary's, and he boasted that he would put him to shame. With this view, he went to the next examination at St. Mary's, and proposed questions to the class of mathematics which he was confident not even the professor would be able to solve. But Martin each time came to the rescue of his students, and triumphantly explained every difficulty.

Father Byrne had unbounded admiration for Martin's talents, and, whenever he spoke of him, he grew eloquent in extolling his high endowments. The great highway between Louisville and Nashville in those days passed within two or three miles of St. Mary's College, and such was, as I have heard from the lips of the oldest living priest in Kentucky, the reputation which Martin had gained, that travellers sometimes went out of their way to see this wonderful boy-professor.

His friends feared lest the flattery and attention which he received might spoil him; and that he came out of this ordeal unscathed is perhaps one of the greatest proofs of the thorough worth and genuine strength of his character. Success and applause could not destroy in him that childlike simplicity which continued through life to be one of his greatest charms.

When he left Kentucky, at the age of twenty, to go to Rome, there was probably no one in the State who was superior to him in the knowledge of mathematics; and, though he never after paid any attention to this science, he never ceased to be ready at accounts, and quick to understand problems in which mathematical calculations were involved. As a student at St. Mary's, he was noted for his application and his eager desire to learn. He never allowed others to assist him in solving the difficulties which presented themselves, but wished to be indebted to his own industry alone for his triumph over them. He was also, as I have said, distinguished for his gentle and loving disposition. In a game of foot-ball, Martin had unintentionally done something which provoked a boy much larger than himself to insult him and to threaten to strike him. One of his cousins who happened to be standing near interfered, and was on the point of punishing the boy, when Martin at once stopped him, saying that he was able to take care of himself, and that he could not upon any account consent to be the occasion of angry words or blows. The person who related this little incident to me added that the noble and Christian bearing of Martin Spalding at that time had made an impression upon him which the lapse of many years had not effaced.

He remained five years at St. Mary's, and graduated with great honor in 1826. Though but sixteen years old, he had already resolved to consecrate his life to the service of God in the priesthood.

He spent the summer vacations at home, and at their close he entered the seminary at Bardstown as a student of theology.

The year in which he began the study of theology is one which is still associated with the happiest memories in the minds of some of the older Catholics of Kentucky. It was the year of grace, the year of the great Jubilee, which, promulgated by Leo XII. in 1825, was preached in Kentucky only in 1826. The entire Catholic population of Kentucky seems to have been awakened to new life and fervor during this holy season. The priests who were engaged in preaching this Jubilee drew up a full account of the fruits of their labors, which they transmitted to the Association of the Propagation of the Faith, in France.

"During the week of the Jubilee," these eye-witnesses relate, "all temporal affairs seemed to be forgotten, and only those of the soul were attended to. As the greater part of the Catholics came from a distance of eight, ten, or twelve miles, they remained during the whole day in the church, without leaving it even for a moment, except to take a frugal repast on the grass or in the neighboring wood. Not only did the laborers and farmers, who constituted the majority of the Catholics, give these beautiful examples of religious fervor, but persons of every condition—merchants, physicians, magistrates, legislators—showed themselves equally eager to profit by the graces of heaven. Human respect, so powerful under other circumstances, had given place to more noble sentiments, and all seemed eager to give open and public evidence of their strong attachment to a religion which was the only source of their consolation and their happiness. Such was the edifying spectacle which Kentucky presented during those days of benediction. Perhaps the fruits of the Jubilee were more abundant here than in any other part of the Christian world, if we take into account the small number of Catholics in this diocese."

This was the first time that the Catholics of the great West had been called upon to unite with their brethren throughout Christendom in the solemn prayer of the Jubilee, and the novelty of the exercises had doubtless something to do with the readiness with which they responded to the voice of the Holy Father; but, apart from this, we cannot but recognize in their fervor and zeal evidences of great religious earnestness and of true piety. The heart of the venerable Bishop Flaget was touched by the devotion and good-will of his people.

"With what pleasure," he wrote, "have I entered upon this apostolic career! If the consolations which I now feel, go on increasing, they will afford me happiness enough for this life."

The Diocesan Seminary, in Kentucky, was established at St. Thomas's almost immediately after the arrival of Bishop Flaget and Father David; but when the new cathedral was consecrated in 1819, it was removed to Bardstown, the Bishop wishing, as far as possible, to live among his seminarians as a father in his family. The Sunday following the dedication of the cathedral, Father David received the episcopal consecration at the hands of Bishop Flaget, and became his coadjutor. The two bishops had rooms in the seminary ; they ate at the same table with the seminarians, and took part in all the exercises of the community.

The day after the opening of the new seminary, Bishop Flaget wrote : " This day will form an epoch in the history of the church in Kentucky ; for I dare hope that from this house will go forth priests who will sustain and propagate the faith." And a few years later, when this hope had been in part fulfilled, he added : " Many priests have already been reared in the seminary, and their piety and talents would distinguish them even in Europe. Some of them are excellent preachers and very good controversialists."

When Martin Spalding entered the seminary, in 1826, he found there a body of men equal to any in the church of the United States to-day.

First of all, there was Bishop Flaget, who, though not remarkable for theological ability, was a model bishop, and the type of a true missionary. He had a heart as tender as a woman's, and a character so perfectly formed after the model given by his divine Master that he himself was a living example of all that the young Levites who were gathered at his feet were to aspire to. The master, he was as the servant; the bishop, he was in garb and bearing as his humblest priest. When he spoke to them, he could, without mockery, bid them be self-denying, poverty-loving, humble, lowly in their walk; for such he was. The children of his apostolic love grew up to be the crown and honor of his old age, and the pride of the church of Kentucky.

Then there was Bishop David, less expansive and less demonstrative of affection than Bishop Flaget, but a man of the soundest judgment and of great learning, and, above all, a thorough disciplinarian. Francis Patrick Kenrick was also there, fresh from the Propaganda, already then the most learned theologian, as he was destined afterwards to become the brightest ornament of the American Church. For him Martin Spalding at once conceived the highest admiration, which soon ripened into a friendship which during many succeeding years remained unshaken, until, when his early friend had been removed to a better world, he was destined to succeed him as the head of the first and oldest see of the United States.

There, too, was Father Reynolds, afterwards the successor of Bishop England in the see of Charleston—a man of profound thought, and an orator.

The Rev. George Elder, the founder and first President of St. Joseph's College, whose character was as lovely and gentle as his mind was cultivated and refined, completes the group of remarkable men whom Martin Spalding found at Bardstown in 1826.

At that time, the seminary was connected with St. Joseph's College, and the seminarians were required to teach and perform other duties in the college. Archbishop Spalding, in his *Life of Bishop Flaget*, says that this state of things had its advantages, but that they were probably more than counterbalanced by the inconveniences necessarily attendant upon such a system. The vocations of some of the seminarians were shaken by this intimate contact with youths of the world, while scarcely a candidate for the ministry was obtained from among those who were educated in the college. This, of course, greatly distressed Bishop Flaget, who made use of every means to correct the evil, and finally established at St. Thomas's a preparatory seminary for young men who gave indication of a vocation to the ecclesiastical state.

Martin Spalding remained in Bardstown four years, dividing his time between the study of philosophy and theology and the duties of a professor in the college. He soon proved that he possessed an aptitude for theology and languages scarcely less remarkable than that which he had shown for mathematics whilst teaching at St. Mary's. His talents and exemplary conduct won for him such favor in the eyes of Bishop Flaget that, at the end of four years, he determined to send him to Rome to complete his theological studies in the Urban College.

After the high privilege of a vocation to the priesthood, Martin Spalding deemed it the most fortunate circumstance in his life that he was permitted to finish his theological education in the Holy City, where he drank in all the sacred doctrines and traditions of the Christian religion at their fountain-head. His eagerness to go to Rome was increased by his admiration of Dr. Kenrick, who had studied there; and his conversation, and the glowing pictures which he drew of the advantages offered in the Eternal City to the aspirant to theological science, helped to influence Bishop Flaget to send the young Kentuckian to the Propaganda.

The clergy of the diocese of Bardstown were not, however, of one opinion concerning the advantages of a Roman education. Some held that the habits of thought and action which young Americans would be likely to acquire during a course of studies in Rome would not be such as to fit them in the best manner for fulfilling with success the duties of missionaries in the backwoods of Kentucky. From this opinion, as we shall hereafter see from his letters written from Rome, Martin Spalding wholly dissented.

He set out on his journey to Rome, in company with James Lancaster, in April, 1830.

A few days after his arrival in Baltimore, he wrote the following letter to his father:

"DEAR FATHER:

"Your parental solicitude makes you anxious, I am sure, to hear from a son whom you so tenderly love. When I left you, dear father, I did not expect to go to Baltimore; but in Louisville we met with Colonel Brent, a former member of Congress from Louisiana, who was on his way to Washington City, and who informed us that it would be safer for us to accompany him thither, as we might otherwise find difficulty in obtaining our passports. We also learned from him that Commodore Porter had been recently appointed Minister to Algiers, and was expected in a short time to sail out to the Mediterranean in a vessel belonging to the navy, in which we, in all probability, would be able to obtain passage by applying at Washington. Since our arrival here, John Rowan has been very active in his efforts to obtain this favor for us, and Major Barry has likewise taken an interest in the matter. In Washington, we were hospitably entertained by the Rev. Mr. Mathews; and, after visiting the public buildings, we left for Baltimore in the company of the Rev. Mr. Hughes, of Philadelphia. I conclude, dear father, by giving expression to my love for you, and my gratitude for the great regard which you have ever shown for my true welfare. I trust that your hope in me will be realized, and that I shall become a zealous priest, and one eminently useful to the church. Do you, dear father, continue to comply with all your religious duties, especially that of bringing up your family in the love and fear of God."

On the following day, the first of May, he wrote to his old professor, Dr. Kenrick, who had just been appointed to the see of Philadelphia:

"RIGHT REVEREND AND DEAR FRIEND:

"The style of my address is expressive at once of your promotion and of my sincere affection for you. You have doubtless ere this heard of your appointment to the Bishopric of Philadelphia, since you have probably received the bulls sent you by the Archbishop of Baltimore. I congratulate the church upon your elevation, and hope that you will receive the burden cheerfully, though I perfectly understand how ungrateful to you the intelligence of your promotion must have proved. What a sacrifice for the good Bishop of Kentucky! Your appointment has excited great interest in Baltimore and Washington. All speak of it as an era in the history of the American Church. I have had the good fortune to meet with the Rev. Mr. Hughes. I handed him your letter, to which I am indebted for the kind manner in which he received me. He is a gentleman of the most polite and engaging manners, blending the amiable modesty and reserve of the priest with the easy deportment of the man of the world. He has, I think, a brilliant future before him. He introduced us to the professors of the seminary and college in Baltimore. In his company, I have been very pleasantly occupied in viewing the various objects of interest here. We ascended together the monument erected by Catholic Maryland to the memory of Washington, from which we had a fine view of the city and its picturesque surroundings. I have also visited the charitable institutions of Baltimore, which do honor to the generosity and benevolence of the Catholics of Maryland, as also to the devoted zeal of the Sisters of Charity, who are so nobly employed in ministering to the suffering members of Christ. The Rev. Mr. Elder has introduced me to some relations here whose acquaintance has given me great pleasure.

"All seem anxious to be informed of every particular concerning the church in Kentucky. They wish especially to hear how the Rev. Mr. Abell stands as a preacher. Here in Baltimore he is considered an orator not unworthy of his native backwoods. I dined with the Archbishop at his invitation, and was received with great kindness. He has some pamphlets for Dr. Wiseman, of the English College in Rome, and he promises to give us letters of introduction to him. The Archbishop expects that you will be consecrated in Bardstown by Bishop Flaget. He asked me how the priests in Kentucky wore their hair, intending, as I perceived, to give a hint to the Rev. Mr. ——. He also asked me whether the Bishop of Bardstown approved of coats with straight collars like ours. When I replied in the affirmative, he informed me that in Maryland this is the distinctive mark of Methodist preachers. James Lancaster was actually mistaken for one of these gentlemen on his way from Washington to Baltimore; whilst I was probably indebted to my youthful appearance for my escape from a like suspicion. The Rev. Mr. Pise, whose acquaintance I have made, is a very active young man, who is thought to possess great talent. He hopes that you will become a regular contributor to the *Metropolitan*, now that you are to be so near the Rome of America."

Although these letters of our young Kentuckian, who had for the first time left his native woods, are not in themselves remarkable, they are yet not without interest, since they give us an insight into his character, and show the bent of his youthful thoughts and aspirations. His mind is eager for knowledge, and he has a keen eye for whatever has a bearing upon the all-absorbing object of his devotion—the church of God, to the service of which he has consecrated his life. The aspiring hopes of the young heart, untaught by disenchanting experience, and uncurbed by adversity, belong to him, but they all concentre in the church; and when visions of the future present themselves to his mind, and he beholds himself such as he hopes to be in after-years, the ideal present to his imagination is that of the "zealous and useful priest." He proves himself not a bad judge of character when he predicts a brilliant future for the Rev. Mr. Hughes, who was as yet unknown to fame.

He and his companion remained in Baltimore two weeks, anxiously waiting for Commodore Porter to sail, until at length, growing weary of delay, they determined to embark in a vessel bound for Gibraltar, which was to sail from Baltimore on the 12th of May.

On the eve of his departure, Martin wrote to Father Byrne, whom, of all his teachers and early associates, he most loved:

"KIND GUARDIAN OF MY YOUTH:

"I write to you from the scene of your former trials and labors. To-morrow we shall commit ourselves to the mercy of the waves and the protection of Heaven, and, after having passed through the purgatory of sea-sickness, we may get our sea-legs, and become, for aught we know, trusty sailors. The captain of the ship on which we are to sail is a Catholic and a gentleman of good standing here in Baltimore, of which he is a resident. We have been very kindly treated during our stay here. The Rev. Mr. Elder has shown us great attention. In manner he reminds me of yourself. Among other privileges, we have had the pleasure of seeing the venerable patriot, Charles Carroll, the last of our Revolutionary heroes. Though ninety-three years of age, he is quite vigorous and remarkably cheerful. He is still able, he says, to mount his horse and ride six or seven miles without great fatigue.

"It is a source of gratification to us to have received the good-will and benediction of the venerable patriot just on the eve of leaving our native land. I have seen some of your old friends in Baltimore. The Rev. Mr. Tessier is as mild and modest as when you knew him. He talks through his nose, laughs merrily, eats heartily, and is as innocent as a child. I went to confession to him, and I am much pleased with his character. The Rev. Mr. Damphoux is always the same eccentric, excellent person.

"When I view my present situation and the advantages which appear in every way to be offered to me for the completion of my education, I naturally recur in thought to him who, under Providence, has been the cause of all my success, and the first link in the chain of my improvement. Believe me, then, dear father, when I say that I shall ever remain, with sincerest love, your devoted son."

Martin Spalding had completed his twentieth year two days before he set sail for Europe. Nearly half of his life had been passed at college or in the seminary, and his great application had somewhat weakened his naturally feeble constitution. This, however, did not at all discourage him; he was still eager for work, and seemed never to doubt that God would give him strength to complete his education, and to become, as he expressed it, a zealous priest, and one eminently useful to the church. In person, he was slender, something above the average height, with a countenance which, for regularity of feature, softness of outline, and perfect purity of expression, might have passed for that of a beautiful girl. His character, too, was singularly affectionate and gentle; his whole nature frank and confiding, unsuspicious of evil, because he himself was innocent.

He had never, I think, felt even the shadow of a sentimental attachment, but carried from the backwoods of the far West to the shrines of the apostles a virgin heart untainted by even the breath of passion.

He had all the enthusiastic love of country which belonged to the young Americans of that day, when the purity of republican manners had not been corrupted by the evil influences of wealth and luxury. To be an American citizen was, in his mind, the highest honor after that of being a Roman Catholic. He looked upon Charles Carroll, as we have seen, with a reverence akin to religion, because in him he beheld one of that band of patriots who, as he had been taught to believe, had risked everything in a cause only less sacred than that of Christ. But the dream of his soul was the church of God, the spouse of Christ, who is all fair, without spot or wrinkle; who, though old, is ever young; and to this, his first love, he never in after-life proved untrue.

CHAPTER III.

STUDENT LIFE IN ROME.

ARTIN SPALDING arrived in Cadiz on the 20th of June, 1830, after a voyage in which the monotony of sea-travel was not broken by any incident worth recording. After waiting two weeks in Cadiz, he found a ship bound for Marseilles. He took passage on this vessel, which, he wrote, was laden with the relics of all the bull-fights that had taken place in Spain within the last ten years. Sailing through the Strait of Gibraltar, he beheld the opposing coasts of Europe and Africa. The favoring breeze filled the canvas, and the travellers expected to be in Marseilles within four or five days. But the winds fell asleep, and the ship was becalmed off the coast of Spain for nearly a month.

When Martin and his companion at length arrived in Marseilles, they embarked with as little delay as possible for Leghorn. But fortune was again adverse, and they were eight days in crossing the Mediterranean. From Leghorn they proceeded to Florence, and, after visiting the churches and art-galleries of the Tuscan capital, continued their journey through Sienna, where they stopped to admire the cathedral, and finally, in company with a Roman gentleman and his lady and two ferocious dogs, they arrived safely in the Eternal City on the 7th of August, just four months from the time they left home. We can hardly realize that a trip to Europe forty years ago could have been attended with so many delays and difficulties.

"If travel have delights," Martin wrote, shortly after he

reached Rome, "which compensate for its many vexations and disappointments, I certainly have not experienced them."

But steam has revolutionized the world, and brought us eight times nearer the central city of Catholic faith than our fathers were.

The vacations were just beginning when Martin arrived in Rome, and he therefore went at once to the summer-house of the Propaganda, near Tivoli—one of the most delightful and picturesque spots in Italy. Here he applied himself to the study of Italian, and by the end of vacation he was able to speak it without much difficulty.

In November, he returned to Rome, and entered upon the routine of Propaganda life. The students of this institution are divided into companies or camerate, the members of one camerata being allowed no communication with those of another.

In the camerata in which the young Kentuckian was placed, there were two Irishmen, two Germans, two Dutchmen, two Constantinopolitans, a Scotchman, a Dalmatian, an Albanian, and a Bulgarian.

His studies were divided into four classes. In the morning, he had church history and moral theology; in the afternoon, Hebrew and dogma.

"How full are my days," he wrote, when he had got thoroughly to work, "and how rapidly they pass! It is impossible to describe my happiness here in the Propaganda. The kind indulgence of my superiors, the cheerfulness and freedom encouraged in the students, the brilliant examples of piety and learning which I behold around me, the almost maternal care with which I am provided with whatever my health may require, the admirable facilities offered for the cultivation of heart and mind, all conduce to render me perfectly happy, and to make me for ever grateful to those who have helped to procure me such blessings. My health, indeed, was not good for a while, the fatigue of travel having proved injurious to me; but God permitted me to be thus tried only to purify my intention, and to cause me to give myself wholly into his sacred keeping. I have made the act of entire self-abandonment, and my health is rapidly improving. I have every confidence that I shall be able to complete my studies, and to prepare myself to be of use to the church, to the service of whose altar I have been called, and to promote whose interests is the chief desire of my heart. Dear brother, let us unite in this glorious work. The vineyard is large, and the laborers are few."

A few months after his arrival in Rome, he received the following letter from Bishop Flaget, in which we perceive both the great piety and the affectionate character of that venerable man:

"MY DEAR SON:

"How I envy the happiness which you enjoyed when you entered into the Holy City!

"Oh! what delight for me had I been in your company when you were presented to the Cardinal-Prefect, to the Rector and Professors of the college, and were received with such kindness! Many a time have I expressed my wish to visit the Limina Apostolorum, but my entreaties have proved vain. My lot is cast; Europe is not to be seen by me again; I am wedded to Kentucky. Here I must live; here I must die. The holy will of God be done. I submit to it with joy, since, by coming to Kentucky, I have been the occasion of your visiting the Holy City, where I hope you will drink in greater learning and piety than I could have ever acquired. The details you gave us in your letter of your fellow-students, of their different nationalities, manners, and colors, and yet all united in the same faith and in the reception of the same sacraments, were both entertaining and edifying. Yet we would have been glad to see what manner of countenance you put on when you sat by those black brothers of yours. My dear Martin was truly witty when he related how they administered a second baptism to him in the gardens of the Holy Father. His Eminence Cardinal Cappellari has written most favorably of you. For God's sake, my dear son, do not frustrate the high expectations of this venerable man and of your old Bishop, who has always loved you like an affectionate father. No doubt, in sending you to Rome, I had your own good in view; but I must confess, as I said to you before your departure, that the honor of our holy religion in Kentucky was the first object I had in contemplation in procuring for you the extraordinary advantages which you now enjoy. Study, then, my dearly beloved child, but study at the foot of the crucifix, having nothing in view but the glory of God, the sanctification and instruction of those who will one day be committed to your care, and your own perfection. Be punctual in the observance of your rules; obey your superiors as you would obey Jesus Christ; be obliging and condescending in your intercourse with your fellow-students; suffer not the mean vice of jealousy to enter your heart; bear with the failings of others as they have to bear with yours; respect national prejudices, customs, and usages, and do not quarrel with any one who does not entertain for your native land the high ideas which have been instilled into your heart from infancy; be more ready to praise than to blame; bear with jokes, and take up daily your cross, and follow in the company of our blessed Saviour."

In a letter to his sister, who was a Lorettine nun, and who had made enquiry concerning the religious orders in Rome, he says: "Nearly all the orders of the church are represented in Rome. The convents of women are very numerous. The Rector, however, tells me that there is no order of Lorettine nuns either in Rome or in Italy. We never see the nuns, as they are all cloistered; but we see the friars every day, who are also quite numerous, and, in general, very exemplary. There are gray friars, and white friars, and black friars; bearded friars, and shaven friars, and hooded friars; lean friars and fat friars; barefoot friars, and shod friars, and slippered friars; clean friars, and dirty friars, and begging friars—but you must really excuse me; I cannot tell you of them all." And then, with that *naïveté* which always characterized him, he adds: "Understand me, my dear sister, I do not make this short litany to ridicule the monks, but to make you laugh. I esteem and venerate the friars. They are very exemplary, give the perfect example of the contempt of worldly goods, "having their conversation in heaven," and they form, at the same time, a most useful body of reserve, which the church calls to her aid in case of need, as there are among them not only most pious but also most learned men."

The brief term of twenty months, during which Pius VIII. sat in the chair of Peter, was drawing to its close when Martin Spalding arrived in Rome. He refers to the death of this Pope in one of his letters:

"The death of our Sovereign Pontiff, Pius VIII., has awakened universal sorrow in the Catholic world. This amiable guardian of the church expired on the 30th of November, after an illness of nearly two weeks. He was greatly esteemed for the gentle qualities which, together with his name, he seems to have inherited from his illustrious predecessor, Pius VII., whom he sought to imitate. Among other incidents illustrative of his kindness of heart, the conversion of an English officer is spoken of, who had solicited an audience, expecting to verify in the person of the Pope all that he had heard of the man of sin. But he was received with such gentleness and cordiality that his mind and heart were completely changed, and, prostrating himself at the feet of his Holiness, he declared his intention to embrace the Catholic faith. The body was embalmed, and then, clothed in pontifical robes, with mozetta and stole, cap of red and white soutane, it was exposed for two days in the chapel of the Quirinal, where it was visited by immense crowds of people. I also had the sad privilege of beholding the mortal remains of the Father of the faithful.

"In the interval between his death and burial, the cardinals, bishops, and prelates of Rome wore mourning, and the soldiers carried their arms reversed. On the 2d of December, the body was borne to St. Peter's with military pomp and full attendance of the cardinals and princes of Rome in carriages. Here it was again exposed for two days in the Sixtine Chapel, and again visited by vast crowds. Finally, on the 6th of December, after all the ceremonies had been performed, the body was placed in a wooden case, enclosed in one of iron, which was surrounded by a third of lead, and was then deposited in the place destined for the temporary reception of the mortal remains of the Pontiff till the death of his successor."

The confident hopes with which Martin had entered upon his studies in Rome soon proved delusive. His health, instead of improving, continued to decline, and in a short time he was brought to the very brink of the grave. In this condition, he dictated a letter to his faithful companion, James Lancaster, in which he informed his relations and friends of his death, told them that he had died happy, and that they should rejoice rather than grieve that he had gone to a better world. This letter was sent to Kentucky, and for more than a week it was supposed that Martin was dead. When the report arrived, Bishop Flaget was sick at

Loretto. He immediately grew worse, and gave way to uncontrollable grief. He kept in his hands a rosary which Martin had chained for him, and repeatedly kissed it and bedewed it with his tears. He, however, consoled himself with the thought that Martin had served God from the days of his youth, and was now certainly in heaven. But God, whose minister he was to be, brought him back from the jaws of death. As soon as he had partially recovered, he wrote the following letter to his father:

"BELOVED FATHER:

"You had, I suppose, given up all hope of ever hearing again from your son. Having been unwell the greater part of the time since my arrival in Rome, as you already know, I was taken ill with cholera-morbus on the 5th of January. The disease continued without abatement for fifteen days, bringing me to the point of death, and causing all to despair of my life. In the letter which I then wrote to the Bishop by the hands of my good companion, I exhorted you to lay aside all solicitude for me, told you that I had died happy, and desired you to wipe away the tears which the news of my death might occasion. Yes, dear father, thanks to God and to the principles of his holy religion which your parental love had taken care to have instilled into my mind from my earliest infancy, I was happy and filled even with the sweetest joy when told that my hour had come, that the prison of my wretched body was to be broken, and that my soul was destined soon to be with her Heavenly Father for all eternity. No language can paint the peace and happiness of mind which I enjoyed during the month in which I was confined to my bed. I suffered, it is true, but religion rendered my sufferings sweet, and the more I was weakened by disease, the more, thanks be to God! to whom alone all the glory must be given, was I filled with joy at the appearance of the near approach of death. Dear father, fear not for me; I shall be happy, for I have given myself without reserve to God and his holy church. I may again see you if it be the holy will of God, and, if it be not his will, I gladly make the sacrifice of that which would be most agreeable to my heart, trusting to see in heaven for all eternity him whom I was not allowed to behold again on earth. Let us endeavor to meet in that blessed abode, where nothing can separate us. Even should I not be permitted to finish my studies here, you will have no reason to regret having sent me, as I shall have seen enough of the religion and glory of this holy city amply to compensate for the expenses you have incurred in sending me to Rome. The Holy Father, Gregory XVI., recently visited our college, and, when I was presented to him, he enquired particularly concerning my health; and, when I answered that I was fast recovering, he expressed the wish that I might soon be restored to perfect health."

There is something singularly touching in this gentle thoughtfulness of the visible head of a church whose children number two hundred million souls, with regard to a simple young man, a stranger from the wild woods of America, whose only merit was that he was a Catholic, and had devoted his life to the service of God in the church.

"I know not," says Cardinal Wiseman, "how a dignitary of any other religion, though holding no royal power and majesty, would receive a body of youths about to devote themselves to the service of his creed, or whether he would think it worth while to admit them at all to an interview. But to Rome there flock from every region of earth aspirants to the ecclesiastical state, in boyhood and well-nigh in childhood, speaking as many languages as are attributed to the apostles on the day of Pentecost; and yet, perhaps, hardly one fails to come into personal contact with him towards whom from infancy he has looked up as the most exalted person in the world. Soon after his arrival, he receives an early blessing on his future career, accompanied often with a few kind words, unfailingly with a benign look. That brief moment is an epoch in life, perhaps a starting-point for success. For the general attachment that united him with millions to the head of his church, there is established a personal bond, an individual connection. It is no longer awe and distant reverence, but an affection as distinct in character as that to one intimately related. And this relation is strengthened in the youthful mind at every succeeding year of his course. He knows that every professor whose lectures he hears has been directly and immediately appointed, after careful selection, by the Pope himself; that every class-book which he reads has received the same supreme sanction; he feels himself almost under the direct tuition of the Holy See; however pure and sparkling the rills at which others may drink, he puts his lips to the very rock which a divine wand has struck, and he sucks in its waters as they gush forth living."*

Shortly after his arrival in Rome, Martin Spalding obtained from the Cardinal-Prefect, through the mediation of the Rector, a place in the Propaganda for his brother Benedict, who was still studying and teaching in the seminary at Bardstown. He at once wrote to Bishop Flaget, and begged him to allow his brother to come and join him in Rome. To this the Bishop himself did not object, but some of his advisers hesitated to give their consent. They seemed to think that theology could be learned as well in Bardstown as in Rome, and that they understood better than their Italian brothers what practical training was necessary to form successful missionaries for Kentucky.

* *Recollections of the Four Last Popes,* p. 29.

These objections were communicated to Martin, who, in reply, wrote a long letter, in which he set forth the special advantages of a Roman education.

"In the past," he asks, "what nation has not felt the influence of religion issuing from the centre of Christian unity, and guided by the august head of the Christian hierarchy? And in her train have followed science and the arts of civilization. The Eternal City still wields an influence in the world not less powerful, certainly more glorious, than that which once belonged to the iron sceptre of her imperial rulers. The Pope is the immediate superior of the Propaganda, which, according to the expression of a cardinal who frequently honors us with his presence, may be rightly called the seminary of Christendom. Here, under the same roof, are assembled young men from all parts of the world. Here we behold the rare spectacle of thirteen distinct nationalities united in the bonds of charity. How advantageous must not such an assemblage prove to the ecclesiastical student who, whilst having before his eyes a striking proof of the catholicity of his faith, is at the same time thereby enabled to gain an accurate knowledge of the state of the church in the various parts of the world? The young men who come here usually possess more than ordinary talent, and, in the collision of opinion or in the ardor of dispute, genius is awakened. A laudable freedom in proposing difficulties is encouraged in the classes, in which the language adopted by the church in her ritual is in constant use. Premiums are annually distributed to those who have signalized themselves, and this year the Holy Father himself presided over these exercises. If we consider our spiritual advantages, they are not less evident. All our superiors are most exemplary. No one more amiable than our Rector; no one more fatherly than our Confessor; no more perfect models of virtue than all our professors. In fact, the Roman clergy in general are a most learned and religious body of men. How can we visit the shrines of the martyrs or the Limina Apostolorum without feeling a glow of the sacred flame which burned in their bosoms—without resolving to imitate their virtues in order to be able to emulate their usefulness?

"As for the difference of the two countries in manners and customs, I, for my part, can see no good reason why the roughness of a Kentucky backwoodsman should not receive a touch of European polish; or how, if he should acquire something of the piety, politeness, and the *gravitas condita comitate* which are characteristic of the Roman clergy, he should thereby be rendered less apt to become a useful missionary. In my own case, I am sure that my attachment to the institutions of my own country has been increased by my absence from it, and I feel confident that no American can travel in Europe without being more thoroughly convinced that the United States, in natural and civil advantages, is inferior to no country in the world. Is there not something in the constant conversation of persons of so many different nations and dispositions which tends to give an acquaintance with human nature, and to impart that spirit of accommodation and conciliation which may dispose us to become all things to all men, after the example of the model of missionaries? Is there not also something in the absence from parents and friends which tends to purify the affections and to ennoble the motives of action? What I have written, my dear brother, has been prompted by the purest love of religion, and I am sure that the gentlemen of Bardstown are not more ardent in the sacred cause than myself. If they wish to send you to Rome, come cheerfully, persuaded that it is the will of God; if not, it is better for you to remain in Bardstown. God speaks by the mouth of those whom he has placed over us. If you come, make an entire sacrifice of yourself to God previous to your departure. Bring nothing with you but good health, a cheerful and brave heart, and a will prepared to yield obedience to whatever may be enjoined."

This letter seems to have produced the intended effect, since, shortly after its reception, Benedict Spalding set out to join his brother in the Eternal City.

By the beginning of his second year in the Propaganda, Martin had entirely regained his health. He again took up his studies with renewed earnestness, and at the close of the year received the first premiums in all his classes, in consequence of which he was decorated with the gold medal. He even began to grow stout about this time, which caused Bishop David to give him certain hygienic admonitions. "I must tell you," he writes, "that I am not pleased to hear that you are growing fleshy. This corpulence alarms me, and causes me to fear that you do not conform to my prescription, which you praise greatly in one of your letters. I have sometimes told those who enquire after my health that I can not but be well, since I always carry my physician with me; and, upon their asking who that physician is, I answer that it is hunger. The venerable Charles Carroll, when asked what means he employed to preserve his health in such perfect condition, replied that he always left the table hungry."

CHAPTER IV.

LAST YEAR IN ROME—PUBLIC DEFENCE OF THESES FOR THE DOCTOR'S CAP.

HE Rector of the Propaganda during the four years which Martin Spalding passed there was Count Reisach, who was afterwards made Archbishop of Munich, and who died a cardinal of the Roman Church just before the assembling of the Vatican Council. He was one of the gentlest of men, and his warm-hearted frankness of manner soon won the confidence and affection of his young American pupil. Dr. Cullen, the present Cardinal-Archbishop of Dublin, taught him Scripture. His spiritual director and confessor was Father Vincent Pallotti, one of the most saintly men of his age. "The good odor of his virtues," wrote Archbishop Spalding of Father Pallotti nearly forty years after he had left the Propaganda, "still sweetens my memory, and clusters like a halo around my heart."

Mezzofanti was also a frequent visitor at the Propaganda at this time. "In appearance," Martin says in one of his letters, "he is not remarkable, but, as a linguist, he is the prodigy of the age. He speaks thirty languages with ease and fluency, understands forty, and can learn a new one in a few days. It is quite an ordinary occurrence, when he is here in the Propaganda, to hear him speak in seven or eight different tongues almost in the same breath. He has read all our best English authors, and frequently recites long passages from our poets. Within the last few weeks, he has learned the Congo language, which he is now engaged in teaching to some missionaries who are to be sent to evangelize the savages of that country." He was, here in the Propaganda, for the first time thrown into contact with the fathers of the Society of Jesus; and the evidences which he beheld of their great learning and virtue soon won his enthusiastic admiration. "They are," he writes, "the brightest ornaments of the clergy, as they are, in my opinion, the most noble, the most learned, and the most useful auxiliary corps which the church has ever been able to summon to her assistance."

From his correspondence, we perceive that his mind was dwelling with unusual interest already then upon the relation of the church to European civilization—a subject which he afterwards labored with such earnestness to develop and elucidate. In one of his letters, he sketches a plan for a history of Italian literature, which, starting from the causes that led to the neglect of letters after the fall of the Roman Empire, should describe the religious, social, and political conditions which brought about their partial revival in the twelfth and thirteenth centuries. He would then show how, in the fifteenth century, Italy became the centre of intellectual activity—the focus whence the rest of Europe received its light. The whole investigation should prove that Europe owes its religion, its laws, its arts and sciences, to Italy, who is indebted for this pre-eminence to the beneficent influence of the church, and, above all, to the fact that Rome had been the home of the Vicar of Christ. Although this plan is imperfect, it nevertheless shows a predilection for those studies which regard the historical and practical side of the church's action upon society, which to the end of his life continued to have a special charm for him.

In the spring of 1834, while Martin Spalding was still a student in the Propaganda, Bishop England arrived in Rome to give an account of his mission to the republic of Hayti. He had left the Eternal City about a year before, with power of apostolic legate to settle the affairs of the church in that island, and he now returned to make a report of what he had seen and done.

Although his efforts had been but partially successful, still he had attended to the business upon which he had been sent with a despatch and energy that excited the admiration of the officials of the Roman Court, who are proverbially slow and deliberate in all affairs of importance. His arrival in Rome was preceded by the rumor that, as a reward for his many and signal services to the cause of religion, he was to receive the cardinal's hat. The Dublin *Evening Post* had first given currency to this report, which was copied by the journals of Paris; and when Bishop England passed through France on his way to Rome, he was everywhere congratulated by the French bishops upon his elevation to the Roman purple. The rumor, like others of more recent date concerning the appointment of an American cardinal, proved to be without foundation; but the fact that it was so generally believed to be true shows the high opinion which the Catholics of Europe had formed of Bishop England's talents and labors in the cause of the church. The American students in the Propaganda were, of course, proud of Dr. England, and enthusiastic admirers of his genius as a writer and speaker. Their letters of this date are filled with the praises of this wonderful man, whom the Italian cardinals called *il vescovo a vapore*—the steam-bishop; meaning probably something similar to what Sydney Smith sought to express when he called Webster a steam-engine in breeches.

It was during this visit of Bishop England to Rome that Martin Spalding, having completed the full course of studies as prescribed in the Propaganda, made a public defence of two hundred and fifty-six propositions, chosen from universal theology, church history, and canon law.

Defence of Theses for the Doctor's Cap. 51

It is seldom that a candidate for the doctorate defends so large a number of theses embracing so wide a range of subjects.

Martin Spalding was the first American student in Rome to whom this honor was granted, and since his time but one or two Americans have received the doctor's cap after a defence of propositions chosen from universal theology, Scripture, and canon law. Bishop England was present when the young Kentuckian stood up to make good his two hundred and fifty-six propositions against any and every foe who might see fit to enter the lists against him; and from his graphic pen we have an interesting account of the closing scenes in Martin Spalding's student life.

The defence of the grand thesis is by no means a mere ceremony of formality and display. Only the best students are selected, and they enter the field in fear, not knowing whether victory or defeat awaits them.

"There is a formidable Jesuit here," wrote Bishop England, "who is a professor of dogmatic theology at the Roman College, who has lately swept, in a comparatively short encounter, half a dozen of these youthful aspirants from the field of fame; and their teachers were neither insensible nor inactive on and after the encounter. The effects of this carnage are not yet at an end; gauntlet after gauntlet is flung down, and the judges of such feats are in continual requisition. On the present occasion, John Martin Spalding, a Kentuckian, and the senior student of the United States of North America, a pupil of the Urban College, published a respectful and manly Latin address to the Congregation of Cardinals presiding over the affairs of the Propaganda, in which, after wishing their eminences happiness and health, he informs them of what he considers the blessings diffused by their institution, for which they deserve thanks: and, as he has finished the usual course of studies, he has determined to express publicly his gratitude by sustaining his theses, expressing the doctrines which he shall endeavor to teach in those distant regions to which he is about to return. For this purpose, he will appear, God willing, in the morning, in the great hall of the college, when and where it shall be lawful for any one who thinks proper to controvert what he undertakes to defend; and, in the afternoon, he will appear in the college chapel, where three select champions will successively make their assaults, after which he will be ready to meet any other that may be disposed to try his strength. Then follows a list of two hundred and fifty-six propositions which he undertakes to defend. They are taken from the several treatises of theology and canon law. Copies were sent to the other colleges, and special invitations were given to several individuals whose attendance was particularly desirable. About half-past eight o'clock on Thursday morning (July 17, 1834), I arrived at the gate of the college, on the pavement in front of which was a profuse scattering of sweet-smelling green leaves; the bay and myrtle predominated; the gate itself was open, and this fragrant path marked the way to the interior.

"The strewing continued up the great staircase, along the open gallery of the first floor, to the great door leading to the principal corridor, along this passage to the gate of the principal hall. This room, about eighty feet in length, by perhaps forty wide and twenty in height, has its walls decorated with paintings of students of this college who had borne testimony to the faith under the inflictions of the deadly pain by which they were in remote regions martyred for their discharge of duty; thus exhibiting to the youth who are therein educated the constancy which the church expects from them under similar circumstances. At the further extremity, opposite the door, was a carpeted platform, elevated two steps; upon this the young Kentuckian was seated, with a small table before him, having also seated by him on one side his professor of theology, a Roman, and on the other his professor of law, a Bavarian count, who is a priest and rector of the college. The renowned scholar, Angelo Mai, presided, being seated on your right as you entered the hall, near this platform. A range of chairs extended on either side, leaving a passage of about ten feet wide in the centre. These chairs were intended for cardinals, bishops, or other prelates and professors who might arrive; ranges of benches parallel to these on each side, behind, were pretty generally thronged by students of that or other colleges, and by strangers. No cardinal was present in the forenoon; the Bishop of Charleston was the only prelate of the episcopal order; but several others of various grades, secular and regular, amongst whom were the rectors and professors of several colleges, occupied most of the chairs.

"The first argument had been concluded when I arrived; it was conducted by an Italian secular priest, whose name I could not learn. The second was made by a Dominican friar, a man of very great talent and ingenuity; he had also nearly concluded. An Infirmarian, or Crutched friar, conducted the third with considerable spirit and ability. Next succeeded an Irishman, a student of the Roman Seminary, who did argue most lustily against the real presence and the sacrifice of the Mass. The next was a German Jesuit, well known in the United States, Father Kohlman, who for nearly half an hour argued eloquently against the primacy of the Holy See. He was followed by Signor Rosa, one of the minutanti and a professor of theology, who argued against the power of remitting all sins in the sacrament of penance. Dr. Wiseman, Rector of the English College, next argued for the figurative meaning of the words of our Saviour in the institution of the eucharist, introducing various analogies from Persian, Arabic, and other Asiatic writers, some of which are pompously brought forward in the preface to ponderous tomes of polyglots by an Oxford doctor of modern celebrity. The celebrated Monsignor Mezzofanti then followed up with considerable subtlety and acuteness, when the great bell announced midday.

"The young American had now been upwards of four hours sharply engaged in scholastic disputation, in the Latin language, with men of various nations and of no ordinary calibre, and had not failed or hesitated in a single answer.

"To a stranger, the style of this mode of disputation is altogether a novelty. You are carried back by the introduction of the argument to all the pompous style of ancient heraldry and regulated courtesy of disputation. The disputant generally commences by a high-wrought compliment to the institution, its various officers, to the particular professor of the science against which he is to make his assault, to the genius and erudition of the defender; then speaks of his own defeats, how reluctant he is to couch a lance against so powerful an opponent; but if he makes a pass or two, it is not in the vain hope of victory, for which there is no chance, but that, taught by the prowess he will elicit, he may improve. He then commences his attack, and presses on generally with great vigor.

"The defendant, in turn, professes the high estimation in which he holds his opponent, introducing in his description an enumeration of the offices he has held, the honors he has obtained, and the great qualities for which he is remarkable. Then he briefly recapitulates the argument, dissects it, and takes its separate parts for successive examination, and, after having thus disposed of it, he says he is inclined to think it not so strong as at first supposed.

"There was a recess for rest, dinner, and preparation for the afternoon. But on this occasion the assembly was more solemn. The disposition of the church was similar to that of the hall. The dresses were, for cardinals, bishops, and other prelates, what are called robes of the second class—the cardinals in red, the bishops in purple, and such of the other prelates as were entitled to it in the same color. The cardinals, of whom only seven were present, sat on very rich chairs on the right side of the chapel. Three chosen disputants occupied the first places on the opposite side; then the bishops and other dignitaries. The Swiss Guard formed at the door and lined the passage. The exercises began with an exceedingly ingenious argument against the primacy of St. Peter, made with great tact and skill by the prelate Raffaelle Fornari, Canonist of the Penitentiaria, former Professor of Theology in the Propaganda, and a man of the very first ability. This lasted nearly three-quarters of an hour. The second was on the subject of Grace, by Father Perrone, a Jesuit, Professor of Dogmatic Theology in the Roman College. This is a man of the most profound research and great logical powers, with an admirable memory. This engagement lasted half an hour. Nearly as long again was occupied in an argument against the divine character of Christianity by Father Modena, Assistant to the Master of the Sacred Palace, and a Dominican friar.

"The cardinals rose and shook hands with the Kentuckian, who was carried away by his fellow-students in triumph." *

We shall now for a moment turn our attention to ecclesiastical affairs in Kentucky during the time that Martin Spalding was in Rome.

Bishop Flaget, who was of an extremely sensitive disposition, which caused him to suffer greatly from disappointments and afflictions, had several times during the quarter of a century in which he had so successfully labored in Kentucky desired to be relieved of the responsibilities and cares of the

* *Bishop England's Works*, vol. iv. p. 131.

episcopal office, thinking, in his great humility, that he was unable to bear so weighty a burden.

After repeated solicitations, he at length succeeded, in 1832, in obtaining from the Holy See the acceptance of his resignation, and the appointment of Bishop David to the see of Bardstown, with Dr. Chabrat as coadjutor.

The intelligence of these changes, which was received during the absence of Bishop Flaget from the diocese, produced very general and great dissatisfaction both among the clergy and the laity of Kentucky. Bishop David protested against his unexpected promotion, and the whole diocese was filled with grief at the loss of Bishop Flaget, who was loved and revered by all as a father.

Bishop Flaget, when the news of the excitement in Kentucky reached him, was in St. Louis. He perceived the necessity of returning at once to his old diocese, and persuaded Bishop Rosati to accompany him, in order to assist in averting the storm which seemed to be brewing. They found, upon their arrival, that the report of the general discontent among both priests and people had not been exaggerated. The new state of things had been brought about so unexpectedly that the bishops seemed doubtful what course to take. Bishop David was resolute in his *nolo episcopari*. Bishop Flaget was convinced that age and infirmity rendered it impossible that he should again assume the duties of the episcopal office; and all seemed to feel that Dr. Chabrat would not be acceptable either to the priests or people of Kentucky. Something, however, had to be done, and the bishops, after having considered all the bearings of the case, finally determined to petition the Holy See to accept the resignation of Bishop David, and to dispose at will of Bishop Flaget and Dr. Chabrat.

The following spring, an answer to the petition was received from the Holy Father, in which he accepted the resignation of Bishop David, and reinstated Bishop Flaget as Bishop of Bardstown. Nothing was said concerning the appointment of Dr. Chabrat. Thus Bishop Flaget's efforts to get relief from the cares of his office resulted, for the time at least, in depriving him of a coadjutor and throwing the undivided burden back upon his own shoulders. In his sensitive state of mind, this was very distressing; and he was unable to find peace or rest until he finally succeeded in obtaining from Rome the appointment of Dr. Chabrat as his coadjutor. The bulls arrived on the 29th of June, 1834, and, in precisely a month from the day of their reception, Dr. Chabrat was consecrated Bishop of Bolina, *in partibus infidelium*, and Coadjutor of the Bishop of Bardstown. Bishop Chabrat, though an excellent priest and a most worthy gentleman, was never a favorite with the priests and Catholic people of Kentucky, many of whom were opposed to his appointment. It is to this feeling that certain remarks of Bishop Flaget, in the following letter to Martin Spalding, refer. The letter is dated the 17th of May, 1834:

"DEAR MARTIN:

"The peace and the mercy of God be with you! I must pay you my compliments for having raised yourself above his Eminence the Cardinal-Prefect. In his last letter, he promised that, *ineunte vere*, you should start for your diocese; but it appears that his eminence had not consulted you, as, according to Benedict's letter, you will not leave Rome before next August, after having completed your studies and made a public defence of theses. The holy will of God be done! If this delay turn to your improvement and the good of the church, as I hope it will, I am content; for I have no other aim than the glory of God and the honor of the church. Be sure that a large field awaits you in Kentucky, and, let your learning, piety, and zeal be never so eminent, we will give you abundant opportunity of putting them to use. Your modesty in asserting that, after four years of great application to study, you have scarcely learned the catechism of divinity pleases me very much. You have said nothing that is not true, but to have sufficient candor to acknowledge it is praiseworthy. What must you think of my dear Kentucky missionaries, who have been ordained after three years of theology, having, whilst studying, to teach daily several hours in the college? When you and my dear James return, we will establish the seminary on a better basis, I hope. If you succeed well in your public examinations, and praises are bestowed upon you, receive them, my dear Martin, with gratitude, but immediately refer them to God. It is better to have moderate talents with humility than to have eminent gifts with pride and vanity. Let me say, *en passant*, that my young Propagandist has favored those who opposed the Rev. M. Chabrat's appointment. This, my dear child, is imprudent, to say the least, and calculated to wound my feelings. Yet I forgive you from the bottom of my heart, on account of your want of experience of the ways of the world, having been all your life a stranger to its malice and wickedness. When you visit the Limina Apostolorum, beg all the apostles to obtain strength for me in my trials, which are many and sometimes almost intolerable."

The reply to this letter of Bishop Flaget was written by Martin Spalding, now the Rev. Dr. Spalding, on the eve of setting out on his journey home:

"RT. REV. FATHER IN CHRIST:

"I should have answered your letter long since, but my occupations during the few weeks which preceded my departure from Rome crowded upon me with such pressure that I could not find even a moment's time to devote to my good old father in Christ. After my public disputation, I entered into a retreat which lasted two weeks, to prepare myself for the reception of holy orders. I was ordained sub-deacon on the 3d, deacon on the 10th, and priest on the 13th of August, by a special dispensation of the Holy Father, which I asked myself, and on the 15th I started on my journey homeward. From the hurry in which I received holy orders, and my haste in leaving Rome after my ordination, you may conclude that my delay here has not been voluntary, or because of my having raised myself above his Eminence Cardinal Pedicini, as you seem to think. No, beloved father, the will of my superiors alone, whom I am bound to obey, caused me to delay so long to return to you; though, strictly speaking, I have not delayed at all, since the course of theology in the Propaganda is of four years, and, even counting my first year here, in which sickness prevented me from studying, I have been in Rome but four years. However, I have simply been obedient to the express will of my superiors, to whom, if fault there be, the fault must be imputed.

"Dear father, never have I passed any time of my life in such perfect happiness as the two weeks which I spent in retreat previous to my ordination; nor have I ever enjoyed before the peace and tranquillity which dwell in my soul since I am a priest. I feel as if I were in a new world. I have dedicated myself wholly, entirely, and permanently to God in the priesthood. By the help of his holy grace, I hope to persevere in my present dispositions to the close of my life, and thus to be able to do something for his honor and glory on the missions of Kentucky.

"Be assured, dear father, that you shall have no difficulty with me as regards reverence, submission, and obedience to my bishop, whomsoever God may choose or has chosen to appoint. I have not learned insubordination and disobedience within the walls of the Propaganda. I have always esteemed and loved the Rev. Mr. Chabrat, and my reverence for him will be increased if he is made bishop. In short, I promise that, with the grace of God, I shall ever be obedient to any and all lawfully constituted authority; this promise I made at my ordination, and I hope never to violate it. A few days previous to my departure, I went to say farewell to the Holy Father, upon which occasion I presented him with a handsomely bound copy of my theses. He seemed pleased, received me with the greatest kindness, and sends through me a thousand blessings to you and your whole diocese.

"If God bless my homeward journey, I shall have many things to tell you when the great joy of seeing you again will be given me."

CHAPTER V.

ORDAINED PRIEST—RETURNS HOME—IS MADE PASTOR OF THE CATHEDRAL IN BARDSTOWN—PROFESSOR IN THE SEMINARY—THE "MINERVA."

HE four years which Martin Spalding passed in Rome under the shadow of the Vatican certainly had a most marked and beneficial influence upon his life. The very surroundings of the place taught him lessons which cannot be learned from books. Wherever he might turn, monuments of Christian faith and Christian heroism spoke to him of the glories of the indefectible church. The tombs of the martyrs; their bones; the very ground which they had watered with their blood, in testimony of Christ; the sacred corridors of the Catacombs, where even now one can almost hear the echoes of the footfalls of those generations of Christian heroes who alone, without human aid, strong only in their faith in God and the purity of their lives, stood up and battled for truth and freedom of conscience with the masters of the world, until at last their persecutors came and knelt at the foot of the cross, converted by the very blood they had shed; the temples of religion, whose material structure even lifts up the soul to God, and bows it down in adoration; all the arts, which here have been led captive in the train of religion, and brought each to add a jewel to her immortal crown; the wonderful and inspiring ceremonies of the church, which in Rome alone are seen in all their beauty and perfection—all

this could not but have a beneficent and elevating influence upon the uncorrupted and generous nature of this young American. A new world was here revealed to him, and his soul glowed with a love and enthusiasm which it had not hitherto known. From his letters we have seen how, from the first moment, his heart went out in love to the church in Rome, "whose faith is spoken of in the whole world," even as a child leaps into the arms of its mother. Upon no subject was he more entertaining or did he speak more gladly than upon that of Rome; and even with regard to those Roman manners and customs which, to an American, appear odd, he never suffered himself to indulge in censure or harsh criticism.

In Rome, too, he was thrown, in relations more or less intimate, with men of the first ability and the greatest learning. When he arrived, Cardinal Cappellari, afterwards Gregory XVI.—a man of considerable literary attainments and of great knowledge—was the Cardinal-Prefect of the Propaganda, and, as we have seen, he received the young American with paternal kindness, and never ceased to encourage him to go manfully forward in the way upon which he had entered.

Count Reisach, a German nobleman—the most amiable of men, who to high birth, exalted position, and great learning added the charm and simplicity of manner which Christian virtue alone can give—was his immediate superior, being Rector of the Propaganda.*

Monsignor Mai, afterwards Cardinal, the inventor and restorer of the palimpsests, who, at the age of thirty-seven, had made more additions to the stock of ancient learning

---

* "You may depend upon it," said Coleridge, "religion is, in its essence, the most gentlemanly thing in the world. It will *alone* gentilize, if unmixed with cant; and I know nothing else that will, *alone*. Certainly not the army, which is thought to be the grand embellisher of manners."

than a century had done before him, was Secretary of the Propaganda, which gave the young student opportunity of frequently seeing and hearing this wonderful man, to whom, after his return to the United States, he sometimes wrote.

Occasionally, too, he was permitted to converse with or, at least, to hear famous men who were not immediately connected with the Propaganda. The pontificate of Gregory XVI. was remarkably fruitful of such men. Thus Martin Spalding was made acquainted with Mezzofanti, Wiseman, Theiner, Palma, Perrone, and others of scarcely less note. Nothing awakens the mind of the student like the contact of higher and more perfectly developed intellects; and, in the present instance, the illustrious examples of so many men who, by their brilliant talents and great learning, were doing or had already done so much for the honor and glory of the church filled him with a noble ambition to emulate in the new world their great achievements in the old. He also brought with him from the Eternal City, as he states in his letter to Bishop Flaget, the spirit of obedience to all lawful authority, and, I may add, a special love and veneration for the visible head of the church, without which Catholic obedience, in the true sense, is not possible. His firm hope had proven to be well founded—God had permitted him to finish his studies and to become a priest, and now, at the age of twenty-four, with a mind well stored and a heart all aglow with zeal, he was prepared to return to his native land to enter upon his life-work.

On the 29th of August, 1834, he sailed from Leghorn for New York, where he landed on the 26th of October. "I remember," said Archbishop McCloskey, referring to this, "the day and date full well, because I myself was then just on the eve of departure for that holy city from which he came; and it was during the few days of his sojourn in New York that I first made his acquaintance, which soon ripened into a friendship that grew and strengthened until the last day of his life."

On his way home, he passed through Philadelphia to visit his old friend and professor, Bishop Kenrick, who, when he set out on his journey to Rome four years before, was still a professor in the seminary at Bardstown. In the cathedral of Philadelphia he preached his first sermon in America. He touched the soil of his native State at Louisville, where he remained a few days to take note of the progress which the church was making in this already at that time the most important city in Kentucky.

Mother Catherine Spalding, the first Mother-Superioress of the Sisters of Charity in Kentucky, and the foundress of the St. Vincent's Orphan Asylum in Louisville, had just begun this noble work, which, in the providence of God, was to be the means of saving so many helpless children from ruin in this world and in eternity.

He, of course, visited the asylum. The first orphan whom Mother Catherine ever received, who is now distinguished alike for cultivation of mind and for a life devoted to deeds of charity, has described that visit to me: " I shall never forget (these are her words) the rosy, beaming, almost boyish face, so full of intelligence, so perfectly spiritual in its whole expression, as it appeared in the poor school-room of the orphans. A word of introduction from the beloved mother, a tender blessing, and in a moment the accomplished scholar and the eloquent priest was sitting in the midst of thirty little girls, the oldest of whom was not twelve, relating his adventures in the old world, telling anecdotes of college life, giving graphic pictures of famous scenes and objects of interest in Europe. So entertaining was the narrator, so lifelike yet simple his délineations, that his hearers, as many an audience afterwards, under the charms of his eloquence, lost the sense of the passage of time." Trivial in itself, this little circumstance is worthy of record, as illustrating one of the most marked features in the character of Archbishop Spalding, which was his great love of children, and the wonderful power which he possessed of winning their attention and sympathy.

When an old man, broken by many cares and many labors, increasing infirmity forewarned him of the near approach of death, he requested that the orphan children for whom he had provided a home might follow what of him was mortal to the grave.

It had been Bishop Flaget's intention, it appears, to make Dr. Spalding president of the seminary and college in Bardstown. He had for several years desired to establish in his own diocese a college modelled after that of the Propaganda, in which he would be able to train up a band of efficient missionaries for the great West; and he relied upon his Roman students to assist him in carrying out this plan.

But when Dr. Spalding arrived in Kentucky, the Rev. Mr. Chabrat had been made coadjutor, and Bishop Flaget was preparing for a journey to Europe, which in all probability would cause him to be absent from his diocese for several years. In this state of affairs, Dr. Spalding was unwilling to take charge of the seminary, and he was therefore made pastor of the cathedral. St. Joseph's College was at this time managed by a Board of Trustees, under the presidency of the Bishop as moderator. Dr. Spalding was at once elected a member of this Board, and also accepted the professorship of philosophy in the seminary. The Propaganda bound its students by solemn promise to write to the Cardinal-Prefect once in every two years a full account of their labors and success in the missions. Dr. Spalding was scrupulously faithful to this obligation up to the time when he was released from it by his appointment as Coadjutor of

Bishop Flaget; and from these letters to the Propaganda, copies of most of which I have been able to procure, we have a reliable account of his labors on the missions from 1834 to 1848.

St. Joseph's Cathedral was built by Bishop Flaget, and dedicated to the service of God in 1819. It was, at that time and for many years after, the finest church in the West. The congregation was, with one exception, the largest in the diocese. Four stations, at which Mass was said, were attached to it, and received monthly visits from the pastor. The whole number of souls committed to the pastoral care of Dr. Spalding was about fifteen hundred. Of these, he says, in one of his letters to the Propaganda, nearly eight hundred approached the sacraments monthly. On Sundays, he sang Mass and preached in the cathedral, and during the week visited one or other of the stations, where he also preached and administered the sacraments. He seems to have labored with remarkable success; for, besides the large number of monthly communicants referred to, he occasionally in his letters makes mention of the conversion of Protestants. In two years, he received into the church not less than fifty converts, which was certainly a very considerable number in so small a place as Bardstown.

He devoted much of his time to instructing the young and ignorant, especially the negroes, of whom there was a large number in his congregation.

The tone of his letters at this time shows with what earnestness and healthful zest he had entered upon his apostolical labors. He is not impatient, he is not too eager, but he finds rest only in work; and the more he does, the more he feels the need of doing. Much had been done, but much more remained to be done. The condition of progress is that, as we advance, the still greater effort must we make to go yet further.

He is wholly absorbed in his vocation, and all the currents of his life are tributary to his soul's high purpose. He preaches, he hears confessions, he visits the sick, he teaches the ignorant, and, when he has nothing else to do, he flies back to his dear books, the ever-welcome companions of his vacant hours.

He had but one kind of duty, but one love, but one spouse to whom he had plighted the troth of his soul; his life was undivided, and he was happy. They who think a wifeless man unblest know naught of the life of the soul in itself and in God. There is a manner of life so high, so certain of its course, so perfectly harmonious with the deepest cravings and highest instincts of the heart, that the soul which has tasted of its delights asks for no other blessedness here on earth. It does not crave; it could not bear closer contact with flesh and blood.

The world has not, I believe, a body of men who are more contented, better satisfied with their lot in life and the work which they are doing, than the priests of the Catholic Church,

Shortly after Dr. Spalding's return home, the faculty of St. Joseph's, of which he was a member, began the publication of the first Catholic periodical ever issued in Kentucky, under the title of the *St. Joseph's College Minerva*.

The *Minerva* was a monthly magazine, and, though under the control of Catholics, it was rather literary than religious in its character.

Dr. Spalding was its leading contributor, and made, through its columns, his first appearance as an essayist and reviewer.

He wrote for it a series of papers, in which he reviewed a *Journal of Travels in Southern Europe;* and also an essay on the *Study of History*. In a paper entitled *Thoughts on Man*, he introduces a student, who, after having travelled over Europe, seeks the mountains of Switzerland to indulge his love of solitude and meditation in presence of the sublimest scenes in nature. Where Sovran Blanc, the monarch of mountains, raises his bald and awful head from out the silent sea of pines, he sits him down and communes with the world around him, and from the created rises to the Creator; and then, turning his thoughts back upon his own soul, he argues, from its infinite longings and aspirations, its immortality.

A few passages from this essay will serve as examples of Dr. Spalding's style in his earliest literary efforts:

"Thus situated, he viewed and examined all the beauty and grandeur which nature spread before him. He contemplated the earth, with its mountains, and valleys, and varied landscapes. His mind ranged among the multitudinous departments and branches of the mineral, vegetable, and animal kingdoms, catching glimpses of the principal beauties of each, and feasting upon the general order and symmetry of the great whole. He then endeavored, by the light of reason, to reduce the phenomena of nature to their proper causes, and was delighted to find that these and all that falls under man's observation constitute one splendid and united aggregate, without the slightest break of harmony or the least dissonance of parts. Even those objects which, viewed separately, seemed out of place, tended, when considered in relation to the whole, to increase the general symmetry. Having in spirit traversed the varied beauties of earth, he turned his enraptured gaze to heaven. His unchained thought travelled through those boundless regions of ether, studded with worlds, and, under the luminous guidance of Astronomy, explored, as far as man's contracted span will permit, the various relations and several beauties of those brilliant orbs that roll above us. Yet notwithstanding the vastness and immeasurable grandeur of the universe; notwithstanding the great multiplicity and variety of its parts, what order, what harmony, what unity! Not a single stone is misplaced in the splendid edifice; not a flaw in the noble vase. The unity of the work argues intelligence and design in the artist. Such symmetry could not be the result of blind chance—a name to which no reality corresponds. Who, enquired he, fitted together with so masterly a hand the various parts of the universe?

> "What hand behind the scene,
> What arm almighty, put these wheeling globes
> In motion, and wound up the vast machine?
> Who rounded in his palm these spacious orbs?
> Who bowled them flaming through the dark profound,
> Numerous as glittering gems of morning dew,
> . . . . . .
> And set the bosom of old night on fire?
> . . . . . .
> Who marshals this bright host, enrols their names,
> Appoints their posts, their marches, and returns,
> Punctual at stated periods? Who disbands
> These veteran troops, their final duty done—
> If e'er disbanded?"

Having concluded that "earth, with her thousand voices, calls on God," he asks himself what are his own relations to this Infinite Being. The soul craves for happiness; its desires, like an inverted cone, expand without limit; possession never satisfies it; in the highest state, it seeks a still higher; it swallows up time, and feels the worthlessness of whatever ceases to be; it shrinks back on itself, and startles at the thought of destruction.

> "'Tis the divinity that stirs within us;
> 'Tis Heaven itself that points out an hereafter
> And intimates eternity to man."

In the mountains of Switzerland, the young traveller meets with a sage who, disgusted with the world, had sought solitude, that undisturbed he might commune with God and nature. He had passed through the exciting scenes of the French Revolution, the Consulate, and the Empire, and the conversation turns upon the social state. The various opinions of philosophers concerning the origin of society are discussed, and the hermit concludes "that whatever may be said of the origin of society, its primary end is the welfare of the members that compose it; that however true may be the maxim that individual interest should be sacrificed to the general good, it should not be pushed to the extent of endangering the interests of the majority; and that when a government, in whatever manner it may be organized, ceases to be advantageous to the majority, it should be exchanged for another more suitable to existing circumstances. The obligatory bonds of society, however unjust and tyrannical may have been the means resorted to for its formation, originate in a contract, whether express or implied, between the *governed* and the *governing*—a contract the obligation of which is as sacred as its fulfilment is all-important. And when one party is guilty of a flagrant violation of the contract—of an infringement that involves the most serious evils—the other can, as is of the nature of a contract, reclaim its rights, and sue for indemnity in the highest chancery of either earth or heaven.

"The justness of your remarks cannot be questioned," rejoined Viator, "whatever hypothesis may be made regarding the formation of society, or whichsoever of the many forms of government we may choose to consider, whether monarchical, aristocratical, republican, or mixed. These principles appear to be founded in the nature of things, and are, of course, unchangeable. The governors and legislators are for the people, not these for those."

CHAPTER VI.

THE "CATHOLIC ADVOCATE"—RELIGIOUS JOURNALISM— EFFORTS TO EXTEND ITS INFLUENCE.

HE *Minerva*, as I have already stated, was rather a literary than a religious magazine. The increase of Catholics, as well as the ability which the young editors of the *Minerva* had shown, led many to think that the church in Kentucky was now able to establish and support a journal specially devoted to the defence of Catholic principles. Of the great need of such a journal there could be no doubt.

The Protestant preachers of that day were very active, and had all the impudence of ignorance in the reckless misstatement of Catholic teachings and practices. Books in defence of the church could not be so easily got as at present, and even those which could be had often failed to grasp the precise phase of religious thought with which the Catholics of the West had to contend. Scattered through the State, they were frequently unable, owing to the small number of missionaries, to see a priest more than twice or three times in the year, and hence could not be well instructed in the doctrines of their faith.

The aggressive character of the Protestant population in the days of camp-meetings and jerking revivals, when superstition and bigotry caused thousands to believe in childish credulity that the Pope was Antichrist, and that Roman Catholics had horns and cloven feet, made the defect of thorough religious training among Catholics more keenly felt.

The necessity of establishing a Catholic journal which, whilst inculcating sound doctrine, would be able to lay hold on each calumny as it would rise, and crush it, or at least deaden its effect, was urgent. For these reasons, at the close of the first year of its existence the *Minerva* ceased to appear, and was succeeded by the *Catholic Advocate*, a weekly journal.

Of this paper Dr. Spalding, whilst continuing to discharge his duties as pastor and professor, became chief editor, assisted by the Rev. G. A. Elder, the Rev. H. Deluynes, who afterwards entered the Society of Jesus, and the Rev. William E. Clark.

The first number, which appeared in February, 1835, contained the following straightforward and manly appeal to the public:

"The fact that Catholics are a vigorous and energetic body cannot be denied. Their continued action, like that of their fathers in the faith, derives a new stimulus from misfortune and oppression. It must ultimately be productive of much good or of much evil. The spirit which animates them is powerful, and, it would seem, from the history of eighteen centuries, unconquerable. Its tendency is highly useful, or dangerous in the extreme. If they are what they are said to be, let them be doomed to disgrace and ruin; their fate will be just. If they are honest and slandered men, it is the duty of the liberal and intelligent portion of their fellow-citizens to support and shield them against sectarian bigotry.

"The verdict of public opinion should never be given but after a patient and dignified hearing of the accused. Hence, on the part of the public, the duty of listening to their vindication, and examining into the merits of their cause; and, on the part of the Catholics, the still more sacred obligation of appearing at the bar of their country, and stating their principles, their belief, their practice as Christians and as citizens. In some cases, not to confute is to confess the charges. Silence would be in these circumstances treachery to themselves, a virtual and cowardly abandonment of their rights as free-born Americans, and even a sort of apostasy from the religion which they profess.

"The language of their actions has hitherto been, it is true, clear and strong. Upon all occasions they have proved themselves peaceful, patriotic, and brave; prodigal alike of their blood and of their intellectual resources for the benefit of all. In the hour of danger, they have fought under the banner of their country. In the time of peace, they have devoted their energies to the education of her youth, that vital part of the republican system. But the religious excitement, or hypocrisy of designing men, heeds not or misconstrues that language, so intelligible, we hope, to the majority of our fellow-citizens. It is lost upon those men, in whose breast a holy zeal, as they call it, for the cause of Christianity and the welfare of their country has not left even a faint vestige of the true American spirit. The love of God and mankind is, in these men, incompatible with a sense and exercise of toleration and justice. They form, we know, a minority; but if they are comparatively few, they are vigilant, active, untiring. They penetrate and act everywhere. In the legislative hall and in the humblest cabin, in the pulpit and during the convivial hour, or in the domestic circle, the voice of slander is heard, and solemnly proclaims, or insidiously whispers, dark things of the Catholics. Their institutions are slandered, their tenets perverted, their attachment and fidelity to their country denied, the public indignation and proscriptive measures openly invoked against them; and, did we not know that we live in the nineteenth century—that we tread the American soil—that we breathe

the free air of a republic—that the march of religious toleration is onward—we might fear a return of those dark and bloody times when the fiend of persecution reared his horrid head and appalled the world. The press wafts on her mighty wings, and spreads, in every place, from Maine to Florida, contempt and distrust for Catholic principles, Catholic practices, Catholic institutions, and, what is still more alarming, the persons of Catholics. The journalist, the novel-writer, the essayist, and the divine unite to bring about this same end, and to crush the devoted Catholic.

"In several parts of the Union, our religious papers have done much to counteract the evil. But, as the attack is, so the defence should be, commensurate with our soil. Upon every point stands an enemy, therefore from every point should spring a friend and protector.

"With these views, and with due acknowledgment of the merits of our already established periodicals, we offer the *Catholic Advocate* to the West, to Kentucky, and principally to our brethren in the faith.

"Our object is not attack, but defence. There is no sectarian rancor, no fanatical zeal in us. We cheerfully grant to others what we claim for ourselves—freedom of conscience, freedom of debate, and unmolested enjoyment of equal rights.

"We say to our brethren in Kentucky—Arouse and support your own cause; you will not appeal in vain to the intelligence, equity, and constitutional spirit of your countrymen; an opportunity is now offered you of dispelling the dark cloud of prejudice which overhangs the minds of many. Give the *Catholic Advocate*, by a general support, extensive circulation and power. Let that paper be in the house of every Catholic in this State. If it fail because you will not have supported it; if your name continue to be a by-word of scorn, accuse not Protestant prejudices, charge not the times with error and bigotry, blame not your country, but yourselves, who sit silent and unconcerned whilst your enemies brand upon you—' Traitors and Idolaters.' "

Religious journalism was at this time in its infancy. A quarter of a century before, there was not a newspaper in America devoted to the interests of any church or denomination of Christians. The influence of the press in defending and propagating faith was comparatively unknown. It was but twelve years since Bishop England had established the *Catholic Miscellany*, which Archbishop Hughes called the first really Catholic journal in the United States. When the *Advocate* was founded, there were but four Catholic newspapers in the country. These were the *Catholic Miscellany*, of Charleston; the *Truth-Teller*, of New York; the *Catholic Herald*, of Philadelphia; and the *Catholic Telegraph*, of Cincinnati.*

Others, such as the *Shamrock*, the *Jesuit*, and the *Green Banner*, had come into life, and, after a short and feeble existence, had died. The young editors of the *Advocate* were not, however, discouraged.

> Sperat infestis, metuit secundis
> Alteram sortem bene preparatum
> Pectus.

They had faith in the mission of the religious press in this age, and especially in this country.

With Americans, Dr. Spalding used to say, newspaper reading is a passion which amounts to a national characteristic. In the Propaganda the American students were proverbial for their eagerness to get hold of journals, whether religious or secular. Now, he argued, this craving must be satisfied. If we do not furnish our people with wholesome food, they will devour that which is noxious. He believed the American people to be frank, honest, and open to con-

* There was also a German Catholic newspaper in Cincinnati—*Der Wahrheitsfreund*.

viction. Their dislike or hatred of the church he ascribed to misapprehension or ignorance of her history and teachings. Hence he believed that if the truth were placed before them plainly, simply, and fearlessly, it could not fail to make a favorable impression upon them. He therefore thought that to the Catholic press in the United States had been given a providential mission of the greatest importance.

Americans have not time, or will not take the trouble, as a general thing, to read heavy books of controversy. Comparatively few Protestants ever enter our churches, and, even when there, everything seems strange, and the sermon intended for Catholics most frequently fails to tell upon those who have not faith. And yet we must reach the non-Catholic mind. "The charity of Christ urges us." Apathy means want of faith, want of hope, want of love. Besides, the church must act intellectually as well as morally. If it is her duty to wrestle ever with the corrupt tendencies of the human heart, to point to heaven when men seek to see only this earth, to utter the indignant protest of the outraged soul when they would fain believe themselves only animals; it is not less a part of her divine mission to combat the intellectual errors of the world. We observe in the history of the church that periods of intellectual activity are almost invariably characterized by moral earnestness and religious zeal. On the other hand, when ignorance invades even the sanctuary, and priests forget to love knowledge, the blood of Christ flows sluggishly through the veins of his spouse, and to the eyes of men she seems to lose something of her divine comeliness. Indeed, there is an essential connection between the thoughts of a people and their actions, especially in an age like ours; and, if we suffer a sectarian and infidel press to control the intellect of the country, our words will fall dead and meaningless upon the hearts of our countrymen. When Dr. Spalding entered upon the duties of the ministry, Protestantism was just assuming that aggressive attitude towards the church which finally culminated and, in a great measure, spent itself in the Know-Nothing movement. It was the period that developed the controversies of Hughes and Breckinridge, and Purcell and Campbell, in both of which the foremost champions of the Protestant cause met with signal defeat. The almost unanimous verdict of Catholics at the present time is, so far as I know, that these discussions proved most useful to the church. Protestantism was defiant, Catholics were calumniated, and the doctrines of the church were treated as obsolete superstitions of a bygone, barbarous age, which no one would dare defend before an impartial audience in the nineteenth century. Catholics were not only thought to be idolaters, but in some parts of the country the ignorance of the people represented them even as a kind of monsters. English Catholic literature was extremely poor, the necessary result of three centuries of relentless persecution of the church wherever the English language was spoken—a persecution of such nature that it rendered it almost impossible for Catholics to receive an education and yet retain their faith.

The young men who, in England and Ireland, and even in this country, aspired to the priesthood, were forced to go to the Continent of Europe to prepare themselves for the reception of holy orders. It is not, therefore, surprising that, even as late as the time of Bishop Milner, the priests of England should have been proverbially ignorant of their own language. In our own country, many of the early missionaries were foreigners, who, though admirably endowed with all the qualities that make true apostles, yet labored under the serious disadvantage of being imperfectly acquainted with the language of the people among whom their lot was cast.

That in this state of things God raised up in his church a race of men who were able triumphantly to defend her, even against the most gifted adversaries, was certainly providential. It was already much to be able to show the Protestants of that day that Catholics had nothing to fear from the public discussion of the grounds of their faith. Catholics, however, in this country have never provoked religious controversy, and have reluctantly consented to enter into it, even when compelled to do so. Shortly after his return from Rome, Dr. Spalding had reason to believe that he would be drawn into a public discussion with a Protestant minister who was eager to show his skill in debate. Having mentioned this in a letter to Bishop Kenrick, of Philadelphia, he received from him the following reply:

"Our controversy here is at an end; yours, I hope, is not begun. Little good is to be expected from discussions with men who are resolved at all hazards to win a triumph. Although it is acknowledged that the Rev. Mr. Hughes was vastly superior to his adversary in sound argument and all that should mark clerical debate, yet Catholics generally think and feel that the priesthood is lowered by such contests. I reluctantly tolerated it."

However much the amiable and gentle nature of Bishop Kenrick might cause him to regret the asperities of religious controversy, he could not but feel that, considering the circumstances of the times, it was impossible to remain silent in presence of the belligerent attitude of the enemies of the church. One of the most important works with which he has enriched Catholic literature grew out of a controversy which had been forced upon him.

No one could be more averse to controversy of any kind than Dr. Spalding; but, from the first year of his priesthood down to the day of his death, he never remained silent in the presence of the calumniators of his faith, and he never suffered an attack upon the doctrines or history of the church, proceeding from a source worthy of notice, to pass without reply. Sincerely loving the free institutions of his country, he could not think that, whilst all the world was writing and speaking, Catholics alone should be silent. He had too much faith in the candor and sense of the American people to doubt that anything but good could come of the frank and fearless defence of Catholic truth before them. As free institutions provoke thought, enquiry, and the consequent collision of minds, they render intellectual contests a necessity. And hence, humanly speaking, it is impossible that the representatives of any system of doctrines should maintain their ground in a free country unless they enter into the public thought of the country and meet their adversaries on the broad field of its intellectual life. The great and far-seeing mind of Cardinal Wiseman perceived this truth, and he acted upon it in England with the happiest results. In the Tractarian movement, when the Church of England was divided within itself, and her own children were engaged in the most lively controversies with one another, prudent and timid Catholics counselled their brothers to abstain from all interference in what, as they supposed, did not concern them.

Far from accepting these counsels of fear, Cardinal Wiseman, with the co-operation of Daniel O'Connell and others, founded the *Dublin Review*, precisely that he might be able to enter into the intellectual contest which was then agitating the Anglican Establishment.

Referring to this in after years, when Anglicanism had been forced to give up to the church so many of its most devoted and gifted sons, he wrote:

"But even in that first bud of the rising power, it was impossible for a calm and hopeful eye not to see new signs in the religious firmament which it became a duty to observe, unless one wished to incur the divine reproach addressed to those who note not the providential warnings and friendly omens of the spiritual heavens. For a Catholic to have overlooked all this, and allowed the wonderful phenomenon to pass by, not turned to any spiritual purpose, but gazed at till it died out, would have been more than stupidity—it would have been wickedness. To watch its progress; to observe its phases; to influence, if possible, its direction; to move it gently towards complete attainment of its unconscious aims; and, moreover, to protest against its errors, to warn against its dangers, to provide arguments against its new modes of attack, and to keep lifted up the mask of beauty under which it had, in sincerity, covered the ghastly and soulless features of Protestantism; these were the duties which the new *Review* undertook to perform, or which, in no small degree, it was expressly created to discharge."

The whole civilized world, to-day, is agitated by questions much deeper and more general than those which occupied the thoughts of the Oxford Tractarians. Protestantism has drifted out from among the vital issues of the age. As a system of doctrines, it is a mere wreck. Questions which concern the fundamental and primary truths of all religion now fill the minds of thinking men. These questions are no longer confined to the pages of heavy and unwieldy volumes, read only by students. No sooner does a serious book appear, seeming to throw light upon doubtful points, than its results are epitomized by the reviewer and the essayist, and thus made the theme of conversation in the select circles of the better educated classes. From the quarterlies and monthlies they find their way, in a diluted form, into the daily press, where they are spread before the devouring eyes of the millions. The whole secular press, with its thousand mouths, proclaims, without ceasing, by day and by night, errors which imply the negation of God and of the soul, the subversion of religion and society. May we not say, with Cardinal Wiseman, that it would be worse than stupidity, it would be positive wickedness, for Catholics to remain idle spectators of this conflict of the church with the world, of truth with error? The school question is certainly one of vital importance in our country and age; but is the education received in the school-room the only, or is it even the chief education? Does not society, does not the literature of a country, does not the press educate?

Dr. Spalding, with that practical wisdom which so eminently belonged to him, saw, as by intuition, the great work which the press in this country was destined to perform in defending and propagating Catholic truth; and he therefore, from the very first year of his priesthood, labored earnestly to extend its influence and to elevate its character. He wrote almost constantly for the *Catholic Advocate*, especially during the earlier years of its existence, though his contributions to the press were by no means confined to its columns. He wrote for the *United States Catholic Magazine*, the *Catholic Cabinet*, the *Metropolitan*, and other periodicals. For several years he was one of the editors of the *Metropolitan*, in which many of the essays and reviews afterwards published in the *Miscellanea*, made their first appearance. In his letters to the Propaganda, to which I have already referred, he makes frequent allusions to his efforts to defend and propagate Catholic doctrine by means of the press. In 1858, the *Advocate* having ceased to appear several years before, Bishop Spalding founded the *Louisville Guardian*, which he placed under the editorial control of a committee of laymen.

He communicated his views concerning the new journal

in a letter to Archbishop Kenrick, from which I make the following extract:

"We are about to start a new Catholic paper here—the *Guardian*. It will be edited by a committee of Catholic laymen, who will take control of it under the auspices of the St. Vincent's Society. We intend to work for freedom of education and for the poor, to try to do something towards arresting the great evil of our day—the ruin of Catholic children. The great seat of this ruin is in your Eastern cities. Hundreds and thousands of these youths come out here lost for ever. God help our poor children!"

Notwithstanding the many cares and labors of the episcopal office, Bishop Spalding found time to write something for almost every number of the *Guardian*, down to the time when the occupation of Kentucky by hostile armies rendered the suspension of its publication necessary. No enterprise to extend the influence of the Catholic press ever failed to meet with his most cordial approval. One of the reasons for which he so greatly desired to see a Catholic university founded in the United States, was that he believed it would become an intellectual centre which would give to the Catholic press of this country a position and a power which no efforts that have hitherto been made have been able to obtain for it.

CHAPTER VII.

PRESIDENT OF ST. JOSEPH'S COLLEGE—PASTOR OF ST. PETER'S CHURCH, IN LEXINGTON—DIOCESE OF NASHVILLE.

N 1838, by the unanimous vote of the Board of Trustees of St. Joseph's College, Dr. Spalding was chosen President of that institution. He had been pastor of the cathedral for four years. God had blessed his labors, and he was contented. He, moreover, greatly preferred the duties of the ministry to those which devolve upon the president of a college. He, however, accepted the office contrary to his own wishes, at the urgent request of Bishop Flaget, with the understanding that he should be permitted to resign whenever another capable of taking the position could be found. Bishop Flaget, finding that he was anxious to return to what he considered a more apostolic life, permitted him to retire from the college at the end of two years, and immediately appointed him pastor of St. Peter's Church, in Lexington, Kentucky.

Lexington lies on a fork of the Elkhorn River, in the heart of one of the most beautiful and fertile districts in the world, the famous Blue Grass region of Kentucky. When Dr. Spalding was sent there, in 1840, it was the second city in population in the State. It was also the seat of Transylvania University, the oldest institution of learning in the West. The people were wealthy, and had that kind of pride with which new-gotten riches nearly always infect character; but, above all, they were thoroughly Protestant.

Lexington was the home of Clay, who was Kentucky's hero in those days, when a Kentuckian was nothing if not political. It was the home, too, of the Breckinridges, who, besides being politicians, were the doughty champions of Protestantism. There were few Catholics in that part of the State, and Dr. Spalding's missionary field extended over eleven counties, through which he travelled in every direction in search of the lost sheep that lay hidden in the dense forests, which the feet of them that announce the glad tidings had then but seldom trodden. Many who had practically abandoned the church, having strayed beyond the reach of its influence, were brought back by his untiring labors, and induced to reconcile themselves with God. Many, too, who had contracted marriage contrary to the laws of the church, were induced by his touching appeals to make right what had been faulty in the contract, and thus whole families were saved to the faith.

An incident which happened whilst Dr. Spalding was pastor of Lexington is worthy of record, as illustrating the force of early example, especially in a mother, even after years of sin and forgetfulness of duty have apparently erased all trace of impressions made during the innocence of childhood. A stranger, who had just arrived in Lexington, was taken quite ill. He was a Catholic in name, but for years had done nothing which would prove that his faith was not dead. Dr. Spalding, hearing of his sickness, visited him, and was soon made acquainted with the sad state of his soul. He sent two Sisters of Charity, who had recently established a house in Lexington, to remain with him and to nurse him. No kindness, however, made any impression on him, and he obstinately refused to be reconciled with the church. He rapidly grew worse, and soon saw himself that he had not much longer to live; but still he could not be induced to think of preparing himself to meet God. He left messages for his absent friends, and gave directions as to what should be done with the little articles which he had with him. Among these was a small crucifix, which had belonged to his mother, and which his veneration for her memory had caused him religiously to preserve. This he gave to one of the Sisters, with the request that she would keep it, mentioning the fact that it had belonged to his mother. This incident suggested to the Sister the thought of endeavoring to lead his mind back to the days when a pious mother watched over him, and when the faith which he had been taught by her lips gave peace and happiness to his soul. The Sister's words were not spoken in vain. The memory of his mother had opened his heart to the grace of God, and he at once asked to see Dr. Spalding, from whom he received the sacraments with every sign of the most lively faith and heartfelt sorrow. As he was a freemason, he publicly renounced all connection with the society, and asked to be buried with the rites of the church.

On another occasion, a destitute clergyman, who had just come from Ireland to the diocese of Nashville, and who was travelling for his health, was taken so ill in Lexington that he was unable to go further. Dr. Spalding had but one bed in the little room which he occupied, as a boarder, in a Catholic family. He immediately brought the sick priest to his room, gave up his bed to him, and remained with him almost constantly, even watching by his side through the night, for several weeks, until death relieved his poor brother of his sufferings.

Dr. Spalding was an earnest advocate of popular missions as a means of arousing the slumbering faith and devotion of Catholics. Whilst a student in the Propaganda, he had sought, in an especial manner, to prepare himself to preach retreats, after the plan of St. Ignatius. Shortly after he was sent to Lexington, he caused a mission to be given to his congregation there, which was productive of the most salutary effects. During the fall and winter of 1840, he delivered a course of fifteen lectures on ecclesiastical history, in the Catholic church in Lexington. These lectures were delivered from notes containing an abstract of the views which he proposed to develop. In his first discourse, he sought to establish the supernatural character of the Christian religion, by showing from the history of its struggles and triumphs during the first three centuries that a divine Power must have presided over its birth and early existence. In his second lecture, he took up the history of the New Testament writings, and showed that, in the age of the foundation of the church, the principle of authority had been accepted and acted upon by the apostles and disciples of Christ. He then, in succession, treated of the form of government in the Primitive Church; of the councils of the first three centuries, and the heresies which they had condemned; of the overthrow of the Roman Empire by the Northmen, and of their conversion to Christianity; of Mohammedanism; of the Crusades; of chivalry and the military orders; of the Spanish Inquisition; and concluded with a discourse on the rise and progress of civil liberty in Europe.

These lectures were well received by all classes of persons in Lexington, which, in that day, with true provincial conceit, called itself the Athens of the West. During this year, Dr. Spalding received into the church about thirty converts. His interest in this class of Catholics was always very great. A physician of some prominence, who lived in Georgetown, Ky., and who had been received into the church some years before, apostatized whilst Dr. Spalding was pastor of the church in Lexington, and sent him a long letter in defence of the step which he had taken. To this communication Dr. Spalding made the following reply:

"DEAR SIR:

"I received your letter a few days ago, but my duties have not, until now, permitted me to acknowledge the favor. When I first heard the sad intelligence of your having abandoned the church of all ages and nations, to a knowledge of and belief in which you had been called by a signal providence of God, I could scarcely believe it. My surprise was the greater from the fact that when I saw you a few days before, I had no intimation of any such intention; on the contrary, the impression remaining upon my mind from the conversation I had with you was that you were still a firm believer in the tenets of the Catholic Church. When the news of your defection was confirmed in such way that I could no longer but credit it, I must say that I was pained and grieved to the very heart. My dear friend, I cannot give expression in this short letter to all that I feel; but I hope soon to see you, when we will speak more fully, and I am sure in the spirit of Christian charity, of this whole matter. God alone, of course, knows your heart, as he alone will judge you. In a few years we shall both be arraigned before his dread tribunal to receive from his infallible lips our doom for eternity. On that awful day, I hope that nothing will be laid to my charge, at least on the score of negligence; and that I may comply with my duty in this matter, you will pardon me for proposing in all humility of heart to your consideration the following points: One article of the Apostles' Creed which you profess still to hold is this: I believe in the Holy Catholic Church. Now, can you suppose for a moment that a sect which sprang up but yesterday, and is confined to one corner of the globe, is or can be the Catholic or universal church?

"It has universality neither of time nor place. It is eighteen hundred years too young to be the church which Christ founded and the apostles built up. You will admit that Christ established but one church, which he commanded all to hear under penalty of being considered heathens and publicans; that he so secured this church, which he built upon a *rock*, by his infallible promises, that the gates of hell can never prevail against it; that he sent his Holy Spirit to teach it all truth and to remain with it for ever, he himself at the same time abiding with it all days, even to the end of the world. Is it possible, in the light of these truths, to believe that the whole Christian world has been in error until the present century? You must admit that salvation is attainable in the old church; what assurance have you that it is possible in any other? The Bible, from which Protestants profess to draw their whole religion, can be proved to be the word of God not otherwise than by the testimony and authority of the Catholic Church, from which they received it. If the church is to be heard as to the foundation, why not also as to the details of faith? My dear friend, I beg you to weigh seriously before God these and other considerations which will suggest themselves to you. You will, I doubt not, appreciate my motive in thus addressing you: it is not with a view of giving you pain, or engaging in useless controversy, but solely with the hope of causing you to reflect more seriously upon the course which you have, I fear, too hastily taken."

Unfortunately for the progress of the church in this part of Kentucky, changes took place in the diocese which rendered it necessary to recall Dr. Spalding to Bardstown, after he had been in Lexington but fifteen months.

For some years Bishop Flaget had entertained the idea of transferring his episcopal see to Louisville. He had conferred with the Holy Father on this subject while in Rome in 1836. Bardstown, the cradle of religion in the diocese, and for a long time the centre of the Catholic population of the State, was, at the time of his appointment, the fittest point for the location of the see. A quarter of a century, however, had wrought a great change. Louisville, which when he first came to Kentucky was an unimportant place with a small floating population of nominal Catholics, had now become the largest city in the State; and the Catholics had grown in proportion, both in numbers and religious earnestness. Everything indicated that it was destined to be the great commercial emporium of Kentucky, and consequently the centre of its Catholic population. Hence, however much Bishop Flaget regretted to leave Bardstown, which had been his home for so many years, and where he had founded such splendid institutions, he yet felt that the good of religion demanded the sacrifice. The Pontifical Rescript authorizing the translation of the see to Louisville was received early in 1841, and the Bishop removed thither with his coadjutor towards the close of that year. Father Reynolds, his vicar-general, who had been pastor of the cathedral in Bardstown since Dr. Spalding's appointment to Lexington, had preceded him some months in order to prepare the way. The people of Bardstown naturally felt aggrieved by the removal of the see; and the Bishop, in order at least in some measure to compensate them for the loss, recalled Dr. Spalding, and placed him again in charge of the old cathedral. It was about this time that Dr. Spalding seriously entertained the thought of devoting his life to the missions in the poor and newly-organized diocese of Nashville, Tennessee. When Bishop Miles was appointed to that see, in 1838, there was not a priest in the diocese.

Zealous missionaries from Kentucky had occasionally visited the scattered Catholics of Tennessee, who were in the greatest spiritual destitution. Dr. Spalding himself had gone on this mission of charity through various parts of the State. I have heard him relate how in these journeyings he once stopped at a farm-house, and to his great surprise found that the family were Catholics, still strong in the faith, though they had not seen a priest for many years. He remained with them for several days; instructed and baptized the children, and administered the sacraments to all who were old enough to receive them. Thus, from his own personal observation, he had been made acquainted with the great need of priests in Tennessee. In a letter which he wrote, in the name of Bishop Miles, to the Archbishop of Vienna, to thank him for a gift which, through him, had been obtained for the diocese of Nashville from the Leopold Society, he said: "The Bishop has neither priest nor deacon, neither house nor money, so that to him may be applied in all truth what was said of the Saviour of men—'he has not where to lay his head.'"

Bishop Miles was more than anxious that Dr. Spalding should devote himself to the missions of Tennessee. He represented to him the immense good to be accomplished there, especially by priests who were able to preach in an attractive and forcible manner. Everywhere throughout the State the people manifested an earnest desire to be informed concerning the teachings of the church. Wherever the visit of a priest was announced, it at once became the absorbing topic of conversation, and when he arrived churches and court-houses were thrown open to him, and crowds flocked to hear him. The novelty which everything Catholic possessed for these people had doubtless not a little to do with their eagerness to see and hear the priest. Their minds, however, were not obstinately shut against the light of truth; and we cannot but think that a rare opportunity for doing great things for the church existed at that day in

Tennessee, could priests have been found to do the work. Such, at least, was the opinion of Dr. Spalding, and he willingly consented to turn his energies in this direction. Having informed Bishop Miles of his desire to enter his diocese, he received from him the following letter, dated February 29, 1840:

"REVEREND AND DEAR FRIEND:

"Your very kind and much esteemed favor has been received, and has afforded me great consolation. The very thought that you will, probably before a great while, be among the clergy of my poor and heretofore cruelly neglected diocese, gives me a pleasure which I cannot express. As I expect soon to see you, I shall not now enter into particulars, but desire you to recommend the matter earnestly to Almighty God. The time of the council is approaching, and if you will be kind enough to accompany me as theologian, you will not only add another to the many favors which I have already received at your hands, but you will have a better opportunity of consulting with the assembled prelates on the propriety of joining the mission of Tennessee. . . . The young man whom you sent me has arrived. He seems to be well disposed, and will, I hope, prove useful. Another has just reached here from Georgia, and our seminary has commenced with this small beginning. God will yet bless our efforts."

Dr. Spalding wrote to the Cardinal-Prefect of the Propaganda, setting forth his reasons for wishing to go to Nashville. He also consulted Bishop Kenrick on the subjects from whom he received the following reply:

"I am pleased with the favorable state of things in the West, and wish an increase of that kind feeling which is mutually cherished. Your interest in Nashville is praiseworthy. However, I should deem it inadvisable to move without the approbation of the Propaganda, especially after having consulted the Prefect. I am of the opinion that your removal thither, with the consent of Bishop Flaget, would not be any violation of your duty; but it is better to have the actual approval of the Cardinal."

What the answer of the Propaganda was I do not know; but since Dr. Spalding did not leave the diocese of Louisville, it may be conjectured that it was unfavorable. He, however, remained the lifelong friend of Bishop Miles, and did everything in his power to encourage and assist him in his arduous mission. In the winter of 1843, he delivered a course of lectures in Nashville to crowded and delighted audiences, numbers being unable to find accommodation in the church. Not only the Catholics, but also many of the most respectable Protestants of the city, came to hear him. Such was the impression produced by his discourses that he was waited on by the literary societies of the city, and invited to lecture before them. Glad of any opportunity to announce the truth and dispel error, he accepted the invitation, and a correspondent, writing from Nashville to the *Catholic Advocate*, says that such audiences as attended these lectures had never before been seen in that city. In the fall of 1847, he preached the sermon at the dedication of the Cathedral of Nashville, and delivered there a second course of lectures.

In a letter to the daughter of John J. Crittenden, Archbishop Spalding relates an incident of his first visit to Nashville, in 1840, which portrays the intense political excitement of that time, as well as the enthusiastic fondness for popular eloquence which existed among the people of the Southwest. No Athenian or Roman audience ever yielded themselves to the charms of eloquence with more passionate love than the people of Kentucky, in the day of Clay, and Marshall, and Crittenden.

Diocese of Nashville.

"BALTIMORE, December 26, 1870.
"MY DEAR MRS. COLEMAN:

"As I am not a civilian, but a clergyman, I feel some reluctance in complying with your request to write out the substance of what I related at the elegant breakfast of our mutual friend, Dr. Samuel D. Gross, in Philadelphia, on the 9th of August, in regard to your venerable father, John J. Crittenden. I recalled that reminiscence as a Kentuckian whose State pride was all aglow, when remembering an incident among the popular forensic efforts of one of Kentucky's most eloquent sons. The facts, briefly referred to on that occasion, are, in substance, as follows:

"Finding myself accidentally in Nashville in August, 1840, whither I had gone for purposes of recreation, I was induced by my friends to attend the great Southwestern Whig Convention. Mr. Crittenden was to be the chief orator of the day, Mr. Clay having spoken the day before. I went, not as a politician, for I took no interest in politics, but as a Kentuckian, anxious to hear a brother Kentuckian speak, and I was well repaid. Though thirty years have elapsed, I have not forgotten the deep impression made upon my mind by one of the most brilliant and impassioned bursts of oratory it has ever been my privilege to listen to, either in Europe or America. The whole scene is before me now, fresh and vivid as on that morning when I stood enraptured by your father's eloquence. I still hear his silvery voice; I still hear the acclamations of thirty thousand people, whose very souls he commanded and bore along with him throughout his masterly oration. Mr. Crittenden had taken a low stand on the platform, and I still hear the cry: 'Higher, higher, Mr. Crittenden! Go up; we wish to see your whole stature!' And as he went higher upon the stand, so he rose higher and higher in eloquence. He took up every cry of that vast audience (as, when he was about to close, they threw to him first one and then another of the great political questions of the day) and rang the changes upon it, becoming more and more grand in eloquence at every step of his physical and moral elevation, showing that he and his audience were one. I particularly remember his comparing the outcry of the people for a political change to an avalanche rushing down from the summit of the Alleghanies to the East and to the West, and bearing all before it. This brilliant figure was carried out, till the immense multitude made the welkin ring with their applauding shouts. Seldom have I witnessed such a success. I well remember, also, the acclamations with which Mr. Clay and himself were greeted by the multitude on their departure from Nashville. Mr. Clay spoke first, from the guard of the steamer, with his usual grace and eloquence; then the cry was, 'Crittenden, Crittenden!' Your father stepped forward, and, in his most happy manner, he said (smiling and bowing to Mr. Clay): 'I suppose this flattering greeting is chiefly owing to the good company in which I have the privilege to be found!' 'Not at all!' shouted the multitude, 'not at all; it is for yourself! Come again; come alone next time, and we will prove it to you!' This, my dear Mrs. Coleman, is the substance of what I related at Dr. Gross's of the great Southwestern Convention.*

"Faithfully yours,
"M. J. SPALDING,
"Archbishop of Baltimore."

* *Life of J. J. Crittenden*, by his daughter, Mrs. C. Coleman, page 129.

CHAPTER VIII.

DR. SPALDING IS APPOINTED VICAR-GENERAL—THE LOUISVILLE "LEAGUE"—HIS LABORS AS A LECTURER AND PREACHER.

HEN Bishop Flaget determined to remove the see of the diocese to Louisville, he recalled Dr. Spalding, as I have already stated, from Lexington, and replaced him in charge of the old cathedral at Bardstown, where he remained for three years, doing the work of a parish priest, and, at the same time, writing for Catholic reviews and journals.

The appointment of Father Reynolds to the see of Charleston, in 1844, left the post of Vicar-General in the diocese of Louisville vacant, and Dr. Spalding was called to fill this responsible office. Bishop Flaget was over eighty years of age, and quite feeble. The health of his second coadjutor, Dr. Chabrat, had not been good for some time, and he was now threatened with loss of sight. He had gone to Europe to seek medical advice, but had received little encouragement to hope that he would find relief from the malady from which he was suffering.

Having no reason to believe that he should ever again be able to perform the duties of his office, he wrote to Rome, offering his resignation. The Holy Father referred the matter to the approaching Provincial Council of Baltimore, which was to meet in 1846. The Fathers of the Council declined to advise the acceptance of Bishop Chabrat's resignation. In the meantime, his disease grew no better, and he resolved again to visit Europe.

On his arrival in Paris, the oculist whom he had previously consulted declared that unless he resigned his charge and remained in France, he would in a short time become hopelessly blind. The Papal Nuncio in Paris, to whom the case had been stated, wrote to the Holy See, recommending the acceptance of Bishop Chabrat's resignation, and he was shortly after relieved from his office as Coadjutor of the Bishop of Louisville.

The great age of Bishop Flaget, and the infirmity of Bishop Chabrat, threw nearly the whole administration of the affairs of the diocese upon Dr. Spalding from the very time of his appointment as Vicar-General.

The cathedral in Louisville had already become a point of great attraction, not only to Catholics, but also to a large and intelligent class of Protestants. Its choir was the best in the city, and its pulpit had acquired a name for eloquence of a high order. It had been filled by the Rev. I. A. Reynolds, late Bishop of Charleston; the Rev. John McGill, late Bishop of Richmond, and the Rev. Father Larkin, of the Society of Jesus, all of whom were men not only of solid attainments, but also of real eloquence. Father McGill was still pastor of the cathedral, and he and Dr. Spalding began a course of Sunday-evening lectures, each occupying the pulpit in turn. The success with which lectures of this kind had been attended in Lexington, encouraged the hope that they would here also be productive of good results. The subjects chosen were ecclesiastical history and the dogmatic teachings of the church. On the first night, the cathedral was filled to overflowing, and the interest seemed to increase with each Sunday evening's lecture. Many Protestants went to the cathedral, and the attendance at the ministrations of the preachers was, in consequence, small. These reverend gentlemen took alarm, and called a meeting to devise some plan for counteracting the effect which the discourses in the cathedral were producing.

The result of their deliberations was the organization of the Louisville Protestant League. The members of the League were the Rev. W. L. Breckinridge, a brother of the Rev. John Breckinridge, the opponent of Archbishop Hughes, the Rev. E. P. Humphrey, and the Rev. W. W. Hill, of the Presbyterian Church; the Baptists were represented by the Rev. A. D. Sears and the Rev. Thomas S. Malcolm; whilst the Methodist champions were the Rev. G. W. Brush and the Rev. H. H. Cavanagh.

Each member of the League bound himself to lecture in turn on the abominations of Popery. With the exception of Dr. Breckinridge, they interchanged pulpits. As he had a fine church and a rich congregation, he preferred to hurl his bolts at Antichrist and the Woman of Sin from his own Olympus. One of his lectures was delivered before an audience composed exclusively of men. The subject was, of course, the confessional.

As the exponent of the dogmas of the church, it fell chiefly to the lot of Father McGill to repel the assaults of the League. His logical mind and skill in argument would have rendered him a formidable adversary in any cause. He was thoroughly conversant with polemical theology, and he took great pains to inform himself minutely of the objections advanced by the League preachers. They were marked by the ignorance and blundering which seem to be inevitable whenever Protestants undertake to attack the church. He therefore found no difficulty in exposing their misstatements and confounding their sophistry. Father McGill was also a master of satire, which he used with great effect in this controversy. The crowds that flocked to the cathedral were, if possible, greater now than before. Men and women, unable to get seats, stood in the aisles of the church, densely packed, up to the very railings of the sanctuary. Hundreds of Protestants, who, in other circumstances, could not have been induced to enter a Catholic church, came to hear the persuasive eloquence and forcible arguments of Father McGill and Dr. Spalding, and thus many prejudices were overcome and the seeds of future conversions were sown.*

Another and much greater good effected by these lectures was that they aroused the spirit of the Catholic body, and caused them to feel a pride in their faith, of which they had not hitherto been conscious, and thus they became more earnest, more ready to organize and co-operate with their zealous pastors in building up the church, and helping on the cause of truth and religion.

Dr. Spalding's official duties, now that he was stationed at the cathedral in Louisville as Vicar-General of the diocese, were more onerous than they had hitherto ever been. He nevertheless found time to devote to other works in the interest of religion than those to which his position properly obliged him.

He developed greater activity, both as a lecturer and writer on Catholic subjects, than he had up to this time manifested. He continued to write for the *Advocate*, and also prepared monthly one or more essays for some Catholic magazine. During the winters of 1844-45, 1846-47, 1847-48, he delivered courses of lectures in the cathedral of Louisville on general and special theology, and on Catholic worship. He wrote in full only the first series of these lectures, which he published under the title of *Evidences of Catholicity*. His experience had led him to think that Sunday-evening lectures, in which the plain and forcible statement and proof of Catholic doctrines are made, without

* I am indebted to the Hon. B. J. Webb, of Louisville for this account of the "League."

seeking controversy or assuming an aggressive attitude toward the sects, are generally attended with the happiest results to the cause of Catholic truth, especially in our large cities. Republican institutions develop a fondness for public speaking, and, in virtue of the law of supply and demand, they create orators. Although the art of printing and journalism, and the consequent more general education of the masses, have opened to those who desire to inform themselves upon the various questions, whether of great or small moment, which the current of events presents to the attention or curiosity of men, other and easier channels of knowledge, and have thus taken from oratory somewhat of the charm and influence which belonged to it in Greece and Rome, they have, however, by no means deprived it of its great power over the mind and heart. Orators no longer control public opinion, but they still have something to do with forming it on many of the most important matters which come up for discussion.

In the religion of Christ, eloquence has a special and divine mission. He blessed it and bade it convert the world when he commanded the apostles to go and teach all nations. This high office he entrusted not to the written, but to the spoken word; and, though from him alone comes conversion, yet, in this as in other things, he works through human agencies, which become the occasions of grace. Other things, too, give to the priest special privileges here. The old conception of the orator, which defines him to be a good man skilled in the art of speaking, should be, one would think, more easily and fully realized in him than in other men. He is not, as De Maistre has said of the ministers of Protestantism, merely a respectable man clothed in black, but all the circumstances of his life tend to render him sacred, even in the eyes of the unbelieving. Separated from the world from early youth, devoted to a life of study and prayer, without wife or children or secular entanglement, the very sacrifices which his vocation imposes upon him witness to the sacredness of his character, the elevation of his thoughts, and the power over the hearts of men of the truth which he preaches. That seriousness and earnestness which are so essential to the orator are implied in the very idea of the priesthood. To these must be added the supernatural strength of conviction which Catholic faith alone gives. Who does not perceive here the immense advantages which the Catholic has over the Protestant speaker? To be a Protestant is to hold opinions; to be a Catholic is to have convictions. The wavering, uncertain, and changing nature of Protestantism takes from the ministers of that religion that perfect and undoubting faith in the doctrines which they preach which is so essential to true eloquence. This defect in the preacher is increased by the attitude of those to whom he speaks, who regard him not as a divinely ordained minister, but merely as the more or less plausible advocate of his own religious theories. And yet preaching is the central act in Protestant worship, without which it would have no attractiveness and no life. The true Protestant idea of a church is that of a lecture-hall; and the introduction of Catholic architecture into Protestant houses of worship is an act of unfaithfulness to the fundamental doctrines of the Reformation. This is evident from the fact that, where Protestants imitate the church in the architectural structure of their religious edifices, the natural logic of the human mind inclines them to supply what such a style of architecture implies—as the altar, the priest, the sacerdotal robes, and the ceremonial which these suppose. But, to return, since Protestantism has no sacrifice, no real presence of Christ, preaching becomes the most important feature in its public worship. And, since the preacher is regarded chiefly

His Labors as a Lecturer and Preacher. 101

or solely from a human stand-point, it is essential that he should preach well. Eloquence commands the highest price in Protestant churches. The barometer of a congregation is its pulpit. It rises or falls with the preacher. The law of supply and demand comes into play here, and, since in the great centres of commerce and population the highest price is paid for pulpit oratory, thither the best ability in the Protestant ministry gravitates. Hence, in the large cities of the United States the pulpits of the more wealthy churches are filled, if not always by orators, at least by good speakers. Now, there are vast numbers of people in this country who, on Sunday evening, are as willing to go to hear a Catholic as a Protestant sermon, provided they have a reasonable hope of hearing what they call a good sermon. Firmly persuaded that we have the truth, and earnestly desiring that all men should be brought to the knowledge of it, it is not a little gain to find men willing to listen to us in defence of our faith. Even should we not convert them, we can at least show them that on earth there is nothing grander, more venerable, more worthy of love than the church on whose brow "time writes no wrinkle." Impressions will be made, prejudices dissipated, and thoughts suggested which will gradually, aided by God's grace, work their way into the heart and produce conviction. The preacher himself may never know it, "*alius est qui plantat et alius qui metit,*" but the work is done. To the Catholic orator the world has never presented a finer field than that which lies before him in this country to-day, and if we intend to do the work that God demands of us, we must prepare ourselves with greater care for this mission. The importance of thorough training in the art of public speaking to those who aspire to the priesthood cannot be exaggerated. Although much has been done in this direction—more, possibly, than might have been expected, in view of the difficulties with which our priests have had to contend—still much remains yet to be done. Hitherto, our seminaries, and to a great extent our colleges, have been in the hands of men to whom English was a foreign language—admirable men, from the priceless value of whose labors I certainly do not wish to detract aught, but from whom it would have been unreasonable to expect that intimate acquaintance with the language and habits of thought and expression of our people absolutely required in those who would successfully train the young men destined for the ministry in this country in the art of public speaking. In the future, greater attention will be paid to this important branch of ecclesiastical education. Chairs of sacred eloquence will be founded in our seminaries, and special teachers in reading and elocution will be employed, and thus the influence of the Catholic pulpit over the religious thought of the country will become far greater than it has hitherto ever been.

Whether or not these reflections have any value, the better judgment of my readers will decide. They have been suggested by the example of the subject of this biography. He certainly felt that the priest, as the preacher of God's truth, has a special mission in this country—a mission not to Catholics alone, but, like that of St. Paul, to Jew and to Gentile, to Greek and to Barbarian, to the slave and to the freeman; and again, as in the case of the great Apostle of the Nations—woe to him if he does not preach, for he is bound to preach. No bishop or priest in the United States has probably ever been more indefatigable or inexhaustible as a preacher or lecturer than Dr. Spalding. For more than thirty years he lectured repeatedly on almost every subject in any way connected with Catholic history or teaching, not only in his own native State, but in nearly all the large cities of the country. His voice was heard, time and again, in

His Labors as a Lecturer and Preacher. 103

New York, Philadelphia, Baltimore, Washington City, New Orleans, St. Louis, Cincinnati, and other cities. He lectured also in Canada.

During his long career as a public lecturer, he never lost the popular favor, and rarely ever failed to be greeted by audiences generally composed, in part, of non-Catholics.

Even in Louisville, where he was so well known, and where he so often spoke, his lectures were always well attended. As a preacher, he was even more active. For years he preached at the late Mass in the cathedral of Louisville on Sundays, when not absent visiting the diocese or on other business. In making the visitation of the various congregations under his jurisdiction, he always preached and frequently lectured once or twice in each parish. He was often more really eloquent and persuasive in addressing the simple people of some remote and small congregation than on more solemn occasions. It has frequently happened to me in travelling through different parts of Kentucky to be told by both Catholics and Protestants of sermons preached probably twenty years before by Dr. Spalding. Not only did the impression still remain, but the subject, and even the arguments advanced, or the points made, were remembered. He loved too to give missions, and to preach retreats in convents, academies, and colleges. He gave retreats to his own clergy and to the clergy of Cincinnati, Detroit, Philadelphia, Baltimore, and possibly other dioceses; and, according to the testimony of persons who took part in these holy exercises, he conducted them in the most satisfactory manner. His greatest delight was to preach to the young; and few, indeed, have ever possessed in so eminent a degree the faculty of instructing children. He could at once place himself *en rapport* with them, win their confidence, and hold their attention. His manner was always characterized by simplicity and naturalness; but on these occasions he seemed himself to become a child again, only holier and wiser than the rest. The tone of his voice, his gestures, his sudden exclamations, his merry laugh, all bespoke the untroubled joy and innocence of childhood. For many years he gave the annual retreat to the pupils of Nazareth Academy, conducted by the Sisters of Charity and long known as one of the most successful schools of the West or South; and occasionally he preached the retreat for the students of St. Joseph's College. Dr. Spalding was not an impassioned speaker, nor yet was his manner cold or unemotional. His discourses were seldom characterized by vehement and fervid eloquence, or by those bursts of passion which electrify an audience until it becomes a passive instrument in the hands of the orator, who plays upon it like some skilful musician, now touching the chord that vibrates sweetest joy, and now that which thrills the deepest notes of woe. The style is the man, say the French; and this is certainly true of Dr. Spalding, considered as a speaker. He was direct, clear, and simple. His manner and tone of voice were familiar and natural, but never without grace and dignity.

His appearance was prepossessing. He was above the average height, full-chested, and endowed with a perfectly developed physique. His whole countenance expressed the unpretending, kind-hearted, sympathetic man. His features were finely chiselled; his brow was large and open, and his eye full of intelligence. His voice was pleasant, and his enunciation wonderfully distinct. Every syllable he uttered was heard even in the largest and most crowded buildings. He rarely failed from the very start to win the good-will and confidence of an audience. His personal appearance, his unassuming yet dignified bearing, the frank and straightforward manner in which he took hold of his subject, his love of truth and justice and liberty, his sympathy with whatever was good or noble, all combined to enlist the feelings of his hearers in his behalf. Thoroughly American, without, however, any of the narrowness of nationalism, he loved his country, and was proud of its history. The descendant of forefathers who for nearly three centuries had been forced to suffer in silence every outrage and injustice for their faith, he loved especially those principles of American liberty which gave to Catholics not only freedom of religious worship, but the right to defend and uphold the teachings of their church. Belonging to the first generation of American Catholics whom circumstances had permitted to receive an education in their own country, he was devoted to the struggles and triumphs by which the new state of things had been brought into existence. Especially did he glory in the part which Catholics had taken in the War of Independence. In that struggle with a nation which, while talking much of liberty, has persecuted perhaps more than any other, we received, as he loved to recall to the minds of his countrymen, the timely assistance of Catholic France and Poland; and the "Maryland line" in every battle, from Brooklyn Heights to Yorktown, fought with unequalled heroism; whilst Commodore Barry, whom Washington appointed to form the navy of the United States, was an Irish Catholic. At a time when the national feeling was most intense, when its ardor had not yet been cooled by the horrors of civil war, or weakened by sectional strife, the public was much more exacting in its demands on the patriotism and loyalty of those who sought to win its favor than now, when even the very words by which we would express sentiments of this kind have lost their charm.

CHAPTER IX.

POPULAR OBJECTIONS TO THE CHURCH—DR. SPALDING'S MANNER OF ANSWERING THEM.

HE great objection to the church, in the minds of the American people, during the period of which I am speaking, was historical rather than doctrinal. Absurd notions of Catholic doctrine were, it is true, very common. Still, people were averse to the church rather from what they conceived to be the tendency of Catholic institutions, than from any clear notion that Catholic doctrines were false. The dominant thought of the country, as of the age, was political and social, not religious. Never had so vast a field, one so teeming with wealth and so inviting to enterprise, opened before an active and intelligent race, as our forefathers beheld here in the New World. The natural advantages and resources of the country developed in them an extraordinary energy and industry, which rarely failed to be rewarded with success. Bold, independent, self-reliant, they rose up and with comparative ease threw off the yoke of the mother country, and formed themselves into a Republic under a constitution which, in their estimation at least, embodied the perfection of human wisdom in all that relates to government. The growth and prosperity of the new Republic were unprecedented, and the national pride grew in proportion. When we beheld cities spring up in a night from dismal swamps as by the enchanter's wand, and broad fields, teeming with richest harvests, smile where but awhile ago the primal forest frowned,

whilst our ships covered the seas and our flag waved in every port, it was but natural that there should have been an uncontrollable outburst of national enthusiasm, which caused us to think ourselves the greatest and most favored people of the world. A new people, living in a new world, we had learned to look with contempt upon all that was old. We were the heralds of a dawn which promised a new life to the race. Knowing but little of the history of the past, our ignorance added to our self-conceit. We looked upon those ages which had prepared for us the blessings which we were enjoying as ignorant, superstitious, and barbarous. And the church, which during long centuries had fought for liberty, for law, for order, for civilization, was, in the minds of the American people, associated with the very opposite of all this.

The anti-Catholic prejudices of Englishmen had been inherited by their American descendants, who found it much easier to emancipate themselves from political subjection to the mother country, than to assert their intellectual independence and renounce the legacy of religious hate which had been bequeathed to them. The English Government, not content with murdering Catholics and confiscating their goods, had done all that it was possible to do to make them what it desired they should be—ignorant, superstitious, and disloyal. Public opinion with regard to Catholics had been so thoroughly perverted throughout the English-speaking world by a system of organized calumny, that no crime, however nefarious, could be imputed to them which the misguided masses were not ready to believe. They were persuaded that the Papists had burned London once, and that they only awaited the opportunity to burn it again; that they had planned a scheme to set fire to all the shipping in the Thames; that they were ready to rise, at a signal, and massacre all their Protestant neighbors; that they were plotting to assassinate the king, and murder all the leading divines of England. These lies readily found credence with the masses, and they suited the designs of unprincipled and tyrannical statesmen too well not to be encouraged by them. In the British Provinces of North America, public opinion was scarcely less unfavorable to Catholics than in England.

During the whole period of our colonial history, Catholics were persecuted, not indeed so generally or with the same relentless cruelty as in England, but still they were kept in bondage and regarded with suspicion; and even when they were allowed to live in peace, it was rather from indifference than from any feeling that they were worthy of toleration. In Maryland even, where they had proclaimed civil and religious liberty, they were doomed to see themselves deprived of all rights, and subjected to the most vexatious persecution. By successive acts of the Provincial Assembly, they were denied the right of public worship, were compelled to contribute to the support of the Anglican clergy, were forbidden to teach, and disqualified from holding civil offices unless they took an oath which implied a denial of their faith. This state of things continued almost to the breaking-out of the War of Independence. The Revolution, which sprang from hatred of England, and the emergency of the crisis, for the moment caused internal jealousies to be forgotten, and all united against the common enemy. The Convention of 1774, in its appeal to the country, entreated all classes of citizens, by their duty to God and the nation, to forget all religious disputes and animosities, that they might all assist in the defence of their common rights and liberties. The causes which finally brought about the insertion of the article forbidding Congress to interfere with the freedom of religious worship are enumerated by Archbishop Carroll, to whose wise and enlightened counsels the result is partly attributable. " Many reasons," he says, "concurred to produce this happy and just article in the new constitutions. First, some of the leading characters in the direction of American councils were by principle averse to all religious oppression ; and having been much acquainted with the manners and doctrines of Roman Catholics, represented strongly the injustice of excluding them from any civil right. Secondly, Catholics concurred as generally, and with equal zeal, in repelling that oppression which first produced hostility with Great Britain, and it would have been impolitic as well as unjust to deprive them of a common share in advantages purchased with common danger and by united exertions. Thirdly, the assistance, or at least the neutrality of Canada was deemed necessary to the success of the United States, and to give equal rights to the Roman Catholics might tend to dispose the Canadians favorably towards the Americans. Lastly, France began to show a disposition to befriend the United States, and it was conceived to be very impolitic to disgust that powerful kingdom by unjust severity against the religion which it professed."*

It is evident from this passage that the toleration of the Catholic Church under the Constitution was, in the beginning, the result of circumstances which American Protestants could not control, rather than of any good-will, on their part, towards Catholics; and as the principles, upon which the Constitution rests, began to impress themselves more clearly upon the minds of the people, it became evident to all that they were wholly incompatible with any interference on the part of the state in matters of religion, and thus, the liberty once granted to the church, was consecrated by its association with the fundamental laws of our government. The Protes-

* MS. relation of Bishop Carroll on origin and condition of Catholics in the United States.

tants, however, very generally, still retained the anti-Catholic prejudices of a former generation. At the time of the Revolution, the church had no existence in any of the colonies except in Maryland and Pennsylvania. The few Catholics who had settled in the other colonies, not being allowed to profess their religion, dissembled or became members of some one or other of the sects. Thus, in nearly all the British provinces in America, Protestants held undisputed possession of the religious ground. They had no intercourse with Catholics, and the little knowledge which they had of the church was derived from sources thoroughly tainted and corrupt. English history, for more than two centuries, had been a conspiracy against the truth in all that related to the church. There was no Catholic English literature, or, at least, none accessible to the reading public of this country, or which, even had it been within their reach, was of a kind to attract their attention or meet their objections. The most absurd and preposterous views concerning the history of the church in the Middle Ages were accepted as being beyond dispute, and no one ever thought of questioning their correctness. The church was represented as having always been the ally of ignorance and tyranny, and the enemy of the people. She had kept the nations in ignorance, and had, with the most obstinate persistence, opposed all progress. The civilization, enlightenment, and liberty of modern times were attributed exclusively to the Reformation, which was the herald of the new dawn after the night of ages. To the prejudices of the Old World were added others peculiar to our own social and political condition. The church, it was said and believed by nearly all Protestants, was the creation of emperors and kings, under whose protection she had grown powerful, but without which she could not exist. Hence, it was argued, Catholics must necessarily be hostile to republican institutions. Indeed, so incompatible were Catholicism and republicanism thought to be that our proud countrymen looked upon Catholics with more of contempt and pity than of alarm. It was not considered possible that the church could ever become strong here. Liberty and enlightenment would necessarily prove fatal to her; and her children, it was confidently believed, leaving behind them their political creed to adopt the principles of this free Republic, would soon also disengage themselves from the shackles of their religious faith. Protestantism had not then become in the United States the feeble and intangible thing it now is, and its influence upon the thought of the country was very great. The preachers, made reckless by impunity, hesitated not to impute the most absurd and impossible doctrines and practices to Catholics, and their words were received without questioning by minds prepared to believe anything, however monstrous, of men whom they had been taught to regard as worse than idolaters. The great work of the Catholic apologist in this country, in the generation which preceded ours, was to clear away the *débris* and rubbish with which false history and ignorant prejudices had sought to obscure and disfigure the whole life of the church. And it was to this task that Dr. Spalding addressed himself, both as a lecturer and as a writer. Each country, as well as each age, has its peculiar phases of thought, which must be taken into consideration by those who seek to influence public opinion. One of Dr. Spalding's chief merits as a public teacher was, that he fully understood the character of the persons whom he sought to enlighten. An American, he knew his countrymen, and admired them; a Catholic, he loved his religion, and was convinced of its truth. That, in his person, between faith and patriotism there was no conflict, was manifest. He loved his country all the more because he was a Catholic, and he was all the sincerer Catholic because no mere human authority was brought to influence the free offering of his soul to God's service. He accepted with cheerful courage the position in which God had placed his church in this young Republic, and he asked for her, not privilege or protection, but justice, common rights under the common law; and such was his confidence in God, and in the truth of his cause, that he had no doubt as to the final issue of the struggle of religion, free and untrammelled, with the prejudices of a people who, however erroneous and mistaken their views might be, were still fair-minded and generous. Admiring much in the past, he still did not think that all was lost because that past was gone. Let the old, he thought, the feeble, the impotent complain; those to whom God gives youth and strength must act; and the church is ever young and ever strong. God is infinite strength, and of this attribute, as of his others, his spouse participates. If the latest word of philosophy, both in metaphysics and natural science, is force; if the old theory of inertia has been dropped, since the power of analysis has shown that everywhere there is action, motion, force; let it be so. The church, too, is strength. She has a force and an energy of her own. Daughter of heaven, she has brought on earth some of that divine efficacy by which all things were made. Christ is the strength of God, and from his cross he poured into the heart of his spouse, together with his life-blood, his god-like power.

He knew that the church which sprang from the conflict of the God-man with death, like him, manifests her highest power in her struggles with the princes of this world. Like the life of man, that of the church is a warfare. He had read her history too attentively not to understand that she cannot but take part in the struggle between good and evil, vice and virtue, truth and error; between the cause of God and that of Satan, which is found wherever there are human beings. The march of the church through the world and through the ages is not along pleasant roads, leading through delightful scenes and peaceful prospects; or, if so, only at times and rarely. If she move in pomp and worldly greatness amid the acclamations of peoples and of nations, her triumph not unfrequently ends in sorrow and humiliation. The road wherein her progress is most secure is the way of the cross, because her strength comes from humility, from poverty, from lowliness.

The difficulties of our position in this country forty years ago neither alarmed nor discouraged Dr. Spalding. He had the most living faith in the indefectible vitality of the church. Others might believe that she was feeble with age, that the shadow of death was upon her, that the light of science, thrown into her dimly-lit sanctuary, would dispel the charm which for so many ages had held captive millions of hearts; but he knew that she was strong and beautiful as when first she came from the hands of God, and that, if the veil with which ignorance and passion had sought to hide her divine countenance could but be lifted, the world would again kneel before her and ask to be forgiven.

Without entering into the complex and delicate question of the proper relations of the church and state, he accepted the actual position of the church in this country with thankfulness and without mental reservation. In this matter, he neither blamed the past nor sought to dictate to the future, but put his hand to the work which God had placed before him. He saw all that was to be done, and, without stopping to reflect how little he could do, he began at once to do what he could. Taking a moderate, and possibly a just, estimate of his own ability, he considered that his mission as a writer and public teacher demanded that he should be useful and practical rather than original or profound. Hence he neither wrote nor spoke for posterity, but for the generation in which he lived. His first aim was to remove the prejudices which false history and a perverted literature had created in the minds of his countrymen. The influence of the church on society, on civilization, and on civil liberty was wholly misunderstood; her services in the cause of learning, of art, and of commerce were ignored; her undying love for the poor and the oppressed were forgotten.

She had been the greatest school of respect the world had ever seen; to her woman owed her position in Christian society, and all the sacred privileges with which public opinion surrounded her; to her the family was indebted for its civilizing and sanctifying power; her monks had preserved the literature of the Greeks and Romans, and had been almost the only lovers of knowledge in a barbarous age. They had reclaimed the waste land of Europe, and had been the chief agents in causing the warlike barbarians to settle down and become peaceful tillers of the soil; they too, together with the bishops and popes of the church, had inspired all the wisest and most humane legislation of the Middle Ages. And yet, all these services were forgotten, and in the minds of the masses of the American people the influence of the church upon the world was identified with the opposite of all that is good. Hence it was all-important to place her history in its true light, and to refute the slanders and calumnies with which, during three centuries, she had been assailed with impunity, because Catholics, at least those whose native language was English, had not been allowed to repel the attacks of their revilers.

Dr. Spalding felt it to be his duty to become the apologist of his faith, according to the measure of ability which God had given him, before the American public.

The essentially illogical nature of Protestantism would, he knew, soon undermine its influence, whilst the free institutions of this country would act as dissolvents upon the loose organizations and uncertain doctrines of the various opposing sects, whose only bond of union is the negation implied by their common name. As a system of religious belief, Protestantism was already losing its hold on the minds of the people, who were both confused and scandalized by its hesitating and doubtful attitude towards the positive dogmas of Christianity. It was useless, therefore, to show that the Bible alone, without a living authority, could not form the basis either of religious unity or faith, when the history of the sects was day by day rendering this perfectly manifest even to the most inattentive observers. Hence, he sought less to refute Protestantism than to prepare the way for Catholic truth, by seeking to enlighten public opinion concerning the real nature and spirit of the church. Many of his best essays, such as those on *Literature and the Arts in the Middle Ages*, *Schools and Universities in the Dark Ages*, and *The Influence of Catholicity on Civil Liberty* were written with this view. In these essays, Dr. Spalding presents, in a popular form, and in a style remarkable for simplicity and ease, the facts which show the incalculable value of the services rendered by the church to the cause of progress and civilization during those centuries in which she contended, single-handed, against barbarism and ignorance. That no one may object to his statement of facts, he adduces the testimony of impartial non-Catholic writers of Germany, France, and England to prove that the church was the only safeguard of society at a time when its very foundations seemed shaken.

The following outline will give us some idea of his manner of dealing with this subject:

All the nations of Europe received their religion from the church, who alone converted them from paganism, and to their religion they are indebted for their civilization. Since

Christ, only Christian nations have been civilized. The church saved Europe from Mohammedanism, which would have drowned all the noble aspirations of her Christian people in indolence and debauch.

By placing Mary, the Mother of Jesus, before the eyes of all men as the ideal woman, the church taught them to honor her whole sex; and through this restoration of woman to her proper sphere in society, she exercised a beneficent influence on the morals and literature of European nations.

Even the extravagances of chivalry were not without certain good results. Female influence prompted not only to deeds of valor, but also stimulated to triumphs of intellect; the delicate hand of woman wove not alone the chaplet which decorated the warrior's brow, but also the laurel and the ivy wreath which adorned the brow of genius. To show more fully the great services rendered to society by the church, he enters into details, and proves that all the essential elements of our modern civilization first came into existence during the time when she controlled the destinies of Europe. Long before the advent of Protestantism, the European mind was active in every department of human knowledge; the spirit of invention and discovery had manifested itself; and men were fast attaining to a more thorough knowledge of God's material universe. The modern languages, in all their richness and strength, had been formed, giving certain proof of the progress of the people in refinement and taste. The art of printing had been invented, schools and universities had been founded, the mariner's compass had been applied to purposes of navigation, and America, the land of promise, had been discovered; whilst commerce, under the fostering care of the Italian Republics, had begun to promote that interchange of the products of the earth which was destined one day to bind together the nations of the world in bonds of sympathy and love.

The Christian nations were on the certain road of progress, and had they but remained united in faith, their advancement would have been both more rapid and more uniform. The effect of the advent of Protestantism was to disturb the natural march of European civilization, by introducing elements of discord, which broke up the brotherhood of nations, and led to centuries of persecution and war, the evil effects of which are still felt. Add to this that the religious and political divisions of Europe stopped the progress of the faith among pagan nations, at a time when the day seemed near at hand when all the world would be Christian, and we will be able to perceive how the true progress of the whole race was retarded by Protestantism. This is but a feeble statement of the leading arguments by which Dr. Spalding sought to vindicate the church from the charge of opposition to progress and civilization. Every reader is, at present, more or less familiar with this whole question, which has been exhaustively treated by many and able writers, so that even the more intelligent Protestants are now prepared to admit the great services which the church has rendered to society. This, however, was not the case when Dr. Spalding wrote his essays on this subject, which, though not remarkable for depth of thought or originality of appreciation of facts, had the great merit of presenting, in a popular and forcible manner, the claims of the church upon the gratitude of all honest and fair-minded men; showing, at the same time, that the cause of progress, properly understood, had nothing to fear from her influence. Appearing at a time when the Catholic controversy in this country, especially in its political and social aspects, was at its height, they were read by both Catholics and Protestants, and doubtless produced a salutary effect upon public opinion.

CHAPTER X.

APPOINTED BISHOP OF LENGONE, IN PART. INFID., AND COADJUTOR OF BISHOP FLAGET—DEATH OF BISHOP FLAGET—STATE OF THE DIOCESE AT THE TIME OF DR. SPALDING'S CONSECRATION.

ISHOP CHABRAT'S resignation, as we have already seen, had been accepted by the Holy See in 1847. He was at the time in France, and he never afterwards returned to the United States.

The whole burden of the diocese of Louisville again fell upon the shoulders of Bishop Flaget, who was over eighty years old, and completely broken by his long and untiring labors on the missions of Kentucky. His infirmities and extreme old age rendered him absolutely incapable of attending to the duties of his office, as he, with that perfect humility and self-forgetfulness so characteristic of his whole life, was the first to recognize. To be thus left to bear a weight of responsibility to which, in his helpless condition, he felt himself wholly unequal, caused his exquisitely sensitive nature to suffer most acutely. Speaking of this period of his life, Dr. Spalding says: "He spent most of his time in prayer. From his lips audible sighs would often break forth deploring what he called his utter 'nullity' (*ma nullité*), and the impossibility in which he found himself, from almost continual vertigo, of thinking of any serious business. Yet in all things he was fully resigned to the will of God, and his accustomed ejaculations at the end of all his prayers and sighs were: 'May the good God be praised! May his holy will be done!'"

The interests of the diocese demanded that a new coadjutor should be appointed as soon as possible. There were congregations which the Bishop had not visited for several years, and numbers were, in consequence, waiting to receive the sacrament of confirmation; whilst the slumbering faith and zeal of the Catholic population in general called for some one capable of infusing new life and vigor.

Bishop Flaget, in this state of affairs, naturally turned to Dr. Spalding as the person best fitted to relieve him of a responsibility to which he was no longer equal. Dr. Spalding had now been laboring in the diocese with great earnestness and success for nearly fourteen years. By his talents, his learning, and the blamelessness of his life, he had won the respect and admiration of all. He was still young, but he was already known far beyond the limits of his native State both as a preacher and writer of more than ordinary ability. Identified with the diocese by birth, by education, and by every natural sympathy, his frank, open character and genial manners gave him peculiar advantages for laboring with success amongst his own people, who were not only proud of him, but loved him. He had for several years occupied the second highest position in the diocese, at a time when, owing to circumstances already mentioned, the chief responsibility of the ecclesiastical administration devolved upon him; and his conduct had been characterized by great prudence and wisdom, united with a practical understanding of the details of business. He was thoroughly conversant with the whole history of the church in Kentucky, as well as with the wise and enlightened views of the noble and apostolic men to whom, under God, it was indebted for its present condition. He had grown up at the feet of Flaget and

David, had imbibed their spirit, and was filled with that disinterested and self-sacrificing zeal which, if not found in the bishop, will most generally be sought for in vain in his priests. He was a student, but had never allowed his devotion to books to interfere with the discharge of the active duties of the ministry. Everything, in a word, seemed to point to him as the one destined by God to take from the failing shoulders of the saintly patriarch of the West the burden which they were no longer able to bear. He had, indeed, been thought of in connection with the episcopacy some years previous to this time, as will be seen from the following letter from the Rev. Dr. White, written in September, 1845, with a view to dissuade Dr. Spalding from withdrawing his name as one of the editors of the *Catholic Magazine:*

"I received your very acceptable communication but two days since, and after some reflection on the plan which you have been thinking of, in regard to the magazine, I have come to the conclusion that it would be better for its interests that you should continue your name, as at present, in connection with mine. This can be done without subjecting you to the necessity of furnishing an article every month. As you are, in the public estimation, a '*doctor optimus, ecclesiæ sanctæ lumen*,' your connection with the magazine will contribute to its circulation, while the withdrawal of your name, at the end of the year, would afford a pretext to many persons for discontinuing their subscriptions. . . . I foresee, and *I know from an official source*, that you will be soon, perhaps before the next council, promoted to the episcopacy. Then, I presume, you will withdraw from the magazine, and, in my opinion, this would be the most favorable occasion for doing so. It is to be hoped, however, that you will always co-operate in supporting its usefulness."

Bishop Chabrat had offered his resignation when this letter was written, and the official information concerning Dr. Spalding's promotion was, doubtless, based upon the supposition that Bishop Flaget would at once need another coadjutor. Bishop Chabrat, however, was not permitted to resign until 1847, and Dr. Spalding's appointment was in consequence delayed. When, at length, the time came to select a successor to Bishop Chabrat, Dr. Spalding's promotion met with opposition in certain quarters, as the following letter of Bishop Miles, written in Baltimore, in May, 1848, will show:

"RIGHT REV. AND DEAR FRIEND:
"I reached this city on Saturday, and was very kindly received by the Archbishop, who soon introduced the subject which of late has given your friends so much uneasiness. He showed me a letter from Bishop Flaget, in reply to one which he had written on this vexed question. Bishop Flaget has agreed to leave the whole matter to the Archbishop of Baltimore and Bishop Kenrick of Philadelphia, and they have both written to Rome in terms which will cause all hesitation to cease. I hope your health has improved, and that in our next Provincial Council Kentucky will be represented by one of her own sons."

A few weeks after this letter was written, the Bulls appointing Dr. Spalding Bishop of Lengone, *in partibus infidelium*, and Coadjutor of the Bishop of Louisville, *cum jure successionis*, were made out in Rome, and were received by him on the Feast of St. Laurence, the 10th of August, 1848.

They were handed to him before the altar of the old cathedral, in a very impressive and solemn manner, by the venerable Bishop Flaget, who announced his intention of consecrating him himself in spite of his feeble health, that he might thus, by the last official act of an episcopal life extending over forty years, place the crown upon all his labors, and leave to the church, which he had founded and built up, a worthy pastor in the son who had grown up at his side, and who had been the staff of his declining age.

After receiving the Bulls, Dr. Spalding entered into a spiritual retreat, in order to prepare himself, by prayer and holy recollection, for the worthy reception of the plenitude of priestly power. The consecration took place on the Feast of the Holy Name of Mary, the 10th of September, 1848. The ceremony was performed by Bishop Flaget, assisted by the Bishops of Philadelphia and Nashville. The Archbishop of St. Louis preached the usual sermon, taking as his subject the nature and perpetuity of the apostolic ministry. The day was one of great festivity in Louisville. From an early hour the cathedral was thronged, and many remained outside, being unable to gain admission to the sacred edifice.

The ceremony lasted for three hours, and at its close Bishop Flaget returned to his room, completely exhausted, saying, with evident emotion, "Now will I sing the canticle of holy Simeon—'Now dost thou, O Lord, dismiss thy servant in peace.'" Even the noblest and most Christian souls not unfrequently find great difficulty in realizing that the time has come when they should retire from the responsibility of office, in order henceforth to lead the life of prayer "hidden with Christ in God." We cling with such tenacity to power and the thought of our own importance, that when increasing years and infirmities warn us, to use the expression of Bishop Flaget, of our approaching nullity, we fret and worry, and are loath to confess, even to ourselves, that for us God's providence has sounded the signal of retreat from the active duties of life. Even they who have labored most zealously in the cause of religion are sometimes exposed to this temptation, allowing the evening of lives, which should be devoted to repose and contemplation, to be disturbed by anxious restlessness. To my mind, not the least of the many proofs of the exalted virtue of Bishop Flaget is found in the cheerful readiness with which he resigned the whole administration of the diocese which he had created into the hands of his beloved son in Christ. After the consecration of Bishop Spalding, he at once withdrew into the solitude of his own heart, and dwelt henceforth in undisturbed communion with God. " Looking at his career with the eye of faith," says his biographer, " the portion of it which appears most luminous is that precisely which to the eye of nature would seem the most shrouded in gloom—the months which immediately preceded his final dissolution. The sun of his life sank calmly to rest; but, as it did so, it lighted up with golden tints the clouds which overhung the horizon, reflecting a mild but glorious flood of light over the world it left behind. His whole life may be said to have been one continual preparation for death. He directed all his actions to this great moment on which eternity depends. As the event approached, however, his thoughts turned to it more frequently, and his preparation became more immediate and earnest. To his friends, who often wished him better health and many more years of life, he invariably replied, 'Oh! no; pray not for longer life, but for a holy and happy death.' This was all he desired and asked for. His most fervent aspiration was to exchange this life of toil and trouble for one of never-ending bliss." *

He lived for a year and a half after the appointment of Bishop Spalding as his coadjutor, from whose hands he received the last sacraments on the 11th of February, 1850, and on the evening of the same day, without a groan or

* *Life of Bishop Flaget*, by Bishop Spalding, page 348.

struggle, calmly fell asleep in the Lord, like an infant that gently sinks to rest on the bosom of its mother.

Nine years before, the venerable Bishop David, the founder of the seminary and of the Sisters of Charity in Kentucky, had passed away from earth, in the eighty-first year of his life. Thus the church of Kentucky lost the two apostolic men to whom she owed more than to all others. They had run their course, they had kept the faith, and the just Judge had prepared for them the crown of glory. Not only were they great priests, but they were also noble and generous-hearted men, full of human sympathy and tender affection. They loved their priests and their people, and in turn received from them the tribute of unbounded filial devotion. To them the clergy of Kentucky are indebted for that spirit of obedience and self-sacrifice which has now become with them a tradition; and from them her people learned to associate the priestly character with all that is highest and worthiest of veneration. One of the greatest services that Bishop Spalding could have rendered to religion in his native State, was to embalm the sacred memories of these saintly men, as he has done in his *Sketches of Kentucky* and his *Life of Bishop Flaget*. Though not yet a century old, the church which they founded has memories and examples of heroic virtue which can never be forgotten. Whilst these patriarchs presided over its destinies, Bishop David was its head, Bishop Flaget its heart. In his biographical notice of Bishop David, whom he calls the Father of the Clergy of the West, Dr. Spalding says: " Sincerity and candor in all things were perhaps the most distinctive traits in his character. He was what he appeared to be. He had less of human respect than is usually found among men. He always told you plainly what he thought; and you might rely upon the sincerity of his opinion as much as upon the soundness of his judgment. He was also, as we have already remarked, entirely consistent with his principles. If he taught prompt obedience in others, he always practised it himself, no matter how much pain it cost him; and this even after he had been consecrated bishop. If he was somewhat rigid towards others, he was much more stern with regard to himself, never seeking to impose upon others a burden which his own shoulders were not ready cheerfully to bear."

Bishop Spalding entered upon the administration of the diocese, which at that time embraced the whole State of Kentucky, under not unfavorable auspices. The Jesuits, who had taken charge of St. Mary's College in 1832, had left the diocese in 1846, having been invited by the Bishop of New York to a more extensive field of labor. This was, at the time, the occasion of some inconvenience to the Bishop, who was compelled to withdraw priests from the missions in order to place them in charge of St. Mary's. St. Joseph's College, too, was under the control of secular priests, and the Bishop felt that he was unable to supply two such institutions with professors from the clergy of his diocese; and he therefore determined to engage some religious order to take charge of either the one or the other of these colleges. With this view, negotiations were entered into with the Jesuits of the vice-province of St. Louis, which were soon brought to a successful termination, and they re-entered the diocese and assumed the management of St. Joseph's College in the same month in which Bishop Spalding was consecrated. They at the same time took charge of the free school for boys in Louisville, which had been erected two years before, under the superintendence of Dr. Spalding, who was then the Vicar-General.

A college was built on a lot adjoining the free school, and into these two institutions over three hundred boys were soon gathered, and placed under the judicious and enlightened training of the fathers of the Society of Jesus.

Late in December, three months after the consecration of Dr. Spalding, there arrived in Kentucky a colony of Trappists, from Melleray, in France.

Members of this austere order who had been driven from their homes by the French Revolution, had come to America as early as 1804, and had established themselves at Pigeon Hill, near Conewago, in Pennsylvania. Having remained there little more than a year, they removed to Kentucky in the fall of 1805, and erected a temporary convent near the church of Holy Cross. This, too, they abandoned in 1808, on account of the climate, which did not permit them to practise the austerities required by their rule.

From Kentucky they went to Florissant, near St. Louis, which they left at the end of a year, and established themselves on a farm in Illinois, lying on the Mississippi River, about six miles above St. Louis. But the malaria of this region made their new home even more unhealthy than those which they had abandoned, and, religious freedom having in the meantime been proclaimed in France, the General of the order, in 1813, recalled them to take possession of the convents from which they had been driven.

The colony which came to Kentucky in 1848 was the second attempt to establish the order in this country. The threatening aspect of the political situation in Europe had made them fearful that they should be again driven from France, and they therefore determined to seek, in the forests of the far West, an asylum where they would be permitted to practise the divine counsels of the Saviour in security and peace.

They purchased of the Sisters of Loretto the convent and farm of Gethsemane, lying about fourteen miles southeast of Bardstown, and near the spot where their brethren had settled in 1805. This second establishment, as we shall see, proved to be more fortunate than the first.

Bishop Spalding considered it a special privilege to have in his diocese these holy men, whose lives are so entirely consecrated to the perfect observance of all that is most exalted in the religion of Christ. He looked upon them as living witnesses to the divine and supernatural power of Catholic faith; for the perennial presence of Christ, and the perpetual indwelling of the Holy Ghost in the church, are not perceived in this alone that she teaches a true doctrine, but the divine action is even more manifest in the supernatural lives of her children. Christ must be continually revealed to the world in the persons of those who love him. His purity, his humility, his charity, his gentleness, his compassion for the sinful, his sympathy with the poor and the oppressed, his spirit of prayer and self-denial, his passion and death, must all be perpetuated in the lives of his saints with the same truth with which his divine countenance was impressed on the napkin of Veronica.

His life was one of perfect chastity. Born of a virgin, he himself remained ever a virgin, and though he alone has consecrated marriage, and given to it the sanctifying and civilizing power which has been so fruitful of good results in Christian lands, still he taught, in language which cannot be misunderstood, that virginity—perfect purity of life—is higher, nearer to God, than the married state; and, therefore, at least some of the children of the church must lead this life of consecrated chastity, that she may present to the world this feature in the life of her divine Founder.

Christ was humble, being God—the Highest; he placed himself beneath the feet of the lowest; and, wishing to die for the sins of men, he chose that manner of death which was most ignominious. Indeed, humility was necessarily a fundamental feature in his character, because without humility there is no virtue, since without it there is no self-sacrifice. Pride is the form of every sin, as humility is that of all virtue. God, says Lacordaire, is the humblest of beings. In the church, then, must be found a few, at least, who imitate Christ in his humble, lowly life, who, like him, descend from the high places, shun honor and renown and all worldly dignity, in order to hide their lives with him in God. Christ was obedient unto death, yea, unto the death of the cross; and they who seek to lead the ideal life which he has shown to the world, must crucify their wills. Christ, though he knew no sin, yet led a life of penance. He fasted, he prayed, he had not whereon to lay his head; and in his church this life of penance must be perpetually renewed. Bishop Spalding looked upon these austere monks as witnesses to Christ in his church, and believed that their lives of prayer and self-abnegation would draw down innumerable blessings upon his diocese.

Writing of them two or three years after they had established themselves at Gethsemane, he said:

"These monks belong to the more strict observance of the Cistercian institute, one of the most austere religious orders in the church. They devote their lives to manual labor, to perpetual silence, to fasting and prayer. Seven hours of each day are spent in church, and as many are given to labor. They never taste flesh-meat, fish, eggs, or butter. Their penitential austerities seem incredible in this age of boasted progress and boundless self-indulgence. Their rigorous lives astonish the worldling, who can appreciate nothing which does not contribute to material progress and sensual enjoyment; whilst they are matter of admiration for all true Christians who, enlightened by faith, are able to estimate the awful malice of sin and the absolute necessity of penance. He who, himself, led a poor and hard life, must look down with complacency on these pious recluses, who, to expiate their own and others' sins, devote themselves, for his love, to this life of privation. Yet, in the midst of their labors and austerities, these good monks are remarkably cheerful and happy. The peace of God, surpassing all understanding, beams constantly from their countenances." *

Another great order of the church, which had been established in the diocese more than forty years before Bishop Spalding's consecration, was now in a prosperous condition. The unrelenting persecution of the Catholics in England had forced the English Dominicans to take refuge on the Continent of Europe. They went to Belgium, where they formed an English province of their order, and founded a college at Bornheim. But not even there could they find peace and security. In 1805, the French Revolution, which upturned everything on the Continent, sent its vandals to seize upon the college at Bornheim. Those members of the order who were not thrown into prison made their escape to England. Among these was a young American who, having been sent to Europe to complete his education, had gone to Bornheim, and, after finishing his studies, had taken the habit of St. Dominic. He had been ordained priest, and his genial nature and great virtue had already won for him the love and confidence of his brethren. This was Father Edward Fenwick, a native of Maryland, and a lineal descendant of the noble family of Fenwicks, of Fenwick Tower, in Northumberland. The Dominicans, who had been driven from Belgium, petitioned the General of the order for permission to go to the United States, the native country of Father Fenwick. The request was granted, and Father Fenwick was named Superior. They accordingly sailed for the United States, and, on landing, presented themselves to Bishop Carroll, the only bishop in the American Union at that time. By his advice, Father Fenwick, accompanied by Fathers Wilson, Tuite, and Anger, all English-

---

* *Life of Bishop Flaget*, page 344.

men, started for the wild woods of Kentucky in the spring of 1806, there to build up a home for their order.

Father Fenwick had inherited from his parents quite a rich patrimony, and with this he purchased a large and fertile tract of land in Washington County, near Springfield, upon which he established the convent of St. Rose, and thus became the founder of the Dominican order in the United States. In 1809, Father Wilson opened, near the convent, a college for the education of Catholic youth, which he placed under the patronage of St. Thomas of Aquin. This was the first Catholic institution of learning in Kentucky, and one of the first in the United States. The college flourished for ten years, when the founding of a convent in Somerset, Ohio, in 1819, necessitated the withdrawal of so many of the fathers that its discontinuance was deemed advisable. Under the shadow of St. Rose, and the fostering care of Father Wilson and Father Miles, the future first Bishop of Nashville, a sisterhood of the Third Order of St. Dominic also grew up, and soon sent forth branches to Ohio and Tennessee.

CHAPTER XI.

STATE OF THE DIOCESE, CONTINUED—BISHOP SPALDING'S FIRST VISITATION—THE EARLY CATHOLICS OF KENTUCKY.

HE Sisters of Charity of Nazareth and the Sisters of Loretto had established convents and academies in various parts of Kentucky, in which children of their own sex were brought up in the knowledge and practice of whatever moulds or adorns the character of the Christian woman.

Bishop Flaget, during his last visit to France, was detained by sickness at Angers, where he was made acquainted with the Sisterhood of the Good Shepherd. With his practical knowledge of the wants of the church in this country, he at once perceived that the introduction of this order into the United States would prove highly serviceable to religion and morality.

He therefore asked for a sufficient number of Sisters to establish the community in his own diocese. His petition was granted, and five Sisters, representing five different nationalities, were sent out to Louisville in the fall of 1842. This was the first establishment of the Sisters of the Good Shepherd in the United States. They met with a hearty welcome, and were placed in a house on Eighth Street, which had been bought for them by the Bishop; and their convent was soon filled with unfortunate women, who, like Magdalen, tired of a life of sin, came to seek forgiveness and peace at the feet of Jesus.

An ecclesiastical seminary had been established, as we

have seen, at St. Thomas', near Bardstown, in 1811, shortly after the arrival of Bishop Flaget in Kentucky. In 1818, the seminary was removed to Bardstown, where it remained till 1848, when, the Jesuits having taken charge of the college, the seminarians were sent for a time to St. Mary's, and then brought back to St. Thomas'.

The Catholic population of the State, at the time of Dr. Spalding's consecration, was about thirty thousand. In the diocese there were forty-three churches and ten chapels, served by forty priests. St. Vincent's Orphan Asylum for girls, founded fifteen years prior to this date, by Mother Catharine Spalding, was now the home of more than a hundred orphans. There was, however, no asylum for boys. The contrast between the well-organized church over which Bishop Spalding was now called to rule, and that body of scattered and wandering children of the old Catholic colony of St. Mary's, whom Bishop Flaget found when, not forty years before, he first entered the dark forests of Kentucky—where the war-whoop of the Indian, passing westward, had not yet died out—is indeed most striking. Then there were not more than five thousand Catholics in the whole State. There were but six priests besides the Vicar-General, three of whom were Dominicans; and ten churches or chapels, built of roughly-hewn logs. With the exception of the order of St. Dominic, there was no religious society in the whole West. Bishop Flaget had been obliged to remain in Baltimore for six months after his consecration, for want of money to defray his travelling expenses to his new diocese, and upon his arrival he found, for the accommodation of himself and the ecclesiastics who had accompanied him, two miserable log-cabins, sixteen feet square, situated in the woods, near St. Stephen's. For furniture they contained a bed, two tables, and six chairs, one of the missionaries being obliged to sleep in the garret.

But the hearty welcome with which his children received him, and the evidences which he beheld of their lively faith, more than compensated for the privations which he was made to suffer.

When he arrived at St. Stephen's, he found the faithful kneeling on the grass, singing canticles. The women were dressed in white, and, though it was four o'clock in the afternoon, many of them were still fasting, with the hope of being able to receive communion from the hands of the Bishop. Here, under the overshadowing foliage of the "forest primeval," an altar had been erected, before which the Bishop clothed himself in his pontifical robes, and then proceeded to the rude chapel, where he took formal possession of his diocese, according to the ceremonies prescribed in the Roman Pontifical.

After his consecration, Bishop Spalding at once entered upon the visitation of the diocese. His first thought was given to the little children of his flock, for whom, in imitation of his divine Master, he felt the tenderest and sincerest love. He visited the schools and literary institutions under his jurisdiction, to manifest his great interest in the cause of Christian education, which he held to be of the most vital importance both to the progress of religion and the welfare of the country. He held that there could be no sound morality without religion, and, since the cultivation of the moral faculties enters of necessity into the proper conception of education, that there in consequence could be no education in the true sense without religion. "Education without religion," said he, "is the body without the soul, the building without the foundation, philosophy without fundamental principles. The contrary theory would banish God, with the hallowing influence of his divine government, from his own favorite domain—the human soul, leaving it during the most trying and dangerous period of life—that of youth—to be buffeted at will by the world, the flesh, and the devil. It ignores the very starting-point of all sound instruction, the fountain-source of all true wisdom." Having by his earnestness and zeal reanimated to renewed energy those to whom God had entrusted the education of the children of his diocese, he entered upon the visitation of the parishes of the State, some of which had not been blessed by the presence of a Catholic Bishop for several years. He had arranged to have missions preached in the various congregations which he was about to visit.

Already in youth, he had learned from his old professor, Bishop David, who seems to have been the first to introduce into the church of this country a practice which has since been productive of the best results, to attach great importance to these popular missions, and he had whilst a student in Rome, as we have already seen, studied with a view to fit himself for this work.*

Taking with him two clergymen to assist in preaching the missions, and in preparing the children for first communion and confirmation, he journeyed on horseback from church to church. From the record which was kept of this his first episcopal visitation, I find that he generally took upon himself the task of instructing the children who were preparing for their first communion, without, however, confining himself to this work of love, for he also bore his share in preaching and in hearing confessions. At the close of the mission he generally lectured on the doctrines of the church, especially those to which Protestants most frequently objected.

---

* The *Relation* addressed by the Jesuits of Maryland, in 1638, to the General of the order in Rome, says: "By the spiritual exercises we have formed the principal inhabitants to the practice of piety, and they have derived signal benefits from them." This passage, however, it will be perceived, does not refer to popular missions, the introduction of which into this country Archbishop Spalding ascribes to Bishop David.

His method in doing this was to state plainly, and to confirm by sound arguments, Catholic teachings, without assuming an aggressive attitude towards Protestantism, or giving to his discourses a polemical character. "Kind persuasion," he wrote, "especially in this country, goes much further than hard logic. The appeal to the heart is more effectual than that to the head; this I have learned by long experience.

"In argument, principles rather than men should be kept steadily in view. The spirit of Milner's *End of Controversy* is admirable in this respect. *Fortiter in re, suaviter in modo.*"

The visitation was made, as far as circumstances permitted, in strict accordance with the rules laid down in the Pontifical. He examined minutely into both the temporal and spiritual administration of each parish, and, after consulting with the pastor, made such regulations as the welfare of the faithful seemed to demand. Nothing escaped his attention. The deeds of property belonging to the church were looked over, and, when any flaw was discovered, it was corrected. In various places, he found that the churches and cemeteries had never been blessed, and the defect was of course remedied. The necessity of establishing Catholic schools where they did not as yet exist was always insisted upon. In his instructions to the people, he never failed to exhort them to cultivate a tender devotion to the Blessed Virgin, the glorious Queen of Heaven and the special Patroness of the church in the United States, and to this end he recommended the immediate establishment among them of the Archconfraternity of the Immaculate Heart of Mary, for the conversion of sinners. In places where there are now well-organized congregations, he found only a few isolated Catholic families. The good effect of the missions was specially manifest. Faith and piety revived, night and morning family prayer was introduced, scandals ceased, persons who had remained away from the sacraments for years sought forgiveness in the tribunal of penance, and the entire Catholic population was renewed in spirit. Many Protestants, too, were received into the church—thirteen out of every hundred confirmed being converts.

The pew system had not at that time been introduced into the church in Kentucky, at least outside of Louisville, and, according to a time-honored custom, the men sat on one side of the aisle, whilst the other was reserved for the women. This division of the sexes was also observed in the solemn procession which the Bishop always made to the graveyard, in order to say the prayers for the dead, as prescribed in the Roman Pontifical. The men and boys marched first, then came the women and girls, and the procession was closed by the clergy, followed by the Bishop. In places where there were a considerable number of Catholics but no church, or one too small for the accommodation of the people, he took measures to have a suitable house of worship built at once. Subscription-lists were opened, and, in several instances, sufficient money for the purpose was obtained on the spot.

Many of the wealthier Catholics owned slaves, who attended the missions with their masters, kneeling alongside of them at the confessional and before the altar to receive holy communion. The simple, Christian life of the Catholics in Kentucky in those days, which are gone away never more to return, ought not to be forgotten. Not in Ireland or Tyrol or Brittany was there a more confiding or childlike faith in all that Christ teaches through the church, than amongst those descendants of the old Catholic colony. They were Kentuckians, with the frank and open manliness of character which distinguished their fellow-countrymen ; they had that naïve and boundless faith in republican institutions, combined with unspeakable contempt for what they considered the effete and corrupt governments of Europe, which belonged peculiarly to the American character before any great sorrow had tried our people, taking from them the freshness of hopes undeceived, the brightness of illusions whose unreality misfortune had not taught them. The flag that floated over them was in their eyes the emblem of a new era in the history of the race—the harbinger of a dawn compared with which the brightness of past civilization would be but night. Never have I known a feeling of more intense love of freedom, and devotion to all the principles which secure it, than that which was found amongst those Catholics of Kentucky. And yet the old, old church, which had existed in the beginning, whose pathway through the ages was marked by the wrecks of time and human passions, which had lived everywhere, in the north and in the south, in the furthest east and the remotest west, whose home had been in the palaces of kings, in the great cities of the world, and in the tents of the wandering and warlike barbarian—before whose beauty and majesty the princes of the earth had bowed down, and the rude savage, against whose strength had risen up time and again men of power and men of mind, only to fall broken like the mad waves of the ocean that dash against the rock-bound coast—this noble old church was their mother—the mother of their souls, to whom they turned with a love and devotion intensified by the memory of how their fathers had clung to her through long ages, until, when it had become a crime to love her in their own land, they sought the new world that God had opened to them, and there made for her a home, and built to her an altar, and with those same Catholic hands built an altar to freedom. The church has never had more submissive or obedient children than they were.

In settling in Kentucky, they had frequently chosen the less fertile portions of the State because a church or chapel had been built there. Indeed, at one time, as I have elsewhere stated, many of the early Catholic colonists thought seriously of removing to Missouri, as it seemed impossible to get missionaries to come to Kentucky. They were not deterred from the practice of their religion by trifles. Men and women would ride ten or fifteen miles over the roughest roads to hear Mass, and would remain fasting till twelve or one o'clock to be able to receive holy communion. Their reverence for the priestly character was unbounded. There were no schisms, no disputes with trustees, no contentions about church property, no rebellions of congregations against their priests or bishop. Never did a father receive truer love in the bosom of his own family than that which was given to Bishop Flaget, yea, and to Bishop David and to Father Nerincks and to Father Badin, by the Catholic people of Kentucky. To others they might be foreigners, men of different race and of another tongue, but to them they were fathers most beloved and most dear. The nationality of the priest was a matter of indifference; they scarcely thought of it; he was simply the minister of God. His actions were not misconstrued; he was not surrounded by men anxious to spy out and detect his faults. Even as a child thinks his father perfect, so those early Catholics thought their priests were saints; and some of them were, in truth. They were not a straitlaced race. They were hospitable, and loved enjoyment, and were never better pleased than when they saw the happy and the light-hearted around them. Frequently they would assemble, and whilst the young engaged in the simple country-dance, the old looked on or talked of other days. Father Badin, who, though the best of men, was not wholly free from certain rigid notions that remind one of the period when in some parts of France Jansenistic ideas entered largely into clerical training, delighted to be present on these occasions. Whenever he could learn that an entertainment was to be given, he made it a point to come in unexpectedly when the enjoyment was at its height. When he entered the room, all understood the meaning of his presence, and resigned themselves with great composure to what seemed to them the inevitable. He had heard, he would say, of their social gathering, and, fearing lest they should forget their night prayers, had come to say them in their good company. All would then kneel down, and Father Badin would proceed to give out prayers for an hour or two, until his devotion was satisfied, and then he would dismiss the gathering, saying it was time they were all in bed. And yet such was their reverence for the priestly character that no one rebelled or even complained. Though there was no great choice of food, still the days of abstinence and fast were invariably kept in strict accordance with the requirements of the church. The pious custom of saying family prayers, night and morning, existed very generally; and when the head of the house owned slaves, they too were required to be present at these devotions. All knelt together in the same room, and the father or the mother of the family gave out the prayer, and the others answered.

Before or after these exercises the master would frequently enter into conversation with his slaves, enquiring concerning the health of this one or the occupations of another. The condition of the plantation, the prospect of the harvest, the proper management of the stock, were discussed in a familiar and unrestrained manner, the master sometimes giving directions and sometimes receiving advice. Between the Catholic masters and their slaves there most generally existed real sympathy and affection.

Not to defend or regret a state of things, which happily

has passed away for ever, do I mention these facts, but simply to show how the influence of true religion tends to refine and soften man even in those relations of life which seem fitted only to render him harsh and unfeeling. I doubt if the relations of master and servant, when so little controlled by law, or even by public opinion, have ever anywhere been more paternal or just than among the Catholic slave-owners of Kentucky.

The faith and earnestness of the early Catholics of our State are manifest, too, in the number of religious institutions which grew up among them, and which still exist. No body of native Catholics of equal numbers in this country has ever, I think, produced so many vocations to the priesthood and to the religious life as were found in Kentucky from 1810 to 1830. The colleges, academies, and schools which they co-operated in founding, testify to their interest in the cause of education. Some of the first Protestant gentlemen of Kentucky and of Louisiana and Mississippi were educated in our colleges.

The Catholics of Kentucky, and those of Maryland as well, have been accused, and not without justice, of want of generosity in the pecuniary support which they gave their priests. Without seeking in any way to extenuate this fault, it may not be amiss to examine into the causes to which it is attributable. For nearly a century and a half from the arrival of Lord Baltimore in 1634, down to the War of Independence, the faith was preserved among the Catholics of Maryland by the Jesuits, who were, with possibly a few exceptions, the only priests in the colony—noble and disinterested men, whose praise is still in the church, and whose memory will never be forgotten by the descendants of those to whom they secured the most priceless of all gifts. Land-grants had been made to the early Jesuit missionaries of Maryland on the same terms as to the other colonists. The compact between Lord Baltimore and the colonists, entitled "Conditions of plantation," gave for a nominal consideration, to every settler who brought with him five able-bodied laborers, two thousand acres of land. The Indian kings also, whom the missionaries had converted, made gratuitous concessions of land to the church.

Ample provision was thus made for the support of the fathers, who, leading the rugged lives of travelling missionaries, needed but little. The circumstances in which the early colonists were placed did not call for orphan asylums, hospitals, and other institutions of benevolence, the need of which is the result of the overcrowding of the poorer and laboring classes in the great centres of commerce. The church edifices, too, were rude and simple structures, put up without great expense.

Indeed, in 1704 a law was passed entitled "An act to prevent the increase of popery in the province," which forbade bishops and priests to say Mass, or exercise any other functions of their ministry. This law, which remained in force until the breaking out of the Revolution, rendered all further building of churches impracticable. The Jesuits, however, succeeded in retaining possession of their lands and servants, and consequently needed nothing for their own support.

On the contrary, they were able to offer hospitality to their people, and in the lower counties of Maryland, Catholics who came fasting from a distance, in order to receive holy communion, frequently dined with the good fathers. So little did the Maryland Jesuits stand in need of the temporal goods of their people, that they were themselves able to give pecuniary assistance to the missions of Pennsylvania, as we learn from a letter of the Provincial in England, written in April, 1759.

Thus, during the entire Colonial period, the Catholics

of Maryland were placed in circumstances which rendered generosity towards the church, if not impossible, at least unnecessary, and often unwise; and, from long habit, they had come to look upon the church as self-sustaining, and the priest as a man who wanted nothing, at least from them. The history of the church everywhere proves that her people will not be generous, unless this quality be cultivated in them. The Maryland Catholics who went to Kentucky at the close of the last century carried with them the result of habits which the growth of a hundred and fifty years had made a second nature. And, unfortunately, the circumstances in which they were placed in their new home were scarcely more favorable to the cultivation of a spirit of generosity than those in which their fathers had lived. For years they had, for the most part, to struggle with poverty, and all the difficulties which a new country opposes to those who seek to bring it into subjection. For nearly a quarter of a century, they had but three or four priests, whom they rarely saw, because their missions extended not only over Kentucky, but over Ohio, Indiana, and Illinois. When, at length, priests began to reside permanently among them, they generally chose as their home one or other of the convents that had grown up, where they lived without great expense. When, finally, the diocese was formed, and the more perfect organization of the parishes demanded that the priest should reside near the church and be supported by the people, it was but natural that they should be somewhat slow in conforming to a state of things so different from their whole past experience. The priests themselves did not at first seem to comprehend the situation, or to understand exactly how to act. They insisted, from the pulpit, on the manifest duty of Catholics in this respect, but failed to adopt a plan which would divide the burden proportionately among all, and thus approve itself to the common sense of the people. The more generous Catholics responded to these appeals, whilst the greater number continued to act as though they thought it were simply absurd that a priest should want money. That which had been found necessary elsewhere, even in the large cities, and amongst the most generous people in the world, was finally adopted here; and the renting of pews has in all, except the poorest, congregations of Kentucky, secured to the priest a competent support.

CHAPTER XII.

RETREAT OF THE CLERGY—BUILDING OF THE CATHE-
DRAL IN LOUISVILLE—DIVISION OF THE DIOCESE—THE
FIRST PLENARY COUNCIL OF BALTIMORE—DESIRE TO
SECURE THE SERVICES OF A TEACHING BROTHERHOOD.

ISHOP SPALDING, after returning from his first visitation of the diocese, assembled his priests at St. Thomas', that they might enter into a spiritual retreat. He preached this retreat himself, and one of the most venerable clergymen of Kentucky has told me that it was in these days of prayer and meditation that he first perceived Bishop Spalding's practical knowledge of human nature and power of governing men, though he had long known him intimately.

Not to grow in intellectual vigor and force of character with increase of authority and higher position, is evidence of irremediable mediocrity; whereas, men who have real merit, as they are advanced in place develop qualities which had escaped the notice of even the observant. All who knew Dr. Spalding agreed that he had talent, that he was laborious and zealous; but his gentle nature and simple manners had led some to imagine that he did not possess those sterner qualities required for the government of men and the vigorous prosecution of the work of a young and growing diocese.

Indeed, to be a successful bishop in this country, one should be a many-sided man, fruitful in resources, and endowed with exhaustless latent force. The very great power which the organization of the church here gives to the bishop, renders him, in a measure, responsible for the entire working of the diocese. In the old Catholic countries of Europe, a bishop has simply to keep the machinery of ecclesiastical government moving. Everything is determined and regulated by law, and little is left to the initiative of the man. But here he has to organize and create; and, what is often more difficult, to harmonize the many conflicting elements which are at work within our young and growing church. To him, every difficulty, whether theological, financial, or personal, is referred in the last instance; and, in addition to this, the physical labor which he is forced to do is of itself exhausting.

It is expected that he should be the best theologian, the most eloquent preacher, the most reliable financier, the safest counsellor both in spiritual and temporal matters, and at the same time the most slavish worker in the diocese. To demand of a man that he should know everything and be able to do everything better than anybody else, is rather exacting. But those who doubted Bishop Spalding's ability to govern a diocese, were not sceptical after this retreat. He had placed himself at the head of his priests, and had shown them that he had a perfect understanding of what was to be done, and of the manner in which it should be done.

He had won both their confidence and their affection. During the three last days of the retreat, public conferences were held, in which questions of practical importance, relating to the administration of the sacraments and other sacerdotal duties, were discusssed; and finally, the priests were assembled in informal synod, to give their advice on certain points which were to form the basis of the diocesan statutes.

These meetings were most satisfactory to all, and the result was harmony of action and mutual good understanding amongst the priests of the diocese, who felt assured and encouraged from having learned that he who was to direct them would himself be guided only by counsels of wisdom and prudence.

Shortly after the close of this retreat, a most successful mission was given to the congregation of the cathedral in Louisville, which was at the time the only church in the city for the English-speaking Catholic population. The number of those who received communion was nine hundred and thirty-four. At no previous mission had there been half so many. There were also two German churches in the city: St. Boniface, which had been built several years before, and the Immaculate Conception, which Bishop Spalding had dedicated a short time after his consecration. In these two congregations there were about two thousand communicants, making the total number for the whole city only three thousand, which, however, is not so small when we consider that in 1825 there were but fifty.

Ever solicitous for the children of his flock, Bishop Spalding felt the urgent want of an orphan asylum for boys. The fact of there being already a hundred orphans in the asylum founded by Mother Catharine for girls, was of itself evidence that many orphans of the other sex were left unprovided for. He therefore took steps to establish an asylum at St. Thomas', which was opened in 1850 with ten orphans, the number steadily increasing until it reached one hundred and fifty.

An association, entitled the St. Joseph's Orphan Society, was organized about the same time, with a view to form an asylum for the children of German parents, though in the original constitution it was stipulated that one-third of the inmates might be of Irish or American parentage. A building, known as the Old Seminary, adjoining the church of the Immaculate Conception, was bought, and the St.

Joseph's and the St. Thomas's Orphan Asylums opened the same year, and have both been the means of preserving the faith and virtue of hundreds of helpless children.

The old cathedral in Louisville, which had originally been built for a parish church, when Bardstown was yet the see of the diocese, was not only too small for the rapidly growing congregation, but was also unfitted to the right performance of the solemn and imposing functions of the episcopal ceremonial. Bishop Spalding, therefore, resolved to begin as soon as possible the erection of a cathedral which would not be unworthy of the Catholics of Kentucky. The vote of the congregation was taken as to the site of the contemplated edifice, and the majority were in favor of building it on the spot where the old church stood. The location was central, and, in the minds of the people, was hallowed by many religious associations. The lot, too, was large, with a greater depth than any other that could have been found in an eligible portion of the city. This having been agreed upon, a meeting was held in the basement of the old church in the spring of 1849, for the purpose of raising funds to begin work. Bishop Spalding, who presided, opened the subscription with ten thousand dollars; and the Catholics of the city, encouraged by his generous example, contributed liberally. He then called upon the principal Catholics throughout the diocese, who also responded with generosity to his appeal. The style of architecture chosen was the Gothic. The cathedral was to be two hundred and ten feet in length by about ninety in width, with a clere-story, supported by a row of graceful columns on each side of the main aisle, and surmounted by a tower whose beautiful spire should rise to a height of two hundred and eighty-five feet above the ground, lifting the cross of Christ above the whole city and surrounding country. The corner-stone was laid on the Feast of the Assumption, the 15th of August,

1849, in the presence of an immense concourse of people. The venerable Bishop Flaget, who was too feeble to be able to assist in the ceremony, overlooked the scene from a balcony of his residence, and, at the close, invoked the blessing of heaven on the beginning of a work the completion of which he was not destined to see.

Under the special supervision and management of the Very Rev. B. J. Spalding, to whose good sense and sound judgment the Bishop in this, as in many other things, was greatly indebted, the work was pushed vigorously forward, and on the Feast of the Most Holy Rosary, October 3, 1852, the new cathedral was solemnly consecrated to the service and worship of God, in the presence of two archbishops, eight bishops, one mitred abbot, and over forty priests. The Archbishop of Cincinnati performed the ceremony of the dedication, and Dr. McCloskey, the present Archbishop of New York, preached in the morning, and the Archbishop of St. Louis in the evening.

On the morning after the dedication, the remains of Bishop Flaget were solemnly translated, and deposited in a crypt beneath the high altar of the cathedral. "The relics of a saint," said Bishop Spalding, "reposing in the crypt of our cathedral, God will not fail to bless us."

The total cost of the cathedral—in the building of which the strictest economy, even in the minutest details of the work, was observed—was seventy-five thousand dollars. The debt was soon paid, with the exception of eight thousand dollars belonging to the seminary fund, which was invested in the cathedral, with the condition of the semi-annual payment of the interest.

The bell, which weighs 4,500 lbs., and which cost twelve hundred dollars, was the generous gift of Mgr. La Bastida, Archbishop of Mexico, who christened it *La Purissima*. In 1858, a clock, made by Blin, of Paris, was placed in the tower, at a cost of two thousand dollars. The cathedral was put under the special protection of the Blessed Virgin and of St. Joseph, the patron of the diocese. "By a coincidence not prearranged," said Bishop Spalding, "it happened that the chief events connected with the building occurred on Feasts of the Blessed Virgin. The subscription was opened on the Feast of the Annunciation, the digging of the foundation was begun on the Feast of the Visitation, the corner-stone was laid on the Feast of the Assumption, and the dedication took place on the Feast of the Holy Rosary. Thus," he added, "the Holy and Immaculate Virgin, under whose auspices the cathedral was begun, watched over it to completion. May she continue to smile on it, and on all who will worship within its walls."

By a special rescript from Rome, the feast of the dedication was transferred from the first Sunday of October to the fourth Sunday of September, to prevent it from clashing with the Feast of the Holy Rosary.

In the meantime, the other congregations of the diocese were not neglected. Bishop Spalding, since his consecration, had dedicated the Church of the Immaculate Conception, in Louisville; that of St. Catharine, at New Haven, and the Church of the Holy Rosary, at Manton. New churches had been built in Paducah, Henderson, and Maysville; and in Frankfort, the capital of the State, a handsome church, and house for priest's residence, had been bought from the Presbyterians, and dedicated to divine worship. A community of Magdalens had been founded in connection with the convent of the Good Shepherd, in a house built for that purpose by the first person who took the habit in the new community—Sister Mary, of St. Augustine. In the winter of 1851-52, Bishop Spalding was engaged in writing the life of Bishop Flaget, which, as he says in the preface, was a labor of filial love, though not without its difficulties, especially for one so engrossed by a multiplicity of cares and duties seemingly incompatible with literary occupations.

"If our early missionaries labored much," he says, "they wrote but little. Their time was too much occupied in the discharge of severe ministerial duties to allow them leisure for recording their proceedings. Hence our early religious history is involved in no little obscurity; and the enquirer who wishes to trace the origin and progress of our missions, has to contend with many difficulties. Among these, the principal is the paucity of well-ascertained facts and dates. Materials there are, indeed, here and there, in abundance; but they are scattered, unconnected, often vague in their accounts, and, still more frequently, merely local, personal, or otherwise unimportant in their details." *

Archbishop Kenrick, to whom he had communicated his intention of writing a biography of Bishop Flaget, replied: "I am glad to learn that you intend to write a life of your venerable predecessor. It is truly a reproach to us that we suffer the memory of persons and things so intimately connected with the history of the church, in this country, to lie buried in episcopal archives, without making any effort to give them publicity. I hope that your example will not be without its favorable influence on others." In composing this life, it was necessary to examine three thousand letters, besides thirty-four volumes of a MS. journal kept by Bishop Flaget, which involves an amount of thankless labor not easily appreciated by those to whom a similar task has never been given to perform. The work is a valuable contribution to the early history of the church west of the Alleghany Mountains. The delicate task of writing the biography of one so recently dead, and whose life had been so intimately connected with many persons still living, caused Bishop

* *Life of Bishop Flaget*—Preface.

Spalding to feel anxious lest he should give offence, and he consulted Archbishop Kenrick as to the rules which should guide him, in view of this difficulty.

"In the correspondence of Bishop Flaget," he wrote, "especially with Bishop Dubourg, there are many interesting disclosures concerning the administration of dioceses, the erection of new sees in the West, the nomination of suitable persons for them, and other things of like import. I fear I shall make some blunders and commit not a few indiscretions; but I desire to embody as much information as possible on the early history of our Western dioceses. I wish I had a little of your *Roman* caution. Pray for me, and give freely any advice you have to offer."

The Archbishop, however, declined to make any suggestions, and simply answered: "I must leave you to your own prudence as to both the living and the dead."

Archbishop Eccleston, the fifth Archbishop of Baltimore, died in April, 1851, and in August of the same year Bishop Kenrick was translated from Philadelphia to fill the vacant see. A few weeks later, he received letters directing him to hold a Plenary Council of the entire episcopate of the United States, and appointing him Apostolic Legate, with authority to preside over the assembly. Bishop Spalding felt that the increasing Catholic population of the extensive territory under his spiritual jurisdiction demanded a division of the diocese of Louisville; and he therefore wrote to Archbishop Kenrick on the subject, stating his reasons, which he desired to submit to the council. In his reply, the Archbishop, after giving his opinion in favor of the formation of the new diocese, says: "The number of our sees is likely to reach forty by the action of the National Council; since New Jersey, North Carolina, Florida, Southern Illinois, Sault Sainte-Marie, and other places, are spoken of as ready for sees." And a few days later he wrote: " I beg of you to prepare your views as to the decrees to be formed in the council, since two or three prelates, well prepared, can expedite our proceedings. I think we should sit during two weeks, or at least until Ascension Thursday. I directed the old catechism, as revised by the Bishop of Buffalo, to be sent to you, that you may communicate to him your observations, and thus prepare for the adoption of a uniform catechism. Some Lazarists are preparing a new and much improved edition of our ceremonial. I have directed an extract from the exposition of ceremonies, published at Rome by Bishop England, to be prefixed, since he was charged by the first council to prepare such an explanation. I am also getting out a new edition of my work on baptism, and will be most thankful for your candid remarks and suggestions. Your trip South will, I trust, renew your health, and give you an opportunity of writing a saint's life without distraction. I asked the Bishop of Boston to preach on the day of commemorating the deceased prelates, but have received no reply. If he should decline, I shall rely on you. The venerable Flaget should be the chief subject. You will not feel yourself slighted in getting only this contingent invitation, as I treat my dearest friends with freedom." A week later he wrote again: "The Bishop of Boston declines preaching the funeral, on the plea of being unacquainted with the merits of the deceased, especially of the venerable Flaget, who ought to be the main subject of the panegyric. You cannot put in this plea; so, waiving all excuse, please prepare for that grand occasion. Dr. Fitzpatrick desires to have two new sees erected—one at Portland, in Maine; the other at Burlington, Vermont. I agree with him, and think that Boston ought to be raised to the dignity of an archdiocese, of which he, however, has no idea. The same honor ought, in my opinion, to be awarded to Philadelphia, since both these cities have vast populations, and historical reminiscences connected with our government and independence."

In reply to this letter, Bishop Spalding wrote as follows:

"LOUISVILLE, February 9, 1852.
"MOST REVEREND AND DEAR FRIEND:

"As I intimated in my last, I accept, though with fear and trembling, your invitation to preach at the service for the deceased prelates. Three subjects for one discourse—and such subjects!—will, I fear, be above my strength; but I shall try to do the best I can. The good Bishop of Boston, for so bold a man against heretics, is remarkably diffident. I, this day, write to Bishop Timon my observations on his catechism. As the subject is important, I have received on it the report of three divines, my brother being chairman. With several small changes, the catechism will, I think, meet a want which has been generally felt; and nowhere so much as in the West, where persons come together from the various Eastern dioceses, having been taught every variety of catechism. God grant that a common catechism may be adopted! The want of uniform practice throughout the Union in regard to feasts, fasts, and other observances is also very embarrassing. Here, for instance, on the two sides of the Ohio River, we have two kinds of discipline, which is very awkward, as the people of Indiana are thrown into constant contact with my own diocesans. There should also, by all means, be a uniform discipline adopted for the Germans, who are migrating to the West with their different local practices."

At the recommendation of the fathers of the First Plenary Council of Baltimore, which met in May, 1852, Pope Pius IX. consented to create a new diocese in Kentucky, embracing all that part of the State lying east of the Kentucky River. The see was placed at Covington, and the Rev. George Carrell, of the Society of Jesus, was made its first Bishop.

In one of the decrees (n. 90) of the First Plenary Council of Baltimore, the fathers use the following impressive language: " We exhort the bishops, and, considering the most grievous evils which are accustomed to follow from the faulty education of youth, we beseech them through the bowels of the mercy of God, to see that schools be established in connection with all the churches of their dioceses; and, if it be necessary and circumstances permit, to provide from the income of the church to which the school is attached for the support of competent teachers." Bishop Flaget had, in 1820, received letters from the Propaganda, in which he was urged to found Catholic schools, and, a little later, all the bishops of the United States were exhorted by the Holy Father to have recourse to this as the only effectual means of preserving the faith of their people. The desire to comply more fully with these instructions than it had hitherto been possible to do in Kentucky, was one of the chief motives which induced Bishop Spalding to visit Europe in the fall of 1852. In his *Life of Bishop Flaget*, which had just been published, in referring to this subject, he had said: "This system of parochial schools, wherever it can be carried out, harmonizes well with the spirit and practice of the Catholic Church, and, if fully established, would be attended with immense advantages to morality and religion. Education without religion is a body without a soul—it develops and gives strength to the passions, while it withholds the only effectual influence which can guide and control them for good." Archbishop Hughes had said, in 1850: ".I think the time has almost come when it will be necessary to build the school-house first and the church afterwards."

Division of the Diocese.

Schools for girls existed already very generally throughout the diocese, and the sisterhoods of Nazareth and Loretto were able to meet the demands which were made for teachers. But it was found extremely difficult to establish good elementary schools for boys. It was not easy to find competent lay teachers, and, when found, it was often impossible to pay them the salaries which they demanded. In a letter to one of his brothers in the episcopate, Bishop Spalding said : " *Rem acu tetigisti :* Your letter pictures the great want we all feel in this country—that of teachers for our children, especially the boys, who are going to ruin by hundreds and thousands. As the Holy Father so well says, the machinations of the enemies of Christ are now chiefly directed to misleading and corrupting youth ; and in these satanical attempts on innocence they succeed, alas ! but too well. . . ."

What was to be done to counteract this evil, the existence of which no one could deny? The teaching orders of religious women had supplied, to a very great extent, at least, the remedy for the Catholic children of their own sex, and the question naturally presented itself, Could not brotherhoods be established which would do for boys what the sisterhoods had done for girls? This had been a favorite idea with Bishop Flaget from the time of his arrival in Kentucky. Father Nerincks, the founder of the Sisterhood of Loretto, had, in 1824, matured the plan for a teaching brotherhood, which death prevented him from carrying into execution. Two years later, Bishop Flaget, with the assistance of the Rev. M. Derigaud, succeeded in bringing together a few religious men, who bound themselves by vows for three years, and who seemed destined to realize his anticipations of the good results to be expected from the permanent establishment of a brotherhood in the diocese. A beginning was made at St. Thomas', and in the spring of 1827, the Brothers, under the direction of Father Derigaud, removed to a farm belonging to the church, in Casey County. They had built a house, and had just entered upon the life of a religious community, when Father Derigaud died, and the Bishop, being unable to find a suitable person to assume the direction of affairs, the brotherhood languished and, at the close of the three years for which they had taken vows, was dissolved. In 1847, two Brothers of St. Francis, from Ireland, took charge of the free school in Louisville, which had been recently built. They, however, met with but little success, and did not remain more than a year. The school was then given in charge of the Jesuits, who had just re-entered the diocese. But, in the summer of 1852, they also, for some cause or other, wished to give it back into the hands of the Bishop. Difficulties of this kind, however, were by no means confined to Kentucky. Even in so wealthy a place as New York, with a large and influential Catholic population, the attempt to introduce the Christian Brothers failed at first, though a second effort was more successful.

Another obstacle, which experience had already proven not to be imaginary, to the success of elementary schools conducted by brotherhoods, was the tendency on their part, not always without reasons which, to themselves at least, seemed sufficient, to devote their best talents and energy to select schools, to the inevitable detriment of such as were attended almost exclusively by the children of the poor.

But to have failed once or twice in a good cause is only to have learned how to succeed in the future, and the obstacles which stand between us and the work God has given us to do, are intended to develop our Christian manhood.

Bishop Spalding then determined to visit Europe, to try

to procure teachers for the children whom Christ had committed to his charge. He had another object, not less important, in view in undertaking this journey: he needed more priests, and hoped to find them in the Catholic countries of the Old World.

CHAPTER XIII.

VISIT TO EUROPE — THE XAVERIAN BROTHERS — THE AMERICAN COLLEGE AT LOUVAIN.

ISHOP SPALDING sailed from New York on the 20th of November, and landed in Havre on the 5th of December, 1852, just in time to assist at the solemn inauguration of the Empire, the splendor of whose rise has been surpassed only by the unequalled ignominy in which it has fallen amid the general wreck and ruin of the nation.

In Rouen, he was received by the Archbishop with a cordiality and kindness which, in France, were everywhere extended to him as the successor of the venerable Flaget. In his company, he visited the old Norman cathedral, where Richard Cœur de Lion is buried, and the church of St. Ouen, which is one of the finest specimens of Gothic architecture in the world. He saw also the palace of the Duke of Bedford, where Joan of Arc was condemned to death, and the Palais de Justice, the old Parliament House of the Dukes of Normandy. In Paris, he called on M. Deluol, at St. Sulpice, who thought there was little hope of his being able to obtain priests, at least in that part of France. He met here Cardinal Gousset, whose works on theology have given him considerable reputation. He describes him, in the short jottings which he set down in a kind of journal, as "a rough-looking man of middle age, with very black countenance." From the Cardinal he received no encouragement—he himself had need of an hundred and fifty more priests than he had in his diocese. The impression he received concerning the state of religion in France was unfavorable. He was particularly pained by the very general want of respect for the sanctity of Sunday. From a Jesuit, in Paris, he learned that not one-fourth of the women and not one-tenth of the men in that great city complied with the precepts of the church. He was delighted, however, to hear from the Abbé Gaume that Gallicanism was well-nigh extinct, and that nearly all the French bishops were now in favor of the Roman rite, whereas five years before a considerable number of them had been opposed to it.

He remained in Paris but a few days, and went thence to Amiens, where he saw the Abbé Gerbet, so well known from his having been associated, in editing the *Avenir*, with Lammenais, Lacordaire, and Montalembert, and whose beautiful works on the Sacrament of Penance and the Holy Eucharist have endeared him to all Catholic readers. He describes him as "a tall, elderly-looking man, with a student-like air." He preached here in French in the convent of the Ladies of the Sacred Heart. Although he spoke French with a good deal of ease, he, of course, did not speak it with perfect accuracy; and I remember hearing him relate, as illustrative of French politeness, a ridiculous blunder which he made in one of his sermons during this visit. In speaking of the mingling of the good with the wicked, in the church, he intended to say that even one of the apostles was a traitor, but he used the French word *traiteur*, which means a saloon-keeper ; " and yet," he would add in telling this, " so wonderful is French politeness, that in my whole audience I did not perceive even a smile." Without making longer stay, for the present, in France, he crossed over into Belgium, with the hope that the country which had given Father Nerincks to Kentucky, would be willing to send other apostles to continue the noble work which he had begun.

In Bruges, he found the Xaverian Brotherhood, which had but recently been established, with a special view to the wants of the church in the United States. The Brothers were praying for an opening in America, and the founder and superior had placed in bank the money necessary to defray the expenses of the voyage.

After consulting with Mgr. Malou, the learned Bishop of Bruges, and formerly professor in the University of Louvain, Bishop Spalding entered into an agreement with these Brothers, by which they bound themselves to open schools in Louisville as soon as arrangements for their reception should be made. They came out in 1854, and began to teach in a building which the Bishop had put up in the lower part of the city, on the lot on which St. Patrick's church now stands. Their success, for several years, was but partial. The founder, who had accompanied the infant colony to Louisville, though a man of excellent intentions, did not seem to understand how to adapt his institute to the new circumstances in which he was here placed, and the work began really to prosper only after he had been superseded as superior. Under the new government, the community grew in numbers, until the Brothers were able to take charge of all the parochial schools for boys, both English and German, in the city.

Bishop Spalding gave them a handsome house on Fourth Street, in which they opened a novitiate. Thus he had the consolation of seeing the Xaverian Brotherhood firmly established in the diocese; and the thought that he had made permanent provision for the education of the Catholic boys of Louisville was to him most reassuring. He was also very anxious to have the Brothers of the Christian Schools in Louisville. In 1859, he offered to give them ten thousand dollars, to assist them in establishing themselves there.

They, however, declined to come, on the ground that their numbers did not justify them in opening new schools.

In 1860, Bishop Spalding succeeded in getting the Brothers of Christian Instruction, to whom he gave the care of the orphans at St. Thomas'. It was his wish to place them in Owensboro or Paducah, that they might establish there a novitiate, which would enable them, after a time, to take charge of the parochial schools in the towns and country congregations throughout the diocese. But, in the meanwhile, the civil war broke out; his correspondence with the Provincial, who resided at Mobile, was interrupted, and before any definite arrangement could be made he had been transferred to Baltimore.

Bishop Spalding, during his stay in Belgium, visited the various dioceses, in order to have an opportunity of seeing the seminaries, and addressing the students in behalf of the American missions. He was everywhere warmly received by both bishops and priests.

"How kind and hospitable is Belgium!" he wrote; "how full of faith and sincerity these excellent Catholics are!"

"Belgium has preserved," wrote Montalembert just at this time, "with greater fidelity than any other people, the manners and the institutions of the old Catholic world; the Middle Ages had never there been disguised by the spirit of courtliness. Hence she has been the first called to apply the conditions and to reap the fruits of the Catholic action in the modern world. Her nationality, nobly reconquered, reposes upon a constitution which her Catholic children have had the glory of giving to her, and of defending with fidelity down to the present day. She has consecrated all the vows and all the conquests of Catholicism in modern times; the absolute independence of the church; the free choice of the bishops by the Vicar of Christ; complete liberty in all matters relating to education and religious associations. Her territory has gradually become covered with monasteries, colleges, and pious foundations. She alone in Europe has witnessed the revival of one of those universities, such as they existed in the ages of faith, devoted exclusively to the defence of truth."

It was during this visit to Belgium that Bishop Spalding conceived the idea of establishing an American College at Louvain. He develops his plan in the following letter to Archbishop Kenrick, dated Mechlin, January 7, 1852:

"I have visited several of the Belgian dioceses, and I have seen much in this truly Catholic country to console and edify me. I have every prospect of success in the principal object of my journey; and, should my anticipations be realized, I hope, with the divine blessing, to be able to place my diocese on a new footing. I dined to-day with Cardinal Sterckx, a most holy and learned prelate. Conversing with his eminence on the utility of establishing here a Missionary College, he entered warmly into the project, and promised to second it with all his influence, which is very great, apart from his high position. He suggested the following plan, of the success of which he entertains no doubt. I lay it before you for your opinion and advice:

"The college is to be for the education of young men for the American missions, and is to be established in connection with the University of Louvain, which is in the archdiocese of Mechlin. The students in the beginning will occupy a rented house, and will have the privilege of attending the course of studies at the university free of charge. The discipline of the college will be under the direction of an American missionary, who will teach English, and exert himself to procure the necessary funds for keeping up the establishment, which, the Cardinal thinks, can be easily realized in Belgium; and this is the opinion of all those clergymen with whom I have conversed on the subject.

Students will not be wanting, for in this diocese particularly the number of candidates for the ministry far exceeds the demand for clergymen.

"Such are the outlines of the plan, which, if carried out, will be of great utility to our missions. The studies at Louvain are of a high order; and, perhaps, some of our bishops may send students of talent to perfect their education in this renowned university. The ecclesiastical spirit here is admirable, and the simple piety of the people contrasts strongly with the comparative coldness of Catholics in Protestant countries.

"A hundred young men educated at Louvain for the American missions! Is not the thought enlivening? And yet, it is very far from impossible; and, if the Cardinal's anticipations be well grounded, it may be done with little or no expense to the American prelates."

Archbishop Kenrick did not take a favorable view of this project, and the carrying out of Bishop Spalding's plan was in consequence delayed.

The scheme was not, however, allowed to drop out of thought, and five years after the date of this letter we find Bishop Spalding, with the co-operation of Bishop Lefevre, of Detroit, taking active steps towards establishing a college at Louvain; though the Archbishop of Baltimore was still unfavorable to the project.

"I cannot see," wrote Bishop Spalding to Archbishop Kenrick, in February, 1857, "why Belgium should not have a missionary college, like Ireland, France, and Italy, or why we should not profit by the abundant missionary zeal of her clergy. Bishop O'Connor wrote to me from Philadelphia, on the 6th of December: 'The Archbishop of Baltimore had first declined having anything to do with the project (of the Belgian College); but he has given me a letter to the Cardinal of Mechlin, expressing strongly the interest he feels in it.' I naturally inferred from this that we should have the great benefit of your approval and influence in carrying out a plan which Providence seems to favor at this time, and which, I am confident, promises much good for the future. Belgians have been among the very best missionaries we have had in Kentucky, as you know. I am sure the American College at Louvain will not in the least interfere with that contemplated in Rome; and, if I mistake not, the Rev. Mr. Kindekens informed me that the project would meet with great favor in Rome, he having spoken of it to persons high in station there."

On the 4th of February, 1857, Bishop Spalding and Bishop Lefevre addressed the following circular to the Archbishops and Bishops of the United States:

"MOST REVEREND AND DEAR SIR:

"We take the liberty to forward to you herewith a prospectus of the American College to be established in Belgium in connection with the University at Louvain. As Providence seems at present to favor the founding of this college, in which many eminent and pious persons in Belgium take so lively an interest, we have ventured to move in the matter, after having consulted with some of our brethren—feeling that unless some one took the initiative, no commencement would probably be made. The principles embodied in the prospectus are, in our opinion, those which are best calculated to give the college a solid beginning, and to put it in proper working order, though time and experience may induce several more or less important modifications in the plan now proposed.

"We take the liberty to request that if you should approve the general objects and regulations of the college, and desire to become one of its patrons, you should have the kindness to signify the same to the Bishop of Detroit, at as early a day as possible, as the Rector proposes to leave for Europe early in March, and it will be highly important to his success that he should have the sanction of as many American prelates as possible. Should you feel inclined to contribute towards the foundation of the college, you will please to specify the amount, that the Rector may be able to calculate his resources. The eighth article of the prospectus will indicate the benefits arising to contributors. We also beg to mention, as an evidence of our own confidence in the advantages likely to result from the proposed college, that we have each agreed to contribute one thousand dollars towards its establishment. Should you desire to adopt any students according to the ninth article, you will please instruct the Rector accordingly.

"With great respect, we remain your faithful brothers in Christ,

✠ MARTIN J. SPALDING,
Bishop of Louisville.
✠ PETER PAUL LEFEVRE,
Bishop Zel. Coadj. Adm., Detroit.

DETROIT, February 4, 1857.

This circular did not induce even one Archbishop or Bishop to give the sanction of his name to the new undertaking. This, however, did not discourage the two Bishops who had signed it. The Very Rev. Peter Kindekens had just returned from Belgium with the news that Count Félix de Merode had promised to give sixty thousand francs towards founding the new college. The Cardinal of Mechlin and one or two other Belgian prelates had renewed their assurance of sympathy and aid, as soon as they should learn that at least some of the Bishops of the United States had put their hand to the work in earnest. Mgr. De Ram the Rector of the University of Louvain, had generously offered to permit the students of the American College to follow the university courses of philosophy and theology free of charge.

Under these circumstances, Bishop Spalding resolved to take immediate steps towards establishing the college at Louvain. Bishop Lefevre and himself advanced a thousand dollars each, and empowered Father Kindekens to proceed to Belgium and open a house for the reception of students, even though he should find it necessary to begin the work in a rented building.

In the prospectus which accompanied the circular to the American hierarchy, Bishop Spalding argued in favor of the project, and sought to meet the objections of those who disapproved of it.

"The advantages of such a college," he wrote, "are manifest. Belgium is eminently a Catholic country. The true ecclesiastical spirit is found, in a high degree of perfection, in the seminaries, which there abound. The climate is healthy and similar to our own, while the people are robust in body and mind, industrious and practical in character. These qualities render them most efficient missionaries, and suit them particularly to the habits and wants of our people, as experience has proved. Another important advantage of the proposed college is the facility which it will afford for obtaining suitable German missionaries, thereby supplying a great want. The celebrity of the Louvain University, lying convenient to the provinces of lower Germany, will draw many German candidates for the holy ministry to the American College to be established in connection with that famous institution, where proper care will be taken to train them for our missions. The founding of this college will not, it is believed, interfere with the establishment of a college or of colleges for the higher ecclesiastical studies in the United States, or with the proposed American College at

Rome. Many of the young men educated at Louvain may hereafter be very usefully employed as professors in our seminaries, and thus they will rather aid than impede a taste for such studies in our own country, where it is highly important that the standard of ecclesiastical education should be elevated as speedily as possible. Should the Roman College be established in accordance with the recommendation of the Holy Father, and the consequent wish of the American prelates, there would be no clashing between it and the college at Louvain, for the obvious reason that the former would be chiefly for young men sent from America; whereas the latter, at least in the beginning, would be filled principally with young men from Belgium, Holland, France, and Germany."

When Father Kindekens reached Belgium, he learned that Count de Merode was dead, and that all hope of getting the promised sixty thousand francs had died with him. He was consequently left with nothing but the two thousand dollars given by Bishop Spalding and Bishop Lefevre. Having taken counsel of the friends of the enterprise in Belgium, he bought the Collége d'Aulne, founded in 1629; and there, in the summer of 1857, he opened the American College of the Immaculate Conception. Before the end of the year he had eight students in the new institution, and in April, 1858, he sent two priests to Louisville and two to Detroit. In 1860, Father De Neve succeeded Father Kindekens as rector of the college, and to his zeal and energy much of the good which has been done must be ascribed. In the course of time other American bishops became patrons of the college; especially those who had no seminary of their own. In 1863, the number of students had risen to forty. The college has now, after an existence of sixteen years, sent one hundred and fifty-four missionaries to the United States, who have been educated at comparatively little expense to the American bishops; so that Bishop Spalding's anticipations have been already realized, and more even than he hoped for has been done. To form a correct estimate of the good which the American College of Louvain has accomplished, we must consider that a large number of its priests have been sent to those dioceses where the need was greatest and where it was almost impossible to get missionaries.

As Archbishop of Baltimore, Dr. Spalding continued to do everything in his power to promote the interests of the American College of Louvain. In a letter to Father De Neve, written in 1868, he says:

"I was delighted to learn from your very welcome favor of the 6th inst. how well you were received in Rome, and with what courage you are animated to continue the noble work to which you have devoted your life. Cardinal Barnabo had been fully posted with reference to the nature and object of our missionary college, and I am not at all surprised that he received you so well. You will find the college honorably mentioned in our Plenary Council."

From Belgium, Bishop Spalding went to Holland, where he met with a cordial welcome from Archbishop Zwysen, who generously offered to allow any of his priests, who were willing to devote themselves to the missions, to accompany him to America; and he also proposed to send him a colony of Sisters, capable of instructing the deaf and dumb. In Holland, which had so long persecuted the soldiers of the cross in two hemispheres, and where, but a few years ago, the existence of Catholics was scarcely suspected by the world, Bishop Spalding, to his surprise, found a church whose members constituted more than a third of the entire population of the kingdom, and who, by the gravity of their manners and the fervor of their faith, had already secured for it an honorable position.

Six young Hollanders, either priests or ready for ordination, were received by Bishop Spalding for the diocese of Louisville, and, on his return, accompanied him to Kentucky. He now turned his steps towards Rome, stopping on his way, in Lyons, where he made the acquaintance of the members of the Council of the Propagation of the Faith. In an address, which he was invited to deliver before them, he stated the wants of his diocese so eloquently that a handsome sum was at once placed at his disposal, for the benefit of the church in Kentucky, whose first bishop had done probably more than any other man to increase and extend the workings and usefulness of this noble association.

Whilst here, he visited the famous shrine of Notre Dame de Fourvières, which overlooks the city of Lyons.

His note-book, which never reaches the dignity of a journal, and which was not intended for any eye but his own, bears testimony, on almost every page, to his spirit of faith and prayer, as well as to his special devotion to the Blessed Virgin. It also testifies to his deep interest in the church, its progress and organization, in all the places which he visits. His affections are not confined to his own little diocese, or even to his own country, but they are as catholic as the church itself. Wherever he meets with Catholics, he feels that he is in the house, not merely of friends, but of brothers, to whom he is bound by the higher kinship of soul, which rises superior to differences of custom and nationality. Everywhere he finds that Catholic priests are kind-hearted, hospitable, and sympathetic; which, I imagine, is the experience of all who have been thrown intimately with them. If they have been hated by those who knew them not, they have also been loved more than any other class of men on earth by the people, the poor and the suffering, in whose hearts the tenderness and devotion of the Catholic priesthood have built up the universal republic of souls which stands for ever, amid the ruins of kingdoms and empires, and the wrecks of time.

In Holland, he is delighted to learn that Pius IX. has determined to re-establish the hierarchy, and that the noble-hearted Zwysen is to be raised to the rank of an archbishop. He visits the seminaries, colleges, and schools; the hospitals, asylums, and other benevolent institutions; assists at the services on Sunday in parish churches, and his soul expands in this atmosphere of faith and religion. Like a loving son, he is joyous and glad at beholding the power of his mother over the hearts of her children. And when he sees her ministering to every form of human suffering, his love for her and his love for them that suffer unite to make him doubly happy. He enquires into everything, the number of priests and seminarians, of convents and colleges, of members of religious communities, of parishes and schools; he seeks to become acquainted with the manner in which the various ecclesiastical institutions are conducted and maintained; with the practical means adopted for the relief of the poor and the reformation of the wicked; with the relations of the church to the state. In Belgium, he takes the deepest interest in the contest which was then going on between the Catholic and infidel parties. He applauds the bishops and priests for the firm and bold stand which they had taken in the face of an infidel ministry, which was endeavoring to poison the fountains of religious truth, by introducing a false and pernicious system of education. He glories in the grand old University of Louvain, in which religion and science had made alliance, in order to do battle against the degrading and fatalistic materialism with which the Universities of Liège and Ghent were seeking to infect the minds of the educated classes. He makes the acquaintance of the professors—admirable men, whose learning and wisdom were surpassed only by the beauty of their lives and the humility of their faith; and he beholds in them the living refutation of the ignorant slander that there is antagonism between the spirit of the church and the highest scientific culture. He contrasts the happy, contented faces of those Catholic populations with the eager, anxious look of our own people, who seem as though they were pursued by some demon which will not allow them to look beyond the grave or to hope for rest before. The sight of their robust and healthy women suggests to him the thought that the vitality of European nations is, in great measure, due to them, whilst we in America are doing all in our power to make woman a mere nerve-organism, and, consequently, to unfit her to become a mother.

At Avignon, he visited the palace of the popes, rendered so famous by the great schism of the West. He found that it had been converted into a barracks. The French Revolution has written its history all over the Continent of Europe in ineffaceable lines of eternal ignominy; and that same spirit which led to the destruction or profanation of the grandest monuments of religion and art, still survives in the infidel revolutionary party which sought to burn Paris, and which would gloat with demoniac joy over the smouldering ruins of St. Peter's.

In Marseilles, he visited the benevolent institutions of Canon Tissiaux, the founder of the Congregation of the Priests of St. Peter, whose special mission is to take care of orphans and to minister to the spiritual wants of prisoners. The good Canon had also established reformatories for both boys and girls, in which they were taught the various trades. The introduction of the trades into the education of these children struck the Bishop as an excellent idea, which might be applied with the best results in the United States, and which, as we shall hereafter see, he himself was destined to put to the practical test. In Rome, he found the memory of the atrocious crimes committed in the name of liberty, during the short-lived Republic of the Triumvirs, still fresh in the minds of all, especially the murders of priests and monks by Zambianchi, with the connivance of Mazzini; and the butchery of two peasants, on the Ponte St. Angelo, whom the mob of brutal savages had mistaken for Jesuits in disguise. Rome, at that time as now, was filled with the thieves and cutthroats of Europe, who seem to be drawn to the robber-government of Italian infidels like vultures to the carcass.

Bishop Spalding now for the first time saw Pius IX., who twice received him in private audience, treating him with the paternal and gentle affection which never fails to win the hearts of those who are brought within the magic circle in which he moves.

Bishop Spalding presented various papers to the Holy Father for signature, all of which he signed only after having read them with such attention as to detect in one a verbal error, which he corrected. The Pope spoke with great veneration of Bishop Flaget, and referred in a special manner to the services which he had rendered to the Society for the Propagation of the Faith. In a second audience, he presented a report of his administration of the diocese of Louisville.

In the Propaganda, Bishop Spalding was received with open arms, as a son who, having been sent forth to battle, had not dishonored his *alma mater*. He said Mass and preached for the students; dined with them; and, in the company of the Americans, visited the sacred places where, as a young man in the full fervor of youthful devotion and enthusiasm, he had so often prayed.

He remained in Rome but two weeks. Passing through

the principal cities and exquisite scenery of central and northern Italy, he crossed Mont Cenis, making part of the journey in sleighs, and, after stopping a few days in Lyons and Clermont to make arrangements for the voyage home with some ecclesiastics who were to accompany him, he arrived in Paris on the 2d of April, 1853. On the 25th of the same month, the ten ecclesiastics, whom he had gathered in France, Belgium, and Holland for the diocese of Louisville, sailed from Havre, whilst Bishop Spalding went to Ireland, with the hope of inducing others to follow their example.

CHAPTER XIV.

RELIGION AND NATIONALISM—THE KNOW-NOTHING CONSPIRACY—"BLOODY MONDAY."

THE enemies of the church, in this country, had sought to produce the impression that Catholicism was a foreign religion, and that to be Catholic was to be un-American. Hence the effort was made throughout the land to excite war against the Catholics, as the enemies of American institutions. The danger was, lest Catholics should yield to this pressure, and gradually isolate themselves and lose all sympathy both with the institutions and the people of this country, considering the American state the enemy of their religion. The result would have been deplorable, as regards the interests both of the church and the nation.

It was not the American people who were seeking to make war on the church, but merely a party of religious fanatics and unprincipled demagogues, who as little represented the American people as did the mobs whom they incited to bloodshed and incendiarism. Their whole conduct was un-American, opposed to all the principles and traditions of our free institutions. To have patiently yielded to these dark conspirators, and to have allowed ourselves to be thrust into the position of a spurious and foreign element, would have been worse than cowardice—it would have been madness. This country was not a Protestant country more than a Catholic country, and the Catholic citizen was no more a foreigner than the Protestant citizen. The whole future of the church here, humanly speaking, depended on the recognition of this fact; and those men who, in spite of calumny and violence, remained firm in their attachment to the great principles of American liberty, protesting that they would never admit that the church was an alien body here, or that they, for being Catholics, were the less true and loyal American citizens, rendered a service, both to the country and to religion, for which we cannot be too grateful. Among the foremost of these was Dr. Spalding, whether we consider the influence of his example or that of his writings. "Born and reared up in this free country," he says, in the introductory address to the *Miscellanea*, written in 1855, "we have doated from infancy on the glorious principles embodied in our noble Declaration of Independence, and in those cognate ones set forth in our matchless Constitution. They have been the dream of our youth and the idol of our maturer years. And we have had abundant opportunities to know that those whom choice, and not the accident of birth, has made citizens of our happy country, entertain, without an exception known to us, a fond predilection for American principles scarcely surpassed in intensity by our own." "Who," he asks, in answer to the charge that Catholics cannot, consistently with their principles, be good citizens of a republican government—"who originated all the free principles that lie at the basis of our own noble Constitution? Who gave us trial by jury, *habeas corpus*, stationary courts, and the principle for which we fought and conquered in our Revolutionary struggle with Protestant England—that taxes are not to be levied without the free consent of those who pay them? Are we indebted to Protestantism for even one of these cardinal elements of free government? No; not for one. They all date back to the good old Catholic times in the Middle Ages—some three hundred years before the dawn of the Reformation."

And again: "We are indebted to Catholics for all the

republics which ever existed in Christian times down to the year 1776—for those of Switzerland, Venice, Genoa, Andorra, San Marino, and a host of free commonwealths which sprang up in the 'dark' ages. Some of these republics lingered until a comparatively recent date; some still exist, proud monuments and unanswerable evidences of Catholic devotion to freedom."

To those who feared a conflict of races and danger to the country from the increasing influx of emigrants, he said: "The surest safeguard against danger of this kind, if it really existed, was to be found in the Catholic Church, the tendency of whose institutions is to break down all barriers of separate nationalities, and to bring about a brotherhood of citizens in which the love of the common country would absorb every lesser feeling.

"Catholicity is of no nation, of no language, of no people; she knows no geographical bounds; she breaks down all the walls of separation between race and race, and she looks alike upon every people and tribe and caste. Her views are as large as the territory which she inhabits, and this is as wide as the world. Jew and Gentile, Greek and Barbarian, Irish, German, French, English, and American are all alike to her. In this country, to which people of so many nations have flocked for shelter against the evils which they endured at home, we have a striking illustration of this truly catholic spirit of the church. Germans, Irish, French, Italians, Spaniards, Poles, Hungarians, Hollanders, Belgians, English, Scotch, and Welsh, differing in language, in national customs, in prejudice—in everything human—are here brought together in the same church, professing the same faith, and worshipping like brothers at the same altars. The evident tendency of this principle is to level all sectional feelings and local prejudices by enlarging the views of mankind, and thus to bring about harmony in society, based upon mutual forbearance and charity. And in fact, so far as the influence of the church has been brought to bear upon the anomalous condition of society in America, it has been exercised for securing the desirable result of causing all its heterogeneous elements to merge into the one varied yet homogeneous nationality. Protestantism isolates and divides; Catholicity brings together and unites. Such have been the results of the two systems in times past; such, from their very nature, must be their influence on society at all times and in all places." *

Dr. Spalding was not content with denying that the church is incompatible with republicanism, or hostile to true liberty, but he maintained that the spirit of Catholicity is in perfect harmony with the wants and institutions of our country, whereas between them and Protestantism there is an innate opposition. He looked upon this country as the hope of the future, both in religion and in civil government, firmly persuaded, however, that in the Catholic Church alone could be found those principles of union and strength which would secure permanency to its institutions; and, in his untiring efforts to build up and firmly establish the church here, he was sustained by the generous conviction that he was laboring, not only for the highest interests of religion, but also for the true welfare of his country. This great nation, he was persuaded, needed a great religion, and consequently could not long remain satisfied with the divided and fragmentary Christianity of Protestantism. No one, however, could be more opposed than he to the introduction of nationalism into religion. The church, as he said, is of no nation, and this is one of the marks of her divinity; and hence, he not only applauded the sublime spectacle of the union of all nationalities in the one faith here, but deprecated, as fraught with the most serious danger, any attempt to introduce

* *Miscellanea*—Introductory Address, p. 57.

among the Catholics of this country the question of nationality. To urge Catholics as citizens to identify themselves with the American nation, and to take a living interest in the affairs of the country, was one thing; but it would have been something quite different to hold that it was their duty to seek to build up here a national church differing in spirit, institutions, or traditions from the church universal. Dr. Spalding was an American and a Catholic; but, as his faith did not interfere with his devotion to his country, so neither did that devotion in any way modify his religious convictions. In fact, it was impossible for him to look upon the church from a merely national stand-point, or to seek to compress Catholic truth into the narrow mould of nationalism. No one knew better than he the evil influences of exaggerated nationalism when brought to bear upon the church.

To make religion national would have been, in his eyes, a return to the pagan theory, in which the church was absorbed in the state. Before Christ, religion existed only as a state institution, and to have any other than the national religion was not only heresy but treason. This narrowness was not hurtful to religion alone, but also greatly helped to produce that hatred amongst nations which is characteristic of all antiquity. The pagan state could have no conception of a Catholic and unnational religion—a religion which, being the exclusive privilege of no people, is equally true and salutary for all nations and for all ages. Even the Jewish religion was national. Jehovah was the God of Abraham, of Isaac, and of Jacob—of the Jew, and not of the Gentile. Hence, even among the Jews we do not find the idea of a catholic religion. Their view was that men should adore in Jerusalem, and they knew not that the day would come when the true worshippers of God would adore him in spirit and in truth, without distinction of place or people. Unfortunately, the tendency to nationalize religion did not die with the birth of Christ.

It was precisely this spirit which first led to the persecution of the Christians. The Christian church, in Rome, did not claim to be a national, but a catholic religion, and the Christians were held to be enemies of the state, because their religion was not that of the state. They could not be good citizens of the Empire, it was argued, because they did not profess the religion of the Empire, and refused to sacrifice to the divinity of Cæsar. Hence they were butchered, quartered, thrown to the wild beasts in the amphitheatre, under the approving eyes of the worshippers of the state gods.

This same cause lies at the root of most of the heresies and schisms which have disturbed the church. The heresies of Nestorius and Eutyches were national heresies, the genuine offspring of the Greek mind and spirit, as opposed to that of the universal church; and the separation of the Greek Church from the Church Catholic was effected almost solely by national and political influences. The dogmatic differences supposed to have existed between the two churches were merely shallow pretexts.

The Russian schism is attributable to the same cause. The great schism of the West in the fourteenth century was likewise produced by this exaggerated spirit of nationalism in religion. France desired to get possession of the Papacy, to make the pope a French pope, and the Papacy a French institution; and the result was a disturbance in the whole Catholic world, the evil effects of which have not even yet wholly disappeared. The politico-religious movement of the sixteenth century was, in principle and in fact, a reaction against the universal church in favor of the national state-church theory. Lutheranism was Germanism, and when Protestantism went outside of Germany and the

Teutonic race, it ceased to be Lutheranism. Anglicanism, as the name indicates, is based on the identification of the national and religious spirit. "The Church of England," says Macaulay, "is an institution as purely local as the Court of Common Pleas." It was created by the law, is upheld by the law, and may be abolished by the law. It owes its very existence to the morbid national sensitiveness of Englishmen.

The persecution of the church in Germany, to-day, is but a renewal of the attempt to nationalize religion, and it has been made possible by the outburst of national feeling consequent upon the success of German arms. The church being universal, Dr. Spalding held that she is beyond and above all nationalities, and he therefore, as a Catholic, viewed man from a higher stand-point than that granted to those who look upon him merely as a citizen of the state.

Multiplicity of languages and differences of race are not, as he considered them, primitive facts, but are consequent upon sin ; and therefore the church, which rehabilitates man as a child of God, should also enable him to approach to his normal condition as a citizen of the world, in which all national divisions and hatreds will be merged in the brotherhood of the race, made a living fact by the fuller realization of the fatherhood of God and the motherhood of the one universal church.

And probably not the least important mission of this country, where all the races of Europe are thrown together in friendly contact, is to help on this great work. However this may be, we cannot but see a most hopeful sign for the future in the dying out of the spirit of exaggerated nationalism, and the breaking down of the barriers which separate the peoples of the earth, which, among other good results, will have the effect to diminish the antagonism which has always existed between a false nationalism and the catholic spirit of the church, thus rendering her progress more certain, and less liable to be disturbed by heresy or schism.

In this country, attempts have been made from time to time, as I have already stated, to place the national spirit in opposition to the church, but their miserable failure has taught the judicious, at least, the futility of such efforts.

Bishop Spalding was witness of the rise and downfall of the most fanatical party which has sought to destroy the church in the United States, by rousing against it the spirit of a false and narrow nationalism. Two great political parties had for a number of years contended with alternate success for the control of national affairs, when the introduction of the question of slavery into the Whig party led to discord and divisions which finally caused its dissolution in 1854-55. Between these two parties, the foreign population of the country had held the balance of power, and hence the foreign vote had come to be looked on as forming a distinct and separate element in American politics.

This, together with other causes, had given birth to the Native American Party, which, however, had little or no influence in the direction of national affairs. As most of the foreign voters in the United States were Democrats, there existed a natural sympathy between the Whig party and the Native American faction. Henry Clay, the great leader of the Whigs, confessed the Native American sympathies of his party, in a letter which he wrote to John J. Crittenden in 1844, just after the famous Presidential campaign in which the Democrats had triumphed by the aid of the foreign vote.

"There is a great tendency among the Whigs," wrote Mr. Clay, "to unfurl the banner of the Native American party. Whilst I own I have great sympathy with that party, I do not perceive the wisdom, at present, either of the Whigs absorbing it or being absorbed by it. If either of these contingencies were to happen, our adversaries would charge that it was the same old party with a new name, or with a new article added to its creed. In the meantime, they would retain all the foreign vote, which they have consolidated, make constant further accessions, and perhaps regain their members who have joined the Native American party. I am disposed to think that it is best for each party, the Whigs and the Natives, to retain their respective organizations distinct from each other, and to cultivate friendly relations together." *

When, at length, in consequence of the death of Clay, the disastrous defeat of General Scott in the Presidential campaign of 1852, and its own internal dissensions, the Whig party became thoroughly disorganized, it is not astonishing that its members should have very generally sought refuge in the Native American party.

It was necessary, however, to find something more than mere opposition to the foreigner. The foreign population was, to a great extent, Catholic; and the Bedini riots and the No-popery fanaticism which the infidel refugees of 1848 had succeeded in exciting, led the organizers of the new party to believe that opposition to the church would increase their chances of success.

The most un-American and disgraceful party which has blackened our political record was accordingly organized, and Kentucky, which had been devoted to Clay and the Whig party, became a stronghold of the Know-Nothing conspiracy.

The Louisville *Journal*, the great organ of Clay and the Whigs, sold itself to the new faction, and led in the anti-Catholic crusade. The Catholics of Kentucky had the right to expect at least courtesy and fairness in the attacks made

* *Life of Crittenden*, vol. i. p. 224.

upon themselves and their faith through the columns of the *Journal*, since many of them had for years been the personal and political friends of George D. Prentice, the editor of the Know-Nothing organ. Unfortunately, we do not need this example to show how utterly base and vulgar political journalism is capable of becoming, when the exigencies of party demand the sacrifice of principle and decency.

To stir up the Protestants of Kentucky to fanatical hatred, not only of the church, but of Catholics, whether native or foreign, the vilest calumnies, the most absurd imputations, the most palpable lies, were repeated day after day in the columns of this newspaper, in a style which, in power of sarcasm and invective, in wealth of the vulgar comparisons and analogies which please the multitude, has rarely been surpassed.

By a remarkable confusion of the sexes and disregard of the propriety of things, the church was transformed into "the man of sin" and "the woman of Babylon," "the son of perdition" and "the mother of harlots," "antichrist" and "the mystery of iniquity." She was held responsible for each particular crime that unfaithful and disobedient Catholics had ever committed.

She was made to answer for the Spanish Inquisition, against the cruelties of which she had repeatedly protested; for the Saint Bartholomew Massacre, with which she had had nothing to do; for the Gunpowder Plot, the work of three or four misguided men. She was represented as the enemy of liberty and education, as gloating over the miseries and misfortunes of humanity—in a word, as fiendish in all her aims and purposes. The American bishops, it was asserted, were the secret political emissaries of the Pope, and were plotting the overthrow of the government and the destruction of American liberty.

In the excited state of the public mind this nonsense

passed current, and led to those scenes of violence and blood which, on the 5th of August, 1855, blackened the fair name of Louisville by deeds which, in cruelty and heartlessness, have not been surpassed in the annals of the North American Indians. Into the details of that day's history I have no desire to enter, except as they directly relate to the life of Bishop Spalding.

The insane rumor had been circulated—and it was believed by the rabble, which had been wrought upon to frenzy by designing men—that Bishop Spalding had organized the Catholics of the city, and that they were prepared to defend themselves on the day of the election. Arms, it was said, had been stored away in various churches, and especially in the basement and tower of the cathedral.

About noon on "Bloody Monday," as the day is still called in Kentucky, the mob was hurrying through Shelby Street to St. Martin's church, with the intention of burning it, when John Barbee, the mayor of the city, and one of the leaders of the Know-Nothing party, arrived and sought to dissuade them. His efforts were for a time ineffectual, but the leaders finally consented to remain quiet until the church could be searched. The mayor brought back word that no arms had been found, and persuaded the mob, after having assured them that they had already elected their candidates, to withdraw under the command of Captain Rousseau. During the afternoon and evening of the same day, threats and movements were made which showed that the mad rabble had designs against the cathedral. The mayor was informed of this, and, together with two councilmen, he waited on Bishop Spalding, and asked to be allowed to search the building in order to satisfy the mob. Permission was granted, and the mayor and councilmen, after fulfilling their mission, issued the following notice, which probably saved the cathedral from destruction :

"We, the undersigned, have in person carefully examined the cathedral, and do assure the community that there are neither men nor arms concealed there; and, further, that the keys of said cathedral on Fifth Street are in the hands of the city authorities.

JOHN BARBEE, Mayor.

T. W. REILLY, } Councilmen."
J. A. GILLIS,

The Catholic churches and institutions escaped destruction on Bloody Monday, but inoffensive and peaceable Catholics had been murdered in cold blood in the streets; their houses had been set on fire, and when the helpless inmates had sought to fly from the flames, they were shot down by fiends who stood around to see that none should escape. "We have just passed through a reign of terror," wrote Bishop Spalding to Archbishop Kenrick, " surpassed only by the Philadelphia riots. Nearly an hundred poor Irish and Germans have been butchered or burned, and some twenty houses have been consumed in the flames. The city authorities—all Know-Nothings—looked calmly on, and they are now endeavoring to lay the blame on the Catholics."

The *Journal*, indeed, sought to shift the responsibility of these atrocious crimes to the shoulders of the Catholics, who, it was hinted, had been urged on by the Bishop and priests.

This base calumny was published while the city was still under a reign of terror, and when it was feared that the mob would yet burn all the Catholic churches. Indeed, the threats to burn the cathedral were repeated the morning after its publication; and on the same day over a hundred German families, in dread of their lives, left the city, whilst others were preparing to leave.

The following "card," in answer to the charge made by the *Journal*, was written by Bishop Spalding when there was still the greatest fear that the bloody scenes of Monday should be renewed:

"TO THE PUBLIC.

"FELLOW-CITIZENS: In the Louisville *Journal* of this morning I find the following passage: 'We are not now prepared to say that they' (assaults committed by foreigners) '. . . . were instigated by the direct instructions of men with fiendish hearts, who control, in a great measure, the passions, and are able to dictate the actions, of the Germans and Irish who made these attacks.' If, as some have understood it, this passage was meant to refer to the Bishop and the priests of this city, I beg respectfully, but most distinctly and earnestly, to deny the truth of the injurious insinuation conveyed by its language. I have myself been, until the last day or two, confined to my room for two weeks by illness; and I have the most positive information that none of the Catholic clergy of this city have had any agency, direct or indirect, in bringing about the recent lamentable outrages, which no one deplores more than we do. Our voice has been uniformly for peace. We have not even in any way interfered with the late election, being overwhelmed with laborious duties in an altogether different sphere. I venture, also, to appeal to the sense of justice and fairness manifested for so many years by the editor of the *Journal*, and to ask him to correct an impression so injurious to us, if such was the meaning of the passage, which I am loath to believe. To all whom the influence of my voice can in any way reach, I beg to say that I entreat them, in the name of Jesus Christ, the God of peace, to abstain from all violence; to remain quietly at home or attending to their business; to keep away from all excited assemblies, and, if they think they have been injured, to return good for evil, and to pray for those who have wronged them. I appeal to them and the world, whether this has not always been the tenor of my instructions to them, both public and private, and also that of all the Catholic clergy. I have too high an opinion of my fellow-citizens of every class to believe for a moment that the threats which have been made by some will be carried out. I entreat all to pause and reflect, to commit no violence, to believe no idle rumors, and to cultivate that peace and love which are the characteristics of the religion of Christ. We are to remain on earth but a few years: let us not add to the necessary ills of life those more awful ones of civil feuds and bloody strife.

☩ M. J. SPALDING.

" LOUISVILLE, August 7, 1855."*

---

* From the Hon. B. J. Webb I have learned that four of the leaders of the Know-Nothing party in Louisville afterwards expressed in his presence sincere regret that they had ever had any connection with the movement. As none of them are now living, I may be allowed to state that the persons referred to were George D. Prentice, General Humphrey Marshall, Mayor Barbee, and Judge Caleb W. Logan. The last-named of these gentlemen wrote the articles in the *Journal* in reply to the " Letters of a Kentucky Catholic," in which Mr. Webb has so ably defended the church against the charges made by the Know-Nothing press.

CHAPTER XV.

THE "MISCELLANEA"—CONTROVERSY WITH PROFESSOR MORSE.

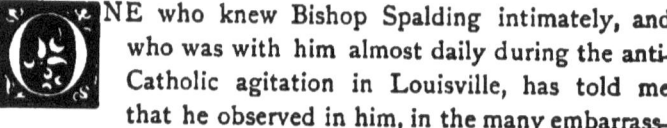NE who knew Bishop Spalding intimately, and who was with him almost daily during the anti-Catholic agitation in Louisville, has told me that he observed in him, in the many embarrassing and trying circumstances in which he was then placed, a more than usual peace of mind. He spent the greater part of his moments of leisure in the sanctuary in prayer, and seemed, through communion with God, to grow unconscious of the trouble which men were seeking to bring upon the church, and which he could not but feel most keenly.

There was not even the shadow of a pretext for accusing him of meddling with political affairs. "We ourselves," he wrote at this time, "'though native here and to the manner born,' have never even voted on a political question, and we believe that most of our brother prelates and clergymen have adopted the same prudent precaution; not, surely, through any want of interest in the country, but chiefly with a view to remove from the enemies of our church the slightest pretext for slandering our religious character. The only influence we have sought to bring to bear on the members of our communion has been invariably in the interests of peace, of order, and of charity for all men, even for our most bitter enemies. Whenever we have had occasion to address our people on the eve of elections, we have counselled them to avoid all violence, to beware of being carried away by passion, to be temperate, to respect the feelings and principles of their opponents, and, in the exercise of their franchise as citizens, to vote conscientiously for the men and measures they might think most likely to advance the real and permanent interests of the Republic." *

The views of Archbishop Hughes on this important subject do not differ from those advanced by Bishop Spalding in the words just quoted. "I hold," he wrote, "and have ever held, that the position of a clergyman forbids him from taking any active part in such questions (political), and that he could not be a partisan without at once endangering and degrading his influence as a priest." And again: "My own principles are, that the American people are able in their own way to manage their affairs of state, without any guidance or instruction toward any class or religious denomination, by either priests or parsons."†

It was during the anti-Catholic agitation of 1855 that Bishop Spalding published his *Miscellanea*.

It would have been difficult to give to Americans a book better suited to the wants of the then existing state of the public mind. The Catholic question was supreme both in church and state. It was discussed everywhere; in bar-rooms, conventicles, lodges, meeting-houses; in the parlors of the rich and around the humble hearthstones of the poor. Men who had never given religion a thought in their lives; who knew nothing of God or Christ, and who did not care to know; who had never even once entered a church, took sides, and were loud in denouncing or defending the Catholic Church. But the question with them was not one of

* *Miscellanea*—Introductory Address, p. 54.
† *Life by Hassard,* pp. 377, 378.

religion, for had it been it would not have interested them at all. Little did they care, for the most part, which was the true church, or whether there was any true church. It was not a question of salvation, but of election. Yet both they who attacked and they who defended were in earnest, not indeed that they might find the truth, but that they might win the victory.

For the first time since the Reformation, vast numbers of Protestants were examining into the history of the church, with a view of defending her against the traditional objections of Protestantism itself. The prevailing prejudices of the non-Catholic mind had given to the controversy its shape and bearing. The church was arraigned before the tribunal of public opinion, and both the indictment and the defence regarded her not in her relations to truth and the soul, but in her influence upon society and the American Republic. That her whole history proved her to be in opposition with the principles of liberty, enlightenment, and progress; that the allegiance which her children owed to the spiritual authority was incompatible with their duties to their country; that she had, whenever it had been in her power to do so, persecuted and employed the most cruel means to perpetuate her rule; that many of her doctrines and practices were immoral, and consequently dangerous to society—such were the chief heads of accusation which her opponents sought to make good against her; whilst, on the other hand, it became the political duty of numberless Protestants to show that these charges were without foundation in fact, and were based on a misconception of her history and a false interpretation of her doctrines and practices. Now, the essays and reviews comprised in the *Miscellanea* furnished an array of facts and arguments bearing upon all these points which could not be found in any other one book in the English language; and they had the additional merit of a free, off-hand, straightforward style, peculiarly suited to the American taste. They covered the whole ground of what was then the Catholic controversy in the United States, and, by facts resting upon unexceptional testimony, by arguments which appeal at once to the good sense and fair-mindedness of the reader, and by the whole spirit and temper in which they are written, furnish a defence of the church, as against the attacks of her accusers, the strength of which could not be easily broken. It was also at this time, and by the prevailing temper of public feeling, that Bishop Spalding was forced into a controversy with Professor Morse concerning the authenticity of the motto attributed to Lafayette: "If ever the liberties of the United States be destroyed, it will be the work of Romish priests."

Little did it matter whether Lafayette had or had not said this. Things as bad had been said of Catholic priests, time and again, by better men than he, who, to take the most favorable view of his character, was remarkable rather for noble impulse than for sound judgment or far-penetrating thought. If a Catholic, as Bishop Spalding put the case, he could not have given expression to the sentiment contained in the motto without being a hypocrite; if an infidel, his opinion has no more weight than that of Voltaire or Tom Paine. He was certainly not a Protestant.*

---

* Shortly after Archbishop Spalding's death, Professor Morse wrote a letter to the New York *Herald*, in which he claimed to have won the victory in this controversy. "I retracted nothing," he says, "for I had nothing to retract." And again: "I also asserted and proved that Lafayette had used nearly the very words of the motto to two Americans, whose names are given, and in his conversations with me had expressed the same sentiments." Professor Morse has since died, and as, by his last words on this subject, he has sought to produce the impression that he had established the authenticity of the motto attributed to Lafayette, I deem it proper to refer briefly

In the spring and summer of 1855, this supposed motto of Lafayette stared one in the face, dressed out in all the impudence of type, from the headings of newspapers innumerable, and from the title-pages of countless no-popery pamphlets. At political gatherings and in torchlight processions, like a thing of evil, it was seen following the American flag, which, as if conscious of the impending danger from popish priests, refused to float on the breeze. In the "Introductory Address" prefixed to the *Miscellanea*, which, as I have said, appeared during the excitement of the Know-Nothing conspiracy, Bishop Spalding had taken occasion to state, upon the authority of a leading political paper in Cincinnati, which was distinctly referred to in a foot-note, that a letter written by Lafayette had been brought to light, in which he denied ever having used the words of the motto.

This was more than could be patiently borne with. No attention was paid to the writer in the Cincinnati *Enquirer*, who was alone responsible; but Bishop Spalding was assailed by three reverend preachers, who pronounced him guilty of a "most high-handed and daring attempt to falsify history"; of "villany, mendacity, and literary forgery."

The only reply which Bishop Spalding made to these charges was to publish the article to which he had referred in the "Address," with the remark that, having given his authority in the first instance, his readers were at liberty to place what value they might see fit upon it: the most that could be said was that it was of no weight. But to denounce him as these reverend gentlemen had done, was simply absurd, and he was resolved to take no further notice of charges so utterly groundless. If his accusers desired to

to the leading points in the controversy between himself and Bishop Spalding. This controversy was not sought by Bishop Spalding; he never sought controversy with any one; it was thrust upon him.

enter into a controversy concerning the authenticity of the letter in question, he referred them to the editors of the newspaper in which it had first been published.

As the Bishop's doughty assailants found themselves headed off in this direction, they at once set to work to move on him from some other point.

To Professor Morse, who had gained considerable notoriety by a very successful application of the discoveries of others in his method of telegraphing, was generally ascribed the honor of having discovered or invented this motto of Lafayette. He had, in 1836, edited a book with this motto on the title-page; and in the preface he had affirmed that Lafayette had made use of the words of the motto in conversation with himself, and that he had expressed the same sentiment in speaking with other Americans.

Professor Morse further stated that he had received a letter from Lafayette a few days after his last interview with him in Paris, in which he urged him, by his sacred duty as an American citizen, to make known to his countrymen the serious apprehensions of the French patriot of danger to the liberties of the Republic from the Catholic priesthood.

As Professor Morse had thus become sponsor for the motto, representations were made to him to the effect that Bishop Spalding, by denying its authenticity, had impugned his veracity. He therefore reaffirmed what he had written twenty years before. Bishop Spalding called for the proof of his assertions, and the controversy began.

Professor Morse adduced in evidence the testimony of an *anonymous* writer, whose name he was not at liberty to give. He then referred to his own interviews with Lafayette in 1831–32: "I cannot," he said, "at this distance of time, of course remember the identical words, but never did he" (Lafayette) "manifest a doubt of the essential antagonism of the maxims and principles of the Papacy and those of republicanism, nor any doubt, if the Papacy were triumphant, republicanism was at an end."

At the urgent request of Bishop Spalding, he proceeded to confirm his statement by the testimony of those other Americans who had heard Lafayette speak the words in question. He first tried to find a military officer in New York who, it was reported, had heard Lafayette use the words, but this gentleman either could not be found or would not testify.

He succeeded better, however, with the Rev. Dr. Vanpelt, of New York. This gentleman had a "vivid and distinct" remembrance of an interview with Lafayette shortly after his return from Boston during his last visit to this country in 1824. These were Lafayette's words:

"My dear friend, I must tell you something that occurred when I was in Boston. I received a polite invitation from the chief Catholic priest or bishop of the Roman Catholic Church in Boston, to attend his church on the Sabbath. I wrote him an apology, saying, as I never expect to be in Boston again, and as during the Revolution, when in Boston, I worshipped sitting by the side of his excellency, General Washington, and as I see that the church and the pews are the same, except as they are decorated with paint, I wish to occupy the same seat in that church on the Sabbath. . . ." And again: "It is my opinion that if ever the liberties of this country [the United States of America] are destroyed, it will be by the subtlety of the Roman Catholic Jesuit priests, for they are the most crafty, dangerous enemies to civil and religious liberty." Such was the testimony of the Rev. Dr. Vanpelt.

Professor Morse brought forward another witness—a certain Mr. Palmer, of Richmond, Virginia, and then proceeded to make good his position by extracts from the speeches of

Lafayette, in which he proclaimed his opposition to a union of church and state, and professed himself an ardent champion of civil and religious liberty.

This is a brief statement of the arguments advanced by Professor Morse to establish the authenticity of the motto. He seemed reluctant to give his proofs, and it was only by the most searching cross-questioning that they were drawn from him.

Bishop Spalding replied by taking up his heads of argument, one by one, and showing the testimony which he had given to be valueless, and his reasoning inconclusive.

The *anonymous* writer, whose name Mr. Morse was not at liberty to give, could not, of course, be admitted as a witness. Besides, since he was put forward as an apostate priest, his testimony was no more above suspicion than would have been that of Benedict Arnold against the patriots of the Revolution, or that of Judas against Christ and the apostles.

The testimony of Mr. Morse himself was unreliable, for various reasons.

By his own confession, he was unable to remember the identical words spoken by Lafayette; and the general statement of Lafayette's opinions, even if accurately made by Mr. Morse, did not affect the question under discussion. But Mr. Morse had spoken of a letter which he had received from Lafayette, in which he was urged to make known to the American people the serious alarm of the French patriot lest the country should be in danger from the machinations of Romish priests. This letter Bishop Spalding repeatedly called for, challenging Professor Morse either to publish it or to produce the original copy. He did neither, but vainly sought to screen himself by declaring that he had never pretended that the motto was in the letter, whereas he had before affirmed that in it Lafayette had urged him to make known to Americans his alarm lest the liberties of the Republic should be destroyed by Catholic priests.

Professor Morse averred afterwards that this letter had been seen by several persons, but he persistently refused to publish it or to produce it before witnesses in connection with this controversy.

There was still another circumstance relative to Mr. Morse's testimony which had an ugly look. Lafayette died in 1834. Professor Morse first published the motto in 1836, whereas Lafayette had, in 1832, earnestly enjoined upon him the duty of warning his countrymen of their imminent danger from "Romish priests." Why had he waited to perform this office for four years after the solemn injunction had been laid upon him, and until Lafayette had been in his grave two years and five months?

And this, too, was not to be forgotten: Mr. Morse had first given currency to this motto during the Maria Monk excitement, when the many "awful disclosures" that were being made would likely cause this revelation to be received without much questioning. But thus far Bishop Spalding had only been gently adjusting Professor Morse on the rack of the inquisition. He was now prepared to apply the crucial test. In the same year in which Professor Morse claimed to have received the message to the American people from Lafayette, that gentleman, in a speech in the French Assembly, had given expression to a sentiment wholly incompatible with that of the motto.

In reply to a motion to expel from France certain refugees, including the English or Irish monks who were living with the Trappists at Melleray, Lafayette had said:

"Mistake not rigor for strength, or despotism for power; then you will not have need of all these precautions, and the Trappists of Melleray will not be more dangerous to you than are the Jesuits of Georgetown to the United States." *

At the very time that he tells Mr. Morse of the danger to the United States from the machinations of Catholic priests, Lafayette publicly declares in the French Assembly that the United States has nothing to fear from even the Jesuits, whom, the Rev. Dr. Vanpelt assures us, he considered "the most crafty and dangerous enemies of civil and religious liberty."

Either Lafayette was the basest of hypocrites, or Professor Morse and the Rev. Dr. Vanpelt were lying under a mistake.

But the "vivid and distinct recollections" of the Rev. Dr. Vanpelt were deserving of more special attention. Lafayette had said to him, such were his vivid recollections, that when in Boston during the Revolution he had worshipped sitting by the side of General Washington, and this circumstance had led to the conversation in which the Frenchman had used the words of the motto or words of like meaning.

Bishop Spalding set to work and showed that Washington and Lafayette had never been in Boston together, and that consequently they could never have worshipped sitting side by side in any church in that city, and that, therefore, the Rev. Dr. Vanpelt had a vivid and distinct recollection of hearing Lafayette say he had done what it was simply impossible that he ever should have done.

Thus the Rev. Dr. Vanpelt was dismissed with a motto very different from that which he had sought to authenticate—*falsus in uno, falsus in omnibus*. One of Professor Morse's witnesses could not be found, the name of another he was not at liberty to give, a third was proven to have borne false testimony, and, finally, his own statement con-

---

* The speech was delivered April 9, 1832, and is found in the *Memoirs and Correspondence of Lafayette*, published in 12 vols., under the supervision of his favorite son, George Washington Lafayette.

cerning the letter which contained the important message from Lafayette he could not verify, leaving the very strong impression that the electric telegraph was not the only thing which he had invented.

In addition to this, Bishop Spalding had shown that Lafayette had publicly in the French Assembly given expression to sentiments in direct contradiction with the motto, and, consequently, that could it be proved that he was its author, the conclusion from the premises would be that his opinion on the subject was absolutely worthless, because self-contradictory. But Professor Morse, by the verdict of the public, had signally failed to establish either the authenticity of the motto, or the trustworthiness of his memory.

This good came of the controversy—it deprived no-popery fanatics of a favorite text, and added another proof, if proof were needed, that when the church is to be attacked, bigots and fanatics will hesitate at nothing, not even fraud and untruth.*

It may be said of the whole anti-Catholic crusade of that day, that the result was favorable to the church. A few narrow-minded bigots, whose ignorance was probably invincible, were really alarmed for the safety of the Bible and the country, and were terribly in earnest in seeking to stamp out from the American soil every trace of Catholicism; they were joined by the mob of European infidels and radicals, and by the rabble formed by the sloughing of our social sores, and this horrid mass of mental obliquity and moral turpitude called itself the American party. The American people rose up and trod it under foot.

---

* Bishop Spalding relates an anecdote of a preacher, who in the midst of the Know-Nothing excitement was hurrying a no-popery publication through the press. He had written a flaming preface, taking the motto as his text, and his manuscript was in the hands of the printer when the reply to Morse appeared. He at once went to his publisher, suppressed the preface, and wrote another, in which no allusion whatever to the motto was to be found.

They felt that Catholics had been wantonly insulted, grossly outraged, and that sympathy which the brave and the manly always have for the wronged took the place of what had been aversion, or, at least, indifference. We have been making rapid strides ever since, with renewed confidence in our fellow-countrymen, increased reverence for the institutions which God has given us, and the abiding conviction that no evil, not self-caused, will ever befall us in this free land.

"The Know-nothing excitement," wrote Bishop Spalding to Archbishop Kenrick, in January, 1855, "after doing us some temporary harm, will finally result in good. *Mary Immaculate, quæ sola cunctas interemit hæreses*, will see to it."

CHAPTER XVI.

THE PROVINCIAL COUNCILS OF CINCINNATI—THE COMMON-SCHOOL SYSTEM.

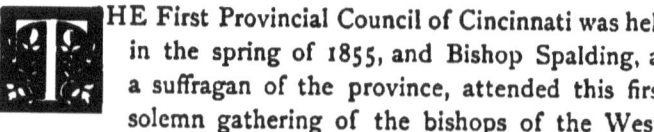THE First Provincial Council of Cincinnati was held in the spring of 1855, and Bishop Spalding, as a suffragan of the province, attended this first solemn gathering of the bishops of the West. He was made Promoter of the Council, and was deputed to write the pastoral letter of the fathers to the clergy and laity of the province. In the Second Provincial Council of Cincinnati, in 1858, and in the third, in 1861, Bishop Spalding held the same office as in the first, and the pastoral letters were also written by him.

These councils, over which the venerable Archbishop Purcell presided, are remarkable for the practical wisdom and thorough ecclesiastical spirit which characterize the decrees therein enacted. They show a perfect comprehension of the wants of the church in the West, as well as of the proper manner of meeting them.

The training of a pious and learned priesthood for the ministry was thought to be of paramount importance. To this end, it was deemed advisable to establish two provincial seminaries: the one to be devoted to preparatory, the other to theological studies. It was not the intention of the fathers, however, that these seminaries should interfere with diocesan institutions already existing. Mount St. Mary's, near Cincinnati, was made the Provincial Theological Seminary, and St. Thomas', in the diocese of Louisville, was raised to the rank of a Provincial Preparatory Seminary.

In the pastoral letter of the Third Council of Cincinnati the fathers say: "We are happy to be able to report that both these seminaries are now in a very satisfactory condition." In the First Council their attention, in connection with the subject of ecclesiastical education, was called to an American College, to be founded in Rome by the munificence of the Holy Father, with the co-operation of the clergy and faithful of the United States. The establishment of theological conferences was earnestly recommended. "Such reunions of the clergy, besides promoting that fraternal feeling which is so sweet a bond of Christian and clerical union, strongly tend to encourage the study of sacred things, to elicit zeal for the salvation of souls, and to establish uniformity of practice in minor rites and observances."

In consideration of the fact that the priests of this country belong to various nationalities, and have been trained in different schools of theology, the effort to bring about uniformity of practice, even "in minor rites and observances," is of the greatest importance.

The holding of spiritual retreats for the clergy, annually, or at least once in two years, was insisted on.

The fathers next turned their thoughts to the subject of the right education of children.

"Earnestly do we desire," wrote Bishop Spalding in the pastoral letter of the First Council, "to see a parochial school in connection with every Catholic church in this province; and we hope the day is not far distant when this wish nearest our hearts will be fully realized. With all the influences constantly at work to unsettle the faith of our children, and to pervert their tender minds from the religion of their fathers; and with all the lamentable results of these influences constantly before our eyes, we cannot too strongly exhort you to contribute generously of your means to enable your pastors to carry out this great work. The erection of Catholic schools is, in many respects, as important an object as the building of new churches." This question of religious education was, in the minds of the fathers of the Cincinnati Councils, the test of fidelity or infidelity to God; and their earnest convictions on this subject have been productive of the most important practical results, as the history and present condition of that province abundantly prove.

In their instructions to the faithful concerning the anti-Catholic movement, then at its height, they say: "To the grievous and utterly false charge of disloyalty to this government, your best answer will be to continue to do what you have all along sought earnestly and sincerely to do—to discharge faithfully all your duties as citizens of the Republic, rendering to Cæsar the things that belong to Cæsar, without, at the same time, forgetting to render to God the things that belong to God. The Catholic religion exists and flourishes under all forms of civil government; it is the visible kingdom of Christ on earth, which is not of this world. It is incompatible with no well-ordered form of human government, because it interferes with none. Its sphere of action is essentially different from and infinitely higher than that of any merely human organization. Its ends, its means of action, its doctrines, its sacraments, and its government all belong or look to the spiritual order. It teaches man the way to heaven, and seeks to wean his affections from this earth. It wages war with the passions, and inculcates self-denial, obedience to constituted authority, humility, and charity. All the Catholic Church asks of the world is a free passage through it to her proper home in the heavens." As to the power of the Sovereign Pontiff, they solemnly declare that it is spiritual in its objects and in its sphere of action, and therefore that it cannot possibly clash with any of the duties which Catholics as good citizens owe to the country in which they live.

The obligation of Catholics to support the religious press, and their apathy and indifference in complying with this sacred duty, were recalled to the minds of the faithful. "We entreat you," say the fathers of the Second Council of Cincinnati, "to awake from your lethargy in this respect, and to extend a willing and generous support to those papers and periodicals which are published, with the approval of your chief pastors, for the explanation and defence of our holy faith; especially to those which are published in your own province or diocese. As the Holy Father, Pius IX., says: 'Providence seems to have given, in our days, a great mission to the Catholic press. It is for it to preserve the principles of order and faith where they still exist, and to propagate them where impiety and cold indifference have caused them to be forgotten.'" The declaration of the fathers, as to the force which they intend these decrees shall have, is most explicit: "The Holy See having approved the decrees passed in our First Provincial Council of Cincinnati, they have the force of law for regulating discipline in this portion of the church of God, and they are as such strictly binding on the consciences of both clergy and laity. The first decree of this council formally accepted and promulgated all the decrees previously passed in the eight Councils of Baltimore, including those of the last or plenary council. These, then, likewise, by the fact of their approbation by the Sovereign Pontiff and of their solemn promulgation here, have the force of law for our province."*

In the *Pastoral Letter of the Third Council of Cincinnati*, held in 1861, special reference is made to the common-school system as it exists in this country.

"We think," say the fathers, "that few candid observers will fail to have remarked the progressive demoralization among the youth of our country, and to regret that the

* *Pastoral Letter of the Second Council of Cincinnati.*

system of common-school education has certainly not succeeded in obviating this downward tendency, to which we may fairly ascribe much in the present alarming condition of our affairs. Under the influence of this plausible but most unwise system, the rising generation has been educated either without any definite religious principles at all, or with false, at least, more or less exaggerated and fanatical principles. The system itself, if carried out according to its alleged intent of abstaining from any definite religious instruction, is well calculated to bring up a generation of religious indifferentists, if not of practical infidels; and if not thus carried out, its tendency is to develop false or very defective, if not dangerous, religious principles. The facts, we believe, sufficiently prove that the influence of our common schools has been developed either in one or both of these directions. We can scarcely explain in any other way the manifest moral deterioration of the country, which is probably the very worst feature in our present troubles. No candid man will deny that public virtue is now very far below the standard to which it was raised in the earlier and purer days of the Republic, when our fathers admired the moral heroism and were guided by the political wisdom of a Washington.

"We have not ceased, on all suitable occasions, to warn our countrymen against the dangerous tendency of this system, as it has been practically carried out, not merely because its operation is very unjust to ourselves, but because we consider it radically defective and wrong; but our appeal has been made calmly, and with due regard for the feelings, and even what we might consider the prejudices, of others. We feel it to be our most sacred and most solemn duty to rear up our children in the knowledge, fear, and love of God; and we regard this as the essential element, as the very foundation, the life and soul, of all sound education among Christians—that which, in fact, distinguishes it from education among pagans. As this religious training is not possible in the public schools as at present organized and conducted, our children are necessarily excluded from them as effectually as they would be by locks and bolts, unless, indeed, we were to become so dead to faith as to be willing to sacrifice the religious education of our children for a merely worldly convenience. . . . .

. . . . In a country so divided in sentiment as ours is on the subject of religion, the only system which would be fair and equitable to all would be that which would make education like religion, and like all important pursuits—*entirely free;* and if taxes are collected from all for its encouragement and support, let them be apportioned fairly among the scholars taught certain branches up to a certain standard, no matter under what religious or other auspices." In further illustration of Bishop Spalding's views on this, socially and religiously, the most important question of our day, I shall here refer to a controversy on this subject which he carried on, in the spring and summer of 1859, with George D. Prentice, the editor of the Louisville *Journal.*

The discussion grew out of Bishop Spalding's review of Joseph Kay's work on common-school education in Europe. Taking the facts as furnished by Mr. Kay, a Protestant, Bishop Spalding had shown, first, that in the matter of common-school education, France stood first among the nations of Europe, and England last, whilst Germany occupied a middle position between these extremes; second, that in the educational system almost universally adopted in Europe, religion occupied the chief place among the branches taught—the principle being generally received that education without religious instruction is, at best, imperfect and of doubtful advantage; third, that to secure religious liberty and safeguard the rights of parents, *separate schools*, supported out of the common-school fund, were allowed whenever the minority, whether Protestant or Catholic, desired to establish them; fourth, that where this plan had been most faithfully carried out, as in France, Austria, Prussia, and Bavaria, the common-school system had worked best, had given most general satisfaction, and had been productive of the greatest good. The logical inference from all this was, that the denominational system of education, adopted by nearly all the states of Europe, was preferable to the common-school system of the United States, which ignores religion and excludes it from the process of education. That a Catholic bishop should affirm this, and, above all, that he should prove it to be true, was of course unpardonable.

Bishop Spalding was therefore accused of being an enemy of American institutions, and an advocate of the despotic governments of Europe, whilst Catholics in general were branded with being disloyal, because they claimed the right to agitate in favor of reform in the common-school system of the country. His assailant did not call in question the facts on which his reasoning was based, but he denied that either they or the deductions made from them were applicable to the educational wants or to the social and religious condition of the United States.

Apart from the general importance of the subject, there were special reasons of a local character which rendered it proper that Bishop Spalding should not refuse to accept the challenge thus thrown out to him.

A sectarian school, established for the avowed purpose of perverting Catholic children from the faith of their fathers, had been recently recognized by the School Board of Louisville, and had received a portion of the moneys of the public-school fund. Catholics had thus been made to pay to help destroy the faith of their own children.

Bishop Spalding entered into this controversy the more willingly, because it would afford him an excellent opportunity of publicly denouncing this outrage upon the most sacred rights of conscience.

To the charge that the continued agitation of the question of common-school education, after it had been settled by the voice of the people, implied disloyalty to the Government, he made answer:

"We regret the useless agitation of settled questions as much, at least, as does the writer; but we have yet to learn that, in this free country, a minority which feels itself aggrieved by the majority has not the clear right, and is not even impelled by duty, to state its grievances, and to continue to do so temperately but boldly until the wrong be redressed. Oppressed minorities surely have rights as well as triumphant majorities; and where they have truth and justice on their side, they have even more sacred and more valid rights. . . . In this country of generous impulses and manly sympathy for the weaker side, there is nothing which awakens greater interest or excites more admiration, than to see an aggrieved minority nobly and persistently battling for its rights."

Having proclaimed the right of agitation for the redress of grievances under a free government, Bishop Spalding took up the objections of his opponent, and showed that there is no reason to be found, either in the social or religious condition of this country, why the denominational system of public schools, which had been found to work well in Europe, should not be introduced here with equal success.

The Government is not asked, he argued, to assume that any form of religion is in itself either true or false. To determine this does not lie within the competency of the state, as the Constitution of the United States expressly admits. The state, however, recognizes the existence of religion, and promises to secure to all its citizens the full and undisturbed possession of their religious rights. Now, when the state forces the members of a religious denomination to pay taxes for the support of schools to which they are not free to send their children, it violates the liberty of conscience which it professes to protect.

"But," objected Bishop Spalding's opponent, "we must have schools supported by taxation; for otherwise, as all experience shows, vast numbers will neglect to give their children any education whatever. It is the part of a wise and well-regulated government to encourage education by every lawful means, for if the corrupt are unfit to be free, the ignorant are incapable of maintaining their liberties. Now, in a country like this, where there are so many opposing churches, the only practicable method of establishing schools to be supported by taxation is to exclude the question of religion."

Bishop Spalding answered these objections, which are probably as strong as any which the friends of our common-school system can make, by applying the great doctrine of free-trade to the business of education. He considered that the minimum of state interference was logically contained in the American theory of government, and that in proportion as we augment the patronage of government, in that same degree do we endanger our political institutions. Legislative and official corruption, which are the principal evils of which we complain, grow out of the too great patronage of the Government, which leads men to look upon political life, not as the road to honor and fame, but as the shortest way to wealth.

The only political remedy for this evil, which has become national and which threatens our life as a nation, is to reduce the influence of the Government to its lowest expression. It is no more the business of the state to teach school than it is to run banks or railroads.

But what does come within its province is the enactment of laws for the proper regulation and protection of all legitimate business, which, provided these conditions be complied with, should be left to the untrammelled competition of all citizens. Now, consider education as a business which the state should protect and foster, but which it should in no case monopolize. Let the state create a fund for educational purposes, by taxation, as under the present system; let it make regulations to which all schools claiming a portion of the public moneys must conform; let it retain a supervision over schools to the support of which it contributes, in whatever relates to secular learning, and then let Catholics, Protestants, Jews, and infidels build their schoolhouses, and receive a rated proportion of the public moneys, provided they conform to the requirements of the law.

Bishop Spalding held that the system, the outlines of which are here given, was not only practicable, but that it would give far greater satisfaction than the one now in existence. The rights of the State would be safeguarded, no injustice would be done to any class of citizens, and popular education, to say the least, would be as universal and of as high a grade as at present. It is not to the purpose to say that this system would make the state a teacher of religion. It would do nothing of the kind. The state under it would do simply what it is now doing, with this difference, that it would not then force a large portion of its citizens to contribute to the support of schools to which they cannot in conscience send their children.

Concerning the reality and serious nature of the injustice which Catholics suffer under the present system of public schools, Bishop Spalding did not think there could be two opinions. To state the case was, as he looked at it, to make it as evident as the most labored argument could render it.

That Catholics have the sincerest conscientious scruples as to the danger of sending their children to the public schools, their deeds more than their words prove. The sacrifices which a man is willing to make in any cause are generally accepted as the test of his sincerity; and if we apply this to the Catholic population of the United States, the perfect honesty of their convictions is at once manifest.

If there were no remedy for this evil, except by withdrawing all state aid for educational purposes, a plausible pretext might be found for this system of injustice. That such is not the case, the example of other civilized nations has proved; whilst the impartial consideration of our own social condition leads to the same conclusion. The Catholic Church in this country has taken a far deeper view of this most vital question of education than that which has been granted to any of the sects; all of which are either wanting in religious earnestness, or ignore the natural laws of religious development in their exclusive and false theories of the special and supernatural action of God in the soul. God has subjected the religious instinct or faculty in man, in some degree at least, to the same law of evolution which governs his other faculties; and consequently, it must be evolved by processes similar to those by which the intellectual and moral faculties are educated; otherwise, man's religious nature will remain to a great extent in a latent and potential state. Now, the whole theory of common-school education in this country ignores this all-important psychological fact. It will not do, in the vast number of cases, to leave religious training to the family influence alone. This is evident for many reasons. The greater number of parents have neither the time nor the intellectual and moral qualifications which would fit them as religious educators of their own children. What would be thought of us were we to insist that the intellectual training which children can receive at home is all-sufficient? All experience teaches that were education left exclusively to the family, ignorance would become universal. In the same way, faith would grow feeble and decay if the religious training of the young were left to the parents alone. It may be objected that we have churches in which the priest can supplement the religious education received at home. Without seeking in the least to underrate the value of this instruction, it must be admitted that it is altogether inadequate to the purpose. As it is the province of religion to control all the actions of life, it follows that it must enter into and form part of the general training of youth. Since the religious faculty requires to be brought out by a process similar to that by which the intellect is educated, it is but natural to suppose that this cannot be done with any degree of success by a few instructions given at considerable intervals of time. Believing that this is the highest and divinest faculty in man, the church holds that at least as much care should be bestowed upon its cultivation as upon that of the other faculties. Indeed, the exclusion of religious instruction from the school-room can be logically justified only on the assumption that religion is false. If all positive religious dogmas are the offspring of superstition, then it is certainly most desirable that doctrines emanating from such a source should be considered as evil, as tending to the perversion of both the mind and the heart. That men who look thus upon all positive religion should wish to exclude it from the process of education is not surprising, but that those who believe that these teachings are revealed of God should concur in this, is altogether incomprehensible. The godless school theory, then, can have its logical basis only in that system of sophistry which holds that all positive religious dogmas had their origin in the credulity, the ignorance and fears, of rude and savage peoples. Were this true, the diffusion of the spirit of unbelief would be most desirable; and for the accomplishment of this end no better means could be found than the godless school system. It is only when we look at the question of education from this higher point of view that we get a right conception of the determined opposition of Catholics to the common-school system as it exists in this country, and that we come to understand how such men as Bishop Spalding, who in other respects undoubtedly admired American institutions, could have no sympathy whatever with this theory of education. He was persuaded that it was based upon an essentially antichristian philosophy, and that, starting out on the implied assumption of the untruth of Christianity, its practical tendency was to undermine faith in Christ himself. No meddlesome or unworthy spirit moved him to protest with such fearlessness and vehemence against the public schools. He felt that the most sacred interests of the country itself were in danger, and that, unless a remedy were applied, the final outcome would be the loss of our character as a Christian nation; and his grief was not greater than his astonishment to find that the leaders of the various Protestant churches were blind to the evils which he deplored, and which did not concern Catholics alone, but all who believe in the divinity of the Christian religion.

The undenominational system of schools which we have here is precisely that which the infidel party in Europe is using every exertion to introduce there, because it perceives how fatal it must prove to religion. "In my opinion," has said one of the leaders of this party, " every church, whatsoever may be the name which it bears or the principle from which it springs, is an obstacle to civilization. Every church, for the reason that it lays down articles of belief and insists upon faith, impedes the development of the human mind. Every church is a hamper upon the free flight of the soul. I desire that the soul be unfettered, and therefore I desire that there be no church. Abolish, then, this whole system which teaches man, from his infancy, to believe in a future state of life. We must learn how to be atheists." *

The great social problem of the age with these men is how to give to man on earth the happiness which he has hitherto been led to look for only in heaven. Underlying all the objections which the various schools of unbelief make to religion, is the thought that whatever induces man to act with regard to a future state is superstition; that, consequently, all positive religious dogmas are hurtful to our true interests, since by inducing us to think of heaven, they cause us to neglect the vital interests of earth.

It is but natural that men who hold such views should wish to exclude all religious instruction from the schools. But these views cannot be said, as yet, to represent public sentiment in this country. Most Americans still believe in God, and have a certain veneration for religion. There is, however, a very general feeling with us that religion is easily distinguishable from creeds and churches; that ecclesiastical organizations are chiefly serviceable as affording a convenient means of teaching morality; that the two sacraments which still remain to, at least, a portion of Protestant Christianity—baptism and the Lord's Supper—are mere rites, void of efficacy and even of meaning; that the minister of religion is only a preacher—a teacher without a divine commission; and, consequently, that church-membership is simply an affair of convenience, and the choice between the different religious denominations of the land merely a matter of taste. Hence, there can be little reason why we should be astonished that the masses of our people

* Carl Vogt: Address before the National Assembly in Frankfort.

attach no importance to denominational religious instruction. They do not, indeed, like the infidels of Europe, look upon all churches as bad, as obstacles to the progress of mankind; but as little do they consider them divine institutions, essential to the progress of religion, to the welfare of society, and the salvation of the soul. Hence, it was altogether natural that in establishing a common-school system, no notice whatever should have been taken of the various religious denominations of the country. Even among the stricter sort of Protestants, the idea, very generally received, that religion must proceed exclusively from the special interference of God, by which the individual, through consciousness of sin, is awakened to repentance, causes them to look upon the teaching of religious doctrines as of little importance. A stray and dissonant voice is now and then raised from the midst of one or other of the sects, to warn against the danger to faith from the exclusion of all religious instruction from the public schools, but it dies away without having awakened even an echo.

Although no one could be more opposed to the public-school system than Bishop Spalding, yet he was by no means in favor of committing the church to party politics in order to effect a reform in this matter or in any other. He appealed to public opinion, and sought to enlighten it, without, however, deluding himself with the hope that any speedy change was to be looked for. He considered that he had done but little when he had written and spoken in favor of the true theory of popular, as of all, education. What God demands of Catholics in this nineteenth century, and in this country especially, is not that they talk, but that they act. He looked upon the agitation of the school question as of very little importance compared with the real work to be done. The remedy which he sought, and which it was in his power to apply, was to build parochial schools, into which he strove to gather the children of his own people, who showed their religious earnestness by generously co-operating with him in this, the most important work of the church.

It will be perceived, from what has been said, that Bishop Spalding's opposition to the common-school system did not proceed chiefly, or to any great extent indeed, from fear lest special or accidental influences prejudicial to their faith should be brought to bear upon Catholic children if allowed to frequent the public schools. He objected to the system itself, which, as it presented itself to his mind, was based upon false principles, and necessarily tended to produce a spirit of religious indifference fatal to Christianity, as understood and taught by the Catholic Church.

The view of religion which common-school education is almost sure to develop, is that it is something quite independent of ecclesiastical organizations, and consequently that it is of no consequence to what church one belong, or whether he belong to any; and this view is in direct antagonism with the fundamental idea upon which the church is founded. To individualize Christianity is to undermine the facts upon which it rests. The humanity of Christ and the objective visible church are correlative facts, and both are essential to the complete notion of the Christian religion. Fellowship with Christ is obtained through communion with his church. She alone is his spouse; she alone the mother of his children. Hence, there can be no more pernicious error in religion than the theory which the common schools, however conducted, must of necessity help to propagate—that communion with the church is not of obligation; and Bishop Spalding therefore held that these schools, even when unsectarian, are still anti-Catholic.

CHAPTER XVII.

DIOCESAN AFFAIRS—TRAITS OF CHARACTER—CORRESPONDENCE WITH ARCHBISHOP KENRICK.

E shall now turn to matters more immediately connected with Bishop Spalding's administration of the diocese of Louisville. A few weeks after his consecration in 1848, he held, as I have already stated, an informal synod of his clergy, in which the outlines of the statutes which were to serve as the basis of his ecclesiastical government were determined. In the next synod, a more definite form was given to these decrees, and they were solemnly promulgated. After declaring that all the decrees of the Councils of Baltimore were to be considered as binding in the diocese of Louisville, the statutes determine the ritual which is to be used in the administration of the sacraments, and the ceremonial to be conformed to in the public functions of the church. They recall the instructions of the Council of Trent to pastors of souls, and the laws of the church, which forbid priests to meddle with secular affairs.

In connection with the administration of the sacraments, the erection of baptismal fonts to be kept under lock and key was made obligatory in all places where baptism is usually given—that is, where there is a resident pastor, and even in other churches this is strongly advised. The custom of administering baptism in private houses, which had been introduced when priests were few, and when Catholics frequently lived at great distances from church, was abolished, except in cases of necessity, or in exceptional circumstances.

The priests laboring on the missions were required to keep baptismal and marriage registers, and their consciences were charged with the obligation of faithfully inscribing in them the names of the parties, as indicated by the formula. The times in which the public exposition of the Blessed Sacrament was permitted by the Ordinary were stated. The statutes required that confessionals should be erected in all churches in which confessions were to be heard. The faithful were to be warned by their pastors each year in Lent of the evils which flow from mixed and consanguineous marriages. The custom of performing the marriage ceremony in private houses where both parties are Catholics, was abolished. Parochial limits and the rights of pastors were to be respected. The duty of instructing children and the negroes was insisted upon. Those charged with the care of souls were required to render annually an account of the state of their missions.

These and other disciplinary regulations embraced in the diocesan statutes were submitted to the priests in synod assembled, and, having been approved of by them, were solemnly promulgated. *Judices causarum*, with jurisdiction *in foro ecclesiastico*, were appointed, before whom all cases within their competency were to be brought. In the second and third synods of Louisville, held in 1858 and 1862, further enactments, tending to complete and perfect the organization of the diocese, were made. Ecclesiastical conferences, to be held in the city four times in the year, and in the country twice, were established, with a view to keep up and cultivate habits of study in the clergy, and also to promote uniformity of action.

The administration of Bishop Spalding, which was based upon the general ecclesiastical polity which is the natural and unhindered outgrowth of the peculiar circumstances in which the church has been placed in this country, could in no proper sense be called arbitrary. The laws which govern the relations of the higher to the lower clergy here form an integral part of the exceptional status of the church in the United States; and to change them in an essential manner would destroy the unity of the whole system. A great portion of the canon law of the church grew out of her relations with the European state, more especially in the Middle Ages, which were so entirely different from those in which she is placed here, as to render the application of many of those laws to our ecclesiastical condition altogether impracticable. Many of them have grown obsolete even in Catholic nations, and the church has acquiesced in the new state of things. Those laws, indeed, which govern faith and morals are of universal obligation. But this is not always the case with regulations which are merely disciplinary. That considerable portion of canon law, for instance, which treats of ecclesiastical benefices, can have no application to the church in this country, nor can that concerning the immunity of clerics. The same must be said of the laws relating to the rights and privileges of patriarchs and primates. We have no primate, and it is not probable that we shall ever have one. There is no patronage and no right of presentation to ecclesiastical livings here, nor is there likely to be any, and, consequently, the canon law on this subject is inapplicable to us. The whole system under which young men are raised to the priesthood in the United States is an exceptional one, not in accordance with the general laws of the church on titles of ordination, and it is impossible that this should be otherwise. To insist on the introduction of this portion of canon law would be to shut out from the sanctuary nine-tenths of the young men who present themselves for orders. And this ought not to be lost sight of in a fair and enlarged view of church polity in the United States, for this *titulus missionis*, which is an absolute necessity here, lies at the root of the relations of the higher to the lower clergy, which by some are thought to be abnormal, whereas they are only the outgrowth of the circumstances in which we have been placed, and which it has not been in the power of any man or body of men to change. These relations are substantially the same which existed in the first ages of the church, when the bishop, as at present in the United States, was the only pastor in the diocese. No one, however, could be less inclined than Bishop Spalding either to exercise arbitrary power himself, or to approve of others exercising it, and he strongly favored, as we shall see, a gradual change in the relations which exist between the two orders of the clergy in this country. He himself was certainly not disposed to remove priests when in *loco parochi*, except for weighty reasons. He was, indeed, from principle opposed to frequent changes, as being hurtful to both priest and people. In one of his letters he refers to a parish in which he had been forced within a brief space of time to make several removals of pastors, and he adds that he feels ashamed to meet the people of that place, for it looked as though he had been trifling with them. He always preferred kind to harsh measures, and seldom had recourse to ecclesiastical censures. In a conversation on this subject, he said that, during an episcopal career of more than twenty years, he had exercised the power of suspension but two or three times.

He rarely if ever took any important step without having first taken counsel of his advisers, who were known and trusted by both the clergy and laity. Even in minor things, he generally consulted with those who were immediately concerned, and, as far as prudence and conscience permitted, allowed himself to be influenced by their views. Whoever had a complaint to make found him ready to listen; and he was always willing to hear both sides before coming to a final decision. He had, however, no conception of the priesthood, especially in this country, except as connected with a life of hardship and self-sacrifice; and he therefore expected his priests to endure much and suffer many things without losing heart, as it was only on this condition that they could be true and useful workers in the vineyard of Christ. He himself had been brought up and had lived under apostolic men, who thought never of themselves, but always of the salvation of souls; and all his views of the priesthood were colored by the impressions made upon him by the example of the noble missionaries who had built up the church in Kentucky. "We should frequently recall to mind," he said, in an exhortation to his priests, "the earnest admonitions of that man of God, the founder and first superior of our theological seminary, Bishop David, who strove in season and out of season to impress upon our minds and hearts the necessity of the priest being a man of prayer, wholly devoted to his duties, and constantly walking before God, meditating upon his law day and night, if he would be perfect, and receive from God the priceless gift of perseverance. Many of us may also remember the oft-repeated declaration of the saintly first Bishop of Louisville, the venerable Flaget, that a priest who does not keep up his spiritual exercises and make his daily meditation, cannot reasonably hope to persevere to the end. A fearful truth, alas! too strongly illustrated by sad experience! These holy men, treading in the footsteps of the saints of God, exemplified in their own lives the truths which they so impressively taught. They were truly the models of the flock and the mirror of the clergy." And again he said: "The salvation of one soul, venerable brethren, is more glorious than the conquest of a kingdom. Of all divine things, says an ancient writer, the most divine is to co-operate with God for the salvation of souls. This is one of the most lofty privileges of our holy ministry; for we are ambassadors of Christ, God, as it were, exhorting by us. Like the apostles, we have been constituted the fishers of men; and if we be so happy as to correspond well with the graces of our vocation, we shall, like them, take many in the Gospel nets, and lead them to life eternal. Our blessed Lord came to send fire on earth, and what does he wish more than that it be enkindled in the hearts of all men? In order that we may be able to scatter this heavenly fire over the earth, we must take care to keep it always burning in our own hearts; for if we be cold ourselves, how shall we be able to warm others? Happy shall we be if, by a constant and living union with Jesus Christ, the Source of the divine fire, we maintain ourselves in the fervor of the holy priesthood, and thus become, like St. John the Baptist, burning and shining lights in God's sanctuary."

His own love for the Blessed Virgin made him desire that his priests should be her most devout servants, as the following words, taken from the pastoral address from which I have been quoting, sufficiently prove: "We exhort you, venerable brethren, to cherish in your own hearts, and to keep alive in those of your flock, a deep reverence and a tender devotion towards the Mother of God our Saviour, who, besides being the elected Patroness of the church in the United States, is in a special manner the queen of the clergy and the tender mother of all the priests of God, as she was and is the mother of the great High-Priest from whom we derive all our ministerial powers. Revered, obeyed, and beloved by her divine Son while on earth, she now shines with brightness unspeakable in heaven, the ever compassionate and devoted mother of all who are the adopted brethren of her Son. Her mother's countenance beams with special interest and kindness on the priests of God's church, who, under Christ, carry on the great work for which he died on the cross. Mary conceived without sin is the master-work of God, more radiant far than was the first mother of the human race, in all the loveliness of her primeval innocence. She is the brightest ornament of heaven as she was of earth ; in her and through her we see retrieved the degradation of her sex, and of the whole human race, brought about by the disobedience of the first Eve. With such a mother in heaven, sweetly smiling on us in our labors, we cannot fail to feel courage and consolation amidst all our tribulations, and to be cheered by the abiding hope that, when the brief days of our sorrowful exile shall be over, she will show us the face of Jesus, the blessed fruit of her womb, in the haven of eternal rest."

Bishop Spalding certainly gave to his clergy the example of a life wholly devoted to the cause of religion. Few men more single-hearted than he have ever lived. Practical experience of life had made him wiser, but he still had all the ingenuousness and transparency of character that belong to childhood. With a faith that not even the shadow of a doubt had ever obscured, with a devotion that had never known any other object than God, with a zeal that never grew cold, he labored to be what he had proposed to himself years ago as a student in the Propaganda—useful to the church of Christ. He was almost a constant sufferer, and had frequent attacks of severe illness; but not even bad health could destroy his energy, or prevent him from performing the arduous duties of his office. If able to sit up, he was sure to be at work, and even when confined to bed he allowed his mind no repose. And yet he was not of a restless or nervous temperament, but could be busy without bustle. He had made it a rule of life not to defer what he could do at the present moment, and what he was, sooner or later, bound to do. I have seen him leave the society of friends, in the midst of an interesting conversation, to say a portion of the office the very first moment it fell due. A year or two before his death he told me that during nearly forty years in which he had been laboring on the missions in one capacity or another, he had never said Mass without having first absolved the matins and lauds of the day.

This fact of itself, as they who are acquainted with the duties of missionary priests and bishops will readily admit, testifies to a life governed by system and order.

He was in the habit of visiting his diocese on horseback, and later in a buggy, which he generally drove himself. But on a smooth and level road his faithful horse needed not a driver, and then the Bishop gave him the reins whilst he said the office of the Breviary.

I shall never forget the pleasant journeys which, when quite a small boy, I had the happiness to make with him. His merry laugh, that might have been that of a child who had never known a sorrow or a care, the simple and naïve way he had of listening to the prattle of children, the whole expression of the countenance showing a soul at rest and happy in the work which he was doing, are still present to my mind, like the remembrance of flowers and sunshine. And I remember, too, with what warmth and reverence and love he was received everywhere, and how his presence was never connected in my mind with anything morose or severe. Eyes that seemed to have looked for his coming grew brighter when he had come, and when he was gone it was like the ceasing of sweet music which one would wish to hear always, but which, even when hushed, keeps playing on in the soul, attuning it to gentler moods and higher thoughts. He was full of human sympathies and human ways. The purple of the bishop never hid the man; nor did he, because he belonged to the supernatural order, cease to be natural. There was, indeed, a certain elegance and refinement about him which no one could fail to perceive— the true breeding of a gentleman; but withal he was as plain as the simplest Kentucky farmer. He rarely talked about learned things; and, when he did, he did not talk in a learned way. He possessed naturally remarkable powers of adaptation, which enabled him to feel perfectly at ease in circumstances and companies the most dissimilar. There was not a poor negro in his whole diocese with whom he was not willing to talk about anything that could be of advantage to him. I remember particularly how kindly he used to speak to the old servants of his father, who had known him as a child. He had a special sympathy with this whole race, and I have known him, whilst Archbishop of Baltimore, to take the trouble to write a long letter to an old negro in Kentucky who had consulted him concerning his own little affairs.

He frequently wrote to children ten or twelve years old, from whom he had received letters. In company where there were children, he never failed to devote himself to their amusement, even to the forgetfulness of the claims of more important persons. When at home, he usually passed the forenoon in writing, or in receiving those who called to see him on matters of business. After dinner, he spent some time in conversation, which he always enjoyed, and then withdrew to his room to say vespers, with matins and lauds for the following day. In summer, he kept up an old Roman habit of taking a short repose in the afternoon. He would then walk out, calling in here and there to visit some school or convent, or to spend a few moments with some Catholic family. On the street, he would stop to greet, with a few pleasant words, almost every acquaintance he chanced to meet. Frequently he would remain to tea at the house of a friend, after which he returned to his room to write or read until the hour for retiring for the night arrived. The rule in his house was, that every one should be in at ten o'clock, when the door was locked. Apart from this regulation, he never interfered with the tastes or hours of the priests of his household. In the cathedral, he had his own confessional, and, when at home, he was generally found there on Saturday afternoon. And it was his custom to preach at the late Mass on Sunday.

The financial affairs of the diocese he entrusted, for the most part, to his brother, the Very Rev. B. J. Spalding, to whose prudence and foresight he was greatly indebted for the freedom from money-troubles which he enjoyed.

When Bishop Spalding wished to engage in serious literary work, he usually left his episcopal residence, and sought some quiet place where he could be free from interruption.

In a letter to Archbishop Kenrick, to whom he was in the habit of writing every few days, he says: "I shall look with much interest for your volume on *Job and the Prophets*. How you can find time, amidst all your labors, to attend to the severe Scriptural studies requisite for the gigantic work you have nearly completed, almost exceeds my comprehension. When I write, I have to run off for a few days, as I have not the knack of doing two or more things at once. I have a snug little country-house at Portland suitable for this purpose."

To Archbishop Kenrick he opened his heart, with the most perfect freedom and simplicity, on all subjects, and in return he received the full and entire confidence of that great and truly Christian bishop. They wrote to one another about their labors, their projects for the good of the church, their literary occupations, making suggestions and criticisms with the freedom which only true and long-tried friendship justifies.

An Episcopal clergyman of Baltimore, who shall be nameless here, had given currency to the stupid slander of the Louisville preachers, to which reference has already been made in connection with the Morse controversy. He had even taken the trouble to send the calumny to England, where it had been published as a striking example of the corruptions of Romanism.

Had Bishop Spalding known his accuser, he would, I think, have taken no notice of him. But as he had never even heard of him, and as the absurd accusation had been made in connection with a controversy which had attracted considerable attention, he thought proper to defend himself.

In writing to Archbishop Kenrick, he had said something about having his defence inserted in the *Mirror*, in case the slander should be repeated. To this the Archbishop replied, in a playful manner, that Bishop Spalding was evidently anxious to involve him in one of those " pugnacious " disputes of which he was so fond. In answer, the Bishop wrote : " I did not wish to involve you in any 'pugnacious' contest, but simply to request that a word of explanation should be inserted in the *Mirror*, in case I should be attacked in Baltimore without my immediate knowledge. I am one of the most peaceable men living—more so, probably, than was the *Doctor Acerrimus* who is canonized ; but I must defend myself when attacked. Sometimes the best mode of defence is to carry the war into Africa, and not always to stand rigidly by the motto in Molière : *Si je me defends, ce n'est, qu'en reculant.*"

This was written in 1859, a short time before the opening of the American College in Rome, and when it was also deemed probable that the Second Plenary Council of the Bishops of the United States would soon be convened; and, in the letter from which I have been quoting, reference is made to both these subjects.

" I was under the impression that Bishop O'Connor was to go to Róme to superintend the opening of the American College. I sent Cardinal Barnabo a check for $1,000, which is all I have been able to collect. Our Kentucky Catholics, as Father Badin used to say, do not belong to the sect of the Donatists; and we need not wonder at their orthodoxy, since we know they came from Maryland. Perhaps at the Plenary Council we may be able to form a general association for the relief of converts, and also to agree upon some plan to give them a *status* in the church, which is even more important. I do not see why such married converts as Dr. Ives and Dr. Huntington might not be ordained lectors, or even receive all the minor orders. They could then, under the direction of the ordinaries, give catechetical instruction in the churches, and superintend the parochial and Sunday-schools, with regular salaries from the congregations. I hope a plan may be matured for the purpose. To have them depend on precarious alms is uncertain and humiliating. I enclose my quota. I am glad you are continuing your revision, but still regret that Dr. Newman and the English bishops do not unite with you in bringing out a common, popular version, which is a great want."

Bishop Spalding, it would seem, afterwards saw fit to modify his opinion as to the work which married converts may be permitted to perform in the church; for I find, in another of his letters, the following sentence: "Rome will never consent, in my opinion, to allow married men to receive even minor orders."

To the subject of the English version of the Bible he frequently refers, in his correspondence with Archbishop Kenrick. Dr. Newman's unequalled knowledge of English could not, he thought, be employed to better purpose than in giving to the great English-speaking Catholic body an idiomatic version of the Scriptures. This was also Archbishop Kenrick's opinion, who was willing to co-operate in the work; and negotiations were, in fact, begun with a view to secure the services of competent persons, both in Great Britain and in this country. Unfortunately, however, owing to causes which I need not here relate, no practical result came of this project.

With reference to the general plan of Archbishop Kenrick's version of the Bible, Bishop Spalding, in his correspondence with that amiable and learned prelate, expresses his opinion with great freedom. "I think," he says in one of his letters, "the notes should be more doctrinal, without, however, being precisely polemical. Some, which are merely critical, might be omitted in the popular, and developed more fully in an enlarged edition. As the people have been so long accustomed to the Douay version, it might be well not to depart from it unnecessarily, or except with a view to make the rendering more English and less Latin, or for the sake of greater accuracy." In a subsequent letter he refers more particularly to the version of the New Testament. "I have just received and examined your New Testament. I am much pleased with it; the small blemishes which had been remarked in the first edition have been removed. I welcome it as a most valuable contribution to our sacred literature. I expect to use it for the first time in the cathedral next Sunday; and gradually to introduce it as a textbook in our other churches. Had I received it before our diocesan synod, in August, I should have officially recommended its adoption to my clergy. The notes must have cost you immense labor; in fact, I can scarcely conceive how you have been able to refer to so many readings and authorities. . . . It is hard for the most perverse critic to censure mildness, especially in a Catholic prelate. Still, I have been tempted to wish that you had been a little more pointed in noticing certain Protestant readings, which have usually been regarded as perversions of the text."

In a letter to Archbishop Kenrick, written in February, 1861, Bishop Spalding returns to this subject, in which he evidently took very great interest. "Our provincial councils will be held this spring, or at least during the course of the present year. Would it not be well to avail yourself of the occasion to secure the co-operation of your brethren in having your version of the New Testament adopted as the standard text for this country?"

CHAPTER XVIII.

HISTORY OF THE REFORMATION—VIEWS ON THE DUTIES OF ECCLESIASTICS IN THEIR RELATIONS WITH THE STATE—EPISCOPAL LABORS.

N his correspondence with Archbishop Kenrick, Bishop Spalding frequently makes allusion to his own literary labors. The first work which he published was the *Review of D'Aubigné's History of the Reformation in Germany and Switzerland*.

He had chosen precisely the kind of writing best suited to his style and habits of thought, for he possessed great power as a reviewer.

The refutation of D'Aubigné, who is little more than a pleasant writer of romance, was complete and unanswerable; and the reception with which Dr. Spalding's book met, at once placed him among the most popular Catholic authors of the day. But his review of D'Aubigné was confined to the history of the Reformation in Germany and Switzerland, and consequently left untouched that portion of the great religious innovation of the sixteenth century, which was of most interest to the public to which his work was more immediately addressed. In 1859, nearly twenty years after the publication of his first volume on the subject, Bishop Spalding determined to write a more complete and general history of the Reformation.

"My essay," he wrote to Archbishop Kenrick, " on the *History of the Reformation* will be published in two octavo volumes, the first of which will contain the original work on Germany and Switzerland, remodelled, and prefaced by a lengthy introduction on the state of Europe before the Reformation.

"The second volume, entirely new, will embrace the history of the Reformation in England, Ireland, and Scotland, the Netherlands, France, and Northern Europe, and will review McCrie's *Knox*, Prescott's *Philip II.*, Motley's *Dutch Republic*, Ranke's *Civil Wars in France*, Fryxell's *Sweden*, and other works.

"I find the gathering of materials more difficult than I had supposed. They accumulate so that it is not easy to know what to select. I have already reviewed Haller's *History of the Swiss Reformation*. Prescott is more prejudiced in his *Philip II.* than in his previous works; he is, however, as an historian, far preferable to Hallam."

From this letter it will be perceived that Bishop Spalding, in his larger and more complete work on the Reformation, did not depart from the plan which he had originally adopted in his refutation of D'Aubigné. He still retained the character and, to a certain extent, the style of a reviewer, which, though subject to disadvantages of rather a serious kind, in historical writing, yet gave him greater facility for correcting false statements and erroneous impressions, which were the more pernicious because of the great authority of the names of those who had given them their sanction.

He was thus able to obtain a double end—to furnish a reliable history of the Reformation, and, at the same time, to call attention to the errors into which even the best and ablest non-Catholic writers on this subject had fallen.

Bishop Spalding does not consider history a bare recital of events; but he looks before and after, and in the past seeks an explanation of the present, which he would have speak words of guidance to the future. He does not belong, however, to what Carlyle calls the class of cause-and-effect speculators, who compute and account for all things in heaven and earth, attempting even to give an algebraical symbol for the infinite, and to reduce the unlimited workings of man's spiritual life within the narrow compass of a formula. The philosophy of history is most generally merely the history of the writer's prejudices and hobbies.

"Speculation," says Bishop Spalding, "however elaborate and philosophical, without a solid basis of facts, is, in our view, wholly worthless, if not mischievous, in an historical writer, as it can scarcely fail to mislead."

In his review of the religious condition of Europe prior to the Reformation, he enters into a comprehensive and dispassionate enquiry into the causes which led to the heresies and schisms of the sixteenth century. In the following brief statement of the question, which covers the whole ground, and at the same time gives a very correct and just insight into the subject, he concludes from the facts which he has developed in this essay :

"1. That the amount and extent of the scandals and abuses complained of during this period (the Middle Ages) have been greatly exaggerated, and that the good more than counterbalanced the evil. Evil always excites more attention and makes more noise in the world than good ; and what contemporary writers, even if they were otherwise good men, say of abuses and of the persons to whom they are to be ascribed, will generally be found to be highly colored; especially if the writers, as is often the case, have their feelings, as partisans, enlisted on the one side or the other. Feelings must be calmed, excitement must pass away, and affairs must fully work themselves out, before a correct and reliable judgment can be formed on any series of events.

"2. That these abuses and scandals generally originated in the world and its princes, not in the church and its chief pastors; most of them being due to the fact that bad men were thrust into the high places of the church by worldly-minded and avaricious princes in spite of the Popes, whose settled policy was to protest with all their might against a line of conduct so very ruinous to the best interests of religion. And such being clearly the case, it is most unjust to charge those scandals on the church or on the pontiffs. If the princes of the earth could have ruined the church, they would have done so by their wicked and oppressive enactments. That they did not succeed in inflicting on her more than occasional and temporary wounds, we owe to the divine vitality of the church, and to the noble and dauntless opposition of the Popes.

"3. That there was a lawful and efficacious remedy for all such evils, which consisted in removing their obvious cause, and giving to the Popes their due power and influence in the nomination of the bishops and in the deliberations of general ecclesiastical councils, the judgments of which had hitherto been always viewed as final; that, in one word, *reformation within* the church and not *revolution outside* of it, was the only proper, lawful, and efficacious remedy for existing evils, and the one which had always been invoked by the wise and the good in all previous ages of Christianity.

"4. Finally, that the fact of Christians having at length felt prepared to resort to the desperate and totally wrong remedy of revolution, was owing to a train of circumstances which had caused faith to wane and grow cold, and which now appealed more to the passions than to reason, more to human considerations than to the principles of divine faith and the interests of eternity."

The History of the Reformation is Bishop Spalding's most valuable contribution to the Catholic literature of our country. It was published in the spring of 1860. The first edition, which was large, was almost immediately exhausted, and a second was called for, which was followed by a third, fourth, and fifth edition. Bishop Timon urged the issuing of a cheaper edition, saying that he thought fifty thousand copies could be sold; and Bishop Spalding was setting about this work when the cloud of civil war loomed above the horizon and directed men's thoughts to the history that was to follow rather than to that which had gone before.

Bishop Spalding's position, during the late civil war, was one which required more than ordinary prudence and wisdom to meet and overcome the difficulties which presented themselves on every side. His people were divided in their views and sympathies, and his diocese was frequently occupied, at the same time, by the armies of both the North and the South.

Whatever his personal opinions may or may not have been on the great questions which, at that time, absorbed the whole thought of the nation, in his official and ecclesiastical capacity he scrupulously abstained from all interference in political and secular matters. In thus seeking to remain aloof from the strife and angry passions of the hour, he was influenced solely by his sense of duty, based upon what he conceived to be the letter and the spirit of the American theory of government. Among the papers which he left, I have found one on "The Church and the Country," in which he discusses this question at some length. As this paper, which was written about the close of the late war, contains a very lucid statement of Bishop Spalding's views on this most important subject, and also furnishes the best commentary upon his conduct during the war, I shall take the liberty of presenting to my readers some of the thoughts which it contains.

"The Catholic Church," wrote Bishop Spalding, "is essentially conservative. She is so both by her origin and divinely established constitution, and by her historical relations to the world. She alone, amid the changes wrought by time, has preserved her integrity unimpaired and her unity unbroken—the seals of her divine origin. She is not only the great *conservative*, but she is the only *union* church. She alone has power to combine and to blend into unity the elements of discord and opposition inherent in human nature. She alone unites all nations, peoples, and tribes in the profession of the one faith, in the reception of the one order of sacraments, and in the one form of ecclesiastical government. And this example of marvellous unity—without parallel in all history—is not merely a phenomenon of the present age, hitherto unknown; it is the ordinary history of the church for eighteen centuries. Catholicity unites; Protestantism divides. History proves this, whether we confine our view to the last three centuries, or enlarge it to the whole period during which Christianity has been acting on the world. In every age, conservatism and union rest with the church, whilst dissensions and divisions are the lot of the sects which rebel against her authority. Protestantism, in all its phases, is but a repetition, under a different form, of the scenes enacted by more ancient sectarism. Everywhere we witness the same love of novelty, the same perpetual and restless antagonisms, and the same never-ending changes of opinion. Having once seceded from the only *union* church, these bodies of fragmentary Christianity find no repose until they dissolve into individualism and nihilism. It is well to bear these truths in mind, in order to be able better to appreciate the past and present position of the Catholic Church towards the American state.

"The influence of the church, in past ages, has been, according to the testimony of the most distinguished publicists, both Catholic and Protestant, highly beneficial to civilization. Her action, however, upon society has been modified by the various circumstances in which she has been placed. Whilst the European populations were in the process of formation, and were as yet like children under tutelage, she was called upon to exert herself more directly in the regulation of their affairs, temporal as well as spiritual. But as the organization of society became more perfect, she retired more and more into her own cherished spiritual domain, in which resided the secret of her wonderful power and influence over the nations of the earth. Whilst these were yet children and needed teachers, she provided them with instructors from the exhaustless body of her clergy; while they were without governors or definite ideas of correct government, she supplied the want by bidding them model their constitutions after her own divinely established system; and if she did not appoint their rulers, she at least exerted a strong influence over them, and thus secured the people from the evils of unbridled despotism. In a word, while they were children, she directed and guided them as such; when they grew up to the age of manhood, and were able to stand alone, her influence over their conduct and civil government underwent a corresponding change, and manifested itself chiefly through moral suasion and example. Having been established for all nations, she must live and does live under all kinds of government. Hence, as a church, she can advocate none to the exclusion of the others. Her kingdom is not of this world, and the chief end which she contemplates is supernatural, and her means and appliances for attaining this end partake of the same heavenly character.

"We may, then, fairly infer that the church of Christ, to be true to her high purposes, should keep herself, as far as may be, within her own lofty sphere; above the region of worldly contentions and human passions, into which she should never descend, except when impelled by a sense of duty or the demands of justice. The church which rises above the strifes and angry passions of the day, and confines herself to her high spiritual office of promoting peace and good-will among men, and of soothing human passions and suffering, in so far shows herself to be the church of Christ. That this has been the course of the Catholic Church in the late war, no one will deny. She has preached religion, not politics; she has advocated love, not hatred. Devoted to the welfare and permanent prosperity of the country, she has thought that she could best promote its interests by confining herself, as a church, to prayer and ministrations for the relief of suffering of every kind, bodily and spiritual. The course almost unanimously adopted by the bishops and clergy of the Catholic Church during the late terrible civil war has been eminently conservative, and worthy of them and of the church of all ages and of all nations. In limiting their action to their own sphere of duties, they have not for a moment thought that they were, in the least, wanting in patriotism, or in the ardent desire to do everything in their power to aid their suffering country in emerging from its difficulties. In the hour of danger, the country has the right to demand that every citizen shall do his duty. The Catholic clergy did theirs, without, however, departing from their proper sphere as ministers of religion. While the Catholic laity were placed in every respect on an exact level with their fellow-citizens of every other denomination and of no denomination, and had the same duties and rights as they; and while they fully discharged their duties as citizens and soldiers, as politicians and officers, in the full proportion of their numbers, the Catholic clergy had also their respective duties, which they were by no means remiss in fulfilling.

"In a country like this, where there is no union of church and state, where the church is happily free, and the state stands pledged by the Constitution not to interfere in matters of faith and worship, there is no sufficient reason, nor even a plausible pretext, for the intervention of the clergy in matters of pure politics. The rights and duties of the church and the state are reciprocal; and as the state has no right to interfere with the church, so the church and its ministers have no right to interfere with the state and its politicians. Such has, in fact, been the settled policy and practice of the church in this country from the very beginning of the Republic; indeed, before its establishment, and during the first movements of the Colonies for declaring and securing their independence of the mother country. We were lately shown a highly interesting paper, in the handwriting of the venerable John Carroll, the first Bishop of Baltimore. It was written early in 1776, fourteen years before he was consecrated Bishop, and contains a copy of his reply to the invitation extended to him by the Colonial Congress to accompany Franklin, Chase, and Charles Carroll on their mission to Canada. Only a fragment of the reply remains; but in the portion which has been preserved the future founder and father of the American hierarchy furnishes some of his reasons for wishing to decline this honorable mission, the principal of which was, that it would involve him in political affairs, for which his education and profession disqualified him, and to which his sacred calling and his sense of honor offered an insuperable barrier. If he was afterwards induced to accompany the envoys, we may be sure that his religious scruples were respected, and that he was allowed to confine his co-operation to duties strictly in accordance with his religious calling. However this may be, the passage which forcibly struck us in the fragmentary paper just referred to is the following: 'I hope I may be allowed to add that, though I have but little regard for my personal safety amidst the present distress of my country, yet I cannot help feeling some for my character; and I have observed that when the ministers of religion leave the duties of their profession to take a busy part in political matters, they generally fall into contempt, and sometimes even bring discredit to the cause in whose service they are engaged.' This sentence states a principle which should be written in letters of gold.

"That it has been faithfully adhered to by the Catholic Church in the United States no one, we think, even slightly acquainted with its history, will be tempted to doubt. No political discussions have been allowed in our ecclesiastical synods and councils, whose deliberations have been exclusively confined to questions connected with the faith, morals, and discipline of the church. So far as we have been able to ascertain, no bishop or priest of the church has even thought of bringing up such matters in our councils, so general and deep was the conviction that these subjects belong to politicians, and would be wholly out of place in ecclesiastical meetings. As the state has not interfered with the church, she has not sought to interfere with the state. She asks nothing of the state beyond the protection of life and property and the freedom of action accorded to all good and law-abiding citizens, which the state in this country willingly grants; and thus, both church and state move onward in their respective spheres in good understanding and harmony. These principles have been officially proclaimed on all proper occasions. I need but refer to the pastoral letters of the fathers of the Provincial Councils of New York and Cincinnati, held about the beginning of the war, and to the pastoral letter of Archbishop Kenrick of Baltimore, of the same date, who was prevented from holding a council by the troubled condition of his province. These official announcements created no surprise, for they simply declared the fixed, time-honored, and well-known policy of the church in this country. They gave no umbrage to the government, for they were but the expression of the logical consequences of the relations of church and state as they exist in the American Republic."

Bishop Spalding has not here advanced any theory as to the natural and proper relations of the church and state prescinding from pre-existing circumstances. He has simply stated what are the actual relations of the two powers in our political organization, and has shown that the church accepts the situation with the most perfect loyalty, without mental reservation, and with the full and explicit purpose of abiding by all the logical consequences of her position in this country.

In January, 1860, Bishop Spalding began to keep a kind of journal, which he continued down to the time of his translation to the see of Baltimore, in 1864. From this journal I shall make such extracts as in my opinion tend to illustrate his character or to throw light upon his history. During the months of January and February, 1860, he was engaged in revising and preparing for the press his *History of the Reformation*. It had been his intention to deliver, during the winter of 1860, a course of lectures in the cathedral of Louisville, on the "Philosophy of Christianity," but he was prevented by ill health and press of business. He proposed, had he been permitted to deliver these lectures, to publish them. The great tendency to deism and naturalism in religious matters, which exists so generally in this country, called, he thought, for a work which would treat, from an American standpoint, the question of reason and revelation. About the middle of February, he went to Washington City, upon the invitation of Professor Henry, to deliver a course of lectures in the Smithsonian Institution.

"I have been invited by Professor Henry," he wrote to Archbishop Kenrick, "to lecture in the Smithsonian Institution. Before accepting, I should feel more at ease to have the advice and approval of the ordinary, though lecturing is not an ecclesiastical function. I wish also to have your opinion as to the subjects which I should treat. I had thought of lecturing on the history and elements of modern civilization, which would give me an opportunity to state what the Catholic Church has done for society without trenching upon controversial ground."

In a letter to the Archbishop, written after his arrival in Washington, he says: "I lectured last evening to a very large and respectable audience. Professor Henry expressed his entire satisfaction, and requested me to prolong the course, which, on account of my Baltimore engagement, I cannot well do. I trust these lectures may do some good." Before returning home, he lectured in Baltimore, New York, Brooklyn, Boston, and other cities.

It was about this time that Bishop Spalding induced the Brothers of Christian Instruction to open a school in Louisville, and to take charge of the male orphan asylum. A new colony of Xaverian Brothers also arrived from Belgium during the summer of this year. The Franciscan Fathers of the order of Minor Conventuals were received into the diocese in the spring, and later they took charge of St. Peter's church, in Louisville, a German congregation which had recently been established. A house for the Magdalenes had just been erected on Eighth Street, and the Bishop blessed it on the 14th of April. During the greater part of this spring he was occupied in visiting his diocese. In June he received a letter from the rector of the American College in Louvain, recommending that it be placed under the direction of the Propaganda. "This," he writes in his journal, "has already been done substantially by a joint letter of Bishops Lefevre and Spalding." In August, Father Smarius, the Jesuit missionary, preached the retreat for the clergy of the diocese, at the close of which two conferences were held, in which the Bishop, who had attended all the exercises, gave his charge, and promulgated the decrees of the Second Provincial Council of Cincinnati. He also gave to each missionary a bound volume, containing the decrees of the two Diocesan Synods of Louisville, of the two Provincial Councils of Cincinnati, and of the first eight Councils of Baltimore. He thought the best way to develop a more perfect system of ecclesiastical law in this country was to observe faithfully what already exists.

In the fall he continued the visitation of the diocese, which had been interrupted during the summer. New churches had been built within the last year or two in Hawesville, Hickman, Bowling Green, Chicago, Clover Port, Shelbyville, at St. Vincent's, and on Casey Creek. These were all dedicated to divine service. In the beginning of November he preached the retreat for the students of St. Joseph's College, nearly two hundred in number, forty of whom were Protestants. On the 22d of November, St. Cecilia's Day, he delivered the address at the opening of the Catholic Institute in Cincinnati, and on the 2d of December he preached at the solemn consecration of the new church of St. John, in Louisville; and a few weeks later he returned to Cincinnati to preach at the dedication of the beautiful church of St. Xavier.

Whilst in Cincinnati he examined the students in theology and philosophy, of Mount St. Mary's. The diocese of Louisville had at this time fourteen students in theology.

Upon his return he began a course of lectures in the cathedral on the Old Testament. Ever solicitous that even the poorest congregations in his diocese should enjoy the greatest possible spiritual advantages, he appointed, in the beginning of 1861, one of his priests to give missions in the remoter parts of the State.

In March of this year, Bishop Spalding visited the diocese

of Fort Wayne, upon the invitation of Bishop Luers, to lecture in various places for churches that were in debt and for other charitable objects.

Returning home, he preached the retreat at Nazareth, beginning on the Feast of St. Joseph; and then, at the request of Archbishop Purcell, he wrote the pastoral letter of the Third Provincial Council of Cincinnati, which was to be held in May.

CHAPTER XIX.

THE CIVIL WAR AND THE CHURCH IN KENTUCKY—STATE OF THE DIOCESE OF LOUISVILLE—BISHOP SPALDING IS APPOINTED TO THE SEE OF BALTIMORE.

THE danger of civil war was now becoming each day more imminent, and Bishop Spalding enjoined that the prayer for peace should be said in his diocese at all the Masses. At the opening of the Provincial Council, he preached on the peace of God. On almost every page of his journal he gives evidence of the great anxiety which the troubled state of the country caused him to feel. After the first battles, he ordered the solemn service for the dead to be held in all the Catholic churches of the city, and in the cathedral he addressed the multitude which had assembled, exhorting them to pray for the return of peace and brotherly love. A recruiting camp had been formed in Indiana, opposite Louisville, in which large numbers of soldiers were enlisted and got ready for service in the field. Bishop Spalding, thinking only of souls, obtained permission of General Rousseau, who was in command, to send priests to the camp to instruct and prepare the Catholic soldiers before their departure for the scene of war.

By the efforts of the missionaries, nearly all of them were induced to approach the sacraments, which, for many, was the first time in years. Quite a number, indeed, had never received communion before.

The church in Kentucky soon began to feel the evil effects of the war, especially in its institutions of learning, which, when the civil strife broke forth, were in a most prosperous condition. St. Joseph's College, which had nearly two hundred students in 1860, was closed in the fall of 1861, and converted into a hospital, by military authority. At Nazareth, which, during the previous year, had had two hundred and fifty pupils, there were now only forty. St. Mary's College, which for several years had been unable to accommodate all who applied for admission, was left almost without students. St. Thomas', which had been raised to the rank of a Provincial Seminary in the First Council of Cincinnati, and which, at the breaking out of the war, was in quite a prosperous condition, soon languished and declined in consequence of the disturbed and unsettled state of things in Kentucky; and the other academies and schools of the diocese suffered in a similar manner.

In the summer of 1861, Bishop Spalding went East. He preached at the dedication of the church of Our Lady of Peace, at Niagara Falls. At Saratoga he preached again and lectured. In Philadelphia, he gave the retreat to the clergy of the diocese.

During this visit, he received from a well-known priest of Philadelphia a burse of two thousand dollars for St. Thomas' Seminary. He arrived home in September, in time to celebrate the anniversary of the dedication of the cathedral, and to preside at the opening of the mission which was to be preached to the congregation by the well-known Jesuit Fathers, Smarius and Damen. Missions were given, about the same time, to the congregations of St. Patrick and St. John. Six thousand five hundred persons approached the sacraments in the three parishes, and fifty converts were received into the church. In the fall and winter of 1861, the outlook in Kentucky was anything but encouraging. A hundred thousand Federal troops lay between Louisville and Bowling Green, and the State, south of Green

River, was held by a large Confederate force. Everything seemed to indicate that Kentucky was to become the great battle-ground of the war.

"My diocese," wrote Bishop Spalding, "is cut in twain by this unhappy war, and I must attend to souls without entering into the angry political discussion."

He did all that lay in his power to provide for the spiritual wants, and, in a measure, the bodily comfort, of the soldiers, without stopping to enquire on which side they were fighting. To General Anderson, the Federal officer in command of his department, he offered the services of the Sisters of Charity, to nurse gratuitously the sick and wounded. The offer was accepted, and the Sisters were soon placed in charge of most of the hospitals. In those of Louisville alone, there were at one time over four thousand sick and wounded soldiers.

What our noble Sisters did around those beds of agony to alleviate human suffering has not been written. Their deeds belong to God's history, and when the final reckoning is made they, perhaps, may weigh more than victories won or battles lost. In the hospitals of Louisville they baptized over six hundred men, who, when the world was fading from sight, sought the light of heaven. These Sisters of Nazareth also ministered in the hospitals at Paducah, and possibly in other places in Kentucky. In January, 1862, it was rumored that the Nazareth Convent was to be taken possession of by the soldiers, which would have left many of the Sisters without a home. Bishop Spalding, upon hearing the report, at once wrote to General Wood, of the Confederate army, to beg him not to allow the Sisters to be disturbed; and in reply General Wood called himself at Nazareth, to assure the mother-superioress of his protection. He behaved, said Bishop Spalding, like a Kentucky gentleman. "I have endeavored," he wrote in his journal, "to do my duty towards the poor soldiers without regard to the exciting political issues." On the 6th of February he made the following entry: "Sister Catharine died at the hospital from fever, contracted in nursing the sick soldiers. She follows to heaven her good sister, Mary Lucy, who died a few weeks ago, at Paducah, a martyr to charity."

In January, 1862, Bishop Spalding went, with Archbishop Purcell, to visit the camp on Green River. They remained here several days, preaching, hearing confessions, and giving confirmation. "Much good," he writes in his journal, "was accomplished. May God arrest this unhappy war. *Dona nobis pacem.*"

February 13: "The Rev. Joseph Haseltine died suddenly about four o'clock this morning, in the seventy-fourth year of his life. He had risen somewhat earlier than usual, and, when found, he was on his knees, his right hand raised to his forehead, as if in the act of making the sign of the cross."

Father Haseltine was born in Concord, New Hampshire, and was brought up according to the strictest sect of the Puritans. When about twenty-five years old, he went to live in Montreal, where contact with Catholics led him to examine into the doctrines of the church. He was soon convinced that it is the only true church, and on Christmas Day, 1818, he made his solemn profession of faith in the parish church of the Sulpicians, in Montreal. Desiring to devote his life exclusively to the service of God, he was advised by the Sulpicians to apply to Bishop Flaget, at Bardstown. For sixteen years he remained in St. Joseph's College, fulfilling the duties of agent and chief disciplinarian; and, after this long probation, was ordained priest by Bishop David, in 1835. He was soon appointed, at the suggestion of Bishop David, Ecclesiastical Superior of the Nazareth Sisterhood, which office he continued to hold to the day of his death. He was remarkable for his scrupulous exactness and regularity in the performance of every duty. He rose punctually at four o'clock, and devoted two hours to prayer, meditation, and the recitation of the divine office before celebrating Mass, which he invariably began at the first stroke of the community bell. Sickness and the infirmities of age had but sweetened and mellowed in him a disposition naturally gentle.

He was a worthy member of the noble band of early Kentucky priests; and the memory of his peaceful and beautiful life is treasured up in the hearts of those for whom he labored so long and so faithfully. The little of this world's goods that belonged to him he left to the orphans.

In March, 1862, a bill was presented to the Legislature of Kentucky, requiring clergymen to take a test-oath, as a preliminary condition to their being allowed to perform the ceremony of marriage. In a letter to the Governor, Bishop Spalding protested against this bill, as an infringement upon the rights of the church. The assistance of the priest at the marriage contract is, he said, in the eyes of the church, a purely religious act, and since under the Constitution there is no union of church and state, the state has no right to impose conditions upon the performance of spiritual functions.

Taking this as a precedent, the Legislature might demand a test-oath as a condition to the performance of any religious office whatever, which is subversive of all freedom of conscience, and directly opposed to the principles upon which our government is based.

This bill, which passed through both Houses of the Legislature, was prevented from becoming a law, during that session at least, by the veto of Governor Magoffin, who, it seems, approved of the views advanced by Bishop Spalding in his letter of exceptions.

The feeling in favor of the bill, however, was so strong,

that in the following year it was made a law of the State, and Bishop Spalding himself took the oath, under the following protest:

"In compliance with the act of the last Legislature of Kentucky, I, as a law-abiding citizen, take the following oath, deeming it my duty, however, to protest against the same as a precedent, chiefly on the ground, among other reasons, that it requires a civil act as an essential preliminary to the performance of a spiritual office—marriage being regarded by the Catholic Church and by all the *old* churches, embracing nearly five-sixths of Christendom, as a sacrament, and consequently as belonging to the spiritual order, and therefore, according to the spirit of our Constitution, not subject, for its performance by a Christian minister, to merely civil laws."

In August, 1862, the clergy entered into retreat at St. Joseph's College, at the close of which the third and last synod of the diocese of Louisville was held. In synod, Bishop Spalding granted full liberty of discussion, and listened with patience to the suggestions of those who had anything to say, it being his desire that his priests should take part in framing the laws by which they were to be governed. *Judices causarum* were appointed, who, in the presence of the Bishop, took an oath to discharge faithfully the duties of their office; and before them, whoever thought himself wrongly censured or unjustly treated had the right to bring his case.

Scarcely was the synod ended, when General Bragg, at the head of a large army, entered Kentucky, and marched without opposition to within forty miles of Louisville, where the Federal troops were not at all prepared to meet him. The wildest excitement prevailed in the city. General Nelson, who was in command, ordered the women and children to be ready to leave at a moment's notice, as the arrival of the

Confederate army was hourly expected. Indeed, it was reported that Bragg had defeated Buell, and was already in sight of Louisville. Men, who had ascended the towers of the churches, announced that they could see the dust and hear the din of the approaching army. To add to the general terror, Nelson, it was said, intended to burn the city in case he should be forced to abandon it. Thousands crossed the Ohio to seek refuge in Indiana, where some died from exposure.

On the day when the panic was greatest, Bishop Spalding wrote in his journal: "God knows what is best for his own glory, and, after chastising us for our manifold sins, he will have mercy and spare us. For myself, I am resolved, with his holy grace, to live and die with my children. I shall not leave my post, nor the sanctuary which I love. There my bones may be laid in the tomb prepared for me by the side of my saintly predecessor. This is my last will and testament, not knowing what to-morrow may bring forth. God help me and my people; may our sweet Mother in heaven smile upon and protect us in this hour of direst need."

September 29, he adds:

"This morning General Nelson was shot in the Galt House. Alas! the poor soul of the fallen."

During this time of tribulation, Bishop Spalding had novenas for the peace and safety of the country offered up in all the churches and religious communities of the diocese. "Christ will hear us," he writes, "and his Mother will be our Mother in this day of our greatest woe. I have the fullest confidence in her, my own sweet Mother in heaven." To add to Bishop Spalding's sorrows, the Jesuits wished, at this time, to give up St. Joseph's College, and to leave the diocese. The college had been closed, and affairs were so unsettled that they preferred to go where they could do greater good. The Bishop, however, could not consent to lose them, and he therefore strenuously opposed them in their desire to leave Kentucky.

A lengthy correspondence between himself and the Visitor of the order took place on the subject, the result of which was, that the Jesuits agreed to remain until the close of the war, provided the Bishop should consent to allow them to withdraw then, in case they should be unable longer to carry on the college.

To this Bishop Spalding gave his assent, upon condition that the question should be left to the final decision of the Metropolitan of Cincinnati or of St. Louis, to both of whom he submitted copies of the correspondence. The matter rested here, and Bishop Spalding was spared the grief of seeing the Jesuits leave Kentucky, so long as he remained Bishop of Louisville.

July 8, 1863, he makes the following entry in his journal: "The greatest, the best, and the most learned of our prelates was found dead in his bed this morning. The venerable Dr. Kenrick is no more in this world, but is doubtless in heaven praying for us."

Little more than a year before, Archbishop Kenrick had written the following note to Bishop Spalding, which almost seems prophetic of his own death:

"I thank you for communicating the intelligence of the death of good Mr. Haseltine, who, I trust, was well prepared to meet his Master. Father Nicholas Steinbacher, S.J., the German translator of my *Primacy*, died still more suddenly, a few days ago, at Boston. He was found dead in his bed. He was a priest of learning and zeal. We know not the day or the hour. Father Steinbacher was of my age."

The suffering and distress caused by the war, which seemed to grow more bloody with time, which brought no hope of peace, threw a gloom over Bishop Spalding's thoughts. "The future of our church, as of our country," he wrote, " is very uncertain. Everything looks dark. But the church will stand, however persecuted. *Deus Providebit.*"

July 17.—" I went to Indianapolis, to lecture to a meeting, over which the mayor presided, with a view to establish a house of the Sisters of the Good Shepherd in that city. Several speeches by Protestant gentlemen, confirmatory of my remarks, and various offers of contributions, were made."

Two days later, he preached at the dedication of the new church in Logansport, Indiana, and in the evening he lectured to a large audience, many of whom were Protestants. He thence proceeded to Buffalo, where he preached twice. Of Bishop Timon he writes: " How I admired his zeal and his works. *Et omnia quæcunque faciet, prosperabuntur.*" In August, he lectured in the cathedral of Cincinnati, before a convention for establishing a normal school. In the same month, he preached at the consecration of the cathedral of Buffalo, and thence went to Canada to deliver lectures in Hamilton and Toronto. Returning home, he made arrangements to have missions given, during the fall, in all the principal country congregations of his diocese. These missions, which were preached by two bands of Jesuit Fathers, reawakened the faith and zeal of the Catholic populations, and also led to the conversion of a great many Protestants.

During the fall and winter of 1863, Bishop Spalding prepared for the press and published the *Eight Days' Retreat* of Father David, who had been his own spiritual director. " I could have wished," he says, with a modesty which was not assumed, " that some one more skilled in the spiritual life had undertaken to edit this work. But, having failed in my efforts to induce some member of the Society of Jesus to

State of the Diocese of Louisville. 253

perform the task, I decided to do the best I could under the circumstances; and for this purpose, I drew on my notes of retreats which were preached to the students of the Propaganda College in Rome, about thirty years ago, by some of the most eminent disciples of St. Ignatius, including the General of the order."

Of the twenty-four meditations which make up the eight days' retreat, three were wanting in the manuscript of Bishop David. These were supplied by Bishop Spalding, who also added whatever he thought necessary to make the manual more complete.

The biographical sketch of Bishop David, which serves as an introduction to the volume, is full of interest, and is another instance of the loving care with which Dr. Spalding has sought to embalm the memory of his early teachers.

This brings us down to 1864, in which year Bishop Spalding was appointed to fill the see of Baltimore, made vacant by the death of Archbishop Kenrick.

In 1848, when he was made Coadjutor of Bishop Flaget, the whole Catholic population of the State of Kentucky was probably thirty thousand. Sixteen years had since elapsed, and within that period Eastern Kentucky had been formed into a separate diocese, with the see at Covington. In 1864, the Catholic population of the diocese of Louisville alone was seventy thousand—more than double that of the entire State in 1848. In 1848, there were but forty-three Catholic churches in the State; in 1864, there were eighty-five in the diocese of Louisville.

There had been a proportionate increase in the number of priests.

During his administration of sixteen years, five new churches had been built in the city of Louisville, including the cathedral, which alone was capable of accommodating as many people as all the Catholic churches of the city at the time of his consecration, whilst two of the old churches of the city had been considerably enlarged.

Parochial schools had been organized, for which Bishop Spalding had secured the services of religious Brothers and Sisters, who had in their charge nearly as many children as frequented the public schools of the city. The diocese was well supplied with colleges and academies for the demands of higher education. The number of religious women in the diocese, belonging to the different communities, and devoting their lives to the service of God and their neighbor, was not less than six hundred.

In building churches and in making other improvements, no debts not easily manageable had been contracted.

Outside of what might in the stricter sense be called church property, the diocese possessed valuable real estate in Louisville and Chicago, which, together with a considerable amount of bank and railroad stock, served as a sinking-fund, whilst it enabled the Bishop to render assistance in starting new churches, and in helping on works of charity.

Conferences of St. Vincent de Paul had been established, which served the double purpose of giving relief to the poor, and of holding the men in the congregations where the society existed to the practice of their religious duties. In the synods and diocesan statutes, Bishop Spalding had done all that could be done to introduce law and uniformity of practice in the government of the diocese, and the result was a union of love and confidence between Bishop, priests, and people.

Slavery and the fanaticism of the Louisville Know-Nothings had, in a great measure, prevented immigration into Kentucky, and the increase of the Catholic population was, in consequence, less rapid there than in some other parts of the Republic; but nowhere were efforts more honest or earnest made to meet the wants of the growing church of this country, than in the diocese of Louisville whilst Bishop Spalding was at its head.

When, therefore, on the 11th of June, 1864, he received the Papal rescript which elevated him to the first and most honorable position in the church of the United States, though this mark of confidence from the highest ecclesiastical authority, which was also a recognition of his services in the cause of religion, could not but be pleasing to a nature keenly sensible to kindness and to the sympathetic appreciation of friends, yet the newly conferred dignity was associated in Bishop Spalding's mind with painful rather than pleasurable feelings. In Kentucky he was at home, surrounded by kindred and by friends, tried and true, who had grown up with him, and whose love from long continuance had become almost a necessity; so that, as he himself expressed it, his very heart-strings were torn and lacerated by this sudden severance.

His relations with his priests were those of an older with younger brothers. They trusted him, and, with but few exceptions, loved him. In the religious institutions of the diocese, which were "his joy and his crown," he was as a father in the midst of the most devoted children, whose eyes were brighter and whose voices were merrier because he was there. Much that he beheld around him to gladden his heart he himself had built up. There were no financial troubles to embarrass or discourage him. In his brother, the Very Rev. Dr. Spalding, who, as the truest of friends, had stood by his side during his whole episcopal life, he possessed an adviser whose business capacity and practical judgment could hardly be surpassed.

No longer young, and in feeble health, every natural sentiment would have inclined him to remain in Kentucky, and to walk quietly down the slope of life, surrounded and supported by those to whom he had given all his best years. But he had never sought his own ease at the price of duty, and though he loved Kentucky and the church of Kentucky, he loved the great cause for which Christ suffered and died still more, and when his Vicar laid the burden on his shoulders, he braced himself with a brave heart to bear it as became a Christian bishop, saying with his patron, St. Martin of Tours, "*Non recuso laborem.*"

He had been a bishop too long to be fascinated by the glitter of the purple, or to imagine that advancement to a higher dignity meant anything else than more labor and greater responsibility. He therefore accepted the appointment to the see of Baltimore in the spirit of the words of Pius IX. in announcing to him his elevation, "as the will of Providence." *Sequere providentiam* was his favorite and oft-repeated motto.

One of his last official acts as Bishop of Louisville was to assemble his council, that the members, as representing the clergy of the diocese, might make known their wishes concerning the choice of his successor.

CHAPTER XX.

ARCHBISHOP SPALDING TAKES POSSESSION OF HIS NEW CHARGE — SUMMARY OF IMPORTANT FACTS IN THE HISTORY OF THE ARCHDIOCESE OF BALTIMORE.

ANY attempt on the part of the state to interfere in the appointment of bishops is irreconcilable with the American theory of government. This question was settled at the time of the establishment of the hierarchy in this country, shortly after we became an independent nation. Before the Revolution, the Catholics of the British Provinces of North America were, in spiritual matters, under the immediate jurisdiction of the Vicar Apostolic of London. But when we had thrown off the authority of Great Britain, the welfare and prosperity of the church here demanded that it should have a separate and independent organization. Representations of the necessity of a change in our ecclesiastical status were made to the Pope, who decided upon the appointment of a Vicar Apostolic for the United States.

So little, however, in that day, was the spirit of the American government understood by even the most intelligent persons, that it was thought necessary first to ask the consent of Congress, and to receive from that body suggestions as to the most suitable person for the new office. With this view, the Papal Nuncio, at Paris, in 1783, addressed a note to Dr. Franklin, who at the time represented the government of this country at the Court of France, requesting him to bring the subject before the Congress of the United States. When the question was submitted to Congress, that body very properly decided that it had nothing to say on the subject.

The precedent thus established of non-interference in matters appertaining to the jurisdiction of the church has been, almost without exception, adhered to by the Government of this country. But when, during the excitement of the late civil war, which seemed to threaten our national existence, the two most important sees—those of Baltimore and New York—became vacant, there seemed for a while to be a disposition to meddle with the liberty of action of the church in the choice of bishops. The urgency of the times had given to the authorities in Washington a power which they had never before exercised; and, as power often gains increase of appetite from what it feeds upon, they were inclined to stretch their jurisdiction as far as possible, without having any very nice regard for the limits assigned to it by the organic law of the land.

Bishop Spalding, under date of February 7, 1864, makes the following entry in his journal: "There appears to be no doubt that the Government has interfered at Rome in regard to the appointments to the sees of Baltimore and New York."

This brief sentence is the only reference which I have been able to find among his papers to a subject to which he seems not to have given more than a passing thought. Whether or not objections were made to him personally, I do not know; nor would the knowledge throw any light upon his history.

The see of Baltimore is not only the oldest in the United States, but it is also the first in point of dignity. For several years after the establishment of the hierarchy, in 1789, it was the only diocese in this country; and when, in 1808, bishops were given to Boston, New York, Philadelphia, and Bardstown, Baltimore was raised to the dignity of an archiepiscopal see. By a decree of the Congregation of Propaganda, confirmed by Pius IX. on the 25th of July, 1858, the prerogative of place is granted to the see of Baltimore, so that in councils, assemblies, and meetings of every kind precedency is given to the Archbishop of Baltimore for the time being, and the seat of honor above any of the archbishops of these provinces that may be present, without regard to the order of promotion or consecration. At the time of the appointment of Bishop Carroll, Baltimore was not thought of at Rome as his episcopal city; but Philadelphia was considered the most proper place for the first see of the country, chiefly no doubt because it was then the seat of the American government. But, for reasons which are obvious, it was finally determined to locate the seat of episcopal authority in the old Maryland colony. "They fixed upon Baltimore," wrote Dr. Carroll, "this being the principal town of Maryland, and that State being the oldest and still the most numerous residence of true religion in America."

The appointment of Bishop Spalding to fill the see of Baltimore, made vacant by the death of Archbishop Kenrick, met with the almost universal approval of the Catholics of this country. Many of the bishops and priests expressed their great satisfaction with the choice made by the Holy Father in terms the most complimentary. "No sooner had Almighty God," wrote Archbishop Odin, "called to himself the great and good Dr. Kenrick, than all eyes were turned towards the Bishop of Louisville as the person in every way qualified to fill that important see." Probably no one could have been chosen who would have been more acceptable either to the clergy or the laity of the Archdiocese of Baltimore. His record as Bishop of Louisville gave assurance of his administrative ability; whilst the honorable name which he had made for himself by his writings and other labors in the cause of the church, inspired the confident belief that he would be a not unworthy successor of Carroll and Kenrick. He came not among the Catholics of Maryland as a stranger. They but welcomed home a not degenerate son of the Pilgrims of Lord Baltimore.

"I have this moment," wrote Father Coskery, the Administrator of the diocese, to Archbishop Spalding, "received a letter from Cardinal Barnabo, announcing the fact that you have been appointed our archbishop. Be assured, beloved Father and Archbishop, that no other appointment could have given an equal amount of satisfaction either to the clergy or the people of your new charge. We have all long loved you, because we have known you either personally or by reputation. In receiving you, it will not seem to us that we are receiving a stranger, but a long-known and tenderly-loved father. With one acclaim of joy, Baltimore will greet you her seventh archbishop."

Bishop O'Connor, in whose death the American Church has lost one of her most gifted and most exemplary sons, wrote as follows to Archbishop Spalding:

"There were rumors of your declining this honor in case it were proffered. I cannot believe that you had any such intention, though the bare possibility of the thing will, I trust, excuse my alluding to it. You have too much wisdom not to see that in such affairs the safest course is to leave one's self in the hands of Providence. You know too much, I am sure, of what such honors imply, to think them worth running from or running after; and, as to any other difficulties that I can see, they should certainly yield to the voice of Providence, which will be manifested in the appointment. It may be no harm for an outsider, whose testimony you may consider in such an affair reliable, to give his opinion, as I do, that your reception by the people of Baltimore will be warm, by the clergy cordial, and that in all you will find sincere support. As a disinterested party, I was able to form an idea on this subject, and my expression of it may carry conviction better than that of others whose feelings may be considered as enlisted."

Archbishop Spalding took possession of his new see on the 31st of July, 1864.

" I consider it a fortunate circumstance," said he, in his inaugural address, "that in the Providence of God I am enabled to begin my duties in the Province of Baltimore on this day, the Festival of St. Ignatius Loyola, the patron of the missions of Maryland"; and, after a discourse, of great breadth of view, on St. Ignatius, and the significance of his work in the church, he applied the lesson thence to be drawn to himself in this new mission which the Vicar of Christ had entrusted to him. The weak things of the world are chosen of God to confound the strong. Though the instrument be poor, yet in the hands of God it may do wonders. " I may not hope," he continued, "to fill the place made vacant by the departure to his rest of the venerated Kenrick; but it must be my aim, with the help of God and the Blessed Virgin, and encouraged by your prayers, brethren, to emulate his bright example, and to follow, if I can, in his footsteps. He was my friend ; I knew him well ; and it is because I knew him so well, that I feel how difficult it will be to fill in your hearts the place which he occupied."

There were many traits of resemblance in the characters of Archbishop Kenrick and Archbishop Spalding, though the two men were very unlike. Both were gentle and simple, innocent and good themselves, and unsuspicious of evil in others.

Archbishop Kenrick was reserved. He gave expression to his sentiments in a quiet, subdued way, as though the outer world were not his home ; and he seemed at once, without effort, to sink back into the sanctuary of his inner life.

Archbishop Spalding, on the contrary, was demonstrative. There was a merry ring in his laugh, suggestive of the undeceived heart of childhood. He had not the art of concealing anything—he thought aloud. He had, too, a plain, blunt way of telling the brutal truth, which sometimes gave offence, and which often astonished those who knew best his perfect gentleness of heart. Both were remarkable for the thoroughness with which their whole nature had been absorbed and remoulded by the spirit of religion. Having come forth from the same school, their theological opinions and views in matters not strictly of faith very generally coincided.

Both of them had found the rare secret of uniting a life of great activity and of manifold external duties with that of the conscientious student, and were thus able, whilst laboring incessantly to build up the church, to become also the guides and directors of Catholic thought, and to enrich the literature of the American church with some of its most important works. Yet Archbishop Spalding was more a man of action than Archbishop Kenrick, and consequently less really a student. The writings of the one were more popular, breathed more the spirit of the busy, moving age; those of the other were more learned, partook more of the fixed and immobile character of the truth which they were intended to defend and illustrate. Archbishop Spalding probably knew more of men, and understood better how to develop and put to proper use the energies of those whom he governed, whilst Archbishop Kenrick was the profounder scholar. Both were alike distinguished by their thoroughly Catholic instincts, which seemed almost unerringly to incline them in thought and action to that which is in most perfect accord with the spirit of the church; and hence they both cherished a tender and filial devotion to the Vicar of Christ as to the visible centre and fountain-head of Catholic unity and life. Apart from the importance which at all times belongs to the see of Baltimore, special circumstances existed when Archbishop Spalding was called to fill it which seemed to demand more than ordinary prudence and wisdom in the person upon whom this honor was conferred.

The Civil war was still raging, and no one could foresee its end or predict what the final result would be. Maryland, like Kentucky, was a border State, which had already been occupied by both armies, and might again become the scene of great battles. The Catholics, like the other citizens of that State, were divided in their political opinions and sympathies.

The death of Archbishop Kenrick had been hastened, as some thought, by the frightful calamities which he saw around him, and by the fear lest still greater evils should come upon his people.

The District of Columbia, too, formed part of the Archdiocese of Baltimore; and, should any misunderstanding arise between the church and the Government in consequence of the troubled and uncertain condition of affairs, it would naturally fall to the Archbishop to represent the ecclesiastical authority.

The manner in which Bishop Spalding had met the difficulties of his position, as Bishop of Louisville, was well known to the Court of Rome; and his appointment to the see of Baltimore, in view of this fact, cannot but be considered as a most valuable endorsement of the wisdom and prudence of his conduct. In other respects, the administration of the diocese of Baltimore presented but little difficulty compared with that which existed in newer and less perfectly organized portions of the church.

A brief statement of what had already been done will serve to throw light upon the task which Archbishop Spalding had to perform.

The history of the Catholic Church within the present territory of the United States reaches back to a time when Protestantism had not yet come into existence. The story of the heroic and saintly lives of the Catholic missionaries who bore the light of faith to the Indians of North America from 1512, when Florida was discovered, down to 1776, when we became an independent people, and even to a more recent date, is fit to be written on the brightest pages of the church's annals. In California, in Texas, in Florida, in the countries that lie around the great lakes of the Northwest, in New York, in Maine, those apostolic men labored with a zeal, an earnestness, often with a success, that recall the first ages of the church.

But with the extinction of the aboriginal tribes, the results of their work, for the most part, disappeared; and their sufferings and their deeds may be hardly said to form part of the history of the present church of the United States. From the landing of Lord Baltimore, in 1634, to the end of the war of Independence, the church scarcely had a recognized existence in the British Colonies, and made little progress.

Outside of Maryland there were no Catholics, if we except a few who were scattered through Pennsylvania, where they received a kind of toleration of contempt. But with liberty of conscience came the signs of awakening life.

Dr. Carroll, in 1788, the year before his consecration as Bishop of Baltimore, laid the foundation of Georgetown College, which was opened in 1791, when Washington City had not yet been laid out. In the same year (1791), M. Nagot founded the Theological Seminary in Baltimore. Down to 1790, there was not a community of religious women in the United States. In that year, Father Charles Neale, the brother of the future Archbishop, brought over from Antwerp four Carmelite nuns, three of whom were Americans, the fourth being an English lady. A house was purchased for them near Port Tobacco, on the Potomac, where they established the first convent of women in this country.*

In 1792, a few members of the order of Poor Clares, who had been driven from France by the Revolution, settled in Georgetown; but they sold their convent to Bishop Neale in 1805, and returned to their native land. In the house which he had bought from the Poor Clares Bishop Neale placed the "Pious Ladies," as they were called, who, without taking special vows or wearing a distinctive habit, led the lives of religious, until they finally adopted the rule of the order of the Visitation. This was the beginning of the Georgetown Convent, which has since rendered such great services to religion. In May, 1805, Bishop Carroll, having previously obtained permission from the General of the order, reorganized the Society of Jesus in the United States. Six fathers, who had been members of the society before its suppression, were readmitted, and others soon arrived from Europe. They at once took charge of the college at Georgetown, which, under their management, soon rose to a high rank among the institutions of learning in the United States.

In 1808, the Rev. John Dubois, afterwards Bishop of New York, opened a college near Emmitsburg, Maryland, to which he gave the name of Mount St. Mary's. The year following, Mother Seton founded the first house of the Sisters of Charity in this country, at a short distance from Father Dubois' seminary.

The influence of these institutions, though by no means

---

* An Ursuline Convent was founded in 1727 in New Orleans, which at that time belonged to France.

confined to Maryland, has been more especially felt in the Archdiocese of Baltimore.

The Sulpicians opened a college in Baltimore in 1799, which prospered for many years, but was finally closed in 1850. Its place was supplied by Loyola College, established by the Jesuits in 1852.

The Brothers of the Christian Schools came to Baltimore in 1846, at the invitation of Archbishop Eccleston, and opened a novitiate and school in Calvert Hall, which had been ceded to them for this purpose by the trustees of the cathedral. In the same year, the Brothers of St. Patrick arrived, and took charge of the male department of the school attached to St. Patrick's Church. Archbishop Eccleston succeeded also in securing the services of the Redemptorists and Lazarists. The former devoted themselves more particularly to the German Catholic population of Baltimore, which was fast becoming an important element of the church's strength in that city. The zeal which they manifested in the cause of Catholic education was especially commendable. Another event connected with Archbishop Eccleston's administration was the founding of St. Charles' College, near Ellicott's Mills. This institution, for which the church is indebted to the munificence of Charles Carroll, is a preparatory seminary, in which boys who give evidence of a vocation to the priesthood are fitted for the study of theology. The college was opened in 1848, and was placed in charge of the Fathers of St. Sulpice. Benevolent institutions for the relief of the various forms of human suffering had been called into existence from time to time by the six venerable men who had successively occupied the archiepiscopal chair of Baltimore. The number of churches and of priests was large, though insufficient for the rapidly growing Catholic population. The cathedral, the cornerstone of which was laid by Archbishop Carroll in 1806, was solemnly dedicated in 1821. Although in the rapid progress of the age it has long since ceased to hold the first rank among our churches in architectural beauty, yet there is none which can compare with it in the number and sacredness of its historical associations, which belong to the entire American church, and which of themselves will be sufficient to preserve it from desecration should the erection of a new cathedral become necessary.

Archbishop Spalding seems to have won the confidence and even the affection of the Catholics of Maryland, from his first appearance among them. Any regrets he may have felt in leaving Kentucky he kept to himself, as not concerning others, and he now had no thought but to identify himself with the people among whom God's Providence had placed him.

It did not take any one long to get acquainted with Archbishop Spalding. His character was perfectly transparent. His thoughts and aims were above reproach, and he spoke them out with entire frankness. He was neither non-committal nor self-absorbed. In his new position, he did not in the least change his mode of life, but remained as simple and unpretending as the poorest priest in his diocese. If people found fault with him, it was because he was, they thought, too plain, and did not attach sufficient importance to ceremony—the pomp and circumstance of office.

He was always ready to see any one who called upon him; prepared to give advice, to speak words of consolation, to talk of business; or, if the occasion required it, to chat pleasantly about the most indifferent things. He himself took the first opportunity to visit his priests and his people, and in a very short time he was quite at home in Baltimore. He made but few changes in the beginning, desiring first to become familiar with the customs and usages of the diocese, as well as with the sentiments and views of his priests, which he wished, as far as possible, to respect. He began by directing his attention to the poor and the children of his charge.

He made appeals in behalf of the various orphan asylums, and established in Baltimore the Conferences of St. Vincent de Paul, whose special mission is to provide for the spiritual and temporal wants of the poor. He visited the various schools, and sought to awaken a more lively interest in the cause of Catholic education.

CHAPTER XXI.

ARCHBISHOP SPALDING'S FIRST WORKS IN THE DIOCESE OF BALTIMORE—THE SYLLABUS—THE SIXTH SYNOD OF BALTIMORE—CORRESPONDENCE ON VARIOUS SUBJECTS.

NE of the first events which marked Archbishop Spalding's administration was the founding of a convent of the Good Shepherd, in Baltimore, by sisters from the mother-house in Louisville, a site having been given for the purpose by Mrs. Emily McTavish.

When he had got rid of the press of more urgent business, he entered upon the visitation of his diocese, during which he administered confirmation in one hundred and twelve places to about eight thousand persons, eight hundred and fifty of whom were converts.

In connection with this visitation, and also to urge the faithful to gain the indulgence of the fifth Jubilee proclaimed by Pius IX., missions were preached to the principal congregations of the diocese. In the cathedral, over six thousand persons approached the sacraments. During the first year of his administration, he finished and decorated the cathedral, which he had found incomplete. A gift of fifteen thousand dollars from one of the most generous Catholic gentlemen of Baltimore enabled him to enlarge the archiepiscopal residence. This was very agreeable to him, as he desired to be able to offer hospitality to his priests when they visited the city. This had been his custom in Louisville, and he desired to keep up the Scriptural injunction in Baltimore.

Besides being proper in itself, it encouraged, he thought, mutual confidence and cordiality. It gave him real pleasure, too, to entertain his priests, and he was never better pleased than when surrounded by them. His soul was in the work which they were doing, and their presence gave him an opportunity of talking of that of which his heart was full. His government was wholly free from anything like espionage. He would have been as unfit for this as he was incapable of it.

When a charge worthy of notice was made against a priest, Archbishop Spalding never failed to make it known to him; not that he believed him guilty, but that he might give him an opportunity of freeing himself from unjust suspicion. When the proof of guilt was too strong to admit of doubt, he was firm in the course which, after a thorough investigation of the case, he thought proper to pursue—above all, when there was danger to souls. *Salus populi suprema lex* was a rule of conduct from which he never knowingly swerved. Charity must be shown to the lambs of the flock, he used to say, not to the wolves. He felt that he could show his priests no greater kindness than by doing all that lay in his power to preserve the dignity and purity of the clerical body free from attaint.

"I did not," he wrote to a clergyman, "attach any importance to the charges made against you, of whom, from all that I knew, I had a good opinion. Still, I thought it due to yourself that you should be informed of them. Your explanation is satisfactory, and I bid you God-speed in your labors, which you should continue for the glory of God."

The knowledge of the various parishes and missions of the diocese, which Archbishop Spalding had gained through the visitation, convinced him that the interests of religion demanded that a greater number of priests should be employed in the work of the ministry.

He therefore sought to make arrangements to get missionaries from All-Hallows, near Dublin; and, with the same view, he became, as Archbishop of Baltimore, a patron of the American College at Louvain, by paying a thousand dollars.

From these sources, as well as from his own seminary, he was soon able to get priests for the more pressing demands of his diocese. During his first visitation, he took measures to have not less than twenty new churches built, nearly all of which were to be ready for service within a year. He preached in all the churches which he visited, and frequently lectured. He was not content with hurrying through the diocese merely to give confirmation, but sought to become acquainted with the people, that he might be able to form a better judgment concerning their spiritual wants. He listened with interest to anything they might propose, and showed himself anxious to co-operate with them in whatever regarded the good of their souls.

His judgment in practical affairs was excellent. Though he cared as little for money as any man, yet no one knew its value better than he. He had the faculty of perceiving almost at once what were the resources of a congregation, and he consequently understood what enterprises were to be pushed forward, and what were to be discouraged.

It is the easiest thing in the world, he used to say, in reference to church enterprises, to contract debts, and the hardest to pay them.

He was also opposed to accepting pious donations clogged with conditions, which, he said, often defeat the end of the donors, and render the gift valueless.

Though prudent, he was never timid in undertaking what his mature judgment led him to believe serviceable to the cause of religion.

Like all men who work, he had great faith in the power of effort, and was not, therefore, easily frightened by difficulties.

In November, 1864, Archbishop Spalding preached at the dedication of the magnificent cathedral of Philadelphia, which had been begun by Bishop Kenrick, continued by Bishop Neuman, and finally completed by Bishop Wood. Whenever he could find respite from his arduous labors, he was still willing to lecture for objects of benevolence.

February 9, 1865, he wrote: "I have just finished my Pastoral on the Jubilee. I attempt to defend the Pontiff and the Encyclical from the American stand-point. In view of the howl of indignation which has gone forth from England and America, I thought a vindication opportune."

The Pastoral to which Archbishop Spalding refers in the words just quoted attracted considerable attention from both the religious and the secular press of the country. The first edition, in pamphlet form, was almost immediately taken up.

"Always learned and eloquent," wrote a leading Catholic editor, "Archbishop Spalding seems to us never so impressive in other writings as in his Pastorals. It is there we find the fervor and power of the ancient doctors and fathers of the church, united with a keen appreciation of the needs of these last days."

The outcry was that the Pope had condemned all the most sacred principles of our Government. To this Archbishop Spalding replied that "to stretch the words of the Pontiff, evidently intended for the stand-point of European radicals and infidels, so as to make them include the state of things established in this country by our Constitution in regard to liberty of conscience, of worship, and of the press, were manifestly unfair and unjust. Divided as we were in religious sentiment from the very origin of our Government, our fathers acted most prudently and wisely in adopting, as an amendment to the Constitution, the organic article that 'Congress shall make no law respecting the establishment of religion or prohibiting the free exercise thereof.' In adopting this amendment, they certainly did not intend, like the European radical disciples of Tom Paine and the French Revolution, to pronounce all religions, whether true or false, equal before God, but only to declare them equal before the law; or rather, simply to lay down the sound and equitable principle that the civil government, adhering strictly to its own appropriate sphere of political duty, pledged itself not to interfere with religious matters, which it rightly viewed as entirely without the bounds of its competency. The founders of our Government were, thank God! neither latitudinarians nor infidels; they were earnest, honest men; and, however much some of them may have been personally lukewarm in the matter of religion, or may have differed in religious opinions, they still professed to believe in Christ and his revelation; and they exhibited a commendable respect for religious observances.*

* "In recent times," these are the words of one of the most thoughtful writers of this century, " European democracy has signalized itself lamentably by its attacks upon religion—a circumstance which, far from favoring its cause, has very seriously injured it. We can, indeed, form an idea of a government more or less free when society is virtuous, moral, and religious; but not when these conditions are wanting. In the latter case, the only form of government that is possible is despotism, the rule of force; for force alone can govern men who are without conscience and without God. If we consider attentively the points of difference between the Revolution of the United States and that of France, we shall find one of the principal to be this—that the American Revolution was essentially democratic; that of France essentially impious. In the manifestoes by which the former was inaugurated, the name of God, of Providence, is everywhere seen; the men engaged in the perilous enterprise of shaking off the yoke of Great Britain, far from blaspheming the Almighty, invoke his assistance, convinced that the cause of independence was the cause of reason and justice. The French began by deifying the leaders of irreligion, overthrowing altars, watering with the blood of priests the temples, the streets, and the scaffolds. The only emblem of revolution recognized by the people is atheism hand in hand with liberty. This folly has borne its

All other matters contained in the *Encyclical*, as well as the long catalogue of eighty propositions condemned in its Appendix or Syllabus, are to be judged of by the same standard. These propositions are condemned in the sense of those who uttered and maintained them, and in no other. To be fair in our interpretation, we must never lose sight of the lofty stand-point of the Pontiff, who steps forth as the champion of law and order against anarchy and revolution, and of revealed religion against more or less openly avowed infidelity. Nor should we forget the stand-point of those whose errors he condemns, who openly or covertly assail all revealed religion, and seek to sap the very foundations of all well-ordered society; who threaten to bring back the untold horrors of the French Revolution, and to make the streets and the highways run with the blood of the best and noblest citizens. Their covert attacks on religion and society are, perhaps, even more formidable than their open assaults. Against the latter the virtuous are really guarded and armed; against the former, which often bear the appearance of good, and whose evil drift is not so easily perceived, we are not so well prepared, and the poison of error is often insidiously instilled into the hearts of the well disposed but simple-minded before they even think of guarding against the danger."

I have found the following reference to the doctrines of the Syllabus in one of Archbishop Spalding's letters:

"Whilst I adhere *ex corde* to the principles enunciated in the Syllabus, I yet look upon them *in concreto et in subjecta materia;* not generalizing what is special, and not stretching

---

fruits; it communicated its fatal contagion to other revolutions in recent times; the new order of things has been inaugurated with sacrilegious crimes; and the proclamation of the rights of man began by the profanation of the temples of Him from whom all rights emanate."—Balmes' *Protestantism and Catholicity*, p. 389.

the meaning of the propositions beyond that inferable from the circumstances to which they were applied. Freedom of worship is condemned when it implies a right not given by Christ, and insists on the right of introducing false religion into a country where it does not exist. It is not only not censurable, but commendable, and the only thing practicable in countries like ours. I reason in a similar manner concerning the liberty of the press, and progress, in the American and Anglo-Saxon, not in the liberal European, sense. There is a wide distinction, and any attempt to confound things so far apart would be wrong and nugatory, putting us in a false position—in an untenable one, in fact. I should say the same with regard to church and state. The principle is right enough ; but its application must vary with the ever-changing conditions of human society."

At the close of the retreat, which he himself preached to his priests in May, 1865, Archbishop Spalding held a diocesan synod—the sixth of Baltimore. In this synod, he urged the pastors to use greater efforts to foster vocations to the priesthood. It was his desire that each of them should select two boys among the children of his parish to be sent to the preparatory seminary of St. Charles. "We trust," he said, in the Pastoral which he published on this occasion, "that faith will be awakened and stimulated to more active exertions, and that Catholic parents will deem it the greatest possible honor and happiness for their families to have one or more of their sons become priests of God. It was so in the early Catholic history of Maryland. Why should it not be so now? Has the spirit of the Neales and the Fenwicks become extinct in the bosoms of their descendants? Should not the uncertainty and vicissitudes of the times tend to convince all reflecting minds blessed with Catholic faith of the utter instability of human affairs, and of the wisdom of choosing the better part? Or is it better for the Christian father and mother to train up their sons to become the votaries and servants of an uncertain and treacherous world than to rear them up with a taste and desire for the sublime ministry of God's altar? At the hour of death, will the wealthy Catholic parent be more comforted by the reflection that he leaves his son heir to his riches—perhaps ungratefully to squander them—or by the thought that he leaves one behind him who will often do what St. Monica on her death-bed begged her dear son, St. Augustine, to do—to remember her at the holy altar?"

A decree was passed in this synod, requiring that children who have not made their first communion shall be heard in confession four times a year during the *Quatuor Tempora*. To encourage greater devotion to the saints, Archbishop Spalding recommended that the festival of the patronal or titular saint of each church should be celebrated with due solemnity.

"Whom God has so honored," he says, in his synodical address, "surely we may honor; whom he has crowned in heaven, we may surely invoke on earth. While the holy example of the saints is a powerful stimulant to our own feeble efforts, the brilliancy of their crowns in heaven fills us with admiration, and inspires us with emulation; and their prayers, poured out to God near his throne in our behalf, will greatly aid us in passing through the perils of this earthly pilgrimage, and in reaching at length the blessed home which they have already entered, and where they are now happy with bliss unutterable. The devout observance of their festivals will tend to keep alive in our hearts these salutary feelings, while it will, moreover, cause us to approximate to the general usage of the church in Catholic countries."

The number of days on which the benediction of the Blessed Sacrament was permitted to be given in the diocese was increased, that greater opportunity of cultivating devotion to our divine Saviour, in the chief mystery of his love, might be offered to the faithful.

Catholics were urged to become members of the Association for the Propagation of the Faith, and of the kindred one, the Society of the Holy Childhood. "Both these associations," said the Archbishop, "will commend themselves to every Catholic heart; and while millions are annually contributed by Protestants in the zealous but wholly ineffectual attempt to convert the heathen, surely Catholics, whose missionaries do succeed, to a marvellous extent, in this blessed work, will not remain behind in their zeal for the salvation of souls and the consequent generosity of their contributions."

A statute of this synod required pastors to explain to the people from the pulpit, at least once a year, the nature and wisdom of the ecclesiastical laws relative to marriage. In his address, the Archbishop referred to the subject of the intermarriage of Catholics and Protestants. "Mixed marriages," he said, "are commonly attended with many inconveniences and difficulties; sometimes with the very worst results to the piety and faith of the Catholic party. The children of such alliances are very frequently reared up without suitable religious instruction, and they often become indifferentists or practical infidels. It is usually difficult enough, particularly in this country, for parents, when both are Catholics, to guard their children against the influence of the pernicious examples by which they are surrounded, and to bring them up as practical and devout members of the church. The difficulty is increased tenfold when one of the parents is not blessed with Catholic faith, and is either an indifferentist or an errorist in religion. The example of such a parent will go very far towards counteracting all the efforts and instructions of the one who is Catholic.

We repeat it, the church is very wise in warning her children against the danger of such marriages; and it is the duty of Catholic parents to guard their children against associations which might entangle them in alliances so fraught with evil to their souls, as it is the duty of pastors to remind parents and children of their obligations in this matter." In conformity with the rubrics and the general usage of the church, the statutes of this synod require that in future all candidates for confirmation shall be provided with sponsors, who must be of the same sex as those whom they present for the reception of the sacrament.

The duty of generously contributing to the support of the Holy Father is also insisted upon. "He labors day and night, with his numerous staff of counsellors and officers, for the spiritual benefit of all Christendom; and it is but fair and equitable that all Christendom should generously co-operate in supporting a necessarily expensive administration, conducted in the spiritual interests of all."

"Finally," continues Archbishop Spalding, in the address from which I have already quoted, "in view of the great number of our children of both sexes who are lost to the church, we have recommended, for general adoption in our congregations, societies of pious ladies, like that lately established in the cathedral parish under the name of the 'Association of St. Joseph.' This society has for its object the care of destitute girls whose faith is endangered because their religious instruction has been neglected. These zealous ladies seek out these poor children, assemble them weekly, and devote several hours to teaching them sewing and the catechism. Within a few weeks, the number of such scholars in the cathedral parish has swelled from twenty to one hundred."

Archbishop Spalding's fondness for historical studies, and his great desire to disseminate correct views on the history of the church, led him, a short time after his promotion to the see of Baltimore, to become responsible for the English translation of Darras' *Church History*, for which he wrote a lengthy introduction. This work gave him not a little trouble. For a time he did the proof-reading himself; but he soon found that this was incompatible with the discharge of the constantly increasing duties of his office. Then, when only a few chapters of the first volume had been done into English, the person who had undertaken the translation was unable to proceed with the work, and Archbishop Spalding was forced to look out for some equally competent person to whom he might entrust the task. Fortunately, a member of the Society of Jesus, of the Maryland Province, was found, who was both able and willing to complete the translation.

Bishop Luers, of Fort Wayne, suggested that a chapter on the history of the church in the United States should be added. This chapter, in the form of an appendix to the fourth volume, was written by the Rev. Dr. White, of Washington City. The entire work, which is a valuable addition to our Catholic literature, was completed in 1866.

Archbishop Spalding had for years carried on an extensive correspondence, which now greatly increased and became really burdensome. He frequently wrote, with his own hand, as many as twenty letters a day, some of them of considerable length, and on almost every conceivable topic.

Bishops consulted him on points of theology or canon law, or as to the manner of meeting some practical difficulties; priests asked his advice on a still greater variety of subjects; others, who wished to refer their doubts to Rome, first sought his opinion. He received letters from members of religious orders and communities requiring answers to all manner of questions relating to monastic life and discipline. Unfledged authors sent him their manuscripts to read, and translators sought his approval of their work. Whoever had a project which he thought of vital interest to the church in this country submitted it to him. People who had got into quarrels and difficulties stated their cases to him. Some asked for letters of introduction, whilst others wished to know whether or not he would advise them to make a change of business. Mothers begged him to intercede for their sons who were in prison, wives for their husbands. Persons who had been impoverished by the war asked for assistance. Children wrote to remind him of his promise to send his photograph. Protestants made endless statements of their objections to the church, and asked to be enlightened. Others sent him criticisms on his sermons, lectures, or books. He was invited to preach here, and to lecture there.

It was not an agreeable task to have to read all the letters which Archbishop Spalding received, and yet he rarely failed to return a prompt answer. He was the most punctual of correspondents. Not to receive an immediate reply to a letter addressed to him meant that he was sick or absent from home.

To a Protestant gentleman who seemed to be honestly enquiring after religious truth he wrote as follows:

"DEAR SIR: Most willingly will I extend to you every aid in my power in securing success to your apparently sincere desire to find out and embrace the true church of Christ. I beg to propose to your serious meditation before God the following remarks, which embody much that is important to you in your present mental and religious condition:

"1. Faith is not merely the result of our human and unaided opinions, but it is supernatural—a *gift of God*, granted only to the humble-minded and simple-hearted. 'Unless you be converted, and become like unto little children, you shall not enter into the kingdom of heaven.' A ray of heavenly light flashes upon our mind when struggling darkly after the truth; and, while it enlightens, it diffuses also a genial warmth, which is the source of divine love. God thus completes the work. This priceless gift, hidden from the wise ones of the world, is granted to the simple-hearted, and it must be sought with humble, trustful, and persevering prayer. 'Without such faith it is impossible to please God,' *Heb.* xi.

"2. The church of Christ is the depository of the saving faith. It is a divine institution, but has in it a human element. Christ is its head, and it is the body of Christ partaking of his divine character. The church is, moreover, the bride of Christ and the only mother of his children. 'No one can have God for a father who has not the church for a mother,' says St. Cyprian.

"3. They who are outside of this church *through their own fault* cannot be saved; for they violate the divine command to hear the church, which is the organ of Christ's communication with the world—'he who hears you, hears me.' They who are outside of this church without any fault of their own will not be condemned for this. Whether or not it is their fault God only, who searches hearts, can decide, and to his judgment we leave them. This is the doctrine of the church on exclusive salvation, and it commends itself by its consistency and reasonableness.

"4. The doctrine of the real presence is perhaps the very clearest thing in all the written revelation of God; and the only logical or possible way of explaining it is through transubstantiation, or change of substance; but the change is hidden, and is thus an object of faith, which is a conviction of things unseen. It is as intelligible as the Trinity or other mysteries, and is perhaps more clearly revealed than any of them all."

To one who was troubled by the opposition of the church to Freemasonry, he wrote:

"For more than a hundred years before the issuing of the late Encyclical, it had been a settled discipline of the Catholic Church to exclude from communion all members of secret societies. This discipline is based upon the principle that it is morally wrong to take an oath of secrecy under the circumstances, and that a society banded together by such an oath is therefore unlawful; and this without reference to the greater or less amount of evil or good that may be supposed to exist in such associations.

"No doubt, as you say, Freemasonry is not so bad in this country as in Europe; but it may be for all this, and even on this very account, the more dangerous, because the more insidious—on the principle that the worst of all counterfeits is the one nearest to the genuine article. The great evil of Freemasonry lies in this—that it is a human substitute for a divine religion; and its high-sounding benevolence is an implied assumption that the church of Christ is not sufficient of itself to render men benevolent and charitable. Religion is the very source and fountain-head of all true charity, and it needs no such helps and can brook no such rivals as Freemasonry and Oddfellowship. The men who belong to these societies may be, as many of them no doubt are, very sincere and excellent persons; but they would be much better had they the additional divine motive of action and the divine grace or help of religion to prompt and guide their natural benevolence. Knowing how well disposed are many of these misguided, or rather imperfectly guided men, I feel like exclaiming: *Tales cum sint, utinam nostri essent!* The natural does not suffice; the supernatural is necessary!"

When the person to whom this letter was addressed hesitated about entering the church, apparently from want of moral courage, Archbishop Spalding addressed him in the following words:

"Is not heaven worth all the comparatively trifling sacrifices which you are called on to make in order to secure its enjoyment? Did not the early disciples leave all things to follow Christ? And after having now for eighteen centuries enjoyed heaven, do they regret the privations which they voluntarily endured? Is this the case with the young man of the Gospel, who, having great possessions, clung to them and went away sad when our dear Lord invited him to become a disciple? Think on these things, and act on those eternal and unchangeable truths. . . . You have rightly interpreted my answer. The church of Christ never compromises where there is question of a principle."

This concluding sentence refers to what he had said concerning Freemasonry in the letter which I have given. Archbishop Spalding was inclined to put as liberal a construction as was consistent with sound principles of morality upon the discipline of the church with regard to secret societies; and, where there was doubt whether a particular association should be looked upon as condemned, he leaned to the side of liberty. He was not, for instance, in favor of visiting with ecclesiastical censures Catholics who are members of trade-unions and similar associations. "In our country," he said, in replying to a person who had asked his advice on this subject, "capital is tyrant, and labor is its slave. I have no desire to interfere with the poor in their efforts to protect themselves, unless it be proved that these societies are plotting against the state or the church."

"You rightly conjecture," he wrote to a Protestant lady, "that I should be gratified to serve you, though you are not a Catholic, and are, moreover, an entire stranger. Christianity inclines us to do all the good we can, without too close scrutiny into persons and things."

And to a Catholic lady he wrote: "You ask me for something which will prove a sensation in this dull and insipid world. I answer you in these words: All for Jesus! Make yourself a spouse of Christ, devoted to him, body, soul, and heart; loving him only and thinking only of him and doing everything for him. . . . Anything short of this will not satisfy your noble aspirations. Be a saint, a sister of charity in the world, trying to do good and to convert all to Christ."

In reply to a request for his autograph he wrote: "You ask me for my autograph and for an accompanying sentiment. My autograph is scarcely worth my giving or your receiving; and I know of no sentiments better than those conveyed by our divine Lord and Master and his beloved disciple, John: 'What doth it profit a man if he gain the whole world, and lose his own soul?' 'God is light, and in him there is no darkness.' 'He who loveth his brother abideth in the light; but he who hateth his brother is in darkness.'"

CHAPTER XXII.

THE SUFFERING PEOPLE OF THE SOUTH—THE DIOCESE OF CHARLESTON—THE CATHOLIC PROTECTORY—SERMON AT THE UNIVERSITY OF NOTRE DAME.

HE assassination of President Lincoln, which was a national calamity, though his personal character, as it will be better understood, is destined to be less admired, called forth the following circular from Archbishop Spalding:

"FELLOW-CITIZENS:

"A deed of blood has been perpetrated which causes every heart to shudder, and which calls for the execration of every citizen. On Good Friday, the hallowed anniversary of our blessed Lord's crucifixion, when all Christendom was bowed down in penitence and sorrow at his tomb, the President of these United States was foully assassinated, and a wicked attempt was made upon the life of the Secretary of State. Words fail us in expressing detestation for a deed so atrocious, hitherto happily unparalleled in our history. Silence is perhaps the best and most appropriate expression of a sorrow too great for utterance.

"We are quite sure that we need not remind our brethren in this archdiocese of the duty—which we are confident they will willingly perform—of uniting with their fellow-citizens in whatever may be deemed most suitable for indicating their horror of the crime and their feelings of sympathy with the bereaved. We also invite them to join in humble supplication to God for our beloved and afflicted country;

and we enjoin that the bells of all our churches be solemnly tolled on the occasion of the late President's funeral."

In the winter of 1864-65, the diocese of Charleston, which at that time extended over the two Carolinas, was temporarily entrusted by the Holy See to the care of Archbishop Spalding. Dr. Lynch, the Bishop of Charleston, was in Europe, unable to return home on account of the blockade of the Southern ports. The Vicar-General, who had been shut up in the besieged city, cut off from communication with the rest of the diocese, was taken sick and had died. Other priests had fallen victims to disease and excessive labor, until in Charleston but one was left who was able to do the work of the ministry. Archbishop Spalding gave him the powers of Vicar-General, and did all that it was possible to do to come to his relief. He sent two priests to Newbern, North Carolina, to attend to the spiritual wants of the soldiers, amongst whom an epidemic had broken out. He succeeded, too, in inducing others to go to Charleston, and interested himself in obtaining passes for them from the Government.

"I thank you," he wrote to Archbishop Odin, of New Orleans, "for your charity in so effectually interesting yourself in behalf of poor Charleston. Please thank the good Provincial [of the Jesuits] in my name. Father N—— expects to start for Charleston to-morrow. His companion is sick in Richmond, very much exhausted, and cannot go now."

On the 30th of June, 1865, he wrote to General Gillmore, to thank him for protecting the churches of Charleston: "I have received your kind favor of the 24th of this month, communicating the welcome intelligence that, in compliance with my request, you have promptly taken measures for protecting the property of the Catholic Church in Charleston."

Archbishop Spalding's sympathy with the suffering people of the South was very great; and he was, I believe, the first Catholic bishop to make an appeal in behalf of those whom the fortunes of war had reduced to utter wretchedness. The cry of distress had gone forth, and, without stopping to consider whether it was politic—whether, in view of the bitter partisan feeling which had scarcely had time to abate ever so little, it was prudent—he issued a circular, calling upon his people to come to the relief of their suffering brethren of the South.

He put the question on the broad basis of Christian charity, and he felt that it was safe to trust the generosity of the American character, which he believed capable of rising superior to partisan feelings when appealed to in the name of humanity.

"Is it not clearly," he said, " a Christian duty for us, who, by a merciful Providence, have been to a great extent freed from the calamities of a war which has pressed so heavily upon our neighbors, to come promptly and generously to their relief? Can we be held blameless before God if our brethren, whom we are solemnly commanded to love even as ourselves, should perish through our coldness and neglect? Most of the sufferers are women, children, and other non-combatants, whose hands are outstretched to implore succor, and whose sighs of anguish ascend to heaven, while their tears bedew the earth. Can we find it in our hearts to resist their appeal?"

The Catholics of Baltimore, in response to these earnest words of their Archbishop, contributed ten thousand dollars, which was distributed among the impoverished people of the South, without distinction of religious faith. The sum, indeed, was paltry, but the example was invaluable. To a Protestant lady who applied for assistance he wrote:

"I take pleasure in enclosing you this check, and I am

only sorry that, from the hundreds of applicants, I am not able to send you much more. . . . It was no doubt through inadvertence that you used the word 'Romish,' which is a nickname. Our true name is Catholic, or Roman Catholic, as the British Parliament and all polite people call us."

Every phase of the question of education attracted the attention of Archbishop Spalding. He was of the opinion that the future of the church in this country depended, humanly speaking, upon this vital issue. The converts to Catholicism do not equal in number, so he thought at least, those who are lost to the faith, especially in our large cities, because of the difficulties with which we have to contend in our ineffectual efforts to secure to our children the blessings of Christian education. He frankly admitted the melancholy fact that a large proportion of the idle and vicious youth of our principal cities are the children of Catholics.

Day by day these unhappy children are caught in the commission of petty crimes, which render them amenable to the authorities, by whom they are placed in sectarian or public reformatories, to be thence transferred by hundreds to distant localities, where they are brought up in complete ignorance of the religion in which they had been baptized. Numerous and active societies also exist, whose sole aim is to snatch from the church these helpless and unfortunate little ones.

In his frequent journeyings through the West, Archbishop Spalding had become acquainted with the extent of the harm which, in this manner, is done to the cause of Catholicism in this country; and he had also learned that the chief source of the evil is in the large cities of the East, where the church finds it impossible to provide for the great numbers of orphan and indigent children who are each year thrown upon her.

One of his first thoughts, therefore, after his promotion to the see of Baltimore, was given to this subject; and, after sufficient deliberation, he determined to found a Catholic protectory or industrial school, as, in his opinion, this was likely to prove the most effectual remedy for the evil.

"For years," he said, in the letter which he addressed to his people on this matter, "we have been losing hundreds of our poor children, particularly orphan and indigent boys. They are taken up from the streets or from the haunts of poverty, and are placed in institutions where their faith is either entirely neglected or artfully undermined. Do we not find all over the country thousands of persons who, from their names, should be Catholics, but who, unfortunately, have abandoned the church, and who rear up their families in ignorance, sometimes in hatred of her sacred principles? Thus the evil is propagated and continually multiplied from generation to generation. Hundreds of thousands, if not millions, who should belong to the church in this country, are now, unhappily, through the criminal neglect of parents and the agencies above referred to, estranged from her communion. The evil is truly great, even gigantic, and it seems to be on the increase. . . . The only practical remedy is the establishment, on a large scale, of protectories or industrial schools, in which poor boys, exposed to the danger of losing their faith, may be religiously educated and trained up to pursuits which will fit them to become useful members of society and ornaments of the church. Such an establishment we have long had very much at heart, even from the first moment after God had constituted us your chief pastor, with the fearful responsibility of answering for your souls; and divine Providence has at length favored us with the opportunity to make a beginning. We have secured the services of an excellent and devoted Brotherhood for this purpose, and we have procured suitable grounds—nearly fifty acres, with the prospect of getting over a hundred—within two miles of Baltimore."

In carrying out this work, into which he had entered with his wonted energy and will, Archbishop Spalding had to contend with serious difficulties.

It was looked upon as something new in the Catholic history of Maryland, and the *nihil innovetur nisi quod traditum* was brought to bear against it. Then, it was said, the plan could not be carried out; it would be impossible to raise the necessary means; the Catholics of the archdiocese had already more institutions than they were able to support, and they were not, moreover, accustomed to being so heavily taxed for their religion, and would not respond to appeals made in behalf of a work the success of which was, to say the least, doubtful.

Such were the views of various prudent persons, who seem to think it their special mission to serve the office of brakes when the church appears to them to be in danger of going forward too rapidly.

Archbishop Spalding, however, was not disconcerted. He had not moved without first considering what was to be done. He seldom, indeed, if ever, began a work from enthusiasm or impulse, and he knew that miracles were not to be looked for where zeal and industry would accomplish the desired result. Though he relied on God's providence, he knew that God's providence is that we should greatly rely on the natural resources which he has given us. If we do nothing for ourselves, God will do nothing for us. Effort he believed to be the first law of progress in the church as in the world. Though eager to push forward whatever he thought would advance the cause of religion, he was not a man to rush rashly into any enterprise. *Festina lente* was one of his favorite mottoes. But then he had great faith in the willingness of the Catholic people to do their duty when it is placed before them in the proper manner.

He did not aim to rouse the enthusiasm of those whom he sought to influence—possibly he had little power to do this—but he appealed to their understanding and sense of right, and, having shown that a project was feasible, he proceeded to explain how its realization became a duty.

Though no one could be more jealous than he of any foreign interference in ecclesiastical matters, he yet believed that the church needs the active and intelligent co-operation of the laity in many of her most important works. Then, he had the rare art of knowing how and whom to consult.

"You should not be so sensitive," he wrote to one of his clergymen, "about the opinions of the people belonging to your charge. You should act in concert with them, asking their advice, and following what may seem most sound; in case of difficulty, referring to me. Thus only can you hope to win their confidence and gain their co-operation. This is my own rule of conduct. Conciliation and kindness are the best."

In projects and transactions where money was one term of the equation to be formed, he always took counsel of business men; and his own knowledge of such matters enabled him to make the best use of their advice. His correspondence shows that he was persuaded that the surest way to make the people generous is to secure their confidence in the practical wisdom with which their offerings are used. He did not believe that, in the financial affairs of the church, there could be any need for secrecy, and he therefore held that, for many reasons, the people should be informed of the precise manner in which their contributions had been employed.

He placed his Protectory, which he had incorporated

under the title of St. Mary's Industrial School for Boys, under the protection of the Immaculate Mother of God.

Mrs. McTavish, of whose generosity I have already had occasion to speak, gave the Archbishop, for the site of the institution, one hundred acres of land lying on the Frederick Road, within a short distance of the city. Temporary buildings were erected here, and the Xaverian Brothers, whom Archbishop Spalding had brought from Belgium for this purpose, took charge of the Protectory on the Feast of the Nativity of the Blessed Virgin, 1866.

They began with one boy; the number, however, soon increased to forty-five, which was as many as could be accommodated in the temporary structure. In April, 1867, the foundation of the permanent building was laid, and it was completed in August, 1868. It is built of hammered stone, and is one hundred and thirty-six by sixty-six feet, five stories high, and capable of giving accommodation to four hundred boys. The entire cost of this structure was not more than sixty thousand dollars.

The treasurer's report from May, 1866, to December, 1868, shows that within that period eighty-one thousand four hundred and thirty-six dollars had been received for the institution. Of this sum, all to about one thousand dollars, which still remained in the treasury, had been spent in the erection of the new Protectory, and in buying implements for the farm, and machinery for carrying on the various trades. In 1871, the institution had received two hundred and sixty-nine boys, who were being taught the trades of printing, shoemaking, tailoring, and carpentering, whilst others were employed as farmers, bakers, and blacksmiths. The boys do not, however, devote their time exclusively to these manual occupations. They have hours for study and recitation, and for instruction in the principles necessary to form faithful Catholics and good citizens.

The great advantage of the industrial school over the orphan asylum is apparent. Orphan asylums, especially for boys, are, for the most part, merely drifting-places, where our children are sheltered, for a time, from the current that is hurrying them on to ruin, to which they must soon again be exposed, scarcely better prepared to battle against its seductive force than when they were first received into the asylum. The boys especially are thrown back into the world without a trade or any certain means of gaining a livelihood, their habits of idleness but ill corrected, their self-respect not increased, and they therefore fall an easy prey to the venal enticements of a mistaken proselytism, or to the allurements of vulgar pleasures. That these objections do not apply, at least with the same force, to industrial schools is evident.

The history of these institutions, not only as conducted by the Catholic Church, but even when under other control, shows that this system tends to develop self-respect, energy, and other noble traits of character. The young men who have grown up in the protectory are frequently proud of their alma mater, and in after-life look back to her with a feeling akin to that with which a scholar regards his college or university. Then they return to the world skilled laborers, with habits of order and industry, able with head erect to elbow their way through the crowd in the great life-struggle. Though Archbishop Spalding was not the first Catholic who sought, by means of the industrial school, to save the abandoned children of our large cities—two converts, Father Haskins and Dr. Ives, having preceded him in this work—yet no one entered into it with greater earnestness, or had stronger faith than he in the results to be expected from institutions of this kind; which, moreover, have received the high sanction of the fathers of the Second Plenary Council of Baltimore. "We, therefore," say the venerable prelates of the American church, "earnestly exhort the Bishops to defend, with every possible care and solicitude, the tender lambs of the Christian fold from the wolves that hang around them. Let them establish industrial schools everywhere, but especially near the great cities, where the number of those in danger is larger. Worthy of praise are they who use every energy to build to God's honor and worship magnificent temples of marble; but a far better and more useful labor is that which prepares for the divine Majesty an eternal dwelling in these living and chosen stones." *

And in their pastoral letter, referring to this same subject, they say: "The only remedy for this great and daily augmenting evil is to provide Catholic protectories or industrial schools, to which such children may be sent, and where, under the only influence that is known to have really reached the roots of vice, the youthful culprit may cease to do evil and learn to do good.

"We rejoice that in some of our dioceses—would that we could say in all!—a beginning has been made in this good work; and we cannot too earnestly exhort our venerable brethren of the clergy to bring this matter before their respective flocks, to endeavor to impress on Christian parents the duty of guarding their children from the evils above referred to, and to invite them to make persevering and effectual efforts for the establishment of institutions wherein, under the influence of religious teachers, the waywardness of youth may be corrected, and good seed planted in the soil in which, while men slept, the enemy had sowed tares."

In May, 1866, Archbishop Spalding, by invitation of the

* Con. Plen. Balt. II., Decret. 446.

Provincial of the Congregation of the Holy Cross, delivered a sermon on devotion to the Blessed Virgin, on the occasion of the unveiling of a monumental statue, and of the consecration of the University of Notre Dame to the Immaculate Mother of God. His devotion to the Blessed Virgin was truly tender and childlike; but he could not bear anything false in the expression of the love which all true Christians should feel for her. " Such faults," he wrote in 1865, " do great harm to the solid and proper devotion to our sweet Mother, who is best praised when the eulogy is strictly true." And in a letter to Archbishop Kenrick, written in 1861, he said, referring to certain books of devotion: " How much devotional trash disfigures our books!" A few passages from his sermon at Notre Dame, while serving as examples of his style as a preacher, will help to show his deep love for Mary. "There are," he said, " two great events, the greatest of all in the world's history. The first was disastrous; the second glorious. In both these events a woman figured, an angel figured, a man figured. In the first, Eve, the mother of all the living; in the second, Mary, the Mother of all the regenerate—Eve, the mother of the fallen; Mary, the Mother of the risen. In the first, an angel of evil took the form of the serpent, and beguiled unto her ruin and unto our ruin our first mother. In the second, the archangel of God addressed another woman, and she obeyed his voice and became the mother of a new race. Man figured in both; he fell in the first; and, immediately after that first fall, the prophecy went forth that God would put enmity between the serpent and the woman, and between her seed and his seed; and that she, through her seed, Jesus Christ, should crush the serpent's head; that she should retrieve by her obedience what had been lost by the disobedience of the first mother of the human race. The parallel is not mine. It comes down to us through the Fathers of the church from the very beginning of Christianity. It comes echoing down the ages, from the days of the apostles until the later times of St. Alphonsus Liguori. Justin Martyr, in the second century; Irenæus and Tertullian, the powerful champions of Christianity in its struggle with infidelity at the end of the second and the beginning of the third century; St. Ambrose, St. Peter Chrysologus, and St. Augustine, who recite the language of Tertullian ; and, indeed, all the Fathers teach that Mary retrieved by her obedience all that Eve had lost by her disobedience; that Mary's becoming the mother of the Man-God crushed the serpent's head, and bade us lift up our heads and look heavenward, for the day of our redemption was near at hand. We may not say that Mary was but a passive instrument in this great work of redemption. She was an intelligent instrument; she was a moral agent, and could have refused her consent. But she was obedient; she assented, and became the mother of her Saviour-God. . . . Do not say that we exaggerate the prerogatives of Mary. The church of the living God never exaggerates. Whatever she says and does is said and done in truth. We are opposed to all exaggerations, for Mary needs no exaggerated eulogy. The simple truth is sublime enough, and sufficient for her votaries, however dearly they may love her, or however much they may wish to exalt her. . . . The church proclaims what we always preach—that Mary is but a creature; that her Son was and is God; and that there is an infinite distance between Mary and her Son. She tells us, and we preach it, that Mary was redeemed by the blood of her Son ; that she has no favor, no exemption, but by and through the blood of that divine Son. . . . All that we have to do is simply to place her in the position in which God has placed her, to honor her as the archangel honored her in the name of God, and to love her as her own

Son loved her. The first pulsation of his heart in his mother's womb, and the first light of love that was in his eye when he came into the world, were given to his dear mother; and the last sigh which escaped him on the cross was breathed out to that same tender, devoted, and loving being. . . . They tell us that in honoring the mother we dishonor the Son. Believe it not. They who make the objection do not themselves believe it. Why do we honor Mary? We honor her because she was *his* mother; we honor her because he loved her, because he is our dear Brother and she is our dear Mother. I look at the beautiful, serene moon, which lights up the night in the heavens, with wonder and admiration; but do I detract in so doing from the brilliancy of the sun? And yet, does not the moon derive its light from the sun? . . . They who scoff at our love of the Blessed Virgin do not understand the feelings of a Catholic heart. . . . There is a mother; she has with her a little daughter, whom she is caressing; her heart is full of love; her words are not marked with logical precision or accuracy; she idolizes the child; her mother's heart knows no bounds; she would seem to prefer that child to God—certainly to all else in the world. These men who sneer at us should carp at that fond mother for the simple outpourings of her mother's heart."

CHAPTER XXIII.

THE SECOND PLENARY COUNCIL OF BALTIMORE.

N a letter to Bishop Timon, under date of August 23, 1865, Archbishop Spalding alludes to his desire to hold a Plenary Council of the bishops of the United States:

"A letter from Rome, dated July 17, states that the question of the Plenary Council to be held next year was agitated in Rome, and that Cardinal Barnabo was warmly in favor of it. This is, no doubt, in consequence of our letter, written June 14, explaining, under four or five heads, the motives for holding such a council. The intelligence is favorable to our project, from which I anticipate much good. Why should we not have a Catholic university? It would be a great thing if we could only agree as to the location and arrangements."

The principal motives for holding a council, to which reference is here made, were, first, that at the close of the national crisis, which had acted as a dissolvent upon all sectarian ecclesiastical organizations, the Catholic Church might present to the country and the world a striking proof of the strong bond of unity with which her members are knit together. Secondly, that the collective wisdom of the church in this country might determine what measures should be adopted in order to meet the new phase of national life which the result of the war had just inaugurated; for, though the church is essentially the same in all times and places, her accidental relations to the world and the state are necessarily variable.

"The customs of men," says Benedict XIV., "vary, and circumstances continually change. That which is useful at one period may cease to be so, and may become even hurtful in another age. The duty of a prudent pastor, unless prevented by a higher law, is to accommodate himself to times and places, to lay aside many ancient usages, when by his own judgment and the light of God he deems this to be for the greater good of the diocese with which he is entrusted." *

Thirdly, that an earnest effort might be made to render ecclesiastical discipline, as far as possible, uniform throughout the entire extent of the United States. The fourth motive I shall give in the words of Archbishop Spalding :

"I think," he wrote, "that it is our most urgent duty to discuss the future status of the negro. Four millions of these unfortunate beings are thrown on our charity, and they silently but eloquently appeal to us for help. We have a golden opportunity to reap a harvest of souls, which, neglected, may not return."

The bishops of the United States very generally agreed that the time was opportune for holding a Plenary Council, and that the interests of religion demanded that it should be convoked at as early a date as possible. Some few, however, seemed to hesitate, on the ground chiefly that the country was still in too unsettled a condition, and that public sentiment with regard to the church, especially in the North, was as yet very uncertain.

Then they feared, too, that unpleasant discussions might arise in the Council.

Archbishop Spalding himself felt no anxiety on these points. The bishops were to meet to attend to their own business, and not to meddle with affairs of state; and he thought he understood the public sentiment of the nation

---

* *De Synod Dioce.* lib. v. c. iii.

well enough to feel confident that in doing this they could have nothing to fear.

As to the other cause of uneasiness, he wrote to one of his brethren in the episcopate:

"I see no reason why we should fear the discussion of agitating topics. The question is closed and need not be reopened."

Pius IX., in his Letters Apostolic of February 16, 1866, after signifying his approval of the project of holding a Plenary Council, constituted Archbishop Spalding its president. "Wherefore," wrote the Holy Father, "having fully examined the subject, we, with our venerable brethren, the cardinals of the Holy Roman Church, who superintend the affairs of the propagation of the faith, have resolved to delegate you, venerable brother, whose piety, knowledge, and profound reverence for the Holy See are well known to us, to the office of convoking and presiding over that Council. . . . We command, besides, all and each of your venerable brother bishops of the United States, that they receive and accept you, whom we have deputed to call together this Council, as its president and director, and that they obey you, assist you, and support you."

As the time for holding the synod had been left to the judgment of the American prelates, Archbishop Spalding, having first received their opinions on the subject, issued letters of convocation, calling all who, by right or custom, should take part in a council of this kind, to meet in Baltimore on the second Sunday of October, 1866.

This delay was deemed necessary for the proper preparation of the matters to be treated of in the Council.

"I know enough about councils," wrote the Archbishop, "to understand that, if nothing definite be prepared, nothing will be done, but all will end in talk."

In another letter, in which he gives his views concerning what should be done in the Council, he says: "I have thought of embodying in the Council a succinct exposition of doctrine, together with the condemnation of current heresies and errors, as well as suitable rules for the regulation of moral conduct and discipline. . . . I have thought, also, of making our approaching Council a complete repertory of our canon law, embracing, in systematic order, all our previous enactments in the Baltimore councils, together with such canons of provincial and diocesan synods as we may wish to make of general application. In a word, of making it a sort of *corpus juris* for the American Church; throwing into an appendix all Roman rescripts and decisions which have reference to our affairs." He adds: "In order to carry out this plan, I shall need the active co-operation of the Metropolitans."

The idea of making doctrinal exposition and the condemnation of current errors features of the Council was new in the history of such assemblies in this country. A national council can, of course, in this matter do nothing more than state the faith already defined, since it does not lie within its competency to make new definitions, which are reserved either to the infallible Pontiff or to the church in œcumenical council assembled, and presided over by him. This feature in Archbishop Spalding's plan was not, however, without precedent or the approval of the Holy See. It is found in several of the principal provincial councils held in Europe, from 1850 to 1860, as in those of Cologne, Vienna, and Prague; and, in one or two instances, the Holy See found the meagreness of doctrinal statement worthy of blame. As each variety of social condition must have its own peculiar phases of error, it cannot but be highly useful to place the truth in precisely that light in which the danger of the error will, by contrast, be best seen; and no more solemn or effectual means of calling the attention of the faithful of a particular portion of the church to sound doctrine, as opposed to the false theories and systems which they hear defended around them, could be found than that which is given in the united voices of the entire episcopate of the nation.

In the fall of 1865, Archbishop Spalding wrote: "I have procured copies of some dozen provincial and diocesan councils, held in Europe from 1850 to 1860, and I must confess that, in comparison with them, ours appear very meagre, especially in moral and doctrinal exposition, which in them occupies much space. We have very much to do to lay deeply and solidly the foundations of our canon law. Until now we seem not to have advanced far beyond the rudiments."

No sooner had the Holy Father given his sanction to the holding of a council, than Archbishop Spalding entered into the work with all the energy of which he was capable.

"My whole heart was and is in the Council," he wrote to Cardinal Cullen; "and, whatever else may be said, I think all will allow me credit for considerable industry. The codification of all previous Baltimore legislation, together with the seeking out and verifying all quotations, was itself a laborious task. But the greatest difficulty was in shaping the new decrees so as to meet the exigencies of so many provinces and dioceses, so differently organized and so remote from one another, with so many nationalities—French and Spanish particularly, besides Irish, German, and American; to harmonize all this, and to present a code of uniform discipline in which all could essentially agree, was not an easy task." "The doctrinal and pastoral portions of the Council," he wrote upon another occasion, "have been drawn up with much labor and care; every quotation having been carefully verified from the original."

The *Acta Concilio Prævia*, containing a brief statement of

the matters to be treated of in the Council, were sent to all whose duty it was to take part in the discussions. Particular *tituli* were assigned to each Metropolitan, who was requested, with the assistance of his suffragans, to prepare them for conciliary action. The first two were written out by Archbishop Spalding himself. The prelates were requested to make any suggestions which might seem good to them, and freely to propose whatever they should deem to be in furtherance of the progress and welfare of the church in this country. "Draw up your bill," he wrote to one of them, "as they say in Congress, and it shall be brought before the house." He desired that the largest liberty consistent with the rules necessary for the maintenance of order in deliberative assemblies should be exercised in the discussion of matters submitted to the action of the Council; and to this end, whoever might choose was permitted in debate to speak English instead of Latin.

When the *tituli* had been returned, Archbishop Spalding called together a college of theologians to assist him in the final preparation of the matters to be proposed to the Fathers of the Council. In connection with the history of this *Cœtus Theologorum*, I may be permitted to quote from a letter of Archbishop Spalding to Bishop Lynch, of Charleston: "I can scarcely thank you sufficiently," he wrote, "for sending me Dr. Corcoran. His services have, indeed, been invaluable." Dr. Keogh, too, was an able member of this body of theologians. Bishop Heiss, at that time rector of the Seminary of Milwaukee, had been invited and had come on to lend the assistance of his learning and experience to the work; but he was unfortunately taken sick a short time after his arrival in Baltimore. The members of the religious orders also added the weight of their great knowledge and wisdom to these deliberations. Indeed, to this work of preparation Archbishop Spalding, with great discernment, brought the very first theological talent of the country. He wished to make the Council as perfect as might be, and he therefore called to his aid the ablest men whom he could find. Nothing gave him greater delight than to place learning and genius in the service of religion. He had not the weakness to imagine that the church is not capable of satisfying all the intellectual wants of even the most gifted minds; or that, because a man is able, he should be looked upon with distrust. If great minds have proved untrue to the church, so have little minds; and in neither case was the fault of the head, but of the heart. Wherever he beheld men of talent battling for the truth, he lent them the aid of a sympathy that was not barren. "*Frater noster es,*" he would say, "*crescas in mille millia.*"

When at length the day on which the Council was to meet had come, everything was ready. Not even the minutest details had been overlooked in the preparation.

On the 7th of October, 1866, seven archbishops, thirty-eight bishops, three mitred abbots, and over one hundred and twenty theologians met in Baltimore to take part in the deliberations of the Second Plenary Council of the church in the United States. This was, at the time, the largest conciliary assembly since the Council of Trent, with the exception of two or three meetings of the bishops in Rome, which, however, were not councils in any proper sense of the word.

Never, in the history of the church in this country, had anything approached in grandeur the opening of this synod. "Already," said Father Ryan, in his eloquent discourse at the Council—" already, during these festive days, you have witnessed the external splendor of the church. You saw her, on Sunday last, at the opening of the Council, as the king's daughter, 'in golden vesture, surrounded with variety'; you heard the rustling of her variegated garments, as the prelates passed in gorgeous procession; you heard the glorious music that almost shook these massive walls, and wafted to the throne of God the profession of faith of the young church of these States—that *Credo in unam Sanctam Catholicam et Apostolicam Ecclesiam* which, for fifteen centuries, from the Council of Nice to the Second Council of Baltimore, has expressed the faith of her children."

The bishops, clad in splendid robes, with mitred heads, each bearing the crosier in hand, attended by a throng of priests and acolytes, recalled, as they moved in solemn procession through the streets to the cathedral, what we read of the religious pageants of the middle ages.

The whole city had crowded to behold the glorious scene. The streets around the cathedral were thronged. Every window and available spot, even the house-tops from which a view of the procession could be had, were filled with eager spectators, who looked on in silent reverence.

The country had just come forth from a most terrible crisis, in which many ancient landmarks had been effaced, and the very ship of state had been wrenched from its moorings. House had been divided against house, and brother's hand had been raised against brother. The sects had been torn asunder, and still lay in disorder and confusion, helping to widen the abyss which had threatened to engulf the nation's life. Half the country was waste and desolate; the people crushed, bowed beneath the double weight of the memory of the past, which could no more return, and of the thought of a future which seemed hopeless. On the other side, there were the weariness and exhaustion which follow a supreme effort, and the longing for peace and happiness after so much bloodshed and misery.

All were ready to applaud any power that had been able to live through that frightful struggle unhurt and unharmed; and when the Catholic Church walked forth before the eyes of the nation, clothed in the panoply of undiminished strength and of unbroken unity, thousands, who but a while ago would have witnessed this manifestation of her power with jealous concern, now hailed it with delight as a harbinger of good omen. Then it must be confessed, too, that during the war men had seen more of the church, and, having learned to know her better, had come to love her more. There was not a village throughout the land where some brave soldier, not a Catholic, was not found to speak the praises of her heroic daughters, who, whilst men fought, stood by to staunch the blood.

The deliberations of the Council were conducted in accordance with the rules of parliamentary debate. The matters prepared for discussion were first submitted to particular congregations of theologians, each of which was presided over by a bishop.

The result of these discussions, gathered by a notary, with the votes and motives alleged for or against, in case of disagreement, were then transmitted to the bishops, who in their private sessions occupied themselves with questions already debated in the congregations of theologians. A new examination was here instituted, a *procès verbal* of which was made by the secretaries. These preliminary discussions, however, decided nothing; but all was referred to the general congregations, and was finally promulgated in the public sessions of the Council. And even then the solemn sanction of the Vicar of Christ was still wanting. "Our legislation is not perfect," said Archbishop Spalding, in his sermon before the opening of the Council, "until it has received the approval of him who sits in the chair of Peter, and who is our chief executive; just as our acts of Congress do not become law until they are approved by the President. Hence, the conciliary acts and decrees will not be published until they will have been confirmed by the Pope. This is one among the great conservative elements and principles of our church, which prevents hasty or injudicious legislation, and secures uniformity of discipline under the guidance of one visible head."

It is the privilege of the church that, notwithstanding her fixed and immutable constitution of faith, and, to some extent, even of discipline, she is yet able, without hurt either to her unity or her Catholicity, to adapt herself to the various modifications of human society with which she is thrown into contact. Indeed, it seems that, precisely because she is so fixed in faith and in essential discipline, she can therefore, with less danger in other things, allow a certain liberty where circumstances demand it. The sects, in trying to fit themselves to new conditions of life, break into fragments. The central life-force in them is too feeble to resist the disintegrating action of the varying influences of nationalism or even of sectionalism. But the church is not so weakly built.

Now, our social condition is so unlike that which is found elsewhere that our church polity cannot be expected to be altogether the same as that which in many particulars is the outgrowth of circumstances wholly dissimilar from those in which we are placed. In the essential organization of the church here, there is, of course, nothing different from that which exists elsewhere—the universal headship of the Vicar of Christ, under him the authority of the bishop in his own diocese, extending over both priest and people; and the mutual relations of these exist substantially here as in other parts of the world. Our faith being Catholic, all those observances, disciplinary and ritualistic, which are but the expression of that faith, are, of course, binding upon us as upon other Catholics.

In fact, any peculiarities of discipline which may exist here concern chiefly matters of detail and certain accidental relations of the two orders of the clergy. I, of course, leave out of the question what may be called the public ecclesiastical law; and, confining the enquiry within the limits thus indicated, a careful study of the Second Plenary Council of Baltimore will, if I am not mistaken, confirm this view of the subject. However this may be, had the Fathers of that Council done nothing more than give a full and methodical statement of all previous ecclesiastical legislation in this country, making, where it seemed proper, what had been particular, general, they would have performed a great work.

They have done this, and much more. They have given us a code of laws, which, indeed, from its very nature could not be either complete or perfect, but which will serve as the fixed and solid foundation upon which to build whatever superstructure the wants of the church in this country may in future demand.

The whole tenor of the Second Plenary Council shows an increasing disposition in the American prelates to conform, wherever it is possible, to the general usage of the church, and, indeed, to comply with certain wise provisions which, even in Catholic countries, have been allowed to fall into desuetude.

They insist, for instance, that the law of the Council of Trent, which requires Provincial Councils to be held every three years, shall be observed in these United States. And in declaring what should be the aim of these synods, they say:

"Wherefore, let the Metropolitans and their suffragans in Council assembled, having consulted together, pass such decrees as, all things considered, may seem to them best for protecting the doctrines of the church against current errors, for reforming the morals of the faithful to them committed, and, in fine, for promoting uniformity of discipline, in accordance with the general discipline of the Catholic Church as it is laid down and defined in the Pontifical Constitutions and in the Œcumenical Councils." *

In enumerating the rights of Metropolitans, too, they evince a desire to return to what, in many other churches at the present day, is to a great extent suffered to remain in abeyance. And in the instruction of the Sacred Congregation, *De Decretis Corrigendis*, the Holy See makes two additions to these rights, as stated by the Fathers of the Plenary Council, which manifest quite significantly the tendency of our ecclesiastical polity.

* P. 47, n. 59.

CHAPTER XXIV.

SECOND PLENARY COUNCIL OF BALTIMORE, CONTINUED—
APPOINTMENT OF BISHOPS—PAROCHIAL RIGHTS—CATHOLIC UNIVERSITY.

THE establishment of the first episcopal see in this country was due to the initiatory movement of the priests of Maryland and Pennsylvania, who, before the Declaration of Independence, had been subject to the Vicar Apostolic of London. Believing that this state of things could not continue without injury to religion, they appointed, shortly after the close of the war, a committee of three to petition the Holy See to erect a bishopric in the United States, and to give them the privilege to nominate a fit person for the episcopal office. This request having been granted by Rome, the clergy selected Father Carroll to fill the new see, and their choice was ratified by the Holy Father.

The sees of New York, Boston, Philadelphia, and Bardstown were created in 1808, at the instance of Bishop Carroll, who, it seems, presented the candidates to fill them, with the exception of Bishop Concannen, who, I believe, was appointed to New York by the Holy See, *proprio motu.*

From this time, when sees became vacant or the erection of new ones became necessary, the bishops themselves generally presented the candidates, though, occasionally, when suitable persons were not found here, the Holy See selected some one in Europe, as in the case of Bishop England's appointment.

In 1834, the Congregation of the Propagation of the Faith determined the manner in which candidates for episcopal sees in this country should be presented, being substantially that which was already in existence.

Slight modifications of this law were made by the Sacred Congregation in 1850, in 1856, and again in 1859. And since, to use the words of the Second Plenary Council, it would seem that this mode of election is capable of being changed for the better, and made still more perfect, the archbishops of the United States were asked by the Holy See whether they could propose any modifications which would be likely to secure greater success in the choice of bishops. Their answer having been received, the Sacred Congregation made certain additions to the decrees hitherto issued on the subject, by which the mode of presenting candidates was still further changed.

The system thus modified, and as found in the Second Plenary Council, is substantially this: Every three years each bishop sends to his Metropolitan and to the Congregation of Propaganda a list of the priests whom he thinks worthy of the episcopal office, accompanied by a detailed account of the qualities which distinguish them. When a see becomes vacant, the bishops meet in synod or in some other way, and discuss the merits of the candidates to be presented to fill it.

Three names are then chosen by secret suffrage, and are sent to Rome, together with a *procès verbal* of the proceedings. From this list the Sovereign Pontiff selects the person whom he thinks best suited to the office. However, in case the person to be chosen is to be an archbishop or the co-adjutor of an archbishop, all the metropolitans of the United States must be consulted.

Archbishop Spalding was, as I infer from his correspondence on this subject, in favor of still further modifying this system, so as, in some way, to give the second order of the clergy a voice in the presentation of candidates for episcopal office. He would have given the diocesan councillors the right to present a list of names to be sent to Rome with that of the bishops. He thought that the Episcopal Council in this country should be looked upon as a quasi-chapter, and that the giving them a vote would bring us nearer the general discipline of the church in this matter. Indeed, he was in favor of introducing the Canonical Chapter, as an element in our church polity, whenever this could be done. The Plenary Council does not seem, however, to have entered upon the discussion of this subject.

Upon the question of instituting canonical parishes and pastors, Archbishop Spalding expressed his opinion in a letter to the Archbishop of St. Louis, written before the opening of the Second Plenary Council.

"While," he says, "I would favor the gradual creation of parish priests, beginning with the large cities, and legislating in that direction, also, for country districts, according to the plan of my venerable predecessor (Synod Balt., 1853, can. 3), I should with him still maintain their movability *ad judicium Episcopi;* and I should deem it premature, and probably disastrous in its consequences, to adopt *at once* the full parochial system, for which we are scarcely prepared."

The legislation of the Second Plenary Council is substantially in accord with these views; for whilst the fathers declare it to be their desire that throughout the States, especially in the larger cities, districts, with accurately defined limits, be assigned to the churches, and that to their rectors parochial or quasi-parochial rights be given, they yet affirm that they by no means intend that immovability be considered as one of these rights. The bishops, however, are exhorted not to use their privileges in this matter, except for grave reasons.[*]

The whole spirit of the legislation of the Second Baltimore

---

[*] *Vid. Con. Plen. Balt. II., Nos.* 124 *et* 125.

Council, as it relates to this question and that of the appointment of bishops, both of which are in a measure vital to the interests of the church in this country, breathes breadth of view and enlightened wisdom.

As we have seen from the letter of Archbishop Spalding to Bishop Timon, quoted above, one of the first subjects, in connection with the Second Plenary Council, which suggested itself to his mind was the founding of a Catholic university. The deep interest which he took in this project is also perceived from his Irish and Belgian correspondence, in which he seeks for information concerning the establishment of the universities of Dublin and Louvain. Among the questions which he submitted to the Fathers of the Baltimore Council was this: Whether the time had not come when, with the sanction of the Sovereign Pontiff, an university should be founded in this country? It was his opinion that an university would give us greater means than we had hitherto possessed for bringing the truths of our faith before the more intelligent class of Americans in a manner which could not but arrest their attention. And now that the church is an ubiquitous fact in this country, he felt that no time should be lost, and that we should at once go to work to create an American Catholic literature, irreproachable both in thought and style, which would deal with all the living problems of the age, and thus furnish a Catholic solution for the doubts by which thousands of those outside the church, who think, are tortured To the attainment of this end nothing would be more likely to contribute than a great central seat of Catholic learning, encircled by the halo of illustrious names, to which the eyes of Catholics from every part of the Union might turn with pride and reverence. It is humiliating to consider how much of what is best in our English and American Catholic literature is the work of men who were educated outside of the church.

To fit our young men for the great vocation of Catholic writers, an university education here at home would possess special advantages over any that could be had in foreign countries.

The thorough knowledge of the general thought of the country, of its peculiar shades and tendencies, the familiarity with what is best and most worthy of study in our own literature, which a Catholic university education here would give, could not be obtained in Europe.

As in helping to found the American College at Louvain Archbishop Spalding did not think he was doing anything that could interfere with the establishment of the Roman College, so he did not in the present case believe that the creation of an university in this country would in any way injure our foreign seminaries. Nor did he accept the opinion of those who hold that an university should not be created, but should grow into being and form. This may have been the general law of its formation in a ruder and more plastic state of the social organism; but in our society, in which every interest is represented by organized bodies, projects which are left to work themselves out are apt to be crushed by coming into collision with passions and prejudices in league with capital, and identified with special interests, which are watched over by jealous and vigilant corporations. With a primitive people, institutions grow up; among a highly cultivated and civilized people, they are created.

Besides, since public instruction intimately concerns faith and morals, and has a direct influence upon the welfare and peace of the church, Catholics have always held that the intervention of the ecclesiastical authority is required for the founding of a university. The history of all the ancient universities, from the thirteenth century down to the establishment of the University of Fulda, in 1732, shows that this principle was never lost sight of. The nineteen universities which came into existence in the sixteenth century were all either founded or confirmed by the Holy See. This historical fact is resumed in the following sentence from the Brief by which Gregory XVI. approved of the Catholic University of Lovain: *Celebriores illustrioresque Europæ universitates non nisi ex sententia et assensu Romanorum Pontificum fuisse constitutas gravissimæ illarum historiæ amplissime testantur.*

But the time when the great work of founding a Catholic university in the United States was to be begun, had not yet come, though the Fathers of the Second Plenary Council of Baltimore express their most ardent desire to see such an institution established here;* and their words concerning the plan of studies which should be pursued in higher ecclesiastical seminaries plainly show the urgent want of a Catholic university in this country.

"We have now no longer," they say, "to contend with the oft-refuted heresies and errors of a bygone age; but with new adversaries—unbelievers of a pagan rather than a Christian character; men who account as naught God and his divine promises, but who do not the less possess cultivated minds. According to them, the things of heaven and earth have no other meaning or value than that which natural reason assigns them. Thus they flatter pride, so deeply rooted in our nature, and seduce those who are not on their guard. If truth cannot persuade them, since they do not care to listen, it must, at least, close their mouths, lest their vain discourse and sounding words delude the simple." †

It was impossible that, in the two weeks to which they had limited their sittings, they should have been able to decide upon all the important matters which it was proposed to submit to them. Then, the urgent wants of the Ameri-

* *Con. Plen. Balt. II.*, n. 451.   † Tit. iii. p. 108.

can College in Rome demanded their immediate attention; and as it was thought necessary that all the bishops should exert themselves to raise a very considerable sum of money, that this institution might be permanently endowed, it was not deemed advisable to enter upon so vast an undertaking as the founding of a Catholic university.*

* The idea of a university is that of an institution whose soul-life is the intercommunion and mutual connection of all the sciences. As the great intellectual work in the church in our day is to show that theology, which is the science of God's revelation as interpreted by the church, is not only not in contradiction with, but is the essential and central point of union of, the whole scientific group, it is at once evident that the mission of a Catholic university is of the very first importance. Or, we may consider the university as the crown of all other institutions of learning. No general system of education can be complete which does not terminate in and receive its complement from the university. As Catholics in this country have a system of education peculiar to themselves and different from that which exists around them, a Catholic university to crown the edifice is of necessity demanded. 'I fear," wrote Bishop Spalding to Archbishop Kenrick in 1856, "we shall never be united in any general object outside the domain of faith and morals." I may be permitted to close these desultory remarks on a subject than which none should be of more interest to American Catholics, with a passage from Dr. Newman:

"I end as I began. A university is a place of concourse, whither students come from every quarter for every kind of knowledge. You cannot have the best of every kind everywhere; you must go to some great city or emporium for it. There you have all the choicest productions of nature and art all together, which you find each in its own separate place elsewhere. All the riches of the land and of the world are carried up thither; there are the best markets, and there the best workmen. It is the centre of the trade, the supreme court of fashion, the umpire of rival skill, and the standard of things rare and precious. It is the place for seeing galleries of first-rate pictures, and for hearing wonderful voices and miraculous performers. It is the place for great preachers, great orators, great nobles, great statesmen. In the nature of things, greatness and unity go together; excellence implies a centre. Such, then, is a university. It is the place to which a thousand schools make contributions; in which the intellect may safely range and speculate, sure to find its equal in some antagonist activity, and its judge in the tribunal of truth. It is a place where enquiry is

My purpose does not lead me, for the present at least, to examine further into the work accomplished by the Second Plenary Council of Baltimore.

It may not be out of place, however, to give an estimate of the wisdom shown by the fathers of the American church in this assembly, as made by a very thoughtful writer in one of the first Catholic reviews in France :*

"We are struck by the wisdom and prudence which characterize the decrees of this Council. . . . We here find evidence of that American good sense, eminently exact and practical, which, in dealing with lofty things, seizes them principally by their positive side, and which, without losing sight of principles, yet adapts them to times and circumstances. If doctrine is greatly represented in this volume, mere speculation occupies but small space. Above everything else, the Council has aimed to be a work of organization. Not less remarkable for what it has not said than for what it has said, it seems to embody the device of the poet: *Semper ad eventum festinat*. No superfluous details, no useless erudition; everything bears the seal of

---

pushed forward, and discoveries verified and perfected, and rashness rendered innocuous, and error exposed, by the collision of mind with mind, and knowledge with knowledge. It is the place where the professor becomes eloquent, and a missionary and preacher of science, displaying it in its most complete and most winning form, pouring it forth with the zeal of enthusiasm, and lighting up his own love of it in the breasts of his hearers. It is the place where the catechist makes good his ground as he goes, treading in the truth day by day into the ready memory, and wedging and tightening it into the expanding reason. It is a place which attracts the affections of the young by its fame, wins the judgment of the middle-aged by its beauty, and rivets the memory of the old by its associations. It is a seat of wisdom, a light of the world, a minister of the faith, an alma mater of the rising generation. It is this and a great deal more, and demands a somewhat better head and hand than mine to describe it well."—*The Office and Work of Universities*, pp. 23-25.

* *Les Etudes Religieuses.*

legislation soberly but firmly motived, wherein nothing is omitted that can enlighten and convince the mind, and nothing is allowed to lengthen what should be short, or complicate what is simple. It is a majestic monument of simple and severe proportions, in which art seems neglected, but is by no means wanting." Much higher authority has also borne witness to the great wisdom manifested in the Baltimore Council.

"Many of the fathers of the Vatican Council," says a well-known writer in the *Catholic World*, himself a member of that august assembly, "seem well acquainted with our Second Plenary Council of Baltimore. More than once it has been referred to with special commendation, as having thoroughly seized the character of this modern age in which we live. And the desire was expressed that its special regulations, on one or two points, for the church in the United States, could be made universal laws for the whole church." *

Cardinal Cullen has expressed his opinion of the Second Plenary Council in the following letter to Archbishop Spalding:

"When last writing, I thanked you for the copy of your Plenary Synod, which you so kindly sent me. Since then I have been able to consult it frequently, and I find that it is a mine of every sort of knowledge necessary for an ecclesiastic. I congratulate you most warmly on your success in bringing out a work which cannot fail to be of the greatest value to the church of America, and, indeed, to every other church."

The closing ceremonies of the Council, at which the President of the United States assisted, were not less imposing than had been those of its opening. Archbishop Purcell, as the senior bishop by consecration of the American

---

* *Catholic World*, April, 1870, art., "Vatican Council."

hierarchy, delivered an address, in which he thanked the Legate Apostolic for the "dignity, impartiality, and learning" with which he had presided over this most important Council.

In reply, Archbishop Spalding said:

"What I have just heard—which I know expresses the feelings of all my venerable brethren—compensates me more than an hundredfold for whatever little labor I have undergone in preparing for this Council. I feel and say from my heart that I am unworthy of the eulogy which the partiality of my venerable brother has passed upon me. I can lay claim only to industry and earnestness. The true secret of all this, I am sure, is that I am the voice or the shadow of him who represents divine unity and authority on this earth; that I am invested, however unworthy, with the authority of Pius IX., through whose voice Peter speaks, and, through Peter, Christ. Herein consists the simplicity, and the beauty, and the sublimity of our faith. We are but the last link in a golden chain, the first of which was Peter, and he was bound to the rock, which is Christ. Never were the unity and the unearthly character of the church shown more strikingly than in this Council. Here we have venerable prelates from all parts of this great and vast Republic, some of whom have come five or six thousand miles—have come at my voice, because in my voice they recognized the voice of Peter and of Christ. They have come together with one heart and one soul, intent only on the great object of beautifying the house of God, of proclaiming his truth and his holiness, and of promoting the salvation of men. All other considerations have been wholly forgotten. During the two weeks of the Council, while we were in session from six to eight hours a day, not one word has been breathed on or one allusion made to the stirring and exciting topics of the day. Our kingdom is not of this world ; we have higher aims—glory to God in the highest, peace on earth to men of good-will.

"We came together to devise ways and means to carry out the purpose for which Christ died on the cross—to save men, to bind them together in unity and charity, and to make them lead holy lives. Absorbed in this great object, we have soared far above the region of storms and clouds, into the pure atmosphere of God, where no controversy or contention is stirred up by human passion; and men, sprung from various nations, have in this Council lost sight of all differences of nationality and temperament, and have been blended into that beautiful unity and harmony which the Catholic Church alone can exhibit."

The fathers of the Second Plenary Council found that the rapid growth of the church justified them in petitioning the Holy See to erect fifteen new dioceses and vicariates apostolic in the United States. The decrees were sent to Rome, where they were submitted to the most thorough examination, and a few slight corrections, partly verbal—*coscrelle*, Father Perrone called them—having been made, they received the solemn sanction of the Holy Father, and became the ecclesiastical law of the United States.

CHAPTER XXV.

THE PAST, THE PRESENT, AND THE FUTURE.

AT the close of this last solemn gathering of the American bishops, I may be permitted to pause a moment, and to consider whether the past and present condition of the church in the United States may not throw some light upon what her future is to be.

The history of the American church contains lessons of the greatest value, not only to ourselves, but it is also full of the deepest interest to Catholics throughout the world. It is the opinion of many thoughtful observers, both in the church and outside of it, in this country and abroad, that our position with regard to the state and society, and, to a certain extent, the mutual relations of the clergy and laity as they here exist, are destined to extend far beyond the limits of our own country, and possibly to become universal. The question is not at all whether this state of things is the best; the enquiry turns upon facts, not upon principles.

The tendency of modern social movements is to give greater power and a wider sphere of action to the people. The reactions which from time to time, with varying success, seek to arrest this tendency, only make its force the more manifest. The masses of the people are being educated now as they have never been before, and the governments of Christendom, willingly or unwillingly, are turning their chief attention to the helping on of this educational movement. Universal suffrage is another form in which this tendency of the age seeks expression.

Again, the qualified independence of church and state is, it would seem, destined to become a feature in the phase of social existence upon which we are entering.

Now, men ask themselves, Can the old church live in this new world which seems to be growing up around her?

They who lose sight of her supernatural character give, for various reasons, a negative answer to this question. The old Protestant theory, that the church is a political machine, the creation of kings and emperors, beneath the shadow of whose thrones alone it is capable of working satisfactorily, still has its advocates, though, intellectually, they are of little importance. There are, nevertheless, men who would fain persuade themselves that the Catholic Church in the nineteenth century is a fossil, whose lifelessness only the dim light of the sanctuary can conceal. Bring it out, they say, into the free atmosphere of liberty, and into the bright light of universal intelligence, and, like some long-buried corpse which seems well preserved when first brought to view, but when exposed to the air crumbles to dust, it will be no more.

Then, the pantheistic evolutionist view of history, which very generally underlies all the non-Catholic thought of the day, gives to its advocates other reasons for thinking that the church of the past cannot be that of the future.

Religious beliefs are, in their eyes, but the necessary results of given psychical and physical conditions of life. When these conditions change, faith is modified; when they pass away, the particular beliefs to which they gave birth die. Now, they say, modern nations are entering upon a new era, socially and politically; general causes are evolving effects hitherto unreached; and, as the result of all this, the religious faith of mankind must necessarily undergo a radical change.

Many Catholics, too, whilst anticipating the new order

of things, yet have unfavorable forebodings as to what the effect upon the general prosperity of the church may be; for God has certainly left the worldly condition of the church subject in part to natural causes.

The church in this country has now for three-quarters of a century been placed in contact with the new order of things, and in circumstances admirably suited to test her real vitality. And as a sequel to the light thrown upon her present condition by the Second Plenary Council of Baltimore, it may not be out of place to examine briefly what her progress has been, and to consider whether it is real or merely apparent. The question whether or not thus far we have numerically lost more than we have gained is, in this connection, altogether of minor importance.

That, to confine ourselves to the period in which the hierarchy has been in existence here, we have lost in numbers by very far more than we have gained, is, if I may express my opinion, beyond all doubt.* But the causes of this are manifest. They are accidental, have already to a great extent disappeared, and must day by day become more and more inactive; so that the number of those who are here lost to the faith is, in proportion to the Catholic population of the country, continually decreasing, whilst the number of converts each year grows larger.

The great problem which we had to solve was whether or not a vigorous but yet orderly and obedient Catholicity could be established in this democratic country, where

* We may, I think, safely accept the opinion of Bishop England, that, during the first twenty years after the erection of the see of Baltimore, though there was an increase of congregations, yet there was a vast total loss of Catholics to the church. He estimated the Catholics of the two Carolinas, in 1832, at ten thousand, whereas he thought fifty thousand of the entire population of the two States were the descendants of Catholics; and he did not think his diocese in this respect an exception, though in this he was probably mistaken.

what are called the principles of modern civilization had found their highest practical expression.

The outlook was by no means flattering to sanguine hopes.

The public sentiment of the country was adverse, and, though Catholics were tolerated, it was only because their toleration formed part of a system which was a necessity, and because they were too much despised to be feared.

In 1785, when Dr. Carroll submitted to the Propaganda a statement of the condition of the church in the United States, he computed the whole Catholic population at twenty-five thousand. The number of priests was but twenty-five. A schismatical spirit existed both among the clergy and the laity.

"Every day," says Dr. Carroll, "furnishes me with new reflections, and almost every day produces new events to alarm my conscience and excite fresh solicitude at the prospect before me. You cannot conceive the trouble which I suffer already, and the still greater which I foresee from the medley of clerical characters, coming from different quarters and of various educations, and seeking employment here. I cannot avoid employing some of them, and they begin soon to create disturbances." *

In New York, Boston, and Philadelphia, selfish and insubordinate priests, instead of promoting union and charity among the people, sowed the seeds of discord and scandal. A deplorable schism occurred in New Orleans in 1805, and, when the diocese was committed to Bishop Dubourg, he was without priests or means to advance religion; and finally, after having encountered many difficulties, he retired to St. Louis.

In South Carolina, the progress of the church was disturbed by miserable dissensions. In Charleston, though

* Letter to Plowden, 1789.

the number of Catholics increased by immigration, yet all real advance in religion was prevented by these scandals. In 1809, but three Catholics, it is said, received the Easter communion in that city. A small colony of Catholics from Maryland had settled in Georgia; but the priest who had charge of them grew negligent, and finally apostatized.

The ill-regulated system of trusteeism was another source of constant disturbances, and seemed at times to threaten to disorganize the church, which, still in its infancy, had so many other enemies to contend with. The trustees not unfrequently sought to extend their power over bishop, priest, and church. The Catholic laity, following the example of Protestants, seemed to be upon the point of demanding that the administration of church affairs should be given into their hands, and that the clergy should become their servants, ready to perform religious services in the manner which they should dictate. This evil continued to be a source of scandals and schisms for many years, and undoubtedly estranged great numbers from the church. There was also danger lest it should serve as a pretext for the intermeddling of the civil authority with church property and other ecclesiastical affairs. Then a vast Catholic immigration began to pour into a country where the church was hardly able to struggle with the difficulties by which it was already surrounded. It was, of course, impossible at once to provide for the religious wants of this new population. These immigrants spread over the country, and very frequently settled where there was no church and no priest.

In such cases, they were necessarily deprived of the sacraments, and their children grew up without religious instructions. The few priests who were laboring on the missions were forced to confine their efforts chiefly to the cities and principal towns, in which the great body of the Catholics lived. It is also worthy of remark, that many of these early missionaries spoke English very imperfectly; whilst they were but little acquainted with the habits and customs of the people amongst whom they were called to labor. Then there was no such thing as Catholic education; and for a long time, the only Catholic schools which existed, with the exception of a few colleges and academies, were of the most wretched kind. Indeed, I think I may be permitted to say that it is comparatively of recent date that many thoughtful and observant minds in the church of this country have comprehended the all-importance of Catholic education. Other agencies, too, worked against the progress of the church. The Catholic immigrants, who were generally extremely poor, suffered of course many hardships and great exposure to the rigors of a climate which was not their own. This increased the mortality amongst them, and, in consequence, numbers of orphans, for whom the church was unable to provide, yearly fell into the hands of Protestants, to be brought up by them in their own faith. We may add to this, that the very people to whom, above all others, the church in this country is indebted, met with special difficulties in the accomplishment of their God-given mission. How this should seemingly have proved an obstacle to the advance of Catholicity in the United States is well stated by Bishop England:

"England has," he says, "unfortunately, too, well succeeded in linking contumely to their name [the Irish] in all her colonies; and, though the United States have cast away the yoke under which she held them, many other causes combined to continue against the Irish Catholic, more or less to the present day, the sneer of the supercilious, the contempt of the conceited, and the dull prosing of those who imagine themselves wise. That which more than a century of fashion has made habitual is not to be overcome in a year; and to any Irish Catholic who has dwelt in this country during one-fourth of the period of my sojourn, it will be painfully evident that, although the evil is slowly diminishing, its influence is not confined to the American nor to the anti-Catholic. When a race is once degraded, however unjustly, it is a weakness of our nature that, however we may be identified with them upon some points, we are desirous of showing that the similitude is not complete. You may be an Irishman, but not a Catholic; you may be Catholic, but not Irish. It is clear you are not an Irish Catholic in either case!!! But when the great majority of Catholics in the United States were either Irish or of Irish descent, the force of the prejudice against the Irish Catholic bore against the Catholic religion in the United States; and the influence of this prejudice has been far more mischievous than is generally believed."* Another source of trouble was the mingling of the various nationalities in the same congregation, where the prejudices and differences of custom and language of each became causes of antagonism and frequently of dissensions. This was a serious evil at a time when the church was struggling for a foothold on the American soil. Then the priests themselves belonged to four or five different nationalities, had been educated in various parts of the world, and hence upon many non-essential points did not think alike. The ecclesiastical organization was imperfect; the five or six bishops of the country, separated by great distances, rarely saw one another; and the individual peculiarities of the priests were frequently not restrained or controlled by a strong central government.

All these difficulties may be said to have belonged within the church of this country, since they proceeded chiefly from the peculiar elements of which the Catholic population was composed. But she had to contend against other trials of a scarcely less serious nature. Contempt, and ignominy,

* *Bishop England's Works*, vol. iii. p. 233.

and disgrace were coupled with the very name of Catholic wherever English rule had been supreme. Catholics were

> "A fixed figure for the hand of scorn
> To point its slowly moving finger at."

Men thought better of Turks and Jews than of us; and the Sultan, in their eyes, was not so hateful as the Pope. If we were tolerated, it was, as I have said elsewhere, the toleration of contempt.

If the church was to triumph over all these obstacles, it could only be by her own innate power and vitality. She had nothing but God's promise. The test could not have been more fairly made. Even her worst enemies could scarcely have asked other conditions than those which were given her.

Three-quarters of a century have hardly passed away since the hierarchy was established here, and the issue of the struggle is now no longer doubtful.

The church in that time has gone steadily forward, and her progress has become, day by day, more real and more certain. She has conquered the elements of discord and disturbance which threatened her young life, and to-day she is the most thoroughly organized and most perfectly united body in all this great country. And perhaps, though it may not be modest to say it, there cannot be found a body of Catholics more zealous for the faith, more self-sacrificing, more loyal to the Vicar of Christ, than the seven millions of the United States.

Whilst freedom has acted as a solvent upon the various sects, which have divided and subdivided, it has only knit us closer together in the bonds of an unconstrained union. Protestantism has been pulled hither and thither by all the to-and-fro conflicting opinions which spring from the teeming mind of our age and country, until it is a mere shred, mere individualism—nihilism. It has lost control of the masses, and has only a sickly and sporadic existence in catering to the morbid sentimentalism of the effeminate rich. So hopeless have its divisions become that it has ceased to believe in truth, and proclaims that the nearest approach to it is to be sought in the conflict of opposing beliefs. Having despaired of religious unity, it calls it an evil, and declares that it is better that Christians should be divided. Unable to formulate a single article of belief, it repudiates the very idea of a creed.

In the midst of all this confusion, the Catholic Church remains undisturbed. The idle theories of men strike against her and fall hurtless at her feet.

Archbishop Spalding, in his day, may be considered the best and truest representative of the oldest element in the church in this country—that of the Maryland colony, which is, I may say, coeval with Anglo-Saxon civilization in North America. The Puritans came with characters cast in an iron mould, fixed in thought, firm in purpose, and with a will intense in proportion to the narrowness of the type they represented; the whole permeated and knit together by a religious enthusiasm which gave color and form to all they thought or did. And yet their religion is dead—their strong and manly faith has become in their descendants a vague and shifting deism, or the sickly sentimentalism of weak and nerve-worn natures. Puritanism, with its immense force and power of resistance, has been unable to withstand the action of time and of freedom. The children of the Catholics who came over with Lord Baltimore are to-day in religion precisely what their fathers were. They hear Mass, they confess their sins, they fast, they pray to the Blessed Virgin and to all the saints, they love and obey the Pope, and believe in One Holy Catholic and Apostolic Church. Voltaire and the Encyclopædists have sneered, and mocked, and laughed. The German pantheists have, as they think, probed to the core, being and existence, and have shown that all reposes on nothing; that in the beginning was nothing, and that the end of each particular existence is nothing, and that whatever is, is only a phase of something that can never be. The scientists, following in their wake, despairing of the soul, have clutched matter, even in its nascent and evolutionary state, and have followed it through all the vagaries of form and life, from the infinitesimal to the infinite. Putting God and the soul aside, with the most reverential and religious air, as the unknowable, because they can neither be seen nor touched, they proceed, with perfect self-complacency, to create the universe.

In the beginning was incandescent gas. In time, a portion was precipitated and began to whirl about most furiously, and other particles were caught up by it, and thus were formed the sun, and stars, and planets. This is very easily understood, since we know bodies move along the line of least resistance.* But as yet there was no life; only a most desperate struggle for life. At length a few inanimate particles of matter, having won the victory, organized and formed a corporation for life, under the express agreement that this corporation should evolve itself until all other possible forms and conditions of life should be involved in it. In other words, it was understood that it should be as voracious and heartless as a railroad or bank corporation. Here we have a clear and satisfactory explanation of the genesis and transformation of species, so that, in case we should not feel disposed to believe that God created man, we can become scientifically superstitious, and hold that this contentious, restless, unsatisfied little animal came of a particular fight which took place several million years ago in primordial matter, and that all things, having begun in

* See Herbert Spencer's *First Principles*, p. 204.

incandescent gas, are likely to end in smoke. But to be serious: in the science of matter, our age has made the most real progress. Everything has been analyzed, every form of matter has been peered into by the patient and laborious eye of the student. The secret places of the earth have been laid open, the "dark, unfathomed caves of ocean" have been made to tell their tale, and we have learned to read and to understand in the earth, in the rocks, and in the air a language which to our fathers was meaningless. The practical applications of our knowledge have given us the means of still further discovery. Whatever anywhere is worth knowing may now be known everywhere. The continents have been crossed, the islands have been visited, the rivers have been traced to their sources. Man has been studied in every phase of his life. The body has been scrutinized from the inception of its existence down to the last stage of decomposition, and the attempt has even been made to express life by a chemical formula—so many particles of nitrogen, oxygen, hydrogen, and carbon. Or, to use the profound language of Mr. Herbert Spencer, "animal life is chiefly a process of oxidation";* and so is the rusting of iron.

The influences that modify human existence, such as climate, laws, religion, have been subjected to the pitiless scrutiny of science; spectrum analysis has even shown us the metals which are found in the sun's photosphere. And now, what has been the effect of all this upon the religious belief of the peoples among whom this scientific development has taken place?

Protestants are tortured by doubt and anxiety. The predominant tendency with them is towards deism or a still more absolute negation of religious truth. A counter-current, but not so strong or so marked, is bearing numbers

* *First Principles*, p. 209.

nearer to the church. Protestant thought has become absolutely chaotic. Hoenighaus wrote a book, in which he proved every Catholic dogma from the confessions of respectable Protestants. To-day a work might be readily composed, which, without going beyond the admissions of the leading and accredited exponents of Protestantism, would infer the negation of every dogma of religion. It is this hesitating, negative, self-contradictory nature of Protestant thought which has made what is called scientific infidelity so loud-mouthed, and led its devotees to believe that they can browbeat Christians into atheism.

But, on the other hand, what impression have the intellectual and scientific achievements of which we boast made upon the church? Are Catholics tortured by doubt? Does a secret and ominous fear pervade the Catholic thought of the age, lest, perchance, science may have undermined the foundations of the church? Has a rationalistic and sceptical spirit found its way into her sanctuary?

Her children have, at least, followed the march of science, and have taken note of its conclusions. Is their faith shaken? No candid and thoughtful observer will give an affirmative answer to these questions.

> "Many a vanished year and age,
> And tempest's breath, and battle's rage
> Have swept o'er Corinth; yet she stands.
>
> . . . . .
>
> The whirlwind's wrath, the earthquake's shock,
> Have left untouched her hoary rock,
>
> . . . . .
>
> The landmark to the double tide,
> That purpling rolls on either side,
> As if their waters chafed to meet,
> Yet pause and crouch beneath her feet."

"Our great antagonist—I speak as a man of science—" says Professor Huxley, "the Roman Catholic Church, the one great spiritual organization which is able to resist, and must, as a matter of life and death, resist, the progress of science and modern civilization, manages her affairs much better." *

The church is able to resist the progress of science, the Professor thinks, because science has been unable to find a weak point in the citadel in which God has placed her; or, possibly, because she is not frightened when Mr. Darwin writes a new book, or Mr. Tyndall proposes to test the medicinal properties of prayer.

The tendency of science must necessarily be to strengthen the faith of men in the universality of law, of method, and of purpose; and, consequently, in the existence of an ever-present, all-wise, beneficent Being. Now, as long as men continue to believe in God, they will believe in Christianity, which finds its full and legitimate expression in the Catholic Church alone. Thus far, at least, she has seen no reason to reverse the sentence which Julian the Apostate, as he took in his hand his heart's blood and cast it against heaven, spoke with dying lips: "Jesus of Nazareth, thou hast conquered."

After all, what is called science can never draw an absolute conclusion; it can deal only with relations, and with these merely in their physical manifestations. Its material hand can never grasp the life of the soul in itself and in God; and its influence upon faith must come rather from its practical applications and discoveries than from any principles which it is able to establish. Now, in no country in the world have the results of science been applied so generally or with such success as in ours.

What has been the effect upon Catholic faith? The children of the church, untainted by popular unbelief, gather around her in serried ranks, and hold out to her the

* *Lay Sermons*, p. 61.

helping hands of sympathy and love. Any danger that might once have seemed imminent of the alienation of the laity from the clergy has passed away, and to-day in no country in the world are priest and people more truly united than here. Parochial schools, in charge of Catholic Brothers and Sisters, are everywhere springing up, and the number of children who receive thorough religious training is yearly becoming larger in a ratio far greater than that of the increase of the Catholic population. In some dioceses, indeed, it may be said that already Catholic children are educated in Catholic schools.

When we educate our own children, we may safely for the rest leave the issue of our cause to God. The number of orphans who are lost to the church is diminishing in proportion to the increase of Catholic protectories, industrial schools, and asylums. What has hitherto been the chief obstacle to the progress of the church—the want of priests —has, in a great measure, ceased to be. At the close of the War of Independence, there were not more than twenty-five priests in the United States. In 1800, there were supposed to be forty. In 1830, there were two hundred and thirty-two priests in the Republic, and some of these had been gained by the cession of Louisiana to the United States. In 1848, there were eight hundred and ninety. In 1861, the number had grown to two thousand three hundred and seventeen; and in 1872, to four thousand eight hundred and nine. The increase in the number of churches has kept pace with that of the priesthood. There can be but little doubt that, by the end of this century, we shall have the most numerous episcopate, and one of the most numerous bodies of priests, of any country in the world. In 1808, there was but a single bishop in the United States; to-day, there are sixty-five dioceses and vicariates apostolic within its limits. In 1800, there were but two convents in the United States; to-day, there are over three hundred and fifty female religious institutions, and probably one hundred and thirty for men.*

As above stated, Dr. Carroll, in 1785, reckoned the Catholic population of this country at twenty-five thousand.

"Upon my first arrival in the United States, in 1820," says Bishop England, "I saw in a public document, coming from a respectable source, the estimate to be one hundred thousand, and this favorable, and from a gentleman by no means unfriendly." † In 1832, he estimated the Catholic population of the country at half a million. "I have since then," he writes in 1836, "made more close enquiries, taken more special notice of details, and received better information; and I think the estimate may be safely fixed at one million two hundred thousand." ‡ Within the last thirty years, opinions widely differing have at various times been advanced as to our Catholic population; and it is to be much regretted that in this matter, which is of the greatest interest, we are still to such an extent left to mere conjecture. However, from the data which we have, we are probably not unwarranted in the statement that there are at present in the United States not less than seven millions of Catholics. The influence of the church upon non-Catholics is also constantly increasing, if we may be allowed to judge from the number of conversions. In a letter dated February 19, 1868, Archbishop Spalding writes: "The precise number of converts whom I have confirmed since the fall of 1864—that is, in less than three years and a half—is fourteen hundred and thirteen! The total number confirmed in the same period is eleven thousand four hundred and eighty-

---

* I of course do not include in this estimate Catholic colleges and academies.
† *Works*, vol. iii. p. 227.
‡ *Works*, ibid.

two; consequently, over twelve per cent. of those confirmed were converts." *

The proportion of converts in the diocese of Louisville was but little below that just given for Maryland. What the proportion may be elsewhere, I have no means of ascertaining; but, unless we are to consider these two dioceses in this respect exceptional, it is evident that these accessions to the church form one of the most important elements of her strength, besides proving, in a way which does not admit of reply, that between her and what the best and noblest in this great nation would aspire to there is no opposition. The question whether or not the Catholic Church, unaided by the state and opposed by popular prejudice, with nothing but common rights under the common law, can maintain herself and wax strong under a free government, in which the most advanced modern principles, as Americans understand them, have been reduced to practice, is not now, if it ever was, doubtful.

---

* In five years, he confirmed 22,209 persons, of whom 2,752 were converts—about 12½ per cent. of the whole number.

CHAPTER XXVI.

THE EMANCIPATED SLAVES—THE CATHOLIC PUBLICATION SOCIETY—THE CENTENARY OF THE MARTYRDOM OF ST. PETER.

IN the spring of 1867, Archbishop Spalding visited Europe for the first time in fifteen years. The Holy Father had invited the bishops of the Catholic world to be present at the centenary celebration of the martyrdom of St. Peter, and, as his health was not good, he determined not to deny himself the pleasure of visiting, possibly for the last time, the shrines of the apostles.

In making the necessary preparations for leaving home, he overworked himself, and was, in consequence, taken dangerously ill. For several days, his physicians thought he could not recover, and, indeed, he seemed to be just hovering between life and death. The announcement of his illness drew forth expressions of sympathy, which proved how warmly he was beloved, not only by his own people, but by thousands of Catholics everywhere, and even Protestants. The enterprising press had already received intelligence of his death, and, on the day on which he sailed for Europe, he had the unusual pleasure of reading his own obituary.

In the pastoral letter which he addressed to his people before leaving home, he alludes to this illness, which came upon him whilst engaged in writing it.

"We had proceeded thus far," he says, "when, in the mysterious providence of God, we were stricken down by an illness which warned us to prepare for a longer journey; and though God gave us, we humbly trust, a suitable measure of resignation, yet he was pleased to listen to the prayers of our faithful people, and to grant us a longer tenure of life. What was refused to our great patron of Tours and his disciples was granted to us, who had but begun our career, had done well-nigh nothing, and were not prepared to die. Coming up from the brink of the tomb, with, we trust, a deeper sense of our responsibility and clearer lights as to the duties we owe to the flock committed to our charge, we now address to you before leaving the few but grave reflections on three points of vital importance to the interests of religion in the archdiocese, which we had in our minds and hearts in beginning this pastoral."

The three subjects to which he alludes are the instruction of the emancipated slaves, the Catholic Publication Society, and the St. Mary's Industrial School. One of the first things he had done after his arrival in Baltimore was to give his hearty approval to the work which Dr. O'Connor was doing in seeking to build up a negro congregation in that city.

"There is no respect of persons," he said, "with God. True to the spirit of this maxim, the Holy Catholic Church has never known any distinction of color or race in her heavenly ministrations for the salvation of all whom Christ, her divine founder, has redeemed."

We have already seen how anxious he was that the Second Plenary Council should devise some practical means for bringing the emancipated slaves within the influence of the church. He now urges the pastors of his archdiocese to put forth every effort of enlightened zeal to secure to them the blessing of Christian instruction. He desires that separate schools be established for them; "since," he says, "experience proves how difficult it is to impart religious instruction to those who cannot read." He wishes also to see more churches built for their use, especially in the cities where they are most needed.

"We must say," he continues, "to the credit of our colored children, that they have been invariably liberal and generous, in proportion to their means, in aiding in the establishment of schools and churches for their benefit. This has been abundantly proved in the case of a church in Washington, and of six or seven colored schools which have been recently established in the archdiocese. The pastors who will determine to labor zealously in their behalf will always find them willing co-operators."

He still further shows his interest in this matter by manifesting his intention to organize a regular system of missions for the special advantage of this portion of his flock—a project which he afterwards succeeded in putting into execution. Indeed, to the end of his life the spiritual welfare of his colored children, as he called them, was one of the things nearest his heart.

In the fall of 1870, he invited all the white Catholic societies of Baltimore to assist at the laying of the cornerstone of St. Francis' School and Orphan Asylum for colored children; and when, at his request, they had all joined in the procession and ceremonies, he spoke to them in the following words, which are so characteristic of his warm and gentle nature:

"MY DEARLY BELOVED CHILDREN: My heart bounds with joy on this happy occasion, and my heart but re-echoes the voice of the Holy Catholic Church. The Catholic Church is of all nations, of all colors, of all peoples! There is no distinction of color with God, and there is none with the Catholic Church. Forty years ago, when I was a student at Rome, there were two colored students in the same college with myself, and one of them was my particular friend. The Catholic Church makes no distinction among its children: and I rejoice to see Germans, and Irish, and Americans here to-day, carrying out the true spirit of the church.

. . . There are no parties in heaven. I want all my children—Irish, German, American, African—I want them all to go to heaven; and I trust that all those who are not yet on the road to that happy place will put themselves on the right path. There are many good people outside of our church, and I want them all to go to heaven."

Several years previous to this, at the request of Archbishop Spalding, two missionaries had been sent to this country by the Holy See, to devote themselves exclusively to the spiritual welfare of the emancipated slaves; and their labors had been crowned with great success.

The fathers of the Second Plenary Council of Baltimore invite, in the name of God's mercy, all priests who may be able to do so to devote themselves wholly to this great work; and they also beg of the Superiors of religious orders to place some of their members at the disposal of the bishops, that they may assign them to the mission of evangelizing the liberated slaves of the Southern States.*

The chief difficulty which prevented the success of this work was the dearth of priests, especially in those States which had large negro populations.

In 1870, Pius IX. directed the priests of St. Joseph's Society for Foreign Missions—a community established by the Rev. Herbert Vaughan, at Mill Hill, near London—to devote themselves to the work of evangelizing the emancipated slaves in the United States.

Having communicated this fact to Archbishop Spalding, Dr. Vaughan received from him the following reply:

"Your letter has filled my heart with joy. I was quite ill when I received it, but it contributed greatly to my convalescence, and I am now nearly well. Please come at once to examine the ground and to make all necessary arrangements for the new colony.

* *Con. Plen. Secund.*, No. 488.

"As Baltimore is the natural and most appropriate point for the mother-house of any institution for the benefit of the colored people, whence it may send forth branches throughout the entire South, you should, I think, begin here.

"In three counties of Maryland, there are sixteen thousand Catholic negroes. . . . You have here a field of action already prepared. . . . I have some sixty acres of good land which I propose to give you, with an ample house, which, with some repairs, might well suit for an humble beginning; and in such works, God blesses humble beginnings."

When, in response to this invitation, Dr. Vaughan, accompanied by four missionaries, arrived in Baltimore, in December, 1871, just two months before Archbishop Spalding's death, he received from him the following letter of welcome:

"DEAR FATHER VAUGHAN: Permit me to welcome you and the four young men whom you bring with you, to labor in behalf of the colored people of the United States. The Archdiocese of Baltimore receives you with open arms, and I have not a doubt that you will be welcomed with similar cordiality by my venerable colleagues throughout the country. . . . Deriving, as you do, your mission to our colored people directly from the Holy Apostolic See, you cannot fail to be blessed by God; and in spite of the difficulties and trials which attend all great enterprises for his glory and the salvation of souls, and which you may therefore reasonably expect, you will succeed.

"With your headquarters for the present in Baltimore, you will be able, with God's help and the fostering encouragement of the respective ordinaries, to extend your labors gradually and successively throughout the entire South, and thus to reap an abundant harvest of souls redeemed by the precious blood of Christ."

The day before his death, I heard him say, in reference to this mission, that it was one of the things which he had asked God to let him see established in his diocese before he died.

It is also, in part, to his aid and encouragement that the colored Catholics of Louisville, his old episcopal city, are indebted for their church. Another subject to which Archbishop Spalding referred in the pastoral letter above mentioned was the Catholic Publication Society of New York, founded by the Very Rev. I. T. Hecker. He had advocated the establishment of a society of this kind as far back as 1854. In a letter to Archbishop Kenrick, written in the month of May of that year, he thus refers to the matter: "Whilst the Methodists and other sectarians have their vast book-concerns and all-pervading tract organizations, it is a shame that we children of the light should be so inert. Let a Catholic institute be established, with its headquarters in Baltimore, the bishops all to be honorary members, and Dr. Ives to be Secretary, charged with the publication of books and tracts. I think we might do something to cope with the vast and, humanly speaking, perfect organization of those who fight in the camp of Satan. I know there are difficulties in the way of carrying out this project; but they grow chiefly out of our own inertness and want of zeal, and could be overcome by a little determination. *Improbus omnia vincit labor.*" When Father Hecker at length undertook the work, Archbishop Spalding gave him his hearty sympathy and efficient aid; and he himself wrote the first tract of the series begun by the Catholic Publication Society. This attempt to organize for the purpose of disseminating cheap Catholic literature was not new in the history of the church in the United States. In 1827, Archbishop Hughes, at that time a young priest, made an effort to found a Tract Society in Philadelphia, for which he wrote the *Conversion* *and Edifying Death of Andrew Dunn*, one of his first essays in the field of literature. " The success of *Andrew Dunn,*" says his biographer, " was much greater than that of the project from which it sprang. It seems to have been the first fruit and the last of the association for the purpose of circulating cheap controversial tracts, from which so much was expected." *

In 1829, the fathers of the First Provincial Council of Baltimore, at the instance of Pope Leo XII., resolved to form an association for the dissemination of Catholic books. † In accordance with this resolution, the *Metropolitan Press* was founded, which continued in operation for several years, and undoubtedly did good, but never came up to the idea of a Catholic publication society. Another association of this kind was begun in 1839, and was called the Catholic Tract Society of Baltimore. It continued its publications for five or six years, and, according to Dr. White, " deserves honorable mention, as having produced some of the best essays that we possess in vindication of the true faith." ‡

When Archbishop Spalding was appointed by the Holy Father to preside over the Second Plenary Council of Baltimore, he invited Father Hecker to lay before the bishops his views with regard to the Catholic Publication Society, which he had just founded ; and he caused special mention to be made of this association in the matters which he had prepared for conciliary deliberation ; and in the pastoral letter issued after the close of the Council, it was earnestly recommended to the Catholics of the United States.

Upon the eve of starting for Europe, in 1867, Archbishop Spalding exhorted all pastors of souls in his archdiocese to

* *Life of Archbishop Hughes,* p. 83.
† *Vide decret.* 35, in General Collection of Baltimore Councils.
‡ Appendix to *Darras' Church History,* p. 653.

establish auxiliary societies, in order to aid the parent society by helping to diffuse its publications. He recommended, however, that these organizations should be of the simplest character, and thought that in many cases it would be found expedient to combine them with religious and charitable institutions already in existence.

"We cannot but believe," he concludes, "that the zeal of our devoted people will be at once and fully awakened to the importance of this subject; and that, under the guidance of their worthy pastors, they will thus be enabled to counteract much evil, and to promote the cause of divine truth. The machinery through which the Holy Catholic Church has been accustomed to work in moving vast masses of men has always been so grand, simple, effective, and silently sublime in its operation that Catholics have, in too many cases, so implicitly trusted to its workings as not to deem their own individual co-operation necessary. On the contrary, those outside the church who would seem to have had no such implicit trust in the divine character of their church organizations, have brought more fully into play the human elements of zeal, activity, and generosity of contributions, and have thereby succeeded in accomplishing what would seem, from their reports, to denote great results. Their zeal and generosity in promoting what they regard as most useful and beneficial, however mistaken their views, should put us to the blush, unless we go and do likewise in the sacred cause of truth, as bequeathed to us by our fathers in the faith."

Having made every arrangement for the proper administration of his diocese during his absence, Archbishop Spalding sailed from New York on the 4th of May, in the French steamer *Pereire*. He was still very feeble, and his friends had the most serious fears for his health. Indeed, many of them did not expect ever to see him again this side the grave; but, as he himself said, his hour had not yet come, and much still remained for him to do. He suffered greatly on the voyage, and was still quite ill when he landed at Havre. In Paris, where he remained for a few days, he grew no better, and, by the advice of his physicians, he went to Vichy, to try the waters. Three weeks' stay here did him some good; and he started for Rome on the 10th of June. It had been his intention before leaving home to visit the Holy Land, and he had written to a friend in Rome, asking him to obtain permission for him to be absent from his diocese long enough to make this journey; adding that, without the express permission of the Holy Father, he should not think his pilgrimage had God's blessing. His sickness, however, took from him all thought of being able to gratify this pious desire. In Lyons, he visited the venerable Cardinal De Bonald, who was then over eighty years of age. In Italy, he was greatly distressed by the many evidences he saw of the sacrileges committed by the Government of Victor Emanuel. In Bologna, he went to the beautiful church of St. Francis to say Mass, and found that it had been turned into a warehouse for carriages and harness. The marble altar was covered with all manner of rubbish. He told the superintendent of the place that God's curse would fall on the sacrilegious government of Italy. He had a Western way of speaking right out whatever he thought without any special regard to consequences, and, when travelling in Europe, took advantage of every opportunity that presented itself to give the apostate Catholics of France and Italy, to use his own words, a piece of his mind. These renegadoes were about the only class of men of whom he ever spoke with bitterness. In passing through the cities and towns of Italy, he never failed to visit the shrines of the saints, and, when possible, to say Mass at the altars where their relics were kept. At Assisi, he went to confession and received communion, as he was too unwell to say Mass in the church of St. Francis. He arrived in Rome in time to assist at the grand celebration of the eighteen hundredth anniversary of the martyrdom of Saints Peter and Paul. Five hundred bishops and not less than twenty thousand priests took part in the ceremonies. Rome had never beheld anything more imposing. But once before in eighteen hundred years had she seen so many prelates gathered within her walls; and never before, I believe, in the whole history of the church had so many priests assembled in one place. The celebration began on the evening of the 28th of June, with the illumination of the dome of St. Peter's. In the stillness of an Italian midsummer's night, fifty thousand pilgrims, gathered from the whole earth, looked up to this of earthly sights the most divinely beautiful; and, as it sank into their souls, awakening thoughts of all the heavenly things they hoped for, they felt that, after all, it was but a feeble image of that pillar of light which it symbolized, and which God had set up in the world to be the beacon to their souls' faith when all else was dark and doubtful. On the morrow, when Italy's sun had just begun to tip that dome with gold, all blushing, as if it felt itself powerless to recall the magic scene, the fifty thousand that had stood without were within St. Peter's "ark of worship undefiled." The light of day was shut out by crimson curtains, which, when a puff of wind blew them aside, let in the momentary sunbeams, as if God's angels were peeping through. Then thirty thousand tapers sprang into life, and threw their varying lights over the upturned faces of the vast multitude, where cardinals, bishops, priests, kings, princes, and people were one in the union of a faith that is fixed.

In the centre of the nave hung an inverted colossal cross of prisms of glass, transfigured with light, above it the keys, and still higher gleamed the Papal tiara. And now, Pius IX., his countenance illumined by that smile which is destined to become a tradition, is borne along on his chair of state to the pontifical throne. He, the visible head of a church whose children for eighteen hundred years, when nothing else remained to be done, have known how to die, and through death to rise to a higher life, even on earth, is about to place on the divine roll of honor the names of twenty-five of those martyr-heroes.

In those rich, clear-cut tones which millions have heard, he invokes the assistance of Heaven in the *Veni Creator Spiritus*, and then solemnly pronounces that these holy martyrs are God's saints, and as such are to be honored and reverenced by all his children. The silver trumpets in the dome sing out the glad tidings to heaven, the cannon of St. Angelo re-echo them to earth, and from all the seven hills of the great city, in notes deep and high, in tones silver and golden, that quiver with joy, that languish with love, the glad announcement is made. The Pope intones the Te Deum: " We praise thee, O God! We glorify thee, O Lord!" And as his words die away, fifty thousand voices take them up, and, with a power that seems to lift that whole multitude almost to the very throne of God, shout out, with a noise like that of many waters: " Thee, Eternal Father, the whole earth adores! To thee, the angels all; to thee, the heavens and the universal powers; to thee, the cherubim and seraphim, with unceasing voice, speak! Holy, holy, holy!" And as the sound dies away, the soul sinks back upon itself, fainting, overpowered by the too great manifestation of God's beauty and strength.

It was at this meeting of the bishops that Pius IX. announced his intention of holding an œcumenical council at as early a date as possible.

During his stay of two weeks in Rome, Archbishop Spalding had three interviews with the Pope, from whom he received great marks of esteem and affection.

At the Propaganda, there was a grand reunion dinner of the old students, amongst whom were twenty-five cardinals, patriarchs, archbishops, and bishops. At this celebration, in which part was taken by men from the furthest orient and the extreme west of the New World—men of every shade and color, of every tribe and tongue, for whom the Catholic Church was the only possible point of union—Archbishop Spalding met many of his old friends and companions with whom he had in early youth walked upright before God in the pleasant ways of virtue and knowledge; and, when he now looked upon the silvered heads and bent forms around him, he felt that the night was coming on apace, and that soon they should meet again in the home of Him for whom they had left father and mother, and all that the world loves. All Catholics feel at home in Rome, or were wont to feel so when their Father lived in freedom there. But Archbishop Spalding's love for the Holy City was remarkable. In his early youth, he had looked to her as

> "The fount at which the panting mind assuages
> Her thirst of knowledge, quaffing there her fill."

And when, during his severe illness, shortly after his first arrival in Rome, he thought that he was to die there, and that there his bones were to lie buried, he rejoiced and thanked God. His greatest grief, when that sickness lingered and threatened to prevent him from continuing his studies, was the thought that he should return home without having received a thorough Roman education. Even bad health had no power to sadden or discourage his young soul, which seemed to forget itself whilst breathing in the supernatural world of religion by which it was surrounded. With Rome were associated his earliest and proudest triumphs—victories the most glorious, because won when the dull world has not yet deadened the heart and shown it that it is all of no use; that all earthly victories end in defeat, and are marked by funeral monuments.

In Rome, he had met many of the men whom he had most loved and most venerated, whose services to him he thought of priceless value; and he had a long memory for benefits received. These sacred associations, hallowed by time, all united to strengthen his love for the centre of Christendom, the mother of all the churches, Rome—

> " Parent of our religion ! whom the wide
> Nations have knelt to for the keys of heaven !
> Europe, repentant of her parricide,
> Shall yet redeem thee, and, all backward driven,
> Roll the barbarian tide, and sue to be forgiven."

But the heat of midsummer was already upon the Sacred City, and Archbishop Spalding, who was still suffering, was forced to hasten away.

CHAPTER XXVII.

TRAVELS IN EUROPE — IRELAND — PROGRESS OF THE CHURCH IN THE ARCHDIOCESE OF BALTIMORE — THE AMERICAN COLLEGE IN ROME.

FTER leaving Rome, Archbishop Spalding visited Loretto, and said Mass in the Holy House, to satisfy his devotion to her whom he loved to call his sweet Mother.

In Padua, he visited the tomb of St. Anthony, and thence turned his steps to Venice, where

"Tasso's echoes are no more,
And silent rows the songless gondolier."

Each of the four times he went to Europe he travelled through Italy, and each time he beheld with new delight her marvellous treasures of religion and art. With Ariosto, he might have said:

"Visto ho Toscana, Lombardia, Romagna,
Quel monte che divide, el quel che serra
Italia, e un mare et l'altro che la bagna." *

In Milan, he said Mass on the tomb of St. Charles Borromeo, which lies in the crypt beneath the Duomo — the most dazzling structure on earth. Overlooking fruitful Lombardy, "the pleasant garden of great Italy," and lifting high towards heaven its four thousand marble pinnacles, all shimmering in the golden sunlight, it stands out against the cloudless sky like the vision of a heaven-built palace.

Hastening on across Lake Maggiore and the Borromean Isles, over the Alps, through the St. Gothard's Pass, down Lake Luzerne, whose unsurpassed natural beauty the genius of Schiller has idealized, Archbishop Spalding, on the 13th of July, reached the old town of Luzerne, above which, on either side, in awful grandeur, rise Pilatus and the Rigi—the one fog-covered, the other white with snow.

Leaving Luzerne, he passed through Basel, famous for its Council, and went down the Rhine to Strasburg. Here he visited the seminary, and, with the permission of Bishop Raes, made an address to the students, with a view to induce some of them to devote themselves to the American missions. In Mayence, he dined with Bishop von Ketteler, whose independence of character and earnest devotion to the church he greatly admired. Making his way between the vine-clad hills of the bending Rhine, which heroic deeds, enshrined in scenery "nor too sombre nor too gay; wild, but not rude; awful, yet not austere," have made a consecrated stream, to which, when once beheld, we never bid farewell, he arrived in Cologne on the 20th of July, and, two days later, in Louvain, to visit the American College, to the foundation of which he had so greatly contributed. He saw again many of his old friends in Belgium, and he also went to Holland, where fifteen years before he had been received with so much kindness. Ever anxious to increase the number of his own priests, and also to assist his brother bishops, he never failed, when permitted, to address the seminarians of the cities through which he passed, in order to awaken vocations for the American missions. In many parts of Europe, he felt there were more priests than were really needed; and here the harvest was ripe, and there were no laborers to gather it in. All this while, however, his health was far from being good, and he was really wandering about Europe chiefly with the hope of finding relief somehow or somewhere.

In Brussels, he met with a friend, who strongly urged him to try the baths of Aix-la-Chapelle. In his suffering condition, it was not difficult to persuade him to do anything that promised relief. So he went to Aix-la-Chapelle, and with what result he tells his benefactress in the following note of August 4, 1869:

"DEAR MADAME:

"I drop you a few lines, to return my sincere thanks for having so effectually called my attention to the baths and waters of this celebrated city. I find that all you said and promised has been fully realized; and when hereafter any one will dare tell me that your amiable sex is accustomed to draw upon imagination for its facts, or at least to color extravagantly what has proved pleasing, I shall point to your recommendation of these waters as a sufficient refutation of, or at any rate a most noted and brilliant exception to, the remark. The baths are all you said and more; they are really superb, and just what I needed. In fact, I consider it a special providence that I met you in Bruxelles, as otherwise I should have gone to Paris instead of Aix. Already I am quite relieved, and in another week I expect to be as young and supple as ever. . . . Though I have not yet taken any excursion to the country, I have visited the relics and curiosities of the grand old cathedral, and also the Hôtel de Ville.

"This is one of the oldest cities in Europe, and its inhabitants say with pride: 'After Rome, Aix-la-Chapelle.' The city, with its monuments, carries us back a thousand years, to the brilliant days of Charlemagne, who was a giant, not only morally and intellectually, but physically; for he was over seven feet two inches tall. . . ."

Now that his health was restored, he was anxious to get back to his beloved children. Returning to Paris, he saw the Universal Exposition, then passed through London on his way to Ireland, to pay a short visit to his old professor and friend, Cardinal Cullen. He was received with such warmth and hospitality that he spent three weeks in viewing the various places of interest in the Isle of Saints. He was so pleased with his visit that, a short time after he returned home, he lectured in Baltimore, to an audience of three thousand persons, on his tour in Ireland.

Archbishop Spalding felt the deepest interest in whatever concerned the welfare of Ireland or the Irish people, as he himself says in a letter to one of the most distinguished Irishmen of our day, from motives of religion and of sympathy, natural to one who had Irish blood in his veins.

His most intimate friend amongst the bishops of the United States, and the one whom he most admired—the gentle and scholarly Kenrick—was an Irishman. He recognized the fact that to the Irish people, above all others, is the church in this country indebted for its progress and present prosperous condition. Not only here, but in England, in Australia, in Canada, in Nova Scotia, indeed, wherever the church has gained ground in our day, the Irish race has proved itself the great missionary people of the nineteenth century. Without them he felt the Maryland Colony could have made little or no impression upon the country; and they had already borne the brunt of the battle and gained half the victory, before the German immigration, which now constitutes so powerful an element of the church in the United States, had attained to very great importance.

The Irish people were specially fitted for the work which the church had to do here. She needed men whom nor fear, nor contempt, nor derision could move from the outspoken profession of their firm-rooted faith; and they had too long suffered worse than martyrdom for conscience' sake to be troubled by such trifles. Others might believe that success has power to consecrate crime and blazon evil deeds; might be ever ready to desert the unpopular cause and salute the rising sun; but they were the veterans of the forlorn hope, never so true to the object of their love as when that object is despised and hated by the whole world beside.

Then, she needed a people between whom and their priests it would be impossible to sow the seeds of suspicion or distrust; that their well-knit and love-welded union might stand firm amidst the conflicting elements of a new and but imperfectly organized state of society.

"The priest," said the late Dr. O'Connor, "is the Irishman's great source of consolation in every shape of affliction. In poverty, he lays open to him his wants, and the priest's hand and tongue are ever ready to find any remedy that can be procured. In persecution or oppression, he flies to him for succor, and, if bold or persevering advocacy can find redress, it will be obtained. He is sick, and even relatives and friends abandon him; the priest alone, undeterred by the pestilential atmosphere, will enter his cabin, and remain with him as long as he can render him a service in assuaging his pains or lifting up his soul to God. In a hundred other things, the intervention of the priest is sought, and its beneficial influence is felt. Do differences arise between neighbors, the priest is the umpire, of whose impartiality and justice no doubt ever crosses the mind. If division arise in the family, the priest is sought as one who will pronounce a sentence consistent with justice and consideration, assuaging while he condemns, and pouring oil and endeavoring to heal the wounds which he is compelled to open. Does a mother tremble for the virtue of a daughter, charmed by the serpent whose glittering spots have attracted her fancy, while she cannot believe in the poison hidden under the tongue? It is to the priest she recurs, and his venerated words dispel the delusion, and save her beloved child from the wiles of the charmer." *

There is nothing in the whole history of the church more beautiful than the unbroken affection which, for so many centuries, has, in Ireland, bound together priest and people; and the same feeling which so generally exists between the clergy and the laity in this country is doubtless, to a very great extent, a traditional continuance of that old love.

In the history of probably every other people unfortunate divisions have arisen, which have at times changed the sacred name of priest to a term of reproach, and, in the popular language, have associated it with opprobrious epithets; but through all their strange, eventful history, whether the heavens smiled or lowered, whether they were freemen or slaves, with the name of priest, the Irish people have ever coupled a title of endearment, and the "sogarth aroon"—*priest dear*—like the English " sweet home," is one of those phrases created by the great heart of the people, which, in their deep meaning, epitomize all that is most precious and consoling in a nation's experience.

No one more admired the harmony and friendly familiarity which, in this country, characterize the mutual relations of bishops, priests, and people, or felt more keenly the all-importance of preserving this sweet concord, than Archbishop Spalding. Both by example and precept, he sought to strengthen these bonds of love; and his correspondence with his brother bishops is evidence both of his great concern in this matter, and of the high wisdom which guided him in dealing with cases of practical difficulty.

As an instance of Archbishop Spalding's interest in whatever concerned the welfare of the Irish race, I may quote here from a letter which he wrote to John Francis Maguire

* *The Irish Priest*—A Lecture.

whilst he was engaged in preparing his book on *The Irish in America:*

"I would suggest," wrote the Archbishop, "that you take special care not to commit your countrymen here to any party in politics, or to either side in the late civil war; and that you avoid any expression which might indicate that they constitute a class apart, with interests different from those of their fellow-citizens in general. . . . In fact, in the late war, they fought nobly with their respective sections, and were among the bravest soldiers on either side. So in politics; though the great majority of them have always been Democrats, yet there have always been many exceptions."

He also states that it is his opinion that emigrants to America should be urged to seek the country and engage in agricultural pursuits, and not to remain in the cities and towns, where they are almost necessarily brought into contact with vice and corruption.*

---

* Father Thébaud, in his excellent work on *The Irish Race*, advances the opinion that the crowding of vast numbers of Irish Catholic immigrants into the large cities of the United States has been providential. The first result of this has been, he thinks, "the sudden and necessary creation of many new episcopal sees."

Now, it seems to me that the erection of a new episcopal see is demanded, not so much because a certain number of Catholics are found in some central point, as because they dwell within the limits of a given territory. The episcopal see of a prosperous and well-organized diocese may be, and even in the history of the church in this country has been, a small and unimportant place; in more than one instance, the cathedral has been the only English-speaking congregation in the city.

Another consideration to which Father Thébaud attaches great importance is that, in the early ages of the church, the Gospel was first preached in the large cities, the populations of which had often to a great extent become Christian before even an attempt was made to convert the inhabitants of the rural districts; and he thinks there is a fundamental law governing facts of this kind. "Christianity," he says, "is a growth, and conse-

"The necessity of temperance," he adds, "cannot be too strongly inculcated. No Irishman who is temperate and industrious can fail to succeed."

On the 6th of October, 1867, Archbishop Spalding preached in the Metropolitan Church of Dublin, and on

---

quently, like everything that grows, must develop itself from a central point outward." But does not Father Thébaud mistake the point at issue? The first and great work of the church in this country was and is to preserve the faith of her own children. In comparison with this, the conversion of non-Catholics is merely of secondary importance. Now, the overcrowding of the poor in the great centres of population tends to develop disease of both body and soul, increases the death ratio, and, consequently, the number of orphans, for whom the church is unable to provide. It renders the proper education of children, who from their earliest years are necessarily thrown into contact with vice, almost impossible, and thus casts upon the world large numbers of young men especially, who, though the children of Catholics, are practically without religion or morality. I may add that it diminishes the influence of the great Catholic body by keeping in squalid poverty thousands who in other circumstances might create for themselves and their children homes that would become the sanctuaries of virtue and self-respect.

That the cities were the strongholds of the Christian religion in the first ages of the church is attributable in a great measure to accidental causes. The Jews were the first preachers and the most zealous disciples of Christianity; they formed the nucleus of the various apostolic churches, and then, as now, lived almost exclusively in the cities. The peculiar organization of the Roman state, and the condition of the rural pagan populations, would furnish other reasons.

The greater facilities offered in the large cities for escaping the pursuit of their persecutors should also be taken into consideration. But that Father Thébaud is mistaken in supposing that the Christian religion is necessarily or even generally propagated from the great centres outward, the conversion of the Irish, the Anglo-Saxons, the Goths, the Franks, and various other Teutonic tribes is proof sufficient.

I should imagine that a man like Father Burke, for instance, might find here a mission as sublime as that of Peter the Hermit or St. Bernard, in preaching to our people the wisdom of leaving the overcrowded centres of population for the vast and fertile districts of the still thinly peopled West.

For Father Thébaud's views, see *The Irish Race*, p. 435 *et seq.*

the same day he took the steamer for New York, where he landed after a voyage of eleven days.

His arrival in his episcopal city was greeted with marked manifestations of joy and reverence by both priests and people; and he began again, with renewed health and courage, the work of building up the church of Christ. His devoted children had not been idle during his absence. Within six weeks after his return, he dedicated four new churches in the city of Baltimore alone. The magnificent building for the Boys' Protectory had been nearly completed, and the Sisters of Charity had purchased a spacious house near Franklin Square for an Industrial School for girls, which had also been recently established. Thus he had the consolation of beholding these two cherished institutions placed on a firm and lasting foundation. The new convent and spacious chapel of the Sisters of the Good Shepherd had been finished and dedicated. The monastery of the Passionists, who had lately come to the archdiocese, was building. Two other institutions had been begun, which are to-day among the most splendid in the United States—the Novitiate of the Redemptorists, at Ilchester, and the Scholasticate of the Jesuits, at Woodstock. The Ladies of the Sacred Heart, at the special invitation of Archbishop Spalding, had entered the archdiocese of Baltimore, and made a foundation at Rosecroft, almost on the very spot where the first Catholic Pilgrims landed.

All these evidences of real and substantial progress rejoiced beyond measure the heart of the Archbishop, who seemed, as he grew older, to understand more and more fully the priceless value of the true faith, and to love it more and more ardently. One of the most important works which required his attention after his return home was the endowment of the American College in Rome.

"The idea of a college for American ecclesiastical students in the Holy City originated," says Mr. Hassard, in his life of Archbishop Hughes, "with Pope Pius IX. 'He proposed it to the bishops of this country in 1855, in his answer to the letter of the prelates composing the First Provincial Council of New York."

In 1857, Bishop O'Connor, of Pittsburg, at the request of the Archbishop of Baltimore, sought, whilst in Rome, to come to an understanding concerning the establishment of the College. The Holy Father then offered to give the ancient convent of l'Umilta to the American Church for the proposed institution; but, as the building was at the time occupied by French troops, he was not able to carry his design into immediate execution. In October, 1858, Archbishop Kenrick wrote to Bishop Spalding as follows: "The Rev. David Whelan has been appointed by me agent to confer with the authorities in Rome as to the erection of a college for the United States, in accordance with the action of the Council [Ninth Provincial of Baltimore]. The Pope urges it in his letter to the Archbishop of New York and in his reply to our Council." The College was not opened, however, until 1859. The bishops of the United States ordered collections to be taken up to defray the preliminary expenses; but the College was not established on a solid financial basis, having to depend chiefly upon uncertain collections, which a few years' experience showed to be inadequate to its proper maintenance.

The question of its endowment was, therefore, brought before the fathers of the Second Plenary Council of Baltimore, who, after considering various plans, finally resolved to raise a sum of money which, properly invested, would secure the College a fixed annual revenue. In January, 1868, the Sacred Congregation, in its instruction *De decretis Concilii corrigendis*, urged the bishops to make no delay in coming to the aid of the College, as it was in imminent danger of being closed for want of funds. In November, Archbishop Spalding, as Chairman of the Metropolitans, and Bishop Wood, as Chairman of the Executive Committee of Bishops, issued an *Appeal to the More Wealthy among the Catholics of the United States*, in which, after referring to the general collection ordered by the Plenary Council to meet the more pressing wants of the College, they recall the traditional generosity of Catholics in the endowment of schools and colleges, especially in ages past, when the great and the wealthy held it as a privilege to be allowed to contribute to such noble and Christian works.

"We urge the matter upon you the more strongly," I quote from the *Appeal*, "as next year the great General Council is to be convened in Rome, and we are to meet the bishops of the whole world in one of those grand assemblies which mark an era in the history of the Universal Church. To the councils of Nice, Ephesus, Chalcedon, Lateran, Lyons, Florence, and Trent is to be added that of the Vatican. Let us, before we go to the Holy City, have the consolation of knowing that, through your munificence, we have a College there to which we can proudly point as bishops of a great Catholic people; let us be spared the disgrace of going thither to find its doors closed and its name blotted out from the list of colleges existing in the Eternal City."

It was proposed to raise from $250,000 to $300,000, to be contributed in sums of $5,000, $1,000, and $500. The Rev. George H. Doane was deputed to call on the wealthy Catholics of the various dioceses of the country. He began with Baltimore. On the 29th of November, 1868, Archbishop Spalding wrote to the Archbishop of New York:

"I am happy to be able to inform your Grace that Father Doane's mission in Baltimore has been successful.

The result of the week's work so far is the subscription —as good as gold—of twenty-one thousand dollars, including three burses, but not including from three to eight thousand dollars additional, which we have well grounded hopes of obtaining. The contribution of Baltimore to the noble work may be safely set down, I think, at $25,000; and it may reach $30,000, as I have strong hopes of another burse. To achieve this result in so short a time, it was necessary diligently to prepare the ground beforehand. This was done by publications in the newspapers, by previous circulation of the *Appeal*, and by announcements from every pulpit in the city on last Sunday. Should other cities and dioceses equal Baltimore, our plan will have attained the end proposed."

His correspondence with various members of the American hierarchy at this time shows with what earnestness and energy he devoted himself to this work. As the oldest Roman student in the episcopate of the United States, he felt a special interest in the American College, which his love of the Holy See, and his unswerving devotion to whatever he thought to be for the honor and good of the church in this country, rendered still more active.

Over two hundred thousand dollars, for the most part in the form of burses of five thousand dollars each, were raised by this *Appeal;* and, although this sum was somewhat less than what had been expected, it was still sufficient to place the College upon a lasting foundation.

CHAPTER XXVIII.

THE DANGERS THAT THREATEN THE DESTRUCTION OF OUR FREE INSTITUTIONS—THE REMEDY—THE CRAVING FOR SENSUOUS INDULGENCE.

RCHBISHOP SPALDING was unrelenting in his opposition to the wasteful extravagance and the morbid craving for sensuous enjoyment which are everywhere invading American life. He himself had been brought up amid the primitive simplicity of our early republican society; and, although he had afterwards studied in Europe, and mingled much with the world, he yet never outgrew the impressions of his plain, democratic training. He considered the modern tendency to pagan sensualism as hurtful alike to the highest interests of true religion and of republican institutions. An effeminate, pleasure-loving people, as he thought, could neither be good Christians nor honest lovers of freedom; and, with St. Augustine, he held that only a virtuous people can long uphold a republican form of government.

He knew the great lesson of history concerning the rise and downfall of free institutions. At first, manners are rude, but pure and natural; faith is simple, but deep and earnest; and the people are poor, but patient of labor, and smitten with the sacred love of liberty. Then, as states grow, either by conquest or industry and commerce, wealth is developed, the arts and sciences flourish, manners become soft and polished. New wants spring into being; the desire of pleasure, the love of luxury, are born. The country blooms as the garden; the city gleams in gold, and flashes in marble. Civilization embellishes existence, and casts its effulgent beams afar; and, at their genial call, the scented, many-hued flowers of life put forth their tender blossoms. But beneath the flowers the serpent lurks. Life, now become so sweet, so pleasant, insensibly enervates the soul. Characters grow less strong and less manly. The virtues of the fathers die with them, and degenerate children cease even to admire that which they can no longer imitate. Egotism takes possession of the heart; the man who lives for pleasure lives for self alone. Corruption spreads, religion grows sickly, modelled after the characters of those who profess it. The disorder passes from the heart to the head. To justify his voluptuous life, man denies the religion which condemns it; and infidelity, like "pitted speck in garnered fruit," soon eats its way to the core of the nation's life. The boundless thirst for gold, the equivalent of all sensual gratification, soon creates two opposite classes in society—the very rich and the very poor. The venality of those clothed with authority renders wealth a protection against punishment for crime. The poorer class grow insubordinate and lawless. Wise men shake their heads, and prophets foretell the coming days of distress, and legislators multiply laws. But all to no purpose. Corruption grows, ascends higher and sinks lower, until all are drawn into its foul, contagious current. Society then calls to its aid force, despotism, and gives itself up into the hands of one man, who will hold all bound in the pitiless chains of tyranny. The people revolt and murder the master whom they had created, and then kneel at the feet of another; and so, from revolution to revolution, from despotism to despotism, the state is hurried on, till, swallowed up in universal chaos, it sinks into the abyss.

Thus great states have grown strong and mighty, thus have they become weak and powerless, until at length Time drew his ploughshare across the plains of their dwelling and the cities of their abiding, leaving only a ruin to mark the place where once they were.

Archbishop Spalding, like other thoughtful men, knew that the American experiment was still, in spite of its dazzling success, a problem. God has never yet given to man a finer stage to strut and fret his brief hour upon than we have here. But shall it endure? Shall the free institutions of this country be of long continuance? This is a question which men who do not reflect will be ready to answer; but others will be less confident.

Many of the most thoughtful men outside the church foresee the dangers which threaten us; but they perceive, too, so they fancy, where the remedy lies. They are smitten with the mania of our age, the idolatry of what they call education. Teach the people how to read and write, they say, make ignorance a crime, and all will be well. Archbishop Spalding, taking the Catholic view, held that the "ills that flesh is heir to" do not proceed from the intellect alone, but that we inherit a depraved will, which no mere intellectual culture can make right.

> "What in me is dark, illumine;
> What is low, raise and support,"

Pope sang; and this is true philosophy. We must enlighten the mind, but we must also raise and support the will.

As a man may "smile and smile and be a villain," so he may read and write, and write and read, and still be the veriest slave to his own wrong-bent heart. The danger which threatens the permanency of our American institutions does not proceed from the want of mental culture. Intellectual training is to-day more universal than it has ever been, but we have not the honest love of liberty our forefathers had.

The founders of this Republic were not immaculate—

they had their faults and their prejudices, as all men have; but however we may judge of them in detail, we must admit that they were men of strong character and of honest purpose, who loved their country better than their private aims. They were earnest men—men of few words and many deeds. God had given them, for the field of their labors, a country unsurpassed in natural resources. He had placed in their hands the printing-press and the steam-engine, to which they bound every implement of human invention. The desert bloomed, cities grew up in a night, and the American continent teemed with the busy life of a great people. In our mountains, we found iron, and silver, and gold; on our boundless plains fattened the finest herds; on our uplands grew the wheat, in our alluvial valleys the maize, the sugar-cane, and the cotton plant. Our country was the refuge of the downtrodden, the breathing-ground of oppressed humanity. But beneath the flower lurked the serpent. Prosperity blinded us, success crazed us, wealth enervated us, the blessings of peace made us long for the curse of war, and the baptism of blood has not purified us.

Corruption still rises higher and sinks deeper, drawing into its foul current every class of society; and I now but repeat what the nation each morning reads—corruption in the high places, and corruption in the lower strata of society, corruption in the halls of Congress, corruption in the State Assemblies, corruption in the judiciary, corruption in the army of officials, corruption in the business circle, corruption in the press, corruption in the pulpit, corruption everywhere. Success is the only criterion of excellence. Everything, even honor, can be bought. Money is impunity before the law. An oath is an empty word. We are more ready to swear than our fathers were to affirm. We read of murders and suicides with less attention than of the price of gold. Nothing is done except by clique and intrigue, which are the forerunners of despotism. But this is not the worst. Crime and sin are not the worst evils of society. Indifference and apathy in crime and sin are the signs of approaching death. Now, the question is, How are we to stay this mountain-wave of corruption which threatens to engulf us? The leaders of an unbelieving generation appeal to popular education; but that portion of the people in which popular education has been carried to the greatest perfection is dying a self-inflicted death. In New England, the increase of population is almost entirely due to the children of foreign parents. A people whose mothers respect not the most sacred laws of life is self-doomed, and can have no part in the future. That the training of the popular intellect is of itself not a sufficient safeguard against the danger that menaces, this is proof enough. Another class of men appeal to political reform to save the country. But with universal suffrage, the representatives of a corrupt people will always be corrupt; and, besides, no merely political reform can regenerate a people which has abandoned virtue. When the masses are depraved, it is not possible that they should have an honest and unselfish love of liberty; and therefore there are conditions of society in which despotism becomes a necessity; in which men are forced to choose between the tyranny of the many and that of one man. Alexander, Cæsar, Cromwell, and Bonaparte were the legitimate offspring of the corruption of the people whom they ruled. There are but two ways of governing men—the method of law and the method of force. When law ceases to command respect, force becomes a necessity. Hence, when pagan nations once became corrupt, there was for them no redemption. They had no power that enabled them to retrace their steps, and to remount the easy way that led to hell. The evil was immedicable. But is it lawful to argue from pagan to Christian society? Has not God, in the Scriptural phrase, made the Christian nations curable? For the corruption of pagan nations there was no remedy, because their religion was null. The Christian nations are curable, but only through their religion. Politicians cannot heal the disorder. They are the quacks of the social therapeutics. It was religion that saved society at the downfall of the Roman Empire. During the middle ages, when Europe was split up into petty principalities, a prey to every antagonism, again it was religion that remodelled and reformed society. When Napoleon stood upon the wreck of the first French Revolution, and bethought him how he might bring order out of the chaos, he at once reopened the churches of France, and recalled religion as the only certain instrument of national regeneration. Popular government can be based only upon popular virtue, which cannot exist without religion. Philosophy, whatever may be its power to control the passions, cannot reach the masses. A nation of philosophers there has never been, nor can there ever be. For the people, religion and the principles of morality are inseparable. Take from them religion, and you take away their only guide of moral conduct.

The religion which is to be the safeguard of morality, and consequently the bulwark of liberty, in this country cannot be the Protestant. To enable us to understand this, two considerations will be sufficient. First, Protestantism in the United States has already lost control of the masses; and, secondly, it has in itself become so wholly a negation that upon it neither a doctrinal nor a moral code can be based. Persuaded of the impotence of Protestantism to preserve in the nation an element of moral strength sufficient to save it from dissolution, Archbishop Spalding looked to the Catholic Church as the only institution which has the vital power to counteract the materialistic and pagan spirit which threatens to infect with its deadly breath the nation's life. He did not, it is true, indulge in dreams about this country's becoming Catholic within a short time; but he held that the church here was destined day by day to increase both in strength and numbers; that she would be able to retain her influence over the millions of her children, and thereby prevent them from abandoning the cardinal principles of Christian morality; and that this great Catholic and conservative element in the nation would be its best defence against the licentious thought and bald materialism which threaten its ruin. The great work of the church in its relation to civil society, according to the theory of government under which we live, was, in Archbishop Spalding's view of the subject, to labor to make her children true to themselves as Catholics, and then it needs must follow they could not be false to their duties as citizens. Hence, in season and out of season, he warned Catholics against the corruptions of the age. He specially feared lest the spirit of worldliness and self-indulgence should with softness infect the rugged hardihood of true Catholic faith, leaving it but the sickly name of what should be a living substance; and, therefore, whilst he encouraged innocent enjoyment, he firmly set his face against all those amusements which in any way offend the most exalted Catholic idea of Christian morality.

He loved the simple ways of the olden time, and could not think that we were better than our fathers because we had become more effeminate and self-indulgent. And when, in the presence of the immense material progress of the age, he beheld men bowed beneath the yoke of the adoration of success, the idolatry of wealth, and the slavish indulgence of passion; when he saw every principle of truth, of justice, and of honor trampled upon by individuals and by nations, and the attempt made to organize society merely for the purpose of giving the greatest amount of sensuous pleasure to the greatest number of animals, his protesting soul almost made him feel, as our philosophers do, contempt for the whole affair.

Though he loved his country, and liberty, and the people, he never had any special admiration for this nineteenth century, in which, as he thought, the predominant power of matter had dwarfed the souls of men.

Few have been so severe as he in denouncing the fashionable dances of the day, which he held to be directly opposed to purity, the immediate jewel of the Catholic soul, which gone, the temple of God is but painted clay. That a Catholic woman, whose model is the Virgin Mother of God, should expose herself to wanton contact and immodest gaze by participating in that which is unseemly in its practice and immoral in its consequences, was so repugnant to his sense of virtue that he could not even think of it with patience. And as for men, he thought an American should be too much of a democrat to dance fancy dances which would more become the harem of a voluptuous tyrant than the republican home of an American citizen. Whilst Bishop of Louisville, his scathing invectives against these immodesties had the effect of almost entirely banishing them from Catholic society, and in Baltimore he continued the crusade against what he considered a recrudescence of paganism.*

---

* I may be permitted to quote here the words of all the bishops of the United States, addressed to those who have charge of souls:

"Choreas immodestas, quæ quotidie magis magisque frequentantur, insectentur ac prorsus damnent. Moneant fideles, quantum non solum in Deum, verum in societatem, et familiam, seipsos denique offendant, qui choreis hisce vel operam, dant vel saltem præsentia sua favore videntur."

"Let them," I translate the words of the venerable prelates of the American Church—" let them inveigh against and wholly condemn the indecent dances which day by day are becoming more and more common. Let them

He was equally bitter in his denunciation of the immodest drama, even that which is patronized by the most respectable classes of society. He could not understand how Christian women could become the public and avowed approvers of the shamelessness of their sex in exhibitions which are sufficient to make men who have souls blush to think their mothers were women. He would have preferred the bullfight to this public desecration of that which is our holiest instinct—the sense of purity.

He probably had something of the natural fondness of priests for exposing the weaknesses of women, may be for exaggerating them. However this may be, he considered the system of female education in this country subject to grave objections. Time has been when woman was degraded by being made the slave of labor; but we Americans degrade her by making her the slave of indolence. The daughters of the rich are brought up like exotics, in a way which develops to the highest degree a finely-wrought and most sensitive nervous system. To this are added all the accomplishments which constitute a merely ornamental education; and the young lady, beautiful, intelligent, refined, so delicate that the winds of heaven may not visit her too roughly, is fit only to sit in the parlor.

The license which the custom of our country permits in the relations of the sexes before marriage, together with the thousand fond dreams that a young woman nurses, satisfies, for a while, her craving nature. Indeed, her life at this period is idle and free as the wind; all that she has to do is, on varied wing and in bright colors, to flit about and sip the honey from the many-scented flowers that smiling nature holds out to her. Her whole education has impressed upon

teach the faithful that they who take part in, or by their presence give sanction to, such dances, sin not only against God, but against society, the family, even against themselves."—*Concil. Balt. Plen. II*, n. 472.

her that her first and highest duty is to please; that her chief use in the world is to be an ornament—a something that will give pleasure to others.

She marries. A life of indolence and nervous excitement has rendered her unfit to be either a wife or a mother. The few children she has, if she have any, are most generally feeble, and hence the American family, as a rule, is the most short-lived of families. Now that life for her has become a serious reality, imposing duties that are not always agreeable, her sensitive nature is shocked by the rude contact of things as they are, and seeks for happiness, not in the fulfilment of duty, but in the indulgence of desire. Before marriage, she lived only to please, and now she thinks it but fair that she should live but to be pleased. Unhappy at home, she goes into society, and her woman's ambition causes her to rush into every extravagance. She must live in a palace and dress like a queen; and, if there be a foreign land of beauty that society talks about, she must visit it; and, to wind up this eventful history, she sometimes succeeds in making her husband a bankrupt in name and fortune.

There can be no doubt but that there is in our society a very solid background of truth to this possibly somewhat high coloring.

Another consideration advanced by Archbishop Spalding, in a sermon on the extravagance of the times, was that this love of display in women checks Christian marriage, and thereby becomes the cause of innumerable other evils.

In the *Pastoral Letter* of the Second Plenary Council, and, indeed, in the *Acts* of the Council also, the shoals upon which virtue too often suffers shipwreck are signalled.

"We consider it to be our duty," say the fathers of that Council, "to warn our people against those amusements which may easily become to them an occasion of sin, and especially against those fashionable dances, which, as at present carried on, are revolting to every feeling of delicacy and propriety, and are fraught with the greatest danger to morals. We would also warn them most solemnly against the great abuses which have sprung up in the matter of fairs, excursions, and picnics, in which, as too often conducted, the name of charity is made to cover a multitude of sins. We forbid all Catholics to have anything to do with them, except when managed in accordance with the regulations of the Ordinary, and under the immediate supervision of their respective pastors."

In the Tenth Provincial Council of Baltimore, which, in accordance with a law promulgated in the Plenary Council, Archbishop Spalding convoked and presided over in the spring of 1869, this subject was again discussed, and in the *Pastoral Letter* reference is made to it in language even still more pointed:

"Prominent among the evils we have to deplore," say the bishops of this synod, "and which are an evidence of the growing licentiousness of the times, may be reckoned a morbid taste for indecent publications, and the frequentation of immoral or positively obscene theatrical performances. No entertainments seem to satisfy the fast degenerating spirit of the age, unless they be highly sensational, and calculated to gratify the most prurient appetites. . . . The church, far from discountenancing, has always encouraged, innocent and moderate amusements, as useful or necessary relaxations; but, while approving of harmless diversions, she never ceases to exercise her sacred influence in censuring all amusements which can be purchased only at the expense of virtue. We deem it particularly our solemn duty to renew our warning against the modern fashionable dances, commonly called *German*, or *round dances*, which are becoming more and more the occasions of sin. These practices are so much the more dangerous as several persons seem to look upon them as harmless, and indulge in them without any apparent remorse of conscience."

In this same letter, reference is made to what the fathers call the "murder of the innocents," which threatens to become the foulest stain on our national character — a crime, say they, which is most prevalent in those localities where the system of education without religion has been longest established and most successfully carried out. They believe that our Catholic population is uncontaminated by this vile infection; but they desire to raise this voice of warning to signal the danger while it is yet afar.

CHAPTER XXIX.

DEATH OF THE VERY REV. B. J. SPALDING—VISITATION OF THE DIOCESE—THE LITTLE SISTERS OF THE POOR—THE VATICAN COUNCIL.

IT was during the summer of 1868 that Archbishop Spalding met with the sad loss of his brother, the Very Rev. B. J. Spalding, Administrator of the diocese of Louisville, whose unexpected death overwhelmed him with sorrow. There was a difference of but two years in their ages. They had studied together at St. Mary's, at St. Joseph's, and in the Propaganda, and afterwards for many years they had labored side by side in Kentucky. Each had been a helper to the other; and the love that united them, if not demonstrative, was of the deepest and truest kind.

The Very Rev. Dr. Spalding had invested the patrimony which he had received from his father principally in real estate in Louisville, which, at the time of his death, had grown to be of some value. In his will, which was drawn up a few months before his death, he bequeathed all that he should die possessed of to his brother, the Archbishop of Baltimore, to be expended, according to his discretion, for charitable objects in the diocese of Louisville.

In carrying out this bequest, Archbishop Spalding, in accordance with what he knew to have been his brother's intentions, deeded the principal part of the estate to a corporation which he had had chartered under the title of "St. Joseph's Industrial School for Boys of the city of Louisville, Kentucky."

What was not bestowed in this manner he divided among

the various benevolent institutions and associations of the diocese.

Three of the new dioceses, and one of the vicariates apostolic, for the erection of which the fathers of the Second Plenary Council had petitioned the Holy See, were in the province of Baltimore. There was considerable delay in Rome in designating the persons who were to fill the new sees. At length, however, the Bulls arrived; and, on the 16th of August, 1868, Archbishop Spalding, assisted by nearly all his suffragans, gave the episcopal consecration, in the cathedral of Baltimore, to the Right Rev. Thomas A. Becker, who had been appointed to the see of Wilmington, and to the Right Rev. James Gibbons, who had been named Vicar Apostolic of North Carolina; and he afterwards accompanied the newly consecrated prelates, both of whom had been attached to his cathedral, to their respective dioceses, and assisted at their installation.

During the summer and fall of this year, he superintended the printing of the *Acts and Decrees of the Second Plenary Council of Baltimore*, which he introduced into his theological seminary as the text-book of canon law.

In the spring and summer of 1869, Archbishop Spalding was occupied in visiting his diocese, preparatory to his departure for the Vatican Council.

From September, 1868, to October, 1869, he administered confirmation over a hundred times, the number of persons confirmed by him during this period being six thousand four hundred and five, eight hundred and forty-seven of whom were converts. It may be stated, as another consoling evidence of the progress of religion, that in June, 1869, he conferred sacred orders upon the largest number of candidates ever ordained at one time in the United States. Twenty-nine were ordained subdeacons; twenty-six, deacons; and twenty-four, priests.

In July, he received special powers from Rome to proceed to Chicago to examine into the state of things in that diocese, and to report to the Holy See.

It was during this summer that he had the happiness of welcoming to Baltimore the Little Sisters of the Poor—one of the noblest congregations of Catholic women that have come to us from France, to whose Christian charity we owe so much. Their mission is to the old, who are helpless, who have nothing of that which should accompany old age, but whom the world, now that they are broken and worn by the weight of toilsome years, has cast aside as no longer fit for its uses. To them, under the habit of the Little Sister, comes the ever-abiding love of Jesus Christ, stretching out the helping hand, speaking the cheery word, all redolent of love, and offering to their abandoned age the comforts of a home.

Archbishop Spalding was most anxious to have in his diocese those institutions of the church whose special mission is to relieve human suffering and to console human sorrow. Whatever his intellectual gifts may or may not have been, he had a great Catholic heart, which went out in love and sympathy to all—to the orphan, to the negro, to the sinful, to the outcast, to the aged, to all who suffered and had none to pity them. He felt that the poor, above all others, need the church, and that she needs them. A religious faith which is confined to the wealthy can have but little force or vitality; for the rich, as a class, are always less earnest in religion than the poor. In our age, above all, which worships only success, they consider their own prosperity in this world as a mark of the divine favor, an especial sign of predestination, and hence they are satisfied with the name of religion, or without religion. A church which is the church of the rich alone cannot be the church of Jesus Christ. The poor alone heard him gladly, and too often they only love to hear those who preach the doctrines which he taught. Present prosperity and joy so fascinate and inebriate men that they become unconscious of the uncertainty of their condition, and forget that "one blast may chill them into misery."

> "Alles lässt sich ertragen
> Nur nicht eine Reihe schöner Tagen."

"The poor you shall have always with you," said Jesus Christ. Possibly he meant that the people would never betray the church. To-day, at least, the kings and princes of the earth have denied her, they that are dressed in brief authority have apostatized, and the church, regretting that of which she is guiltless, stretches out her mother's arms to the people, the children of her earliest love.

"The friendship of the poor," said St. Bernard, in the days when the church ruled the world—"the friendship of the poor makes us the friends of kings." The people is king to-day, and the church that made the people free will make them holy. Infidelity is seeking to found the democracy of disorder and unrule on the ignoble basis of mere animalism; the church will build up the democracy of Christ, which will recognize the inalienable rights of the immortal soul as the only source of human dignity and of human liberty.

"I believe," says M. Louis Veuillot, "that the future belongs to the democracy; that the church will discipline the democratic barbarism as she has disciplined all other barbarisms, which, under different names, are in fact identical; that she will baptize it, that she will educate it, that she will organize it into a body politic, and that, at length, we shall have a Holy Roman Democracy, as we have had a Holy Roman Empire. And perhaps it will then be found that in substance both are the same thing." *

* *Rome pendant le Concile*, p. 495.

The people will belong to them who have the power to love them most, and only Christ and they who believe in him can love the people. This age and country have talked of the people, have flattered the people, in wordy language have sought to raise the people to heaven. The world loves the people when the people can work, when the people can vote, when the people can fight; but when the people are sick, are sorrowful, are poor, only Jesus Christ and they who love him love the people. The world loves beauty, it loves power, it loves money; but only Christ, and they who are his, love the poor, the afflicted, and the suffering. Were it not for Jesus living in his church, again the people would be forced to butcher one another beneath the eyes of a rich, voluptuous world, that the weary, dragging hours might pass less slowly.

The world talks of the people, of the freedom of the people, of the happiness of the people; Jesus Christ alone is the God of the people, the man of the people. Where he is not, the people are nothing; take him away, and there remains but paganism—the many living for the few, the many dying for the few—man without dignity, and woman without honor.

And this is the great question of the future—Who shall have the people? The kings of Christendom with their own hands have profaned the sacredness that did hedge them in. Protestantism is a wreck. In presence of the people, there remain but the church and atheism. Will the people of the future be Catholic, or will they be godless? This is the question. Driven from the palaces of kings and from the seats of worldly power, the church is left with the people alone, and she will entwine her gentle arms around their necks, and they will be her children, and she will be their mother. Christians must believe this, because they are not permitted to despair of the human race.

In connection with the great world-struggle of the future, the most important event which has taken place in our day is the Vatican Council.

It was on the 20th of October, 1869, that Archbishop Spalding bade farewell to his beloved children, in obedience to the voice of Christ's Vicar, in order to take part in the great Council which Pius IX. had convoked to meet on the 8th of the following December. For days before, his house had been thronged with the crowds that came to ask his blessing and bid him God-speed on his way. On the day of his departure, which was lovely as only an American October day can be, the whole city seemed to have turned out to do him honor. The Catholic societies with their banners formed a double line along the streets through which the procession passed. The priests and seminarians of the archdiocese led the way, then came several bishops in carriages, followed by that which bore the Archbishop, and behind this walked the boys of the St. Mary's Industrial School. As the procession moved down the densely crowded street, words of affection and love broke from the lips of the people. "God bless you, Archbishop!" they said, and then, "Good-by, dear Archbishop"; and when something caused a momentary halt, they rushed around his carriage to touch his hand or say a last kind word of parting.

The *Baltimore*, on which Archbishop Spalding was to sail, was lying some distance down the bay. Two thousand people were on the boats which took the Archbishop and his party out to the steamer, which was decked with flags and hung with wreaths of evergreens and flowers. Over the companion-ladder, a beautiful arch had been thrown, in the centre of which was inscribed, "Rome." Under this the Archbishop and party passed to the deck, where they were received by the officers of the ship.

When the signal was given, the *Baltimore* moved off

amid the booming of cannon and the cheers of the multitude. On Federal Hill, where the church of St. Mary, the Star of the Sea, now stands, a large concourse of people had assembled; and, as the boats passed, they cheered lustily. At Fort McHenry, they were saluted by the military band, and by the lowering and hoisting of the flag. At Swann Point, the *Baltimore* laid to; the boats which still accompanied her, came up, the parting words were spoken, the ship moved out to sea, and the boats turned homeward.

The passage across the ocean was as pleasant as a sea voyage can be, favored, as it was, both by pleasant company and fair weather. On the two Sundays on which they were on the waters, Catholic service was held, at which both crew and passengers, with few exceptions, assisted. On the first Sunday, Archbishop Spalding preached on the divinity of Christ, and interwove in his remarks a beautiful tribute to his Immaculate Mother. On the second Sunday, the sermon was delivered by Bishop McGill. As they approached Southampton, on the 2d of November, the bishops and priests joined in singing the *Te Deum*, in thanksgiving for their prosperous voyage.

Archbishop Spalding, in company with several of the bishops who had crossed the ocean with him, after spending a few days in England, passed into France; and, having delayed a little in Paris and Lyons, sailed from Marseilles for Civita Vecchia. It took them four days to make the trip across the Mediterranean, thirty-six hours being the usual time required. Stress of weather forced them to put into the Isle of Elba, where they visited the modest house in which the great Napoleon dwelt during his first exile. When within two hours' sail of Civita Vecchia, the rough sea again forced them to seek shelter in a neighboring port, where they were tossed about in all the agony of sea-sickness. But on the 26th of November, they succeeded in landing in Civita Vecchia, where they were warmly welcomed by the Governor of the city, who entertained the bishops and priests at dinner; and soon Rome gladdened their eyes, and they were again at home.

The chief fact in connection with the history of the Vatican Council is the definition of the infallibility of the Pope.

Although the Council itself remains unfinished, this, the greatest work which it could have accomplished, is complete, and has its own history.

Before the Council assembled, and after it had met, much feeling was called forth by agitations against the definition of the dogma, or in favor of it; and, as it is easy to perceive now, far too great importance was attached to these efforts. No sooner was the Council convoked, than, as by a divine instinct, the whole Catholic world. looked for a clear and explicit declaration upon a point which the vast majority of the bishops, and the great mass of the clergy and laity, believed to be no longer open to discussion, but which, nevertheless, because it had not been clearly defined, was threatening to become a source of division and discord in the church.

The discussions which took place concerning the advisability of defining the dogma are important only inasmuch as they manifest the universal interest in the subject, and show that the declaration of the faith of the church on this point was confidently looked for. In fact, everything else had been settled. This was the only question which remained to be decided. To have recoiled before what men called the spirit of the age, and to have concealed the truth out of respect to modern ideas, would have been to be afraid; but the church has never been afraid.

A concession universally made by the opponents of the

church is that she is the most logically consistent institution that has appeared on the stage of human action. No power, earthly or infernal, has ever been able to make her draw back from the legitimate conclusions from the facts upon which she is built. The Vatican Council is an example of this truth. In an age essentially democratic, when the spirit of the time is seeking to take away prestige and power from the individual, to give them to humanity; when the theory of the divine right of kings has yielded to that of the inalienable rights of the people; when the words of even the greatest thinkers are read in mere idle curiosity by minds that have ceased to believe that it is given to man to know the truth; in an age which has no faith in the individual, even when crowned with the tiara of virtue, genius, and power, the church proclaimed to the world that the Vicar of Christ is infallible. There seemed to be many reasons why she should not then, at least, make this solemn declaration. A European crisis was impending; the temporal power of the Pope was threatened; at any moment he might be driven into exile; many Catholics, eminent for virtue and learning, seemed to doubt and hesitate; the Protestant and infidel press of two worlds was awaiting in anxious expectation the proclamation of the dogma, that it might shout with its hundred mouths to the four corners of the earth that at length the hands of her own children had signed the death-warrant of the church: and yet the solemn promulgation was made. These voices of the children of time passed unheeded by the ear of her whose eye, in enraptured gaze, is fixed on eternity.

Archbishop Spalding had always believed in the infallibility of the Pope. This belief was a tradition with the Maryland Catholics, fostered and rendered stronger by the Jesuit fathers, who for so many years were their only religious teachers. His fathers had taken this faith with them to Kentucky. It was the doctrine which he had received from Flaget and David. Neither the Catholics of Maryland nor their descendants in Kentucky were tainted with even a tinge of Gallicanism. Indeed, it may be affirmed that, as far as we have a tradition in this country, it is thoroughly orthodox. It is the special pride of the American Church that it has not only been faithful to the Vicar of Christ, but has ever had for him the tenderest devotion.

"Thank God," wrote Archbishop Spalding to Cardinal Cullen in 1866, just after the close of the Second Plenary Council of Baltimore—"thank God, we are Roman to the heart." The confession of faith of both the Plenary Councils of Baltimore is as full and complete on this point as it was then possible to make it. When, after the convocation of the Vatican Council, the question, whether or not it would be opportune to define the infallibility of the Pope, first began to be discussed, Archbishop Spalding inclined to the opinion that a formal definition would be unnecessary and possibly inexpedient. He thought that Gallicanism was dead, and that Catholics everywhere believed in the infallibility of the Holy See. Hence, he argued, there could be no necessity for a formal definition. He believed, too, that much time would be consumed in conciliary debate, in case the question of fixing the precise limits of Papal infallibility should be submitted to the fathers.

These considerations led him to think that the most proper way of proclaiming the dogma of Papal infallibility would be to condemn all errors opposed to it; and this was his opinion when he went to the Council. It was, however, merely an opinion, formed, as he himself felt, without a perfect knowledge of all the circumstances in the case, and one which, upon fuller information, he might see cause to change. He was not a partisan. He had in him none of the stuff out of which partisans are made. He was simply a Catholic bishop, who had never belonged to a party either in the church or out of it.

On the 27th of March, 1869, eight months before the assembling of the Council, he wrote as follows to a distinguished theologian who was at that time in Rome:

"I believe *firmly* the infallibility of the Pope, but incline to think its formal definition unnecessary and perhaps inexpedient, not only for the reasons which you allege, but also on account of the difficulty of fixing the precise limits of doctrinal decisions. Where they are formal, as in the case of the Immaculate Conception, there is no difficulty. But are all the declarations of encyclicals, allocutions, and similar documents to be received as doctrinal definitions? And what about the decisions of congregations, confirmed by the Pope?"

And again, in August, he wrote:

"While maintaining the high *Roman* ground of orthodoxy, I caution much prudence in framing constitutions."

In both these letters, Archbishop Spalding seems to take for granted that a definition will be made; and he simply indicates his preference for an implicit rather than a formal definition.

In August, 1869, two months before leaving for the Council, he wrote to Cardinal Barnabo, giving his views on various subjects which he supposed would be brought before the fathers. One of these he designates as "The Infallibility of the Sovereign Pontiff teaching *ex cathedra*." "I have not," he says, "the least doubt of this infallibility, and there are very few bishops who do doubt of it. The only question which may, perhaps, arise will relate to the utility, advisability, and necessity of making an *explicit* definition in the Council. It will have to be considered whether a definition of this kind would not be likely to excite controversies now slumbering and almost extinct; whether an *implicit* definition—an amplification of that of the Council of Florence—which would define the dogma without using the word, would not be more opportune and of greater service to the cause of the church.

"Should the fathers deem it expedient to make a formal definition, its limits should be accurately marked, and, in the accompanying doctrinal exposition, statement should be made whether and how far, in the intention of the fathers, this infallibility should be extended to pontifical letters, allocutions, encyclicals, bulls, and other documents of this nature."

This letter affords sufficient evidence that Archbishop Spalding had all along contemplated the contingency of an explicit definition, and that he did not look upon it with any alarm. In fact, he held that a definition, either implicit or explicit, was necessary. If he did not, in the beginning, advocate a formal definition, he was still less in favor of abstaining from the unmistakable affirmation of the faith of the church on this point.

His views with regard to what was called the opportunity of the definition were, at the time he left home to go to the Council, based upon his knowledge of the state of the public mind in the church of this country. No one with us called in question the infallibility of the Pope; his declarations had always been received by the Catholics of this country with the greatest reverence. Hence, in view of what had been the general practice of the church, he did not see any reason for making a formal definition of a dogma which, as he thought, was not doubted by Catholics.

Of the religious thought and of the precise bearing of the currents of Catholic opinion in Europe, he, of course, could not be thoroughly informed, and his views were therefore subject to the modifications which developments in this direction might produce.

CHAPTER XXX.

THE VATICAN COUNCIL — THE POSTULATUM OF ARCHBISHOP SPALDING — LETTER TO BISHOP DUPANLOUP.

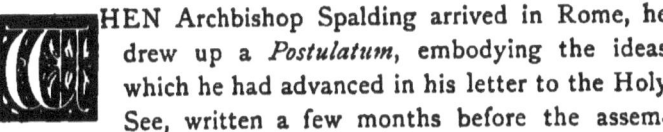HEN Archbishop Spalding arrived in Rome, he drew up a *Postulatum*, embodying the ideas which he had advanced in his letter to the Holy See, written a few months before the assembling of the Council. This *Postulatum*, which was entitled "A Schema for the clear and logical definition of the Infallibility of the Roman Pontiff, in accordance with the principles already received by the Church," is the one which, as I have been informed, all the bishops of the United States had originally intended to sign. It certainly asserts the infallibility of the Pope in the most unmistakable manner, and some of the leaders of "the opposition" objected to it that it was even more comprehensive than would be the simple definition of the Pope's infallibility. The London *Tablet* said that it was evidently from the hand of a consummate theologian, and was another document proving the universality of the belief in the infallibility of the Pope.

The following is a translation of this *Postulatum:*

"In the chapter on the Roman Pontiff, after condemning, in the first place, the errors concerning his primacy, the following or similar words might be added:

"'We altogether reprobate the temerity of those who dare to appeal from the judgments of the Sovereign Pontiff to a general council.

"'In the next place, we wholly condemn the perverse

cavils of those who presume to say that external submission, without the internal assent of the mind and heart, are to be given to the judgments of the Roman Pontiff.

"'Moreover, we utterly reject the method of speaking and teaching adopted by those who, imagining a rash and preposterous division between the collective episcopate and the Supreme Pontiff, dispute as to which of the two is the greater, and thus endeavor to separate and disjoin the head from the body, Peter from the church; as if an assembly of brothers, whom Peter is commanded, even in his successors, to confirm, could ever be severed from him whose faith, by the promise of Christ, shall never fail; or as if they who are to be taught and confirmed by Peter could ever lawfully teach and confirm in opposition to him.

"'Nor do we condemn less severely the opinion and mode of action of those who, in order that they may be able more freely to propagate errors condemned by the Roman Pontiff, are not ashamed to insinuate that the true sense of the books from which the condemned propositions have been taken was not rightly understood by him.'

"These propositions are further explained and confirmed by what follows:

"1. The bishops of nearly the whole Catholic world, lately assembled in Rome, have shown these views to be theirs in the remarkable words in which they addressed the happily-reigning Sovereign Pontiff: 'Your voice has never been silent. To announce to men the eternal truths; to strike with the sword of the apostolic word errors which attack at once the natural and the supernatural order, and threaten to undermine the very foundations of authority, both civil and ecclesiastical; to dispel the darkness with which perverse and recent doctrines have obscured the minds of men; to proclaim without fear; to persuade and recommend whatever is necessary or useful to the welfare, whether of individuals, or of the Christian family, or of civil society—these are the duties which you have considered to belong to your ministry, that all may be brought to know what a Catholic should believe, profess, and practise. We return thanks to your Holiness for this attentive solicitude, for which we shall ever be grateful; and believing that by the mouth of Pius Peter has spoken, whatever for the preservation of the sacred deposit you have said, confirmed, announced, we also say, confirm, and announce; and with one voice and heart we reject whatever you have judged worthy of condemnation, as contrary to divine faith, the salvation of souls, and the welfare of human society.' *

"2. For the living and infallible authority exists only in that church which, built by Christ our Lord on Peter, the Head, Prince, and Pastor of the whole church, whose faith he has promised shall never fail, has its lawful pontiffs, descending without intermission from Peter himself, placed in his chair, the heirs and defenders of his doctrine, dignity, honor, and power. And since where Peter is, there is the church; and he lives ever and judges in his successors, and gives, to them who seek, the truth of faith: therefore the divine words are to be received plainly in that sense which has held and still holds the Roman chair of the blessed Peter; which, mother and mistress of all the churches, has ever preserved intact and inviolate the faith delivered by Christ our Lord, which she has taught the faithful, showing to all the way of salvation and the doctrine of incorrupt truth."

"Reasons why the above *Schema* is thought to be more expedient:

"1. It may be confidently hoped that a *Schema* of this nature would meet with the approval of almost all the

---

* These words are taken from the reply of the bishops to the allocution of Pius IX. on the occasion of the centenary of St. Peter, July 1, 1867. Nearly five hundred bishops signed the address.

fathers, and would be confirmed by their quasi-unanimous suffrage; for it contains the certain and incontestable principles of Catholic doctrine, now received by the universal church, which all acknowledge and profess, the exceptions being so few that no account of them need be taken.

"2. This full consent of all, or at least of nearly all, the fathers is not only expedient, but seems to be altogether required, when the question is one of defining a point of doctrine, especially in a matter of such importance that, if this were possible, it should be defined without a dissenting voice.

"3. At this present time, unanimity seems to be altogether necessary, on account of rumors which have been spread among the people, and are on all sides believed, to the effect that, concerning this matter, there is great discord among the fathers. A definition unanimously pronounced by the fathers would utterly shut the mouths of those who are now so rashly boasting, and it would give the greatest edification to the church. In truth, we have enemies enough outside the fold, without our exciting or appearing in any way to cherish dissensions in the very camp of the church herself.

"4. The proposed method of defining by implication, although it be indirect, seems to excel, both in force and simplicity; for it is clearer, and perhaps contains more than would a formal and explicit definition. The latter will furnish theologians with many opportunities of raising questions. There will be perpetual discussions among them as to where and under what circumstances the Roman Pontiff is to be believed to have addressed all the faithful, and to have pronounced an infallible judgment. All those questions will still remain undecided which hitherto, even among the most pious defenders of the Pontifical infallibility, have been agitated concerning the public and the private teaching of the Pope, the true meaning of the expression, *ex cathedra*, and the matters which strictly relate to faith and morals. Perhaps questions of this kind will burst forth with even greater violence, and will be treated with still warmer feeling.

"5. But in the proposed *Schema* of definition, no express distinction is made, nor is any required; for it joins the inerrancy of the Roman Pontiff with the infallibility of the church herself, and presents it as a logical consequence, and as a corollary of the Primacy itself; so that the infallibility of the church, and the divinely conferred Primacy, are made equally conspicuous, and are contained within the same limits; and these principles of the faith have been sufficiently fixed and determined even from the very infancy of the church. Now, the force of a formal definition would be extended to all past ages, and would easily open the whole field of ecclesiastical history and the entire collection of Pontifical documents to the argumentations of theologians, and to the now nearly extinct accusations of heretics and wicked men against the Roman Pontiff."

SCHEMA PRO INFALLIBILITATE ROMANI PONTIFICIS EX PRINCIPIIS JAM AB ECCLESIA UNIVERSA RECEPTIS LOGICE CLAREQUE DEFINIENDA.

In ipso capite de Romano Pontifice, damnatis primo loco erroribus contra ejus primatum, hæc et similia, si placeat, adjungi poterunt:

1. Omnino reprobamus eorum temeritatem, qui a summi Pontificis supremis judiciis ad concilium œcumenicum appellare audent.

2. Deinde prorsus damnamus perversas eorum cavillationes, qui dicere audent externum quidem obsequium, non autem internum mentis cordisque assensum Romani Pontificis judiciis esse præstandum.

3. Insuper omnino improbamus eorum loquendi et docendi rationem, qui temeraria quadam et præpostera divisione inter cœtum Episcoporum et summum Pontificem excogitata, disputant uter eorum videatur esse major, et sic caput a corpore, Petrum ab Ecclesia distrahere et sejungere conantur: quasi fratrum cœtus, quos Petrus etiam in successoribus suis confirmat ut jubetur, posset unquam ab illo desciscere, cujus fides ex Christi promissione nunquam deficiet; aut iis qui a Petro docendi sunt et confirmandi, ipsum contra docere et confirmare liceret.

6. Neque minus reprobandum judicamus illorum sententiam et agendi rationem, qui, ut errores a Romano Pontifice damnatos in vulgus diffundere liberius valeant dictitare non verentur verum sensum librorum, ex quibus damnatæ hujusmodi propositiones excerptæ sunt, a Pontifice haud rite intellectum fuisse.

Qua quidem omnia illustrantur confirmanturque ab eis quæ sequuntur.

1. Atque ita quidem sentire se luculenter testatus est totius fere catholici orbis Episcopatus nuperrime Romæ congregatus, dum summum Pontificem feliciter regnantem præclaris hisce verbis allocutus est : " Non enim unquam obticuit os tuum. Tu æternas veritates annuntiare, Tu sæculi errores naturalem supernaturalemque rerum ordinem atque ipsa ecclesiasticæ civilisque potestatis fundamenta subvertere minitantes Apostolici eloquii gladio configere, Tu caliginem novarum doctrinarum pravitate mentibus offusam dispellere, Tu quæ necessaria ac salutaria sunt tum singulis hominibus, tum Christianæ familiæ, tum civili societati, intrepide affari, suadere, commendare supremi Tui ministerii es arbitratus : ut tandem cuncti assequantur quid hominem Catholicum tenere, servare, ac profiteri oporteat. Pro qua eximia cura maximas Sanctitati Tuæ gratias agimus, habituri sumus sempiternas ; Petrumque per os Pii locutum credentes, quæ ad custodiendum depositum a Te dicta confirmata, prolata sunt, nos quoque dicimus, confirmamus, annuntiamus ; unoque ore atque animo rejicimus, omnia quæ divinæ fidei, saluti animarum, ipsi societatis humanæ bono adversa, Tu ipse reprobanda ac rejicienda judicasti."*

2. Nam " viva et infallibilis auctoritas in ea tantum viget Ecclesia, quæ a Christo Domino super Petrum, totius Ecclesiæ caput, principem et pastorem, cujus fidem nunquam defuturam promisit, ædificata, suos legitimos semper habet Pontifices, sine intermissione ab ipso Petro ducentes originem in ejus cathedra collocatos, et ejusdem etiam doctrinæ, dignitatis, honoris, ac potestatis hæredes et vindices. Et quoniam ubi Petrus, ibi Ecclesia † ac Petrus per Romanum Pontificem loquitur,‡ et semper in suis successoribus vivit et judicium exercet,§ ac præstat quærentibus fidei veritatem ; ‖ idcirco divina eloquia eo plane sensu sunt accipienda, quem tenuit ac tenet hæc Romana beatissimi Petri cathedra, quæ omnium Ecclesiarum mater et magistra,¶ fidem a Christo Domino traditam, integram inviolatamque semper servavit, eamque fideles edocuit omnibus ostendens salutis semitam et incorruptæ veritatis doctrinam."**

* Responsio Episcoporum ad SS. D. N. Allocutionem, in solemn. sæc. Martyrii SS. Petri et Pauli, die 1 Julii, 1867 ; cui Responsioni subscripserunt quingenti fere episcopi.

† S. Ambrosius in Ps. xl.   ‡ Concil. Chalced., act. ii.
§ Synodus Ephes., act. iii.   ‖ S. Petrus Chrysol., in Epist. ad Eutych.
¶ Concil. Trid. Ses. vii. de Bapt.

** SS. D. N. Epistola Encycl., 9 Novemb., 1846, a Concilio Baltimorensi Plenario II. relata, in Decreto de Hierarchia, cap. ii. pp. 42, 43.

Rationes ob quas schema supra propositum magis expedire creditur.

I. Primo sperari tuto potest, fore ut hujusmodi schema Patribus quasi universis magis arrideat, et eorum unanimi fere suffragio confirmetur. Continet enim certa et inconcussa doctrinæ catholicæ principia jam in universa Ecclesia recepta, quæque agnoscunt et profitentur omnes, paucis exceptis, quorum numerus adeo exiguus est, ut ejus nulla ratio habenda videatur.

II. Plena hæc Patrum omnium (vel saltem fere omnium) consensio non solum expedit, sed omnino postulari videtur, quando agitur de capite doctrinæ definiendo : præsertim in re tanti momenti ; quæ sane nemine (si id fieri possit) dissentiente definiri deberet.

III. Hoc autem tempore ejusmodi unanimitas summopere necessaria videtur, ob voces in vulgus sparsas et ubique creditas, quibus magna inter Patres hac de re discordia esse perhibetur. Unanimis Patrum definitio hostibus nostris sic temere gloriantibus os penitus obstrueret, et maximam Ecclesiæ Dei ædificationem pareret. Profecto satis hostium externorum habemus, quin in ipsis Ecclesiæ castris nova dissidia excitemus, vel ullo modo fovere videamur.

IV. Propositus implicite definiendi modus, quamvis sit indirectus, videtur tamen tum vi tum simplicitate præstare. Clarior enim est, ac plura forsan continet, quam definitio formalis et explicita. Hæc enim plures cavillandi locos theologis suppeditabit. Disceptabitur perpetuo inter eos, quando et quibus rerum adjunctis Romanus Pontifex omnes Christi fideles allocutus fuisse et infallibile judicium protulisse credendus sit. Indecisæ adhuc manebunt omnes illæ quæstiones, etiam inter piissimos Pontificiæ infallibilitatis propugnatores hactenus agitatæ, de persona Pontificis docentis publica et privata, de vera locutionis *ex cathedra* significatione, de rebus quæ ad fidem moresque *vere* spectant. Imo violentius forsan erumpent hujusmodi quæstiones, et longe majori animi contentione pertractabuntur.

V. In proposito autem definiendi Schemate nulla fit nullaque requiritur distinctio expressa ; nam inerrantiam Romani Pontificis cum Ecclesiæ ipsius infallibilitate intime conjungit, eamque veluti logicam ipsius primatus sequelam et veluti corollarium exhibet, adeo ut tam late pateat iisdemque limitibus contineatur ac ipsa Ecclesiæ infallibilitas ipseque divinitus constitutus Primatus ; quæ quidem fidei principia jam ab Ecclesiæ ipsius primordiis satis fixa et determinata sunt. Hujusmodi igitur definiendi ratione, ansa nulla præbetur sive theologis, sive fidelibus, dubitandi aut cavillandi circa jussa et decreta S. Pontificis, cujus sapientissimo consilio, dum pascit tam agnos quam oves, sicut decet filios erga Patrem, omnia reverenter et amanter relinquuntur dirimenda.

VI. Demum hæc definiendi ratio, dum fixa quædum et immota principia ubique recepta asserit, simul hoc commodi habet, ut non solum Christianis omnibus infallibilem in fidei morumque rebus, nullo dubitandi vel cavillandi loco relicto, credendi et agendi normam proponat, sed etiam futurorum præcipue temporum bono prospiciat. Formalis vero definitio, cum vi sua ad omnia etiam retroacta sæcula protenderetur, facile universum historiæ ecclesiasticæ campum totumque Bullarium Theologorum cavillationibus et hæreticorum impiorumque adversus Romanos Pontifices criminationibus, jam fere sopitis, aperiret.

This *Postulatum*, which embodies the views that Archbishop Spalding had held from the time the question first began to be agitated, undoubtedly contains a very clear and forcible affirmation of the infallibility of the Pope. In fact, Archbishop Spalding thought that the terms therein employed would more effectually stop all cavil than a more formal definition. He advocated it, not as a compromise between those who affirmed and those who denied the infallibility of the Pope, but as the most practical and least objectionable form in which the definition could be drawn up.

"The present method," he says, "of defining by implication, although it be indirect, seems to excel both in force and simplicity; for it is clearer, and, perhaps, contains more than would a formal definition." And, in fact, this was an objection made to Archbishop Spalding's *Postulatum* by those who opposed the introduction of the question of infallibility into the Council. From this *Postulatum*, then, and from the letters which he wrote to Rome before the assembling of the Council, it is evident that Archbishop Spalding was opposed neither to the infallibility of the Pope nor to the opportuneness of its definition by the Council, but that he favored a definition by implication in preference to an explicit affirmation of the dogma.

It is only in the light of this certain fact that the *rationes* added to the *Schema*, which afterwards were so prominently brought into the controversy on infallibility, may be properly viewed. They must be taken in the con-

nection in which the author of the *Postulatum* adduces
them. He brings them forward, not as arguments against
a definition of Papal infallibility; on the contrary, he urges
them as reasons for making what he holds to be a clear
and logical definition of this dogma. Others are free to
think that they prove more or less than their author intended they should prove; but since he in this very document makes the clearest statement of what he desires the
Council to define concerning the infallibility of the Pope, it
is simply absurd to seek by refinement of logical deductions
to make him responsible for what he openly rejects. Archbishop Spalding's chief motive, and the only one which in
his own mind was of palmary importance, in favoring an
implicit definition, was that he thought a *Schema* of this
kind would secure the unanimous, or quasi-unanimous, vote
of the fathers, and thus prevent that of which he naturally
had the greatest horror, and which he considered as most
contrary to the spirit of Christ and the church—discord and
strife. What Protestants would think of the definition, or
how it would be received by what is called the spirit of the
age, were matters which did not trouble him. He had lived
too long among Protestants and in the breath of this world
to be frightened by idle theories on these subjects.

A short time after this memorial was drawn up, Archbishop Spalding was made a member of the deputation of
twelve cardinals and fourteen prelates, appointed by the
Holy Father, to whose judgment all *Postulata* had to be
submitted before they could be brought before the Council.
In this new position, he felt that both propriety and
fairness should prevent him from longer taking part in
movements to bring special matters before the Council,
and he therefore abstained from taking further steps to
bring the *Postulatum* to the notice of the Fathers. It was,
however, looked upon as an important document in connec-

tion with the history of the definition of papal infallibility, from the fact that it was generally thought to represent the views of a considerable number of the bishops of the Council, who were called "the third party." As the controversy on the opportuneness of defining the infallibility waxed warmer, and as those who were adverse became more determined in their opposition, they sought to force "the third party," or those who were in favor of an implicit definition, to pronounce openly for their side, since the project of definition by implication had fallen through.

The famous brochure, *Ce qui se passe au Concile*, which appeared in May, after the assembling of the Council, thus speaks of what was called "the third party": "They know now that their separation from the minority, far from serving the cause of moderation, has seriously compromised it; by their concessions, they have only emboldened the extremists, without having been able to restrain them, and without even having obtained respect for their own opinions. The situation is critical. They (the third party) hold within their hands the fate of the Council. What will they do? We shall be greatly surprised should these wise prelates permit to mature in silence the events which threaten us, the irreparable calamity of which they would be the first to deplore."*

Bishop Dupanloup, in his reply to Archbishop Dechamps, dated March 1, 1870, repeatedly makes use of the *rationes* of the *Postulatum* of Archbishop Spalding to prove that the bishops, whose views this *Postulatum* embodied, were or should be opposed to the definition of the infallibility of the Pope. Now, it must be borne in mind that Archbishop Spalding, in his *Postulatum*, expressly demands the definition of Pontifical infallibility. The document was drawn up, in fact, under the firm persuasion that the infallibility of the

* Page 122.

Pope would be defined by the Council. The only question which its author considered open to discussion was whether the definition should be formal or implied. The *rationes* annexed to the *Postulatum* were, indeed, intended to conclude against an explicit definition; but they were not advanced for the purpose of showing that the Council should abstain from defining the dogma of Papal infallibility. Hence, to urge them when the question had been narrowed down to an explicit definition, or none at all, was carrying them beyond the purpose for which they had been drawn up.

It did not follow that Archbishop Spalding, because he was in favor of a definition by implication, should prefer no definition to a formal one.

He felt that the use which had been made of the *rationes* would tend to place him in a false position, and he had no thought of being made to assume whatever attitude might best suit the purposes of the verbal fencers who were waging war at the doors of the Council. He therefore, on the 4th of April, 1870, addressed a letter to Bishop Dupanloup, of which the following is a translation:

"MY LORD:

"In a letter which your lordship has just written to the Archbishop of Malines, you do me an honor for which I cannot thank you. You quote repeatedly a *Postulatum* which, in concert with many of my venerable colleagues, I deemed it my duty to present to the Council at a time when the question of Pontifical infallibility was far from the degree of maturity at which it has now arrived. While several bishops, entirely devoted to the Holy See, still doubted whether it was opportune to introduce this question, we asked, in our *Postulatum*, that it should be defined in such a manner as to obtain the concurrence of all the members of the august assembly. But your citations are so arranged as to lead your readers to suppose that we are averse, if not to the truth, at least to the opportuneness, of this definition; and, consequently, to class us with what certain journals choose to call the 'party of the opposition' in the Council. Your lordship, it is true, does not consider our opposition sufficiently decided, and, after having availed yourself of our proposition in every part of your letter, you finally throw it aside as people fling away a weapon which is no longer serviceable. This mode of action is no doubt very flattering to us; but it does not prevent your lordship from attempting to place us among your allies—a character which we feel compelled to repudiate. There is no justification for the effort which has been made to represent us as opposed to the plain and honest declaration of the general belief of the church with respect to the infallibility of the Vicar of Jesus Christ. The fifth paragraph of our *rationes* expresses the faith of the subscribers on this subject in a manner which leaves no room for doubt. In our project of definition, we intimately unite the infallibility of the Roman Pontiff with the infallibility of the church, and we propose the first *as a logical consequence and corollary of the Primacy*, in such sort that it extends as far as, and acknowledges no other limits than, the infallibility of the church and the divinely constituted Primacy itself, which are principles of faith, fixed and determined from the very origin of Christianity. We believe, then, that this mode of definition has the advantage that it furnishes no pretext, either to theologians or the faithful, of doubting or disputing about the commands and decrees of the Sovereign Pontiff, to whose most wise sentence, by which the sheep as well as the lambs are guided, everything must be lovingly and reverently committed, as becomes children in their relations with a father." *

* In our *Schema*, we also quoted a most significant passage from the

"Such, my lord, was the sole design of those who drew up the *Postulatum*, so incorrectly interpreted by you. Their intention was not to hide the light under a bushel, or to put a veil over the belief of the church. They desired, on the contrary, to find a mode of definition which should guard this belief from every attack, and obtain for it, both from pastors and people, a more unanimous adhesion. They had thought that this end might be attained by fixing the doctrine of infallibility practically and *in concreto*, rather than by affirming it in an abstract formula. They proposed, therefore, to define—

"1. That no appeal from the judgments of the Sovereign Pontiff is lawful.

"2. That every Christian is bound to give to these decisions interior assent, and not merely respectful silence.

"3. That Gallicanism, by separating the body of bishops from the Sovereign Pontiff, and giving to them the right to reform his judgments, destroys the order established by Jesus Christ, according to which Peter is to confirm his brethren, and not to receive confirmation from them.

"4. That the decisions of the Pope are not less sovereign

address presented to the Sovereign Pontiff by the five hundred bishops assembled in Rome at the centenary of St. Peter. Your lordship cannot have forgotten this address, which you helped to compose; and I ask myself, with surprise, how you can to-day think it inopportune to define a doctrine which, at least in substance, was so loudly proclaimed on that solemn occasion. Finally, to remove the possibility of doubt as to our past or present belief, we quoted a decree of the Second Plenary Council of Baltimore, in which, adopting a sentence from the first encyclical of Pius IX., the American episcopate declares that it recognizes no living and infallible authority, except in that church which was built by our Lord Jesus Christ upon Peter, Chief, Prince, and Pastor of the universal church, to whom he promised that his faith should never fail. Is it not strange that any one should attempt to represent *as inopportunists* in Rome, bishops who in their own country have already promulgated such a decree?

in the declaration of dogmatic facts than in the determination of purely doctrinal questions.

"Each of the four propositions here enumerated evidently implies infallibility, and it is therefore an entire misconstruction of the thought of those who solicited this solemn definition to represent them as favorable to the opinion of the inopportunists. And it must be added, my lord, that it is not my doctrine alone that your letter presents under a form so remote from the truth. In a note furnished to you, you tell us, by a learned theologian, belonging to an illustrious order, you quote a certain number of writers as sharing your opinion, and among them you place my venerable predecessor in the see of Baltimore, the Most Rev. Francis P. Kenrick. I know not what your other citations may be worth; and, if I may believe persons who have found leisure to verify them, your lordship, in accepting them blindly, has been the dupe of a too great confidence. What I can affirm is this: that it is impossible, without injustice, to attribute to Archbishop Kenrick a doctrine at variance with that of the immense majority of Catholic doctors. In his *Dogmatic Theology*, that prelate has a special article, entitled *De Definitionibus Pontificiis*, in which he is not content with declaring his belief in the infallibility of such definitions, but refutes, with a conciseness which in no way impairs the triumphant vigor of his replies, the objections which both the earlier and later Gallicans have drawn from the facts in the history of Liberius, Honorius, and other Pontiffs.*

"You will, no doubt, be surprised, my lord, that a learned theologian, belonging to an illustrious order, should have allowed himself so palpable a perversion of the truth in connection with a work which we all have in our hands; and this may lead you to suspect that there is a school of falsi-

---

* *Tract. de Eccles. de Tribunali Doct.*, p. 240, Mech.

fication, quite other than that which defends Pontifical infallibility. One correction more, and I shall conclude. Your lordship turns to good account that passage of our memorial in which we express the desire that the definition of the doctrinal sovereignty of the Pope should be pronounced with perfect unanimity—*quæ sane nemine, si id fieri possit, dissentiente, definiri deberet.*

"The word *deberet*, which you write in capital letters, you translate by *il faut*, and you remark that this is the strict sense of the word, which does not signify, you say, *it would be desirable or preferable;* but, *it must.* The signers of the memorial are thus transformed by your lordship into decided advocates of the new theory, according to which unanimity is required for the validity of doctrinal definitions.

"We earnestly protest against such an interpretation of our thoughts, and to reject it there is no need of our invoking tradition, so plainly contrary to the theory which you impute to us; nor need we trouble ourselves to prove to you that such a theory involves nothing less than the destruction of the authority of the church; it is enough for us to appeal to grammar. Though I am far from pretending to compare myself with your lordship in the knowledge of French, I think I may venture to affirm that the indicative absolute— *il faut*—has not, in that language, the sense of the Latin optative, *deberet;* especially when this optative is still further softened by various attenuating phrases—*si fieri possit, videtur,* etc. It seems to me plain that if we are to choose between the two translations indicated by your lordship— *it must,* or *it would be desirable*—that precisely which you reject is the one which ought to be preferred, as by far the more exact.

"Such, indeed, is our thought. It seems to us most desirable, and more necessary than ever in the present circumstances, that in all the acts of the Council, especially in that which is most fought against, the Catholic episcopate should present itself to the world—to believers as to unbelievers—surrounded with the glory and clothed with the strength which unanimity gives. But from the necessity of this accord, it has never entered our minds to conclude that the majority is bound to yield to the minority. We sought rather to remove the obstacles created, much less by the substance than by the form of the question, which hindered the minority from agreeing with the majority. We have reason to believe that our efforts have not been fruitless. Our project, it is true, was not accepted by the Commission, which put it aside, with all the others that had been presented, and drew up a new one. Though its adoption was not urged with the instance with which others have been pushed, the one which we composed has helped not a little to bring together several members of the Council, and to prepare the happy accord of which everything leads us to hope for the approaching consummation. We have not, indeed, succeeded, according to our earnest desire, in preventing the digging up of materials from the history of the past for scandalous discussions. Rash men have recklessly provoked these scandals, and have thus rendered useless the measures of conciliation which we had suggested. But perhaps there is no reason why we should complain very much of this. The discussion of the truth has been rendered more searching, and its complete manifestation by the Council less difficult. Already the question of opportuneness may be considered settled ; and we have every reason to believe that, when the Council shall be invited to pronounce upon the doctrine itself, its decision will be fortified with that moral unanimity which we continue to regard as most useful. What is certain, my lord, is that all of us, whether we have signed the various *postulata*, or have abstained from doing so, have henceforth but two courses before us—we

must place ourselves squarely either on the side of the Pope or on that of his opponents. The Catholic episcopate has long since made its choice; and the fathers of the Vatican, by proclaiming as an article of faith the duty of never separating from the successor of St. Peter, will walk in the footsteps of their predecessors. With the grace of God, I shall never stray from the glorious paths in which our young church of America has followed up to this hour with unshaken fidelity; and it is in order to render all doubt as to my resolution in this matter impossible, that I think it my duty publicly to repudiate the false impressions which may have been made by your letter. It had been my intention to wait for the discussion in Council before making this protest; but when I saw the increasing number of writings, of a nature to disturb the faith of Christians, I considered that it became the duty of the chief pastors to prepare their flocks to accept with hearty obedience the decisions of the Council. I should regard it as the greatest misfortune of my life to have contributed in any way to encourage even one of my brethren to falter in perfect obedience to the authority of the church. In associating me, in spite of myself, in your own struggles against a definition which has now become inevitable, your lordship burdens me with a portion of that frightful responsibility which nothing can induce me to accept, and thus imposes upon me the necessity of making a public statement of my personal conviction. But in performing this duty of conscience, I am not the less, my lord, your lordship's respectful and devoted servant, ✠ MARTIN JOHN SPALDING,
"Archbishop of Baltimore."

CHAPTER XXXI.

THE DEFINITION OF PAPAL INFALLIBILITY NOT ONLY OPPORTUNE, BUT NECESSARY — DEVOTION OF THE AMERICAN CHURCH TO THE HOLY SEE.

RCHBISHOP SPALDING had, as I have already stated, favored an implicit definition of Papal infallibility, chiefly because he thought such a definition would receive the quasi-unanimous vote of the fathers, and preclude all danger from the agitation of *les questions irritantes*, which had been held, like the sword of Damocles, over the head of the Council.

At the time the letter to Bishop Dupanloup was written, four months had elapsed since the assembling of the bishops, and the *via media* had failed to accomplish the result hoped for by those who had advocated it, and affairs had taken such a shape that, as Archbishop Spalding said, but two courses lay before the bishops—either to place themselves openly on the side of the Pope or on that of the opposition. Not a few events had occurred in the meantime which were not without a very significant bearing upon the question of opportuneness. Undercurrents of thought, especially in Germany, but also in France and in other parts of the world, which had hitherto escaped the notice of all except the very observant, had been brought to the surface by the assembling of the Council. *Qui assemble le peuple, l'émeut*, says a French proverb, and the church was agitated by the gathering together of its representatives from every part of the world.

As the winds of heaven trouble the waters of the ocean even till they rise in rage and fury, and then pillow themselves upon their tranquil bosom, cleansed of "the perilous stuff," so these conflicts brought to the surface some things which had to be swept away, and which, but for the agitation occasioned by the assembling of the Council, might have continued unnoticed to eat their way like a canker to the Catholic heart. God, it is true, is not in the storm or in the whirlwind, but these had to pass by before the divine calm of his presence could be felt. Writings had appeared in Germany and France, under the authority and patronage of great names, the tendency of which was to destroy, not merely faith in the infallibility of the Pope, but all respect for the Papacy. One could almost catch the feeble echoes of Luther's rude phraseology.

As the pseudo-reformers of the sixteenth century represented the church as wholly corrupt, these *illuminati* of our day represented her as ignorant. The old spirit of nationalism, as opposed to Catholicism, cropped out in rude and uninviting forms. The scientific pride of Germany, and what was supposed to be the military hegemony of France, who loved to fight only for ideas, gave infinite confidence to the German and French opponents of the definition. The German science to which they appealed was as complete a sham as the military power of France proved to be a few months later. It would be impertinent, I know, in any man to say aught against the solid learning of Germany; but there existed in that country before the Council a school of what was supposed to be Catholic theology, but which was, in reality, an impossible rationalism, which but imperfectly succeeded in concealing itself beneath the forms of Catholic phraseology. The leaders in this school of thought held in self-complacent vainglory that "German science," represented by them, was the only science; that the lamp of theological knowledge had been removed from Italy, and burned now in Germany alone; that the mantle of the prophets under the old law had fallen upon the scientific theologians, whose office it had become to mould the public opinion of the church, to which her doctrinal decisions would be forced to conform.*

The central point around which the varying shades of opinion of this party were grouped was that which forms the only bond of sympathy among the sects—antipathy to Rome and the successor of Peter, the representative of Catholic unity. The brilliant talents and great learning of some of these men had succeeded in winning for them disciples in France and England, and possibly elsewhere, the tendency of whose writings was very hurtful to the soundness of Catholic faith. The assembling of the Vatican Council revealed many things in this connection which must have been quite new to bishops who had passed their lives in the arduous missionary duties of the United States, where Catholics have never known any other feeling toward the Pope than that of filial love. They at once saw that Gallicanism was not wholly dead, or that, if dead, it had been succeeded by a species of rationalistic nationalism, which was far worse. And—what could as little lay claim to the sympathies of American bishops—the attempt was made to induce the governments of Europe to interfere to prevent the definition. At the instigation of some of

* Dr. Döllinger, in his lectures on the *Reunion of the Churches*, recently published, toward the close of the seventh and last lecture makes the following statement:

"I have found it the almost universal conviction in foreign countries that it is the special mission of Germany to take the lead in this world-wide question [the fusion of the Catholic, Greek schismatic, and Protestant churches into one], and give to the movement its form, measure, and direction. *We are the heart of Europe, richer in theologians than all other lands.*"

Hannibal Chollop says to Mark Tapley: "We are a model to the airth, . . . We are the intellect and virtue of the airth, the cream of human natur', and the flower of moral force."—*Vide Dublin Review* for January 1873, p. 207.

the leaders of the German "scientific theologians," the Bavarian Government, through Prince Hohenlohe, had begun a systematic agitation against the Council, in order to induce the European powers to agree upon some plan by which the definition of the infallibility of the Pope might be prevented. The avowed aim of the well-known *Janus* publication was to rouse the civil governments against the Council.

After Prince Hohenlohe's note to the various so-called Catholic governments, the Spanish minister, Olozaga, threatened the church with the hostility of a league to be formed by France, Italy, Portugal, Spain, and Bavaria. General Menabrea addressed a circular to his diplomatic agents, proposing to the powers to prevent the assembling of the Council, on the ground of their not having been invited to it. A joint despatch was sent by Prince Hohenlohe and the Italian Government to their representatives in France, urging the withdrawal of the French troops from Rome during the Council, *to insure freedom of deliberation*.

After the Council assembled, Count Daru, the French Minister of Foreign Affairs, addressed a letter to the Holy See, with a view to prevent the definition; Von Beust, the Protestant Chancellor of Austria, sought to bring his influence to bear in the same direction; and their example was followed, more or less openly, by most of the other governments of Europe.

When Archbishop Spalding saw this alliance of the liberal or rationalistic Catholics with the governments of Europe for the purpose of preventing the definition of what, he held, had always been the faith of the church, he considered, as he says in his letter to Bishop Dupanloup, the question of opportuneness at an end. The opposition had created the opportuneness, and had made the definition necessary. The church defines the truths of revelation when they are denied, and the hour had come when she could no longer remain silent upon this all-important article of faith. "*Error, cui non resistitur, approbatur, et veritas, cum non defenditur, opprimetur.*" "If the Gnosticism," says Archbishop Manning, "of what has well been called the Professordom of Germany had been allowed to spread its mixture of conceited illuminism and contemptuous rationalism for a few years longer, the faith of multitudes might have been irremediably lost; and Germany, which now presents the noblest fidelity and constancy in its episcopate, in its priesthood, and in its laity, might have been a prey to the Old Catholic schism, or to the tyrannical liberalism of those who deify the civil power."*

Still another phase of the question had been revealed by the opposition. Though scarcely one of the bishops of the Council had opposed the definition for any other reason than that of inexpediency, yet the arguments which had been employed to establish this, had they been conclusive, would have had a much wider bearing.

"The historical difficulties," which were made to bear the heat and brunt of the battle on the side of the inopportunists, had they been of any value, would have proved, not only that it was inopportune to define the infallibility of the Pope, but that it was impossible to define it, since popes had erred in what must be considered as *ex cathedra* definitions. What other conclusion was it possible to draw from the inopportunist interpretation of the facts in the cases of Popes Liberius, Honorius, Pascal II., and others? When the controversy had assumed this shape, the Council was forced either to declare the Pope infallible, or by its silence to admit that he was not infallible; because, *de facto*, he had been guilty of error in the past. Here, again, the opposi-

---

* *Sermons on Eccles. Sub.*, vol iii., Introduct., p. 39.

tion had created, not only the opportuneness, but the necessity of the definition.

To that portion of his letter to Bishop Dupanloup in which he spoke of the unswerving devotion of the church of the United States to the Vicar of Christ, Archbishop Spalding added the following note: "If a special duty of gratitude obliges all the churches of the West to unbounded devotion to the Holy See, to which they owe all their privileges and their very existence, there is not one of them all which may be less permitted to forget this duty than the church of the United States, which but yesterday came forth from the maternal and ever-fruitful bosom of the Church of Rome. We were accordingly most happy, on the occasion of a recent visit of the Holy Father to the American College of the North, to assure him, in the name of our venerable brothers, who surrounded us, of our lively gratitude and entire devotion to the Papacy. The acts of all our Councils, said we, and the letters addressed to your Holiness and to your predecessors by the episcopate of our country, are evidence that we have always made profession of the greatest respect and the most ardent love for the successor of Peter. We have ever remained united with the chair of Peter, and nothing can separate us from it. And how could this not be, since from the very rise of religion in our country we have been watched over by the Sovereign Pontiffs with a constant and truly paternal solicitude? For the rest, our veneration and our filial obedience have been abundantly blessed of God; and under our eyes the promise of the Holy Ghost is fulfilled—' The obedient man shall recount his victories.' Sixty years ago, there was but one bishop in the United States; to-day we have sixty dioceses and vicariates apostolic. To popes who bore the name of Pius our church is especially indebted for its progress. Pius VI. gave it its first bishop; Pius VII. established the hierarchy and constituted the first ecclesiastical province; Pius IX. to this first province has added six others. Pius has planted; we have watered the vineyard according to the measure of our strength; and God has given the increase. . . .

"The sentiments which we expressed on this occasion had been proclaimed with much more solemnity and with greater authority in the various *Acts* of the Second Plenary Council of Baltimore, and especially in the letter to Pius IX., signed by the seven archbishops of the United States in the name of all their suffragans. Let it suffice to quote the final sentence of this letter, in which the fathers of the Council 'submit their decrees to the examination and correction of the Holy Father, resolved to recognize his voice as the voice of Peter speaking to them by the mouth of his successor.'"

In the question of opportuneness, great weight was attached to the views of the American bishops. The church of the United States, all admitted, was growing rapidly. America was destined to be the home of civilized populations more numerous than those which at present inhabit Europe; and Catholics there, were already living under social conditions toward which Europe seemed to be approaching.

The opposition felt that the support of the bishops of the New World would be most opportune. Archbishop Spalding said: American Catholics are Roman Catholics; and they will stand with the Pope, if such a thing were possible, against all the bishops in the world; and his words were grand, not because he uttered them, but because they were spoken in the fit hour, and proclaimed the living faith of a young but great and vigorous church. Why, we Catholics of Irish and English descent had been baptized Papists in three centuries of blood and cruelty; and were we now, in mere wantonness, to give up the glorious title of our nobility? "O Church of Rome!" exclaimed Fénelon, in the days of an older Gallicanism, "O Holy City! O dear and common country of all true Christians! There is in Christ Jesus nor Greek, nor Scythian, nor Barbarian, nor Jew, nor Gentile. All are made one people in thy bosom. All are co-citizens of Rome, and every Catholic is Roman." *

This was the confession of faith made by Archbishop Spalding—simple enough, but sublime because it was made in the right hour.

"When the history of the Vatican Council comes to be written," wrote a well-known Englishman, "not many names will be mentioned with more honor than that of the wise and prudent Archbishop of Baltimore; nor will any extra-conciliary document be recorded in future generations with deeper satisfaction or warmer gratitude than the letter in which Mgr. Spalding vindicated himself and his colleagues from all complicity with Gallican doctrines and intrigues." †

"Your grace has earned the gratitude of millions," wrote Dr. Marshall, the author of *The Christian Missions*, "whom your noble letter will console and instruct. Every one seems

* Deuxième Mandement sur la Constitution Unigenitus.
† *The Vatican*, p. 258.

In referring to the letter of Archbishop Spalding to Bishop Dupanloup, the Roman correspondent of the *Pall Mall Gazette* made an observation which it may be worth while to record here: "The violent pamphlet" (this is his language) "of Mgr. Spalding, Archbishop of Baltimore, in favor of Pontifical infallibility, has drawn attention to the fact that the three champions of the dogma—Dr. Manning, Mgr. Spalding, and Mgr. Dechamps—come from *the three freest countries of the world*—England, North America, and Belgium. . . . Nearly all the opponents of the dogma," he continues, "are from States which have concluded concordats with the Holy See, which recognize the Catholic religion as that of the nation, and either directly pay its clergy, as in France, or maintain it, as in Austria, Hungary and Germany, in possession of vast estates."

to feel that it is the most formidable blow hitherto inflicted upon that deplorable school whose final condemnation seems to be at hand. It is a matter for special congratulation that this lesson should have been given by an American prelate. The world imagines that your countrymen are too free and independent to accept the light yoke of truth, and that, if they are Catholics, it can only be a *diluted* Popery which such men profess. Their chief pastor has dispelled effectually this popular delusion. . . . Our American brothers will feel a just pride that such a voice has gone forth from the see of Baltimore, and that one whom they love, with so much reason, has delivered such a testimony in the face of Europe and of all Christendom. Your letter, my dear Lord Archbishop, will go to the ends of the earth, and it will always remain one of the conspicuous facts in the history of the Vatican Council, that the American Church was so nobly represented in it by one who is already in fact, and who will soon, I hope, be in title and honor, its Primate."

As Archbishop Spalding felt that special ties of gratitude should bind us to the Holy See, he also perfectly understood that the highest interests of the church in this great Republic, even more than elsewhere, demanded that this union of love should be cherished and in every possible way strengthened.

The whole edifice of the church, indeed, is knit together under the headship of Peter, cemented into imperishable durability on the divinely-adjusted rock, which crumbles not at the touch of all-destroying time, moves not in the universal upheaval of human things, but, like the foundations of the everlasting hills, remains for ever. What in ages past has held the church together, prevented it from being broken up into national, sectarian, fragmentary parts, without unity of doctrine or bond of communion, a prey to all the vicissitudes to which human affairs are subject? The see of Peter, the centre of unity, the bond of charity, the keystone to the arch that spans the earth and reaches to heaven, like the rainbow, a perpetual symbol of God's ever-enduring love and truth. Now, this traditional and conservative authority of the Holy See is, such at least was the opinion of Archbishop Spalding, even more necessary for us than for any other portion of the Church Catholic. In our active and restless society, everything is in a state of chronic transition. Manners, customs, and opinions change with the same rapidity with which we cause splendid palaces and vast centres of commerce to spring up from the bosom of the miasmatic swamp or through the dense foliage of the primeval forest. We have no landmarks of the olden time, no ancient moorings, no anchor sunk in the strata of bygone ages. Religious opinion here outside the church, more universally than in Europe, is fast resolving itself into deism, atheism, pantheism—into that philosophy, in a word, by whatsoever name you may call it, by which God is made an abstraction, and man becomes to himself his own supreme law.

Protestantism with us is certainly adrift on the wide, wide sea, driven hither and yon, torn, and rent, and twisted by every wind of human opinion. In it there is nor unity, nor strength, nor beauty. The crucial age is upon it, and, like a circle in the water, it will never cease to enlarge itself, that it may take in every phase of human opinion, until it disperse into naught. Catholics, like other men, are more or less influenced by the circumstances in which they are thrown; and in this irreverent age and country, in which we do not sufficiently respect anything, and least of all the persons of those clothed with authority, a true and abiding devotion to the Vicar of Christ, the centre of unity and the pillar of strength, is the only safeguard against the disintegrating action of the repulsive and centrifugal forces, which the license of the times, the spirit of nationality, the difference of customs and ideas, and the increasing disrespect for authority, will bring to bear against the unity of the church in this country. In the past, our relations with the Holy See have been all that could be desired; and it was but natural that this should have been, since, so long as we were a young and infant church, we instinctively felt the need of a father's guiding and protecting hand. But now that we have grown stronger and feel less our dependence, it is all the more necessary that we should cling, with the tender love of a child to its mother, to the centre of our unity, and consequently of our strength.

"I should regard as the greatest misfortune of my life," wrote Archbishop Spalding, "to have contributed in any way whatever to cause even a single one of my brothers to falter in perfect obedience to the authority of the church."

These words contain the spirit of his life. He had the most unbounded respect for anything, however trivial and unimportant in itself, that came from the Holy See; and no one could be more careful than he was in carrying out to the letter the various regulations sanctioned by the Holy Father for the government of the church in this country. His zeal in this respect may have seemed to some excessive; but he felt that in his position he could do no greater work for the church than to give the highest example of perfect respect for authority.

Archbishop Spalding, as I have already stated, was appointed by the Holy Father a member of the Commission on *Postulata*. He was also elected, by a majority of the votes of the bishops, a member of the Commission on Faith.

These were among the principal congregations of the Council, and in them was prepared much of the most delicate and important matter which was afterwards submitted to the bishops.

During the eight months in which the Vatican Council was in session, Archbishop Spalding labored almost incessantly, and he bore the fatigues of the trying deliberations of those months remarkably well, much better, indeed, than many of his brothers who were younger and more vigorous than himself. He had the gift of being able to throw his whole soul into whatever he undertook to perform; and this power of concentrating his energies often sustained him in the midst of labors which his naturally feeble health would not have otherwise borne. He remained in Rome until after the fourth and last General Congregation, which was held on the 18th of July, 1870, and in which the final vote on the infallibility of the Pope was taken—five hundred and thirty-three of the five hundred and thirty-five bishops present voting in favor of the definition.*

---

* The last preliminary vote in the public Congregation, held a few days previously, stood: Placet, 451; non-Placet, 88; Placet with modifications, 62. Most of the last class voted Placet at the session, while most of the non-Placet voters chose to absent themselves, though they were perfectly free to vote, as the example of two of their number proved. Comparing the total number of voters on this occasion with that of the fathers who originally belonged to the Council, there is a falling off of two hundred and twenty-nine, of whom probably twelve had died, and the remainder, with the exception above indicated, had been permitted, for legitimate causes, to return to their dioceses. The great majority of these were in favor of the definition.

CHAPTER XXXII.

THE MANNER IN WHICH THE DISCUSSIONS OF THE VATICAN COUNCIL WERE CONDUCTED—THE INFALLIBILITY OF THE POPE—LIBERTY AND LIBERALISM—TOUR IN SWITZERLAND.

"DISCUSSION," wrote Archbishop Spalding, "is characteristic of all deliberative assemblies, of which the oldest and best models have been the councils of the Catholic Church. From that of Jerusalem, presided over by Peter, to that of the Vatican, presided over by his successor, Pius IX., there has always been, first, 'much disputing,' and then later, after the matter had been discussed and Peter or his successor had pronounced sentence, a great silence and peace." *

Immediately after the final vote had been taken, Archbishop Spalding addressed a *Pastoral Letter* on the Papal infallibility to the clergy and laity of the archdiocese of Baltimore. The irresponsible correspondents of the press had sought, by the reckless perversion of facts, to bring the Council into disrepute. They desired to produce the impression that the intellect, the virtue, and the independence of spirit in the Council were to be found exclusively among those who were opposed to the infallibility of the Pope. These far-seeing and heroic men were represented as overwhelmed by the noisy and tyrannical majority, who were described, to use the words of Archbishop Manning, as a Dead Sea of superstition, narrowness, shallowness, ignorance, prejudice; without theology, philosophy, science, or

* Pastoral Letter on Infallibility.

eloquence; gathered from "old Catholic countries"; bigoted, tyrannical, deaf to reason; with a herd of "Curial and Italian prelates" and mere "Vicars Apostolic."

Freedom of discussion, we were told, there was none; for the thrilling eloquence of the minority was drowned by the violent ringing of bells and intemperate interruptions; by outcries, menacing gestures, and wild clamors round the tribune.

Archbishop Spalding, who was perfectly familiar with the laws and customs that govern deliberative assemblies, and who was an eye-witness of what he describes, and intimately acquainted with even the minutest details relating to the Council, gives the following plain and matter-of-fact statement as to the manner in which its deliberations were carried on.

"Never," he writes, "has there been a council in which there has existed fuller latitude or greater freedom of discussion, or one in which greater decorum and dignity have been observed. Every subject, or *Schema*, has been thoughtfully examined, in its most minute details, and in all its possible bearings. The regulations provided for a triple discussion; the first in writing, the other two by word of mouth. After the distribution of the *Schema*, the fathers were invited to hand in, in writing, within a specified period, their objections or modifications to the appropriate deputation or committee, which thereupon instituted a searching examination, and reported back the result of their deliberations in the shape of a revised and reprinted *Schema*. Then the oral discussion began; first, in general, or on the general matter and form of the *Schema;* and next, in particular, on each chapter, and even on each phrase and word; the speakers at the same time presenting in writing the amendments which they deemed opportune. These amendments were printed and distributed among the fathers, who were advised of the day assigned for voting on them. The vote taken, such of the amendments as were adopted were embodied in the reprinted *Schema;* and then the fathers were called upon to vote, first, on each separate part or chapter of the revised text; and, next, on the whole. The last vote was most solemn; it was taken by calling separately all the members of the Council, each of whom might answer in one of three ways—either by *placet*, or yea; by *non-placet*, or nay; or by *placet juxta modum*, or yea with a modification. These modifications handed in, in writing, were printed and sent back to the deputation for examination, and, on their report to the Council, the final preparatory vote was taken in the general Congregation, preliminary to the solemn and conclusive vote in the public session.

"The great mass of these debates regarded the forms of expression rather than the substance of the things themselves; though some of them, especially on the last *Constitution*—to which we shall soon refer—touched to a greater or less extent the substance itself, or at least the opportuneness of the definition. Every sentence, every phrase, every word, every comma even, was searchingly examined; and with a triple discussion and a triple preparatory vote, even humanly speaking, there could scarcely be room for a mistake. The judgment of the church on matters of faith and morals, when confirmed by the Roman Pontiff—as they necessarily must be—being irreversible and infallible, and regarding all time as well as all nations, all these precautions are wisely taken as a preliminary to the promised presence and assistance of the Holy Ghost, who then puts the seal of his infallible truth on the results of human research and industry. These are not only not excluded by the divine promises, but they are regarded, not, indeed, as a condition of infallibility, but as a moral duty of the assembled fathers, who are bound to search the Scriptures and the traditions of the church before rendering their decision." *

After paying this tribute to the fairness with which the proceedings of the Council were conducted, Archbishop Spalding, in a few concise and lucid paragraphs, disengages the question of infallibility from the misconceptions with which ignorance and prejudice had sought to obscure it, and then gives a clear conception of its real scope and nature. He shows that the Vatican Council has not set up a new doctrine, but has merely proclaimed in the most solemn manner a truth that was coeval with the founding of the Christian church, which is a divinely established organism in which the separation of the head from the body is impossible without the destruction of that work against which, by God's promise, the gates of hell shall never prevail. "From the Catholic stand-point," he concludes, "we cannot logically believe in the infallibility of the church without admitting the official infallibility of its visible head, the Roman Pontiff.

---

* Friedrich, in his *Documenta ad Illustrandum Concilium Vaticanum, anni 1870*, gives the original draughts or *Schemata* as first submitted to the bishops. A comparison between these draughts and the *Constitutions* as finally adopted shows that hardly a sentence has been left standing in the latter as it stood in the former. Except in the general titles, "On Faith" and "On the Church," everything is altered—the arrangement, the titles of the chapters, the matter of the chapters—not a little entirely eliminated, not a little entirely new introduced. In the *First Constitution*, the matter is cut down to about one-half its original dimensions—eighteen chapters reduced to four. The *Second Constitution* is reduced to about one-third its original compass—four chapters instead of fifteen; and a great deal of very weighty matter is left out altogether; whilst the chapter on the Papal infallibility, not in the *Schema* at all, is inserted, and a series of canons are expunged. This, of itself, furnishes most undeniable and palpable proof that the *Constitutions* are the free and deliberate work of the bishops; and, at the same time, it affords a striking instance of the utter untrustworthiness of those who have attacked the Council. "Lie! lie!" said Voltaire; "something will always stick."

And it is not at all to be wondered at that this cardinal point of Catholic doctrine should have been defined in the Council of the Vatican, as it had been so publicly impugned, with so much evil to the church, since the close of the last General Council; particularly as the opposition to it has lately been reawakened in a manner so fierce and so determined. It was surely time to settle finally a question which has produced so much excitement, to the great embarrassment and disedification of the faithful."

To the oft-repeated objection that the definition would shock the prejudices of non-Catholics, and retard or prevent their conversion to the true faith, Archbishop Spalding replied: " A long acquaintance and a friendly discussion with intelligent and candid non-Catholics, running through a period of more than a third of a century, has impressed us with the conviction that what they admire most in the Catholic controvertist is candor, directness, and an openness which leaves no suspicion that anything is left in the background or meant to be concealed. They admire a man who feels strong enough to accept the whole position, and who is bold enough to meet every issue and to decline no responsibility. The first things which strike a cultivated non-Catholic, when his attention is called to the Catholic Church, are its world-wide grandeur of extension, its superhuman and marvellous unity of faith, and its tenacious consistency in so steadily adhering to principle amid weal and woe; and above all, its wonderful antiquity, indicated so strikingly in its long line of Pontiffs, reaching back through the wreck of kingdoms and the vicissitudes of human affairs to the time when Peter and Paul first came, poor strangers, to the Eternal City, to set up the standard of the cross in the magnificent metropolis and mistress of the world. The range of human history can present no parallel to this line of venerable Pontiffs, through whose energetic exertions and untiring zeal, apostles were ordained and successively sent out to convert the nations, and to knit them, as fast as converted, to the great Roman centre of unity; so that, in the course of a few centuries, the world became Christian even far beyond the boundaries of the Roman Empire. Thus was accomplished the promise of Christ, the divine Shepherd of the flock, through the agency of his delegated chief shepherd: 'And other sheep I have, which are not of this fold; them also must I call, and there shall be *one sheepfold under the one shepherd.*'

"The chief agents, under Christ, of this marvellous transformation were manifestly the Roman Pontiffs; and to them, whenever it is a question of the church, all eyes are spontaneously directed. Now, in discussing with Protestants, we take this high stand-point as our beginning, and from it we easily survey the whole field, and point out all its bearings, with the official infallibility of the Pontiffs established, and along with it the necessary adherence of the body to the head; we explain at once the secret of that wonderful unity and tenacity of faith which so puzzles the unbeliever in supernatural interposition and guidance. The fidelity of Christ in fulfilling his promise, that the gates of hell shall not prevail against his church, built upon Peter as a rock, and that his faith shall not fail, that he may safely and securely confirm his brethren, makes clear what else would be well-nigh, if not wholly, inexplicable. . . .

"While professing their belief in the divine mission of the apostles and in the inspiration of the New Testament, evangelical Protestants admit the infallibility of Peter and of the other apostles, at least of such of them as were inspired writers. Why was this gift of infallibility conferred on them? Plainly that the whole body of Christians, who would be instructed by their writings, might not be necessarily led into error. It was for the security and common good of Christendom that this extraordinary gift was divinely bestowed. The infallibility of the other apostles did not descend to their successors, the individual bishops, because these were to have charge of only particular and local churches; and their error would thus not affect or mislead the whole body, and might, moreover, be readily remedied by the ordinary powers left by Christ with his divinely constituted church. The case was widely different with Peter and his successors, whose jurisdiction was to remain world-wide, and whose error—if official error there could be—would necessarily taint and ruin the entire body of the church. For from the very beginning of the church, from and before the days of Irenæus, in the second century, it was a generally received axiom and rule of conduct that 'all other churches—that is, the faithful who are everywhere—*must of necessity agree with the Roman Church.*'"

Archbishop Spalding next turns to the objection that the definition of the infallibility of the Pope will prove hurtful to the cause of civil liberty; and, after referring to the foundation of all liberty, the liberty of the soul—" if, therefore, the Son shall make you free, you shall be free indeed "—he continues: " The second kind of liberty, and the highest possible type of it in civil governments, is that in which, whatever be the form of government, the rights of all citizens are respected and protected alike; in which, if it be a republic, the majority rules while respecting the rights of the minority; in which the taxes are equitably·levied upon all citizens in proportion to their ability or means, and do not exceed what is necessary for carrying on the government; above all, in which the property and the rights and laws of the church are respected and left inviolate, and in which all citizens, ecclesiastics included, are equally protected by the law, not only as written, but as executed; in which, in a word, without discrimination, especially as between the rich and the poor, all are equally protected in their legitimate rights, all are equal before the law, and all are equally governed and equally benefited by the law. This theory of liberty was, in substance, laid down by the Catholic schoolmen of the middle ages ; but it has seldom, if ever, been fully realized in this imperfect world."

To this view of liberty, which has been developed and given to the world by the Catholic Church, the infallible Pope can never be opposed. "Governments," continues Archbishop Spalding, "like garments, must fit or suit the people for whom they are formed. Some may need a monarchy, others may prefer a republic. The church leaves all this to regulate itself, according to the choice of the people or the circumstances of time and place, confining herself to teaching both sovereigns and people their respective duties as laid down by the law of Christ. She teaches boldly and fearlessly, though she may sometimes be able only to cry out in the wilderness to those who will not heed her voice.

" It is well known that the great reigning Sovereign Pontiff, first of all sovereigns in modern times, inaugurated a system of free government, even to the extent of establishing a deliberative assembly, in which the delegates of the people might fully and freely express their sentiments on matters which concerned their civil well-being. It is also, alas! but too well known how the enlightened benevolence of our great and good Pius IX. was thwarted by the wicked and repaid with ingratitude by those very men whom he had amnestied and loaded with favors! His Prime Minister basely assassinated, at mid-day, on the very steps of the Chambers; his private secretary, the lamented Palma, shot down at his side by a cowardly assassin ; himself imprisoned in his palace by a furious and blood-thirsty mob, and finally forced to fly from his capital, and become an exile and a wanderer on the earth."

But when we cease to speak of liberty, and come to *liberalism*, he shows that the question assumes a wholly new aspect. Between Liberalism and Catholicism there is a necessary conflict, because Liberalism affirms that there is no absolute and immutable truth, whereas the church makes this principle the very cornerstone of all knowledge and of all justice. Liberalism is want of principle. It respects Rome because she has preserved the temples and statues of paganism, and scorns her because she has built asylums for purity and obedience; for the murderer and the assassin it has only words of tenderness, and would fain change their prisons into palaces; but upon the monk who obeys and is pure it pours out the wrath of diabolic hatred; it builds temples to Venus, where the flesh is adored; and it drives the Catholic virgin from the home which her own heart chose. It calls itself the friend of the people, and it seeks to tear from their hearts their only hope—that of a better life; the protector of the poor, and it shuts them up in gloomy prisons, where a cold and venal hand deals out to them wherewith to fill the stomach, but where no word of love is spoken to make them feel that they are men—are loved. It proclaims the inviolability of the human conscience, and around the bed of the dying man it places fiends in human shape to force him to die as he has lived—God's enemy and his own. It desires not the homage of blind faith, and in midnight lodges it extorts from its victims an oath to believe and act according to principles of the real nature and tendency of which they are to be kept in ignorance. It in turn befriends and betrays all governments, and loves none. It sits on the throne with Cæsar; it strengthens the hands of absolutism in the person of a heartless and crafty minister; and it leads the rabble under the banner of the Commune. It betrays every cause it advocates, and is as incapable of honest dealing as of disinterested love. To the church it holds out a seeming hand of friendship, whilst with the other it filches the alms of the poor. It palters in a double sense, and breaks the promise to the hope, whilst keeping it to the ear.

A deep and true instinct caused the French Revolution to give to what it meant by liberty the form of a prostitute; for Liberalism, which, intellectually, is want of principle, is, morally, the worship of lust; and the symbol of lust is woman, venal, degraded, stripped of modesty and purity, which alone make her free and beautiful. Liberalism is the most hollow and sounding sham of this age. Between the church and it there can be no reconciliation, as there can be none between God and Satan. With liberty the church needs not to be reconciled—she is never greater than when free with the free; but could she shake hands with the polluted idol of libertinism, she would not be the spouse of Christ. Not among the least of the benefits conferred upon the world by the Vatican Council is this, that henceforth there can be no more liberal Catholics—Catholics who in any way sympathize with Liberalism, or who hold that reconciliation between it and the church is possible.

The sessions of the Council of the Vatican were suspended after the vote which was taken on the 18th of July; and Archbishop Spalding immediately left Rome to escape the oppressive heat, and went to breathe the mountain air of Savoy and Switzerland, until, as was then thought, the Council would reassemble in the fall. He visited the tomb of St. Francis de Sales at Annecy, and many other scenes of the labors of this great apostle, who was his ideal of a Catholic bishop. He gave a brief account of this pilgrimage in the following letter, written from Geneva to Mother Frances Gardiner, Superior of the Sisters of Charity of Nazareth:

"My Dear Mother:

"I have thought that I could not better spend my vacation, during the suspension of the Council, than in making a pilgrimage to all the places rendered sacred by the lives and deaths of two of your patrons—St. Francis de Sales and St. Jane de Chantal. I have just returned from this consoling visit, and enclose to you relics of both saints, which you may divide among your friends, keeping the best part for yourself.

"I visited Annecy, where I said Mass at the shrines where the bodies of the two saints repose in splendid caskets behind the respective altars. I went to Thorens, where St. Francis was born, baptized, and consecrated bishop; and also to Thonon, where he began his apostolic labors, where his life was so often exposed to the attempts of hired assassins, and where he prepared the way for the conversion of seventy-two thousand Calvinists. I was everywhere received with open arms by the Bishop and clergy, and was greatly edified by the piety of the people, who still remember and revere St. Francis as their father in God. How much better to be a saint, and have one's memory kept always fresh, than to be a sinner and be forgotten!

"With the aid of your continued prayers, I hope to be much better after this pilgrimage. I am sure St. Francis and his friend will pray for me."

In Geneva, Archbishop Spalding spent several days.

"Geneva," he wrote, "is the Protestant Rome no longer, simply because it has ceased to be Protestant in any proper sense of the term. Nearly one-half of the city, and considerably more than half of the canton, are now Catholic, while nine-tenths of the remaining portion have gone off into the ranks of Unitarianism and rationalism, the latter verging on downright infidelity. The name of John Calvin is now seldom heard, and his last resting-place is utterly unknown ; and the same may be said of his predecessors and co-workers in iniquity under the mask of religion—Viret, Farel, and others. Their memory is wholly gone, their very names have well-nigh perished. The principal and real non-Catholic patron saints of Geneva are Jean Jacques Rousseau, a native of the city, who has a statue erected to him on an island of the Rhone, in a position prominent and central, and Voltaire, a foreigner, the philosopher of Fernaix, in the immediate vicinity; while the secondary patrons may be said to be two other infidel foreigners, Gibbon and Byron."

"In Geneva," he adds, "the Protestant churches are usually called *temples*—a not unsuitable designation for houses of worship dedicated to what may be called, without any exaggeration or breach of charity, a system of vague and bald Christianity, dashed with a revived paganism. Plato, Socrates, and Epictetus might well preach in these *temples*, if they could only school themselves—which they might readily do—to speak respectfully of Christ as a great reformer and philosopher."

Of St. Peter's Cathedral, in Geneva, which, like nearly all the magnificent churches of the world, was built by Catholics, he wrote :

"Stripped of its altars, its paintings and statuary, it appeared to us a grand picture of desolation, a temple instead of a church, a shell without a kernel, a body without a soul! How our heart sank within us at the sad spectacle of desecration, especially when, in reply to our implied question, while we pointed to the empty and desolate sanctuary, and said, 'There once stood the high altar,' the elderly female sexton said, with a lurid smile worthy of John Calvin, 'We Protestants have no altar'! Cold walls and empty benches—that was all. And here, within these hallowed walls, which once resounded with the *Gloria in*

Excelsis and the Psalms of David, are now heard but lifeless canticles and sermons filled with the platitudes of Socinianism and rationalism! God and Christ has been driven from his own holy sanctuary, and *man*, with his pigmy but grandiloquent humanitarianism, has been enthroned in his place! And this thing has been called *reformation!*

"From the church of John Calvin we went to his house, and here our spirits were suddenly refreshed. What a change, and how unexpected! The Sisters of Charity, with their angelic ministrations, now occupy the ample residence where the once great apostle of *uncharity* had his abode, and where he planned his heartless system. Hundreds of Catholic children fill the religious schools taught by them, and receive in the very *salons* of Calvin the elements of a sound Catholic education!"

In connection with his tour through Switzerland, Archbishop Spalding refers to the oft-repeated assertion that the Protestant are far superior to the Catholic cantons in culture, productiveness, and general prosperity. Were the assertion founded in fact, he asks, what would follow? Christ certainly did not establish his religion to enable men to lay up more easily and abundantly treasures on earth. They who seek only this world may succeed better than others in finding what they seek, but a divine voice has declared that "they have received their reward." "We believe," he continues, "that whatever difference exists between the Catholic and Protestant cantons, in point of culture and progress, may be fairly traced to other causes than difference of religion. In general, it may be said that, at the time of the so-called Reformation and thereafter, the Protestants took possession of the plains, which constituted the most fertile portion of Switzerland, leaving to the Catholics the mountainous, and therefore least productive, portions; or, to speak more accurately, that the inhabitants of the plains, being already more wealthy, and probably more worldly-minded and corrupt, became Protestants; while those of the mountains, for a contrary reason, remained steadfastly attached to the faith of their fathers. We believe the impartial tourist will come to the conclusion that, other things being equal, there is very little, if any, difference between the general appearance and cultivation of the two classes of cantons. We ourselves passed through eleven out of the twenty-two cantons, and we could remark no striking difference of the kind referred to."

CHAPTER XXXIII.

THE SACRILEGIOUS INVASION OF ROME — ARCHBISHOP SPALDING RETURNS HOME—HIS RECEPTION IN BALTIMORE AND WASHINGTON CITY—A RETROSPECT.

HE sessions of the Council of the Vatican had hardly been suspended, when events occurred in Europe which seemed to betoken that the fathers would not be able to reassemble again in the fall. The war which had broken out between France and Prussia had led to the withdrawal of the French troops from Rome, and it was easy to foresee that the Italian Government would not long hesitate to crown its many infamies by taking possession of the Holy City. Of the consummation of this sacrilegious crime, Archbishop Spalding received the news whilst in Switzerland. "Finding our position at Albano insecure," wrote Dr. Chatard, the Rector of the American College, immediately after the capture of the city, "from the approach of the invading troops and consequent troubles, I brought all the community to Rome on the evening of the 12th and morning of the 13th of September. The next morning, the gates were closed; and on the 14th occurred the first skirmish at Monte Mario between the lancers and the zouaves and dragoons. The next three days saw the Italian forces arrive in great numbers. The interference of Baron von Arnim delayed the attack to the morning of the 20th, although there was little more than words in the whole matter of intervention. At five o'clock on the morning of that day, we were awakened by fearful cannonading. The

points first assailed were the Porta Pinciana, the Porta Salara, the Villa Macao, and the Porta San Lorenzo. After three hours and a few minutes of incessant firing, the attack on the Porta Pancrazio was made, and bombs began to fall in the city. Whether it was that our flag, which I had placed on the highest point of the college, protected us in part, or our central position placed us beyond range, we were not struck at all, nor, as far as I know, did any shot strike near us. . . . The firing lasted until half-past ten o'clock, when a white flag was run up at the cross of St. Peter's, at Castel Angelo, and at St. Mary Major's. It seems the Italian troops endeavored to enter the city before the result of the parley was made known. The zouaves fired on them, and this exasperated the enemy. The fighting ceased, however, and the troops poured into the city. . . . We have passed through three days of terror, we may say. The populace have had things pretty much their own way. Papal soldiers have been beaten and killed in the streets. Ecclesiastics were not safe; many have been insulted and threatened with personal violence. To do the Italian troops justice, they took no part in this, but uniformly kept order and defended those who were molested. The returned *emigrati* and the element introduced into Rome before the siege, together with the dregs of the people and the Jews, are those to whose door this violence is laid."

These events made it evident that the Council could not continue its labors in Rome. Archbishop Spalding did not, however, at once abandon the hope of seeing the fathers reassemble in the fall. He thought that some city of Belgium might be chosen in which to resume the work, and in this view he was supported by several leading bishops of the Council. But the state of Europe was so unsettled, and the French and German bishops were surrounded by so many difficulties, that this project was not taken into serious consideration. Not wishing to return home without positive instructions from the Pope, Archbishop Spalding, as soon as he had heard of the capture of the city by the Italian Government, wrote to Rome to ask what he should do; and, in reply, received the following letter from Cardinal Bilio, one of the Presidents of the Council:

"In answer to your esteemed letter of the 29th of September, I have the honor to inform you that the Holy Father, to whom I carried it this morning, not only permits, but desires, that you return to Baltimore; since, owing to the sad state to which we are reduced, the Council is suspended *de facto*, and soon will be *de jure*. The Holy Father, though greatly afflicted, is in good health, and sends you his most especial blessing, both for yourself and your diocese, whither the esteem and love of all who have had the honor to know you, among whom I hold myself to be one of the first, will accompany you."

Upon the reception of this letter, Archbishop Spalding at once prepared to return home, and towards the close of October he sailed on the City of Paris from Liverpool to New York, where he arrived early in November. In Baltimore, fifty thousand people assembled to welcome him home. This imposing demonstration of popular reverence was not less an evidence of the love and veneration in which Archbishop Spalding was held by the Catholics of Maryland, than a proof of their filial devotion to the church and her infallible Head on earth; and it is thus of historical importance as an example of the unfeigned delight with which the Catholics of the United States received the definition of the Papal infallibility. His arrival was announced by the booming of cannon, and the bells of all the Catholic churches of the city rang out the welcome tidings. The Catholic societies, with floating banners and gay badges, formed in line, and passed before the open carriage in which the Archbishop sat. The streets along which the procession passed were decked with flags, and from the windows beaming faces and the waving of handkerchiefs betokened the heartfelt joy that welcomed home one beloved and dear. The sidewalks were thronged, and the streets around the cathedral were filled with crowds patiently awaiting the arrival of the procession. In the address of welcome, Judge Mason, after giving expression to the gratitude which all felt for the safe return of the Archbishop, and to the pride with which his course in the Council had filled the Catholics of Maryland, turned to what was the more immediate sentiment of the occasion:

"We have not come together," he said, "to welcome home the great champion of truth, who has left the impress of his vigorous mind upon one of the most important, as it will be one of the most enduring, pages in the world's history; but we have assembled in the spirit of that simple love which prompts little children to meet and welcome with outstretched arms a father whose long absence made their home cheerless and desolate, and whose return brings joy and gladness. We come to receive a father's blessing; to conduct you, dear Archbishop, once more to your old familiar seat in the midst of a devoted household; and again to resume those tender and affectionate relations which, even more than the honor and dignity which attach to your character as Prelate, have endeared us to you."

The address in the name of the clergy was delivered by the venerable Father Coskery.

"Most reverend and beloved father," he said, "your children, of both the clergy and laity, hail with delight the return of their Archbishop, of whom, assuredly, we have reason to be proud, if ever a devotedly attached flock had reason to be proud of their chief pastor. The testimony of the Catholic world 'beareth witness' to our own, and convinces us that we speak not merely the language of filial love and pride, but also that of truth, which will be historic, when we assert that amid the illustrious lights which shone so conspicuously in the great Vatican Council, few have done more than our own Archbishop, in the fulfilment of the episcopal office, to enlighten in the things of God 'every man that cometh into the world.'"

To these addresses Archbishop Spalding replied, in his simple way:

"DEARLY BELOVED:

"I thank you all for this kindly greeting; I have loved you all very much, but now, after this testimonial of your affection, I must love you more than ever."

In Washington City, he was received with scarcely less enthusiasm than in Baltimore. Here, again, he was met by the clergy and the Catholic societies, who conducted him in solemn procession through the streets of the national capital, thronged by thousands, who extended to him a cordial welcome home.

The demonstration was not unlike that which is witnessed on Inauguration Day, except that there was no military parade. These popular gatherings did not have as their end the mere idle ceremony of pomp and display. They were a public profession of faith, and an evidence of the hearty readiness with which the children of the church in this country obey the voice of their mother. They also furnished an opportunity of entering a formal protest against the sacrilegious crime which the Italian Government had just consummated. This, in fact, was done at the reception of the Archbishop both in Baltimore and in Washington City.

The thousands who had assembled to welcome him home organized themselves into a mass meeting, and passed resolutions, of which the following was the preamble: "We, the Catholics of the Archdiocese of Baltimore, in general meeting assembled, to the number of more than fifty thousand, in order to welcome the return from Rome of our beloved Archbishop, wish to avail ourselves of this impressive occasion to give expression, in the face of all Christendom, to our earnest, solemn, and unanimous protest against the late invasion of the Roman States by the Florentine Government." They then give as their reasons for making this protest that this invasion had been made in violation of solemn treaties, by which the independence of the Sovereign Pontiff in the government of the small territory that he still possessed was secured; that Rome belonged, not to Italy, but to Christendom—to the two hundred millions of Christians scattered over the world, who had given their money to build it up and enrich it with splendid monuments of religion; that the Papal territory stood in the same relation to the united states of Christendom that the District of Columbia bears to the United States of America; and as no State of the Union could have the right to take possession of the District of Columbia, so no nation can have the right to take possession of the Papal territory.

They also affirm that since Rome is not only the sanctuary of religion, but the capital of literature and art as well, it is greatly to be feared lest its precious treasures should be scattered or destroyed by the ruthless invader.

At the mass meeting in Washington City, similar resolutions were drawn up and unanimously adopted.

In a letter addressed to Archbishop Spalding at this time, through the columns of the press, by the Bishop of Wheeling, that Right Reverend Prelate said:

"I wish to express in the most public manner my gratification at the grand ovation given you recently in the capital of the United States. It was a most flattering demonstration of filial regard to your person by the Catholics of your diocese; but it has acquired an interest for the population of our entire country, as being made the occasion of sending forth a protest from that capital against the action of the robber government of Italy for daring to seize upon the patrimony of the Holy See."

Archbishop Spalding, a few weeks after his return, delivered a lecture in Philadelphia on the temporal power of the Pope, in which, after reviewing its origin and early history, he pointed out its intimate relations with his spiritual sovereignty. The church, being Catholic and not national, must have an unnational head. Place the Pope in France, and he will become a French Pope; place him in Spain, and he will become a Spanish Pope; make him the subject of Victor Emanuel, and he will become an Italian Pope. The interests of the church require that the Pope, whatever his nationality may be, shall be of no nation.

Since two hundred million Catholics yield to him the highest obedience as to the immediate representative of Christ, they have, beyond question, the right to demand that not even the shadow of suspicion shall be thrown upon his perfect freedom of action. They cannot have this assurance whilst he is the subject of any government whatever. His spiritual power, the greatest on earth, renders it impossible that he should be a subject with impunity.

"The Pope is outside of Paris," said the great Napoleon, who, when his reason was undisturbed by some dream of mad ambition, was as far-seeing as it is given to man to be,—" the Pope is outside of Paris, and it is well; he is not either at Madrid or Vienna, and it is for this reason that we support his spiritual authority. At Madrid, at Vienna, they would be warranted in saying the same. Do you believe that, if he were at Paris, the Austrians, the Spaniards, would consent to receive his decisions? We are, therefore, but too happy that he resides far away from us, and that, at the same time, he does not live with our rivals, but dwells in freedom in time-consecrated Rome, far from the control of the German Emperor, from that of the kings of France and Spain; holding the balance among Catholic sovereigns, leaning a little to the strongest, but at once assuming an erect posture when the strongest seeks to become unjust or oppressive. The ages have done this, and they have done well. For the government of souls, it is the best, the most beneficent institution that can be imagined."

Were it possible that the Pope should be the subject and at the same time the friend of any earthly government, this state of things would be precisely the most dangerous of all to the peace and unity of the church. Whilst he is persecuted, whilst he is a prisoner, Catholics can suffer with him and be patient; but to see him a subject, humbly kissing the hand of some sensuous and lust-besotted Italian king, meekly receiving from the polluted mouths of ignorant ministers suggestions as to how Christ's world-wide church should be administered, is what God will never permit; and they who think that the church will grow accustomed to the state of things which now exists in Rome little know the temper of her divine mind. If she were like the world, she would doubtless bow down before accomplished facts, and applaud whatever is; but, fortunately for the dignity of human nature, there is still left on earth at least one institution in whose eyes success cannot consecrate crime. So long as the Italian Government remains in Rome, so long will it be the enemy of all Catholics, the hated robber of the only temporal good which they possess in common; and with the divine patience which drove the Cæsar of a former paganism from the Eternal City will they work and wait till this modern toadstool growth shall rot from off the soil it infects. When the savage triumph of German pride, the brutal delirium of the Paris Commune, and the cowardly theft of the Italian Government will be remembered only as warnings of God's wrath, the infallible Pope will still be King of Rome.

"Have not, then," asks Archbishop Spalding in this lecture, "the Roman people, like the other peoples of the world, the right to change their temporal rulers? To this I answer," he replies, "first, that the late change was made, not by the Roman people or on their demand, but by a foreign power and by overwhelming force of arms. The Romans were simply forced by the bayonet to accept one ruler for another; and the *plébiscite*, or popular vote, which followed was manifestly a farce and a sham, enacted under the influence of their new masters, at the head of their victorious battalions. Every observer of recent events in France and Italy is well aware of the manner in which these *plébiscites* have been managed. They deceive no one except those who wish to be deceived. In Rome, especially, everything was done under the open terror of the bayonet. Hence, the voting was naturally almost entirely on one side. Vast numbers of camp-followers and of men from other parts of Italy, the very scum of the cities, who clearly had no right of suffrage—even boys under age— were allowed to vote; whilst many of the Romans were induced to do so through a terrorism which they had not the courage to resist. Finally, the counting of the votes was altogether in the hands of the interested military leaders, and no reliance whatever could be placed on its accuracy. In these United States, we know something of the machinery requisite for obtaining a successful vote; but we are only infants in a science in which the Italian and European Liberals are so thoroughly proficient. I answer, secondly, that even if they desired to do so—which they did not—the Roman people have no more right to vote away a territory which clearly belongs to the whole Catholic Church--to the united states of Christendom, as the consecrated residence of its chief—than have the people of the District of Columbia to vote away to one or more of the States a Territory belonging to the whole United States, as the seat of their General Government. In both cases, the soil is necessarily neutral ground and the common property of all; and it cannot be alienated without common consent. Suppose the barbarous inhabitants on the borders of the Isthmus of Suez, or those along the Panama Railway, should attempt to vote away that great international canal or railway, or should assume to themselves the right to administer its commerce for their own advantage, would England, would France, would the United States, would any nation in Christendom submit to such an outrage? Private convenience and local claims must yield to the public good and to vested rights."

Shortly after his return from the Vatican Council, Archbishop Spalding dedicated two new churches in Baltimore, and one in the immediate vicinity. He also made arrangements to have three other churches built in the city, one of which was intended for the Bohemian Catholics, whilst another was to be commemorative of the Jubilee of Pius IX., in honor of his twenty-five years of Pontificate. He built within this year two new parochial schools for the cathedral parish. He was anxious to give a thorough organization to the parochial school system of the city, by which all the Catholic elementary schools should be placed under the supervision of a board of directors. He had not, however, matured this plan, which was one of the chief subjects of his thoughts, when his last sickness warned him that his work was done. He began again the visitation of his diocese, and, during the spring and summer of 1871, he gave confirmation in Baltimore, Washington City, and various other places. The proportion of converts confirmed was about thirteen per cent. He continued to preach frequently, and occasionally he lectured for some charitable object. His last lecture was delivered for the benefit of the negro Catholics of Baltimore. As the twenty-fifth anniversary of the elevation of Pius IX. to the chair of Peter drew near, Archbishop Spalding issued a circular to the Catholics of the archdiocese, inviting them to commemorate the event with appropriate observance.

The celebration, both in Baltimore and Washington City, surpassed his fondest hopes. On Sunday, June 17, there was a general communion in all the churches for the Holy Father, and Monday, the 18th, the celebration took place.

"We have had," the Archbishop wrote a few days later, "the grandest possible celebration here in honor of the Jubilee. Nothing like it has ever been seen in Baltimore or in the United States. Indeed, I have never seen such enthusiasm. Rich and poor alike illuminated their houses, and the Catholic churches and institutions flamed with light. Over a hundred thousand people were in the streets to view the procession, which was two hours in passing a given point."

Archbishop Spalding was greatly pleased by this splendid proof of the devotion of the Catholics of his diocese to the Holy Father; for, apart from other and more important considerations, he had a special love and veneration for Pius IX.

The following letter was written in reply to one which had been drawn up and sent to the Holy Father in the name of the Catholics of the archdiocese of Baltimore, on the occasion of his Pontifical Jubilee:

"PIUS P.P. IX.

"VENERABLE BROTHER AND BELOVED SONS! HEALTH AND APOSTOLIC BENEDICTION:

"We have received your very dutiful letter of the 21st of June, by which, in the name of your fellow-Catholics, you convey to us the expression of your congratulation, and of the filial love with which you celebrated our Pontifical Jubilee, by a very large and enthusiastic meeting, and public testimonials of your rejoicing. Though we have already taken measures that our feelings of gratitude and benevolence towards our children, who have done so much for us, should be made known to all in common, yet we desire to give to you, by this letter, a special token of our affection for you, and to signify to you that your zeal and devotion towards us and the Holy See, of which you have given repeated proofs, have afforded us great comfort and consolation. But especially do we commend your hope and the confidence which you place in our Lord, and to which, without doubt, his many favors should excite all the faithful. And now, venerable brother and beloved sons, whilst we are assured that your zeal for religion is boundless, and your prayers for us unceasing at this perilous time and in these afflictions which beset us, we beseech the divine Majesty that he would give you courage to strive in his cause, and bestow an abundant reward for the good works which you perform in his honor. As a signal mark and pledge of our affection, and an earnest of heaven's favor, we lovingly impart the Apostolical benediction to you, venerable brother, who lead your flock with sacerdotal zeal; to you, also, beloved sons, to your families, to all our dear children of the archdiocese, the clergy, and their faithful people.

"Given at St. Peter's, the 2d of August, 1871, the 26th year of our Pontificate.   PIUS P.P. IX."

Little remains now for me to do but to tell how Archbishop Spalding, having lived a brief span, breathed out his soul to God. But before the shades of night have gathered around his life, in the twilight, with its solemn stillness, we may pause a moment to ponder over its course and its meaning, or to recall its characteristic and cherished features.

All the currents of his life set to the church, which, for him, had the promise of the life that is and of that which is to be. He was unable even to conceive of a better state of things here on earth than that in which all men, united in faith, in hope, in love, would be gentle, true, and charitable, in life; brave and trusting, in death. In his eyes, in comparison with this soul-life, subject and aspiring to God, the hurry, the rush, the eager rivalry, and the weary unrest of them that seek pleasure and of them that seek power, were not of great moment. If we should fly in the air, if we should tunnel the earth, if we should walk on the bottom of the ocean as in our native element, if we should convert every baser metal into gold, the infinite yearnings of the soul would be unsatisfied as now. Hence, he was never infected with the idolatry of material progress; nor did he believe that any possible modification or perfection of matter could help us to solve the problem of human life. Philosophy, too, he thought was insufficient. In the knowledge of absolute truth, we have made no progress since Plato and St. Augustine. Then, we want something more than speculation. You can no more fill the all-devouring mind with abstractions than you can

> "Cloy the hungry edge of appetite,
> By bare imagination of a feast."

And as for physical science, cold and pitiless, with the hard, unrelenting features of its brazen face, its feet are of clay, and they rest on sand. It can, at best, be but a phase in human thought, and all the eternal questionings of the soul will remain after it as they were before. I remember hearing Archbishop Spalding say, a year or two before his death, that, as he grew older, he realized more fully the truth of his faith, and saw more clearly that, if it were not true, nothing was. He believed that the teachings of the church contain the highest lessons of truth and wisdom for the human race, now and for all time to come; and, believing this, he labored honestly and faithfully to build up the church of God. There was in his life, what is found in so few lives of Americans, perfect unity and harmony. In the way in which he set his face in early youth he walked even to the end; and to this end were directed all his labors of mind and body.

Few men, I think, have had a clearer insight into the wants of the church in this country than he. His mind was practical, and he attached but little weight to mere speculation; and hence his attention was given almost exclusively to those questions which have an actual bearing upon the progress of the church. Catholic education, for instance, was, in his opinion, the essential condition of any real growth of the church in the United States. In comparison with this, he held every other issue of the present day to be of minor importance; and though he sought to propagate his views, and to prove their correctness in essays, lectures, and controversies, the real manner with which he dealt with the question was more practical still. Not political agitation, not discussion, but honest, Catholic work was what was wanted. The bishops and priests, he thought, should everywhere, without delay, go to work to build up parochial schools; and he sought to urge on this movement by legislation in the national and provincial councils and in the diocesan synods. And though he looked upon primary education as the most important, because it regards the greatest number, he felt the imperative necessity of raising the standard of the higher education, and thought the time had come when we should found a Catholic university. He was also a most strenuous advocate of that practical education which is given to orphan and abandoned children in protectories and industrial schools. Some one has called him the friend of children, and I think no other title could have pleased him so much.

Archbishop Spalding also thoroughly appreciated the mission of the press, and the importance of creating a Catholic literature, by which we would be enabled to enter into and influence the thought of the age; and his own labors in this direction have been productive of good results. His views on the relations of the church to the state in this country, with reference to their bearing upon the duties of ecclesiastics, as also his opinions concerning the manner and direction in which our ecclesiastical polity should be developed, were, I cannot but think, both wise and prudent. His great desire to promote perfect uniformity of discipline and harmony of action, as well as the scrupulous care with which he sought to have the enactments of our various councils observed, may be adduced also as evidences of his practical good sense. "The best way," he said, "to create a more perfect system of canon law is to observe faithfully that which we already have." The best laws become useless when the idea of the sacredness of law has been destroyed by habitual disregard of authority.

A sufficient proof of the real ability of Archbishop Spalding, as it is the surest test of that of any man, is the fact that he was never placed in a position, however high or responsible, to which he did not prove himself equal.

His moral character is above reproach. If he was ever guilty of an act over which even his dearest friend should wish to throw the mantle of concealment, I have been unable to discover it. His character was as transparent as that of an innocent child, and, had there been even a breath upon its purity, it could not have escaped notice.

Some thought he was ambitious; if so, it was a noble ambition; but they who knew him best will admit that he was simply zealous and laborious. He was pleased by the sympathy and attention of friends; but this is a pardonable weakness, and one which leans to the side of virtue. He was without policy and devoid even of tact, except that which comes of good sense. His piety was without cant, his charity without sentimentalism, and his devotion to the church without pretence. He hated shams, and reverenced honesty and sincerity even in an enemy. His sympathies, like his faith, were Catholic, and he thought every human being was his neighbor. He loved the people, without being a demagogue; and his country, without being an office-seeker; and freedom, not for himself alone, but for all men. If he did not cultivate individual affections with special care, he was all the freer to devote himself to truth, and justice, and every high interest of humanity.

Though he was simple and ingenuous, and, one would think, easily imposed upon, he yet possessed an accurate knowledge of character, and was seldom mistaken in his judgment as to what the men whom he wished to employ in the service of the church were able to do.

He knew perfectly well the value of money, and was a prudent and far-seeing administrator of the finances of the church; but he was wholly free from any personal love of gain. His hand was always open to the poor; and he died, I may say, in poverty. Some one owed him two or three thousand dollars, which he would have given away had he been able to get hold of it; and he left instructions that this money should be used for the benefit of the poor children, whom he so loved.

He was, I think, very free from prejudice. There was in his character nothing of the narrowness and one-sidedness of nationalism. He believed that God had made all the peoples of the earth of one blood, and in the Catholic republic of souls he acknowledged no distinction of race or color. He had no class-prejudices. Plebeian in his origin, simple and severe in his tastes, he neither affected contempt for high birth, nor sought to ape the manners of the great. Though he had been much in Europe, and had there mixed with many refined and cultivated people, he remained to the end a plain, blunt American citizen. He would have been the last man to desire to see the spirit of courtliness introduced into church or state in this country. He did not blindly admire either the sacred eld or these modern days; but thought that every condition of human society has been, is, and must be imperfect: "*Optimus ille est qui minimis urgetur.*"

The flippant sciolism of the day, which blasphemes whatever it is unable to understand, will say that Archbishop Spalding was not free from sectarian prejudice, because he believed in the Catholic Church. Prejudice is a leaning to one side of a cause for some reason not founded in truth and justice; and hence, as the truth is one and error manifold, it is of the nature of prejudice that it should be indefinitely variable in time and place. Individuals, families, nations, races, epochs, have their prejudices, and, of the myriad forms of this phenomenon, no two are alike. But the Catholic faith has been held, for many centuries, by hundreds of millions of men, differing in individual characteristics, in nationality, in race, in every possible accidental condition of life. There must be some deeper, universal, more persistent cause underlying this historic fact than the whim of prejudice. Take another view of the subject. It is not every one, as Napoleon said to Bertrand, who can afford to be an atheist. The belief in a personal God is the most universal and irrepressible fact in the history of the human race. The most perfect and exalted idea of God which has been given to men has come through Christ; hence, if we believe in God, reason demands that we should believe in the God of Christianity. But the only logical Christianity is Catholicism. In the face of revelation, the human reason can take but two attitudes: it must constitute itself either its judge or its disciple.

The Protestants said: We believe the Scripture; but each man's reason must decide what its meaning is.

The Socinians added: Therefore, we must believe only what is conformable to reason.

The Deists subjoined: Reason, then, of itself, suffices to teach us the truth. Hence, revelation is useless and consequently false.

The Atheists reply: What you tell us of God and the soul is contrary to reason; we will therefore accept only matter.

The Sceptics conclude, in closing up the procession: Materialism contains more absurdities and contradictions than all other systems, and we will therefore doubt everything. Between Catholicism and scepticism there is no logical foothold.*

As Archbishop Spalding was not prepared to be a sceptic, he could not think that prejudice made him a Catholic.

To be a Catholic, as he perfectly well understood, can mean only one thing; and he thought that the most pitiful of men is one of those namby-pamby nondescripts, who, whilst holding to the name of Catholic, seeks to be an eclectic. Archbishop Spalding belonged to the class of men who are most serviceable to a good cause. He was

* Bergier, in his introduction to the *Traité de la Vraie Religion*, has developed this argument in the fullest and most forcible manner.

honest, unselfish, laborious, hopeful, and conciliating. He was good rather than great; his mind was solid rather than brilliant; and he was a worker, and not a theorist. His instincts were generous, his impulses noble, and all the motions of his spirit were gentle. He was kind without weakness, firm without obstinacy; and, having power, he was neither haughty nor tyrannical.

Of his sincere piety and tender devotion no one could doubt. All his thoughts and aspirations were colored by religion and tended heavenward. In the performance of his ecclesiastical functions, his humble, serious bearing indicated his reverence of soul; and his whole deportment in the house of God was of a kind that cannot be assumed for a purpose. In the pulpit, he was grave and earnest, and would have thought it "pitiful to court a grin when he should woo a soul."

And yet he did not believe that, to be pleasing to God, we should make ourselves disagreeable to men, or that a gloomy brow and long-drawn face were evidences of piety. He knew when to be serious and when to be joyful. In his moments of recreation, surrounded by his friends, he could be as light of heart and gay of voice as if he had never had a care. He laughed; he talked; he indulged in badinage and repartee; he told anecdotes, and told them well; and, what is rare, in this he did not overstep the modesty of nature.

He was, in fine, a man who made those who knew him well, think better of human nature.

CHAPTER XXXIV.

LAST ILLNESS AND DEATH OF ARCHBISHOP SPALDING.

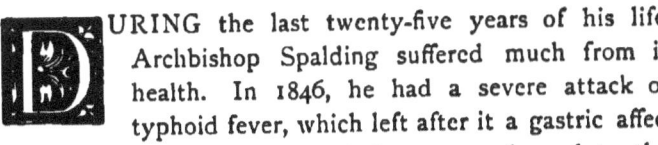URING the last twenty-five years of his life, Archbishop Spalding suffered much from ill health. In 1846, he had a severe attack of typhoid fever, which left after it a gastric affection, from which he never entirely recovered; and to this was added chronic bronchitis, which was aggravated by his almost incessant labors as a preacher and lecturer. Though not in good health, he had great vital power, by which he was enabled to rally from the frequent spells of illness to which he was subject. Suffering did not take from him the capacity to work.

He was so often ill, especially in the latter years of his life, that he began to look upon sickness as his normal state. "I do not see how I am going to die at all," he wrote in October, 1871, just after recovering from an attack which his physicians thought would certainly prove fatal. "This is the fifth time that I have been brought to the very brink of the grave by this same kind of gastric affection, and each time I have been restored to life by novenas and prayers. But as the Scotchman, who, being condemned to be hanged by his chief, and availing himself of the privilege of his clan, which allowed him to select the tree on which he was to be suspended, chose a bush not three feet high, answered, when taunted with his stupidity, 'I am in no hurry—I can wait till it grows,' so I will wait till God calls me."

We have already seen how cheerfully, and even gladly, he accepted death, when he thought his hour had come, shortly after his arrival in Rome in 1830. It does not appear that it ever occurred to him to think that it was hard to die thus in the very blush of youth, in a strange land, thousands of miles away from friends and kindred, who would not be allowed so much as to look upon his grave.

"I was happy," he wrote to his father, "and even filled with the sweetest joy, when told that my hour had come, that the prison of my wretched body was to be broken, and that my soul was destined soon to be with its heavenly Father for all eternity."

The frosts of many winters had whitened his head since he wrote this, but the innocent and brave heart was young as ever, ready to die, and also willing to live. I do not believe there was ever a time, after his elevation to the priesthood, when he would not have cheerfully laid down the burden of life; and yet he found the most intense pleasure in living and working for the church. In fact, he never looked upon life gloomily. Of a hopeful, sanguine nature, he saw rather the bright side of things, and always retained something of that unsuspecting responsiveness which peculiarly belongs to those who have never known the world.

His kindly nature went out in grateful return to the feeblest call of affection, as the violet opens all its beauty to the faintest ray of sunshine.

He loved his friends, he loved his kindred, he loved his work, and, above all, he loved God's church. Not, then, from apathy or weariness was he willing to die; but he looked upon death as God's minister, who may come to us at any moment, and whom we should therefore be prepared to receive at all times. For at least two years before he died, he had the response of death within himself, and frequently spoke as though he were fully persuaded that he had but a short time to live. "The machine is worn out, he used to say; the doctors have patched it up time and again, but they are about at the end of their trade." It was only the machine which was failing; for his mind and heart were vigorous and sound as they had ever been. After his return from the Vatican Council, when his friends urged him to write or lecture, he generally replied that his day had passed, and that his work was done. But he nevertheless continued to preach, and occasionally to lecture, almost to the very time when his last illness came upon him.

"A good soldier," he wrote, "does not abandon his post until regularly relieved; and the only discharge for a soldier of the cross is death."

His interest in whatever concerned the welfare of the church was as living the day in which he died as it had been in the first flush of his youthful zeal. We have seen with what joy he received the missionaries of St. Joseph, who arrived but a short time before his death, and how hopefully he looked forward to the result of their labors among the emancipated slaves of the South. The favorite projects of his life still occupied his thoughts.

"May God bless the good work and you!" he wrote to Father Hecker, referring to his efforts for the diffusion of Catholic books and tracts. "I need scarcely say how cordially I go with you in all this, and how cheerfully I will co-operate.

"But, alas! our Catholics are not a reading people, and they will have to be educated up to the point. They seem to feel that all is finished, and that nothing remains to be done; that the church being divine, no exertion is needed to extend its influence, and to ward off evil and scandal. I wish there could be infused into them, not, indeed, the restless and feverish activity of Protestants, 'always learning, and never arriving at the knowledge of the truth,' but something of that steady Catholic zeal which, with suitable organization, may achieve wonders."

Again, three months before his death, he wrote: "While I was sick, I so greatly appreciated the sweet unction of the Psalms that I thought we neglected them too much, and that our piety was decidedly too dull and prosy; and I almost made up my mind that, if I recovered, I would get up a new Prayer-Book, with Prime for morning prayer, Compline for evening prayer, and the full Psalter of David done into English. Our English Prayer-Books have but little of the unction, and none of the poetry, of the Psalms, which have been adopted by the church as her official standard of prayer."

A few days later, he wrote to Cardinal Barnabo: "I am just convalescent from an illness which brought me to death's door. God has wished to keep me longer here. *Eheu! nimis prolongatus est incolatus meus!* However, whilst I live, I shall not cease to work. Having completed the parochial schools near the cathedral, which have cost nearly thirty thousand dollars, I am about to begin the erection of a large church, in a quarter of the city where there is great need of one, which is to be dedicated to the service of God, under the patronage of St. Pius. I intend that this church shall be a perpetual memorial of the Jubilee of the Holy Father."

During the last months of his life, he began to prepare a new edition of his *Sketches of Kentucky* and the *Life of Bishop Flaget*, which he intended partly to rewrite and condense into one volume. He worked at this even during his last illness. At the end of his course, he looked back, with the greatest tenderness and love, to the spot where it first began. The scenes which had witnessed the labors of the best years of his life grew again before his eyes; he dwelt, with the fondness of a child, upon the places which are the whole world to his young heart; and he found relief in occupying himself with thoughts of the days that were no more, in recalling to mind the labors and sufferings of those apostolic men who were the guides of his youth and the models of his maturer life. He thought again of the simple manners of the good old times, when, if hands were rough, hearts were brave and true; when the noble courage and more than the purity of the matrons of Rome, in her best days, asked not other adornment than the home-spun gown. Again he wrote of Father Byrne and old St. Mary's, buried deep in the dark woods, the peaceful home of religion and science, where one would have least looked for such an asylum; and where, as the boy-professor, he won his first triumphs, and first felt his soul lifted heavenward on the wings of high aspiration and generous resolve.

He loved to talk of the peaceful cloisters and convents, homes of all that God most loves, which are scattered through the old Catholic counties of Kentucky—of Gethsemane and St. Rose, of St. Joseph's and St. Thomas's, of Nazareth, of Loretto, of St. Catharine's, of Holy Mary's, and of Bethlehem.

A short time before Christmas, he felt that it was his duty, though he was quite unwell, to go to New York, in order to be present at a meeting of bishops, in which matters of some importance were to be discussed. In returning home, he took cold, which brought on an attack of acute bronchitis of a very aggravated form. For six weeks, he suffered from partial suffocation, which often threw him into agonies of pain. During these six weeks, he was rarely ever able to lie in bed, but was obliged to sit in his chair.

On Christmas morning, he said Mass for the last time, on a little altar which he had caused to be erected in the hall before his bedroom. When the Sisters of Charity, who were nursing him, expressed the fear lest he should not be able to stand so long, he replied: "Pray that God may give me strength; it would be a great sacrifice not to say Mass on the Feast of Christmas. Since my first Mass, God has given me great devotion in celebrating the divine mysteries." He remained all night sitting in his chair, and at six o'clock prepared for the Holy Sacrifice. His left foot was considerably swollen, and he seemed to suffer intensely during the celebration of the Mass. When the sister asked him how he felt, he smiled and said, "The sweet little Infant pressed on my foot during the Holy Sacrifice." From this time, his sufferings increased almost daily and the frightful spells of suffocation grew more frequent.

He was in sickness, as in health, demonstrative, and could not easily remain quiet whilst any one was with him; but Dr. McSherry, his physician, and the Sisters of Charity who nursed him, declare that his patience and resignation were perfect. He was willing to die, he was willing to get well, or he was willing to live and suffer, as it might please his divine Master. He united each pain with the different stages of our Lord's passion. When able to speak, he gave frequent utterance to acts of faith, hope, and resignation. "Not only will I suffer patiently and cheerfully," he would often say, "but, oh! how lovingly, my sweet Jesus! May thy holy will be done for ever and ever!" "Grant me, O my God! patience and resignation, but, above all, thy love; for patience and resignation may be pagan, but *love* is Christian." He did not seem to feel any anxiety as to God's judgment. "For well-nigh forty years," I heard him say the day before he died, "I have labored for God; there may have been some little human vanity in some of my deeds, but, in the main, all was done with a right intention." "My sweet Jesus!" he would often say, "I go to thee full of confidence; not that I rely on any merits of my own, but solely on thy mercies, which are above all thy works."

The red sash which he had worn as a student of the Propaganda, and a crucifix, which had been blessed for the hour of death and given to him by Gregory XVI. after his ordination, he kept constantly with him during this sickness. In a hasty application of cups, when he was in danger of suffocating, heat was used in the absence of an exhausting-pump, and his chest was burned by the blazing alcohol. "This," he said, "is like purgatory; but it is all right, I can bear it." Upon another occasion, his sufferings became so intense as to blunt for a time his consciousness; respiration had almost ceased, and the physician thought it well to apply a powerful galvanic battery to his chest. When he came to himself again, and was told of this, he said: "This, doctor, is a regular case of assault and battery." His habit of making playful remarks to visitors often deceived them as to his real condition. They could not believe that one who was consciously dying could be pleased to have smiling faces about him. Yet so it was. Archbishop Spalding spoke cheerfully and even gaily twenty minutes before he died. Death, though it approached him without disguise, had no terrors for him. He looked it in the face with a courage as heroic as it was unpretending.

On the 3d of January, Father Coskery, thinking that he might die at any moment, determined to give him the Holy Viaticum and extreme unction. When he told the Archbishop of his intention, he thanked him, and added that it would give him the greatest satisfaction; for he had always prayed that he might not die without the last sacraments. About midnight, Father Coskery, accompanied by the other priests of the cathedral, entered his room and gave him Viaticum and extreme unction. After the reception of these holy sacraments, he spoke a few words of exhortation to those around him, blessed them, and in their persons all his priests and children, and then remained for the rest of the night sitting in his chair, absorbed in prayer and meditation. He passed the night before Epiphany, which he called the great feast of the Propaganda, in a continual act of love and desire to receive holy communion. Father Coskery frequently gave him communion, during his illness, just after midnight. On these occasions, he would often ask what hour it was, and, when told, he would say: "The time is fast approaching when my sweet Jesus will come to me. Oh! that I could die and be with him for ever! But not my will, but thine, be done, O Lord!"

He retained the perfect use of his faculties, and remained conscious, I think, to within five minutes of his death.

One day, when Dr. McSherry was trying some new remedy to ease his intense suffering, he said: "It is useless, doctor; I am worn out, worn out." The doctor replied: "Your head and your heart, Archbishop, are not worn out." "No," he answered, "my heart is certainly not worn out, but my lungs are."

It would be difficult to suffer more than he suffered during those six weeks in which he sat in his chair, without sleep and without rest, and literally choked to death. "If I get well," he said, the day before he died, "I intend to write a treatise on the art of choking to death." He, however, had no thought of recovering, but had said from the very beginning of his sickness that his hour had come; and no favorable symptoms ever deluded him for a moment into the belief that he would again be restored to health.

The consulting physician one day assured him that, notwithstanding his great suffering, he would soon be better. He made no reply; but when the doctor had left the room, he said to the Sisters: "I will soon be better, indeed, but not in the way that he means."

On the feast of the Purification, he heard Mass, sitting in his chair, and received again the Holy Viaticum. He spent the whole day in tender devotion to the Blessed Virgin. He had lost his own mother, he said, when he was five years old, and he had then taken the Blessed Virgin for his mother, and she had had care of him through life.

He several times spoke of his mother during his last illness, of whose size, features, and gentle ways he said he had a very distinct remembrance, though she had died when he was so young; and he related to the Sisters the anecdote about her calling him her little bishop.

The following incident I shall give in the words of the Sister of Charity* who nursed the Archbishop during the last five weeks of his life: "On Sunday night (February 4), he seemed to be much easier, and asked us to say prayers for him. When we had finished, he continued to move his lips in silent prayer. All at once he raised his eyes and hands towards heaven, his countenance lighted up, and in an ecstasy of delight he exclaimed: 'O my beautiful mother! my sweet mother! how beautiful thou art!' He said to me: 'Oh! do you see her?' But all that I saw was his countenance, so radiant that I know not how to describe it. After remaining thus transported with joy for three or four minutes, he closed his eyes, and said: 'Now, my sweet Jesus, I know for certain that thou art going to take me to thyself; for thou wouldst not permit me to see that light and leave me in this miserable world. O my God! that light alone is worth, not only one, but many lives.' I then asked him what he had seen. Hesitating for some moments, he said: 'Well, I will tell you, but you must say nothing of it, for the world would only laugh at it. My blessed Mother has deigned to visit me, and I saw her divine Son at a distance. She smiled on me, and said: "Courage, my child; all will be

* Sister Louise Collins.

well; I will soon come again." But she did not tell me when.' Then, looking at the pictures of the Blessed Virgin he said: 'Take them away; I can no longer see in them any trace of my beautiful mother.'"

"I cannot," continues the good Sister of Charity who writes this account, "give an idea of my feelings while this heavenly scene lasted. I was afraid to breathe, and I kept my eyes steadily fixed on his countenance, which shone with a most brilliant light. On my way home the next morning, I asked the sister who had been present with me what her impressions were at the time. She replied: 'I was awe struck and astonished at your reply when the Archbishop asked you if you did not see the light. You answered, No.' 'Well,' said I, 'did you see it?' 'I did not see the light he spoke of,' she answered, 'but I saw it reflected on his countenance.'"

Archbishop Spalding had never in his whole life, I think, had even a temptation to doubt of the truth of his faith. In fact, the only arguments which Catholics ever have against the church are their own sins. These are their only reasons for doubting. The Catholic faith, lived up to, is never doubted of. With Archbishop Spalding, faith and act had gone hand in hand; and he had not trod the primrose path of dalliance whilst pointing out to others the steep and thorny way that leads to heaven. His faith was therefore strong, as his life had been pure. But in his last illness, he seemed almost to realize the truths of the unseen world, and to contemplate them as though the earthly veil, that symbolizes but hides them, had been withdrawn. During the six weeks of intense suffering that immediately preceded his death, his conversation was in heaven, and he seemed to be as an aged exile, who, after long years of weary wanderings, at length catches a glimpse of the home where his eyes first beheld the light of heaven and the created image of

God's beauty. He prayed almost without ceasing, and when he spoke, unless he said some playful word to make others cheerful, it was always of God and his divine Son, of the ever Blessed Virgin and the saints. Each time that he took his medicine, he made a special act of obedience, and always blessed it with the sign of the cross before receiving it from the hand of the sister.

On Tuesday night, February 6, he thought he was near death, and he sent for his good and devoted priests, as he loved to call them; and, when they had gathered around him, he made them kneel down and recite the prayers of the church for the departing soul. The next morning (Wednesday, February 7), he was suffering less than usual. When some one asked him how he felt, he answered: "I am much easier, and entirely relieved of the choking sensation; but I am now dying of exhaustion." A little later, in reply to the same question, he said: "I am nearer heaven." He remained perfectly calm, and during the forenoon talked in a very pleasant and cheerful manner. About half-past three o'clock in the afternoon, he said that he would like to lie on the lounge which was in his room. After he had been placed on it, he told the Sisters to kneel and say the *Our Father* and the *Hail Mary* five times, in honor of the five wounds of our Lord. He then blessed them and bade them good-by, saying that he would pray for all his children and friends in heaven. The Sisters saw that he was dying, and sent for Bishop Becker and the clergymen who were in the house. They immediately entered the room. The Archbishop raised his eyes and saw one of them kneeling near him, and he made a sign to the Sister that he wished to say something. She bent over him, and he whispered, as if excusing himself for not speaking, "Tell him that I have lost my voice, and cannot speak." Bishop Becker then gave him the last blessing, and in five minutes

Archbishop Spalding's mortal life was over. He died without a struggle, so calmly and peacefully that it was impossible to tell the precise moment when the soul parted from the body; and the sweet smile that had cheered so many a weary soul still hovered about those lips which had pleaded only for truth, and justice, and mercy.

His body was embalmed and laid in state in the parlor of the episcopal residence, which had been converted into a *chapelle ardente*.

The public was admitted to view the remains on Friday morning, February the 9th; and during this and the two following days, a continuous stream of human beings passed around the catafalque on which the body was lying. The whole city seemed to mourn. All creeds, colors, nationalities, and conditions of life were represented in the vast crowds that gathered to look for the last time upon all that remained of one whose goodness and purity of life no one doubted. Even the breath of envy and of sectarian bitterness was silenced, and, from one end of the land to the other, all bore testimony to the noble character and spotless life of Archbishop Spalding.

The funeral took place on Monday, February the 12th. From early morning, the square around the cathedral was packed with people, anxious to assist at the last sad rites, and thousands turned away, despairing of being able even to obtain a sight of the procession. Fourteen bishops and probably two hundred priests took part in the ceremonies. The funeral sermon was preached by Archbishop McCloskey. When all was over, the body was borne down the central aisle of the cathedral into the vaults beneath, and was laid under the sanctuary, by the side of the remains of Archbishop Kenrick.

Gloriosi principes terræ, quomodo in vita sua dilexerunt se ita et in morte non sunt separati.

INDEX.

Ability, the, of Archbishop Spalding, 444.
Accusations against priests, Archbishop Spalding's manner of dealing with, 270.
Advocate, the Catholic, 72.
Aix-la-Chapelle, 352.
America, the Church of, 403.
Annecy, 425.
Anniversary, twenty-fifth, of the elevation of Pius IX. to the chair of Peter, 440.
Archbishop Spalding, characteristic features in the life of, 442; his clear insight into the wants of the church in this country, 443; his knowledge of character, 445; the willingness with which he accepted death, 449.
Asylum, St. Thomas' Orphan, 146; St. Joseph's, *ibid.*
Avignon, 171.

Badin, Father, 138.
Baltimore, archdiocese of, 263.
Barbee, John, 185.
Barnabo, Cardinal, letter of Archbishop Spalding to, 384.
Becker, Right Rev. Thomas A., 375.
Belgium, 161.
Bilio, Cardinal, letter of, to Archbishop Spalding, 432.

Bishops in the United States, difficulties of their position, 144 *et seq.;* mode of appointing, 310; number of, in the United States, 334.
Books of devotion, 295.
Bragg, General, 249.
Brotherhoods, the teaching, 155 *et seq.*
Brothers, the Xaverian, 160; of Christian instruction, 161; of the Christian schools, 266; of St. Patrick, 266.
Byrne, the Rev. Wm., 21.

Calvin, John, 426.
Cantons, Protestant and Catholic, of Switzerland, 428.
Cathedral, St. Joseph's, Bardstown, 66; of the Assumption, in Louisville, 147 *et seq.*; of Baltimore, 266, 269; of Philadelphia, 272.
Catholicism the only logical Christianity, 447.
Catholics of Kentucky, 17 *et seq.;* habits of, 136 *et seq.;* their want of generosity explained, 140 *et seq.;* reverence of, for the priestly character, 139.
Catholicity, evidences of, 98; and nationalism, 176.

Carroll, Charles, 33, 47; Archbishop, 238.
Centenary of the martyrdom of St. Peter and St. Paul, 346.
Ceremonies, closing, of the Second Plenary Council of Baltimore, 318.
Chabrat, Bishop, 57; his resignation accepted, 96.
Chapter, Canonical, 312.
Character, moral, of Archbishop Spalding, 444.
Charleston, diocese of, 286.
Chatard, Dr., letter of, to Archbishop Spalding, 430.
Chicago, diocese of, 376.
Church, Protestants defending the, 190; history of, in the United States, 264; the, and the country, 234; the strength of, 112; her services to the cause of civilization, 114, 116; influence of, 235.
Civita Vecchia, 380.
Clay, Henry, letter of, 181.
Cœtus Theologorum of the Second Plenary Council of Baltimore, 303.
College, St. Mary's, 21; St. Joseph's, 28; Georgetown, 264; Sulpician, Baltimore, 266; Mt. St. Mary's, Emmitsburg, 265; Loyola, 266; American, at Louvain, 162 *et seq.*; number of missionaries which it has sent to the United States, 167; American, of Rome, 358.
Commission, the, *de fidei*, in the Vatican Council, Archbishop Spalding a member of, 414.
Concannen, Bishop, 310.
Confessions of children who have not made their first communion, 276.
Consistency of the church, 382.
Convent, of women, first in the United States, 265.
Conventuals, minor, 241.
Converts, Archbishop Spalding's interest in, 86 *et seq.*; their status in the church, 227; number of in Kentucky and Maryland, 335.
Corcoran, the Rev. James A., 303.
Correspondence of Bishop Spalding and Archbishop Kenrick, 225; of Archbishop Spalding, 279.
Corruption of American society, 363.
Coskery, Father, address of, 433.
Council, the First Plenary of Baltimore, 151 *et seq.*; the Second Plenary of Baltimore, 298; the Episcopal, 312; the Second Plenary of Baltimore and Papal infallibility, 399.
Councils, Provincial, of Cincinnati, 200; law of the Council of Trent concerning, 308.
Country, the, and the church, 234.
Covington, diocese of, 152.
Crittenden, John J., 93.
Crusade, anti-Catholic, favorable to the church, 198.

Cullen, Cardinal, 48, 353; letter of Archbishop Spalding to, 383.
Dances, immodest, 360.
Darras, translation of the *Church History* of, 279.
D'Aubigné, 230.
David, Bishop, 27, 56; his death, 124; biographical sketch of, 253.
Death of Archbishop Spalding, 459.
Dechamps, Mgr., 411.
Democracy, difference between European and American, 273; Christian, 377.
De Neve, Mgr., 167.
Devotion to the Blessed Virgin, 296.
Difficulties, the historical, brought against the Papal infallibility, 408.
Diocese of Louisville, condition of, in 1864, 253.
Discussions in the Vatican Council, manner in which they were conducted, 417.
Doane, the Rev. G. H., 360.
Döllinger, Dr., 406.
Dominicans, the, 129.
Dubois, the Rev. John, 265.
Dupanloup, Bishop, letter of Archbishop Spalding to, 397.

Eccleston, Archbishop, 266.
Education, Roman ecclesiastical, 44, 45; of woman, 370.
Elba, Isle of, 380.
Eloquence of the pulpit, Catholicity and Protestantism compared in their influence upon, 99 *et seq.*
England, Bishop, 49 *et seq.*

Europe, visit of Bishop Spalding to, 158.

Faith a gift of God, 280.
Fénelon, 411.
Finances of the diocese of Louisville, 225.
Flaget, Bishop, 27; resignation accepted, 56; the last months of his life, 123.
Founders of the American Republic, 364.
Franklin, Dr., 257.
Freedom of Discussion in the Vatican Council, 417.
Freemasonry, 282.
Friedrich, Dr., 419.

Gallicanism, 159, 406.
Gardiner, Mother Frances, 425.
Gaume, the Abbé, 159.
Gazette, the *Pall Mall*, 411.
Geneva, 426.
Gerbet, the Abbé, 160.
Gibbons, Rt. Rev. James A., 375.
Gousset, Cardinal, 158.
Government, interference of, in the appointment of bishops, 257.
Governments, the, of Europe, 406.
Gregory XVI., 43.

Habits, personal, of Bishop Spalding, 222.
Hallam, 231.
Haseltine, the Rev. Joseph, 247.
Haskins, Father, 293.
Health, ill, of Archbishop Spalding, 449.
Hecker, Very Rev. I. T., 342.

Heiss, Bishop, 303.
Henry, Professor, 240.
Heresies of Sixteenth Century, causes which led to, 232.
History of the Reformation, 230.
Hohenlohe, Prince, note of, 407.
Holland, 168.
Holy Childhood, Association of, 277.
Hospitality, episcopal, 269.
Hospitals, the military, in Kentucky, 246.
House, the, of Calvin, 428.
Hughes, Archbishop, 31, 189.
Huntington, Dr., 227.
Huxley, Professor, 332.

Illness, last, of Archbishop Spalding, 453.
Indianapolis, 252.
Indians in Kentucky, 16.
Industrial School for boys, St. Joseph's, 374.
Infallibility, the, of the Pope, Archbishop Spalding had always believed in, 382; a logical consequence of the Primacy, 398; not a new doctrine, 419.
Institute, Smithsonian, 240; Catholic, of Cincinnati, 242.
Institutions of learning in Kentucky, 245; religious, number of, in the United States, 335.
Invasion, the, of Rome by the Italian Government, 430.
Irish Catholics, prejudices against, 326; the love of, for the priest, 354.
Italy, 350.

Ives, Dr., 227, 293.

Jesuits, the, 49; in Kentucky, 125, 140, 250.
Journal, the Louisville, 182.
Journalism, religious, 75 *et seq*.
Jubilee of 1825, 25.

Kenrick, Most Rev. Francis Patrick, 27, 227; compared with Archbishop Spalding, 261; his doctrine on Papal infallibility, 400.
Keogh, the Rev. James, 303.
Kindekens, Very Rev. Peter, 167.
Know-Nothings, the, 184.

Ladies of the Sacred Heart, 358.
Lafayette, General, 191.
Law, canon, 218.
Lazarists, the, 266.
League, the Louisville, 97.
Lecturer, Bishop Spalding's labors as a, 102.
Lectures, Sunday evening, 98.
Lefevre, Bishop, 167.
Legislature, the, of Kentucky, 248.
Letter of Bishop Miles, 91; of Bishop O'Connor, 260.
Letters of Archbishop Spalding to his father, 30, 42; to Archbishop Kenrick, 30; to Father Byrne, 33; to his brother, 37, 45; to his sister, 39; to Bishop Flaget, 58; to Mrs. Coleman, 93; of Bishop Flaget, 38, 57; Apostolic, 300.
Lexington, Dr. Spalding pastor of, 83 *et seq*.

Liberalism and Catholicism, 424.
Liberty, civil, and Papal infallibility, 422.
Lincoln, Abraham, 285.
Little Sisters of the Poor, 376.
Logan, Caleb W., 187.
Louisville, transfer of the see of the diocese to, 89.
Losses of the church in the United States, 323.
Luers, Bishop, 279.

Magoffin, Governor, 248.
Maguire, John Francis, 355.
Mai, Cardinal, 62.
Manning, Archbishop, 408.
Mason, Judge, address of, 433.
Marriage of Catholics and Protestants, 277.
Marseilles, 171.
Marshall, General Humphrey, 187; Dr., 411.
McGill, Bishop, 97.
McTavish, Mrs. Emily, 269.
McSherry, Dr., 454.
Merode, Count de, 165.
Mezzofanti, Cardinal, 48.
Milan, 350.
Minerva, the St. Joseph's College, 67.
Miscellanea, the, 189.
Miscellany, the *Catholic*, 75.
Missions, popular, 86; by whom introduced into this country, 134.
Monday, Bloody, 184.
Monks, Irish, 196.
Montalembert, 161.
Morse, Professor, 191.
Motives for holding Second Plenary Council of Baltimore, 298.

Motto, the, attributed to Lafayette, 191.
Murder of the innocents, 373.

Nagot, the Rev. M., 264.
Nashville, diocese of, 89 *et seq.*
Nationalism and religion, 174 *et seq.*
Nations, the law of the rise and downfall of, 362 *et seq.*
Neale, the Rev. Charles, 264.
Negroes, Bishop Spalding's sympathy with, 224.
Nelson, General, 250.
Nerincks, Father, 155.
Newman, the Rev. Henry H., 227.

Objections to the church, 106.
O'Connor, Bishop, 226.
Odin, Archbishop, 259.
Orders, the religious, witnesses to the supernatural power of Catholic faith, 127.
Ordination, largest ever held in the U. S., 375.

Pallotti, Father Vincent, 48.
Pantheism, 330.
Party, the Native American, 181; the Whig, 182; the Know-Nothing, 182 *et seq.*; the Third, in the Vatican Council, 396.
People, the, of the South, 287; of Ireland, 353; the, 378.
Persecution of Catholics in this country, 108.
Philosophy of History, 231.
Picnics, 371.
Pius VIII., 40.

Pius IX., 172; letter of, to Archbishop Spalding, 441.
Plébiscite, 438.
Politics, Bishop Spalding's aversion to, 188.
Polity, ecclesiastical, in the U. S., 307.
Pope, the, duty of contributing to the support of, 278; cannot be the subject and at the same time the friend of any earthly ruler, 437.
Population, Catholic, of Kentucky, 132; of the U. S., 335.
Postulatum, the, of Archbishop Spalding, 387.
Power, temporal, of the Pope, 435.
Prayer-books, English, 452.
Prerogative of place granted to the Archbishop of Baltimore, 259.
Prejudice, Archbishop Spalding free from, 446.
Prejudices, Protestant, 107.
Prentice, George D., 183.
Prescott, Wm. H., 231.
Priests, parish, 312; number of, in the U. S., 334.
Pride, scientific, of Germany, 405.
Primate, none in the U. S., 218.
Professordom, the, of Germany, 408.
Progress of the church in the U. S., 328 et seq.; of science, 331.
Protectory, St. Mary's, 292.
Protest of the Catholics of Baltimore and Washington City against the invasion of Rome, 434.
Protestantism in the U. S., 328, 413.
Purcell, Archbishop, 318.
Puritans, the, 329.

Question, the, of the future, 378.

Reasons for an implicit definition of Papal infallibility, 389.
Reception of Archbishop Spalding in Baltimore, 432.
Redemptorists, the, 266.
Reformation, the causes that led to, 232.
Reisach, Cardinal, 62.
Relations of the two orders of the clergy, 218.
Religion the only safeguard of American society, 367.
Republics founded by Catholics, 176.
Residence, archiepiscopal, of Baltimore, 269.
Retreat, eight days', of Bishop David, 252.
Review, the *Dublin*, 79.
Reynolds, Bishop, 95.
Rich, the, religious character of, 376.
Rights, parochial, 312.
Rome, Archbishop Spalding's love of, 348.
Rousseau, Jean Jacques, 427.
Ryan, Rt. Rev. P. J., 304.

Saints, patronal, 276.
Salvation, exclusive, Catholic doctrine of, 281.
Schism, the Old Catholic, 408.
School, industrial, for girls, 358.

Index.   467

Schools, industrial, 289, 293; for the emancipated slaves, 338.
Science, effect of the progress of, on religious faith, 331.
Sciolism, 446.
See, the Holy, conservatism of, 413; the first episcopal in the U. S., 310.
Seminary, Theological, at Bardstown, 27; Mount St. Mary's, Cincinnati, 200; St. Mary's, Baltimore, 264; Preparatory, St. Thomas', 200; St. Charles', 266.
Sermon on the Blessed Virgin, 295.
Seton, Mother, 265.
Sisterhood of the Good Shepherd, 131; in Baltimore, 269.
Slaves, the emancipated, 338.
Societies, secret, 283.
Society of Jesus, reorganization of, in the U. S., 265; of St. Joseph for Foreign Missions, 340; the Catholic Publication, 342.
Soldier of the Cross, 451.
Spalding, Archbishop, his knowledge of mathematics, 23, 24; illness in Rome, 41; is ordained priest, 59; president of St. Joseph's College, 83; pastor of St. Peter's Church, Lexington, Ky., 84 *et seq.*; vicar-general of the diocese of Louisville, 95; his manner as a public speaker, 104; appointed coadjutor of Bishop Flaget, 121; his consecration, 122; his *Life of Bishop Flaget*, 149 *et seq.*; Mother Catherine, 64; Very Rev. B. J., 225; death of, 374.
St. Francis de Sales, 425.
Sulpicians, the, in Baltimore, 266.
Syllabus, the, Archbishop Spalding's defence of, 272.
Synod, the Sixth, of Baltimore, 275; the Third, of Louisville, 249.
System of common schools in the United States, 204 *et seq.*

Tablet, the London, 387.
Tendency of modern social movements, 321.
Thébaud, Father, 356.
Theses, defence of, 50 *et seq.*
Thonon, 426.
Thought, undercurrents of, in France and Germany, 404.
Timon, Bishop, 252.
Tissiaux, canon, 171.
Titulus missionis, 218.
Toleration of Catholics in the United States, causes which led to, 109.
Trappists, the, 126 *et seq.*
Trusteeism, 325.

Umilta, Convent of, 359.
Unanimity not required for doctrinal definitions, 401.
Union of church and State, 237.
University, Catholic, for the United States, 298, 313 *et seq.*; idea of, 316; the, of Louvain, 170; of Notre Dame, Indiana, 295.

Vanpelt, the Rev. Dr., 197.

Vatican, the, Council of, 379.
Vaughan, the Rev. Herbert, 340.
Version, English, of the Bible, 227.
Veuillot, M. Louis, 377.
Vicar Apostolic, of London, 257.
Virgin, the Blessed, devotion of Bishop Spalding to, 169, 221.
Visitation, Order of the, 265; the episcopal, Bishop Spalding's manner of making, 134.

Vocations to the priesthood, 275.
Vote, the final, on Papal infallibility, 415.

Washington City, reception of Archbishop Spalding in, 434.
Webb, Hon. B. J., 98.
Whelan, the Rev. David, 359.
White, the Rev. Dr., 279.
Woman, false system of education of, 370.
Wood, General, 246; Bishop, 360.
Worship, freedom of, 275.

Archbishop Spalding's Works.

New and Uniform Editions in 3 and 5 Vols.
VARIOUS BINDINGS.

☞ These Volumes ought to occupy a conspicuous place in every library, as complete and reliable works of reference.

Miscellanea:

Comprising Reviews, Essays, and Lectures on Historical, Theological, and Miscellaneous Subjects. By the Most Rev. M. J. Spalding, D.D., Archbishop of Baltimore. Fifth revised and greatly enlarged edition. In 1 vol. of upwards of 800 pages 8vo, cloth, ... $3 50

Another edition, fine paper, 2 vols. 8vo, cloth, bevelled, ... 5 00
   Library style, ... 6 00
   Half calf, ... 7 00

The History of the Protestant Reformation

In Germany, Switzerland, England, Ireland, Scotland, the Netherlands, France, and Northern Europe. In a Series of Essays, reviewing D'Aubigné, Menzel, Hallam, Short, Prescott, Ranke, Fryxell, and others. Sixth edition revised. With a New Preface and a New and Complete Index. By the Most Rev. M. J. Spalding, D.D., Archbishop of Baltimore. In 1 vol. of 1,000 pages 8vo, cloth, ... 3 50

Another edition, fine paper, 2 vols. 8vo, cloth, bevelled, ... 5 00
   Library style, ... 6 00
   Half calf, ... 7 00

Lectures on the Evidences of Catholicity.

By the Most Rev. M. J. Spalding, D.D., Archbishop of Baltimore. Fifth revised edition. 1 vol. 8vo, cloth, ... 2 00

Another edition, on fine paper, cloth, bevelled, ... 2 50
   Library style, ... 3 00
   Half calf, ... 3 50

The Complete Set, in 5 vols. 8vo. Fine edition, cloth, extra, bevelled, with appropriate back and side stamps. Put up in neat box, ... 12 50
   Library style, ... 15 00
   Half calf, ... 17 50

JOHN MURPHY & CO., Baltimore.

The Catholic Publication Society, New York.

BOOKS PUBLISHED
BY
The Catholic Publication Society,
9 WARREN STREET, NEW YORK.

☞ Attention is called to the following Catalogue of our Books. The prices given are the retail ones. A large discount is allowed to Clergymen, Booksellers, Religious Institutions, and Library Societies.

☞ All the books in this list sent by mail, postage paid, on receipt of price.

☞ All the publications of the several Catholic Publishers, both in this country and in England, kept in stock.

"A wonderful book."—*Boston Pilot.*
My Clerical Friends, and their Relations to Modern Thought. Contents: Chap. I. The Vocation of the Clergy.—II. The Clergy at Home.—III. The Clergy Abroad.—IV. The Clergy and Modern Thought. 1 vol. 12mo, ... **1 50**

By the same author.
Church Defence: Report of a Conference on the Present Dangers of the Church. By the author of "My Clerical Friends." Members of the Conference: Canon Lightwood, Archdeacon Tennyson, Rev. Cyril Hooker—Ritualists. The Regius Professor of Chaldee, the Bishop of Rochester, Rev. Prebendary Smiles—High Churchmen. The Bishop of Brighton, Archdeacon Softly, Rev. Silas Trumpington—Low Churchmen. Dean Marmion, Rev. Prebendary Creedless—Broad Churchmen. Rev. Mark Weasel—Anglican Unattached. 1 vol. 18mo, cloth, **60 cts.**

The Comedy of Convocation in the English Church. In Two Scenes. Edited by Archdeacon Chasuble, D.D., and dedicated to the Pan-Anglican Synod. 8vo, cloth, ... **1 00**

Bibliographia Catholica Americana. A List of American Catholic Books published up to the year 1825. By Rev. J. M. Finotti. 1 vol. 8vo, ... **5 00**

Nellie Netterville; or, One of the Transplanted. A Tale of the Times of Cromwell in Ireland. By Miss Caddell. 1 vol. 12mo, cloth, extra, ... **1 50**
Cloth, gilt, ... **2 00**

Wild Times. A Tale of the Days of Queen Elizabeth. By Cecilia Mary Caddell. First American edition. 1 vol. 12mo, . **1 50**
Cloth, gilt, ... **2 00**

The Progressionists and Angela. From the German of Bolanden. 1 vol. 8vo, **1 50**
Cloth, gilt, ... **2 00**

The Nesbits; or, A Mother's Last Request, and Other Tales. 1 vol. 12mo, . . **1 25**

Peter's Journey, and Other Tales, and Wilfulness and Its Consequences. 1 vol. 12mo, frontispiece, ... **1 50**
Cloth, gilt, ... **2 00**

Little Pierre, the Pedlar of Alsace. Translated from the French, and illustrated by 27 first-class woodcuts. (This makes one of the handsomest premium books ever issued in this country.) Cloth, extra, **1 50**
Cloth, full gilt, ... **2 00**

Maggie's Rosary, and Other Tales. (CONTENTS: By the author of "Marion Howard." Maggie's Rosary—The White Angel—Mabel—Old Morgan's Rose-Tree. From the French of Souvestre, translated by Emily Bowles: The Sawyer of the Vosges—A Meeting on the Alps—The Godson.) 1 vol. 12mo, **1 00**

The Catholic Publication Society

The Threshold of the Catholic Church. A course of plain Instructions for those entering her communion. By Fr. Bagshaw. With preface by Mgr. Capel. 1 vol. 12mo, ... **1 50**

Sermons on Ecclesiastical Subjects. Vol. I. By Archbishop Manning. Cloth, extra, ... **2 00**

The same, Vol. II., ... **2 00**

A Winged Word, and Other Stories. By the author of "The House of Yorke," etc., ... **1 50**

Cloth gilt, ... **2 00**

The House of Yorke: A Story of American Life. Cloth, extra, . . **2 00**

Cloth, full gilt, ... **3 00**

Myrrha Lake; or, Into the Light of Catholicity. By Minnie Mary Lee. 1 vol. 16mo, ... **1 00**

Only a Pin. Translated from the French by a Graduate of St. Joseph's Academy, Emmittsburg. 1 vol. 16mo, cloth extra, ... **1 00**

Cloth, gilt, ... **1 50**

Constance Sherwood: An Autobiography of the Sixteenth Century. By Lady Georgiana Fullerton. With four illustrations. 1 vol. 8vo, extra cloth, . **2 00**

Cloth, gilt, ... **3 00**

The Betrothed. From the Italian of Manzoni. 1 vol. 12mo, ... **1 50**

Cloth, gilt, ... **2 00**

French Eggs in an English Basket. Translated by Emily Bowles. 1 vol. 12mo, ... **1 50**

Two Thousand Miles on Horseback. A Summer Tour to the Plains, the Rocky Mountains, and New Mexico. By James F. Meline. 1 vol. 12mo, . . **1 50**

Mary Queen of Scots and Her Latest English Historian. A Narrative of the Principal Events in the Life of Mary Stuart. With some Remarks on Mr. Froude's History of England. By James F. Meline. 1 vol. 12mo, ... **1 75**

The Life and Times of Sixtus the Fifth. Translated from the French by James F. Meline. 1 vol. 16mo, . . . **1 00**

All-Hallow Eve; or, The Test of Futurity, and Other Stories. 1 vol. 8vo, ... **2 00**

Cloth, gilt, ... **3 00**

Impressions of Spain. By Lady Herbert. 1 vol. 12mo, fifteen Illustrations, cloth extra, ... **2 00**

Cradle Lands. Egypt, Syria, Palestine, Jerusalem, etc. By Lady Herbert. Illustrated by eight full-page Illustrations. 1 vol. 12mo, vellum cloth, ... **2 00**

Cloth, full gilt, ... **2 50**

Half-calf, ... **4 00**

Life of J. Theophane Venard, Martyr in Tonquin. Translated from the French by Lady Herbert. 1 vol. 16mo, . . **1 00**

Three Phases of Christian Love. The Mother, the Maiden, and the Religious. By Lady Herbert. One vol. 12mo, . **1 50**

Gilt, extra, ... **2 00**

The Life of Henry Dorie, Martyr. Translated from the French by Lady Herbert. 1 vol., 16mo, ... **75 cts.**

A Sister's Story. By Madame Augustus Craven. Translated from the French by Emily Bowles. One vol. crown 8vo, pp. 528, cloth, extra, ... **2 50**

Cloth, gilt, ... **3 00**

Anne Severin. By the Author of "A Sister's Story." 1 vol. 12mo, cloth, . **1 50**

Cloth, gilt, ... **2 00**

Fleurange. By Madame Augustus Craven. 1 vol. 8vo, ... **1 50**

Cloth, gilt, ... **2 00**

Visits to the Blessed Sacrament and to the Blessed Virgin, for every day in the Month. By St. Alphonsus Liguori. 24mo, cloth, new edition, ... **60 cts.**

Way of Salvation, in Meditations for Every Day in the Year. Translated from the Italian of St. Alphonsus Liguori by Rev. James Jones. 24mo, cloth, . . **75 cts.**

Hours of the Passion; or, Pathetic Reflections on the Sufferings and Death of our Blessed Redeemer. By St. Liguori. New edition. Translated by Right Rev. W. Walsh, Bishop of Halifax, with a sketch of the Life of St. Alphonsus Liguori. 18mo, cloth, ... **60 cts.**

Love of Our Lord Jesus Christ Reduced to Practice. By St. Alphonsus Liguori. Translated by the Right Rev. W. Walsh, Bishop of Halifax. New edition. 18mo, cloth, ... **60 cts.**

Short Treatise on Prayer. Adapted to all Classes of Christians. By St. Alphonsus Liguori. The holy author of this treatise says: "Were it in my power, I would publish as many copies of this work as there are Christians on earth, and would give each a copy, that each might be convinced of the absolute necessity of prayer." New edition. 24mo, cloth, ... **40 cts.**

Spirit of St. Alphonsus de Liguori. A Selection from his Shorter Spiritual Treatises. Translated from the Italian by the Rev. J. Jones. With a Memoir of the author. 24mo, cloth, ... **60 cts.**

The Catholic Publication Society.

The Glories of Mary. Translated from the Italian of St. Alphonsus Maria de Liguori. Second edition. Revised by Rev. Robert A. Coffin, C.SS.R. 1 vol. 12mo. **1 25**

Life and Letters of Madame Swetchine. Translated from the French of the Count Falloux. One vol. 12mo, . **2 00**

The Writings of Madame Swetchine. Edited by Count de Falloux. 1 vol. 12mo, **1 50**

Oakeley on Catholic Worship: A Manual of Popular Instruction on the Ceremonies and Devotions of the Church. By Frederick Canon Oakeley, M.A., Missionary Rector of St. John's, Islington. 1 vol. 16mo, **60 cts.**

Oakeley on the Mass. The Order and Ceremonial of the most Holy and Adorable Sacrifice of the Mass explained in a Dialogue between a Priest and a Catechumen. With an Appendix on Solemn Mass, Vespers, Compline, and the Benediction of the Most Holy Sacrament. By Canon Frederick Oakeley. 1 vol. 18mo, . **60 cts.**

Manresa; or, The Spiritual Exercises of St. Ignatius. For General use. New Edition. 1 vol. 12mo, . . **1 50**

Dr. Newman's Answer to Dr. Pusey's Eirenicon. Paper, . . **75 cts.**

An Essay in Aid of a Grammar of Assent. By John Henry Newman, D.D., of the Oratory. 1 vol. 12mo, cloth, . **2 50**

Apologia Pro Vita Sua; Being a Reply to a Pamphlet entitled "What, then, Does Dr. Newman Mean?" By John Henry Newman, D.D. New edition. 1 vol. 12mo, **2 00**

Exposition of the Doctrine of the Catholic Church in Matters of Controversy. By the Right Rev. J. B. Bossuet. A new edition, with copious notes, by Rev. J. Fletcher, D.D. 18mo, . . **60 cts.**

Letters of Eugenie de Guerin. Edited by G. S. Tébutien. 1 vol. 12mo, cloth, ... **2 00**

Journal of Eugenie de Guerin. Edited by G. S. Trébutien. 1 vol. 12mo, **2 00**

Letters to a Protestant Friend on the Holy Scriptures. By Rev. D. A. Gallitzin. 18mo, cloth, ... **60 cts.**

Defence of Catholic Principles. By the Rev. D. A. Gallitzin. Fourth edition. 18mo, cloth, . . **60 cts.**

Spiritual Director of Devout and Religious Souls. By St. Francis de Sales, **50 cts.**

Introduction to a Devout Life. From the French of St. Francis of Sales, Bishop and Prince of Geneva. To which is prefixed an Abstract of his Life. 18mo, cloth, **75 cts.**

Think Well On't; or, Reflections on the Great Truths of the Christian Religion, for every day in the Month. By Right Rev. R. Challoner. 32mo, cloth, . **30 cts.**

Catholic Christian Instructed in the Sacraments, Sacrifices, Ceremonies, and Observances of the Church, by way of question and answer. By the Right Rev. Dr. Challoner. 24mo, cloth, flexible, . **25 cts.**

Catholic Christian Instructed. 12mo edition. Cloth, ... **50 cts.**

Christ and the Church. Lectures delivered in St. Ann's Church, New York, during Advent, 1869. By Rev. Thos. S. Preston. 1 vol. 12mo, ... **1 50**

Reason and Revelation. Lectures Delivered in St. Ann's Church, New York, during Advent, 1867, by Rev. T. S. Preston. One vol. 12mo, ... **1 50**

Little Treatise on the Little Virtues. Written originally in Italian by Father Roberti, of the Society of Jesus. To which are added, A Letter on Fervor by Father Vallois, S.J., and Maxims from an unpublished manuscript of Father Segneri, S.J.; also, Devotions to the Sacred Heart of Jesus. 32mo, cloth, ... **45 cts.**

Lenten Sermons. From the Italian of Father Segneri, S.J. Vol. I. 12mo, **1 50**

A New and Enlarged Edition, with Maps, etc. **An Illustrated History of Ireland,** from the Earliest Period to the Present Time; with several first-class full-page engravings of Historical Scenes designed by Henry Doyle, and engraved by George Hanlon and George Pearson; together with upward of One Hundred Woodcuts, by eminent Artists, illustrating Antiquities, Scenery, and Sites of Remarkable Events; and three large Maps—one of Ireland, and the others of Family Homes, Statistics, etc. 1 vol. 8vo, nearly 700 pages, extra cloth, . **5 00** Half-calf, ... **7 00**

The Life of St. Patrick, Apostle of Ireland. By M. F. Cusack, author of "The Illustrated History of Ireland," etc. Illustrated, one vol., ... **6 00**

The Patriot's History of Ireland. By M. F. Cusack. 1 vol., . . **1 25**

The Works of the Most Reverend John Hughes, first Archbishop of New York, containing Biography, Sermons, Lectures, Speeches, etc. Carefully compiled from the Best Sources, and edited by Lawrence Kehoe. 2 vols. 8vo, cloth, . . **8 00** 2 vols., half-calf, extra, . . **12 00**

Poor Man's Catechism; or, The Christian Doctrine Explained, with Short Admonitions. By John Mannock, O.S.B. 24mo, cloth, ... **50 cts.**

Poor Man's Controversy. By J. Mannock, author of "Poor Man's Catechism." 18mo, cloth, ... **50 cts.**

Catholic Tracts. Fifty Catholic Tracts of "The Catholic Publication Society," on various subjects. 1 vol. 12mo, cloth extra, **1 25**

Irish Odes, and Other Poems. By Aubrey de Vere. 1 vol. 12mo, toned paper, **2 00** Cloth, gilt, ... **2 50**

No. 9 Warren Street, New York.

The Catholic Publication Society.

May Carols, and Hymns and Poems. By Aubrey de Vere. Blue and gold, **1 25**

The Liquefaction of the Blood of St. Januarius. Cloth, . . . **1 00**

History of the Old and New Testaments. By J. Reeve. 8vo, half-bound, embossed roan, ... **1 00**

Compendious Abstract of the History of the Church of Christ. By Rev. Wm. Gahan. With continuation down to the present time, by John G. Shea, LL.D. 12mo, **1 25**

The Life of Mother Julia, Foundress of the Sisters of Notre Dame. 1 vol. 12mo, cloth, extra, with Portrait of Mother Julia. **1 50**

Cloth, gilt, ... **2 00**

History of England, for the Use of Schools. By W. F. Mylus. Continued down to the present time by John G. Shea, LL.D. 12mo, . . . **1 25**

Life of Mother Margaret Mary Hallahan, founder of the English Congregation of St. Catherine of Siena, of the Third Order of St. Dominick. By her Religious Children. With a Preface by the Right Rev. Bishop Ullathorne. 1 vol. 8vo, . . **4 00**

Early History of the Catholic Church in the Island of New York. By the Right Rev. J. R. Bayley, D.D. With four Steel Plates of the four first Bishops and a woodcut of old St. Peter's. 1 vol. 12mo, cloth, **1 50**

History of the Society of Jesus. Daurignac. 2 vols., . . . **3 00**

The Life of Father Ravignan, S.J. By Father Ponlevoy, S.J. Translated from the French. 1 vol. crown 8vo, toned paper, **4 00**

Life of St. Vincent de Paul. 32mo, cloth, ... **45 cts.**

Life of Blessed Margaret Mary Alacoque. With some Account of the Devotion to the Sacred Heart. By the Rev. George Tickell, S.J. 1 vol. 8vo, . . **2 50**

Our Lady of Litanies. By Rev. X. D. McLeod, ... **1 00**

The Sacramentals of the Holy Catholic Church. By the Rev. W. J. Barry, **1 00**

Lenten Monitor; or, Moral Reflections and Devout Aspirations on the Gospel for each day, from Ash-Wednesday till Easter Sunday. By Rev. P. Baker, O.S.F. 24mo, cloth, new edition, . . . **60 cts.**

The End of Religious Controversy. By Rt. Rev. John Milner, D.D. 1 vol. 12mo. **75 cts.**

FATHER FORMBY'S WORKS.

Pictorial Bible and Church History Stories. An easy, continuous narrative for the Young, from Adam and Eve in Paradise down to the Middle of the Reign of Pope Pius IX. Profusely illustrated by over 500 Woodcuts from original designs by the most eminent artists. Crown 8vo.

I. The Old Testament Stories. Containing 200 illustrations and 6 maps, 520 pp., ... **3 00**

II. The Life of Christ. Containing 100 illustrations, 186 pp., . . **1 00**

III. The History of the Church. Containing 200 illustrations, 540 pp., **3 00**

The above beautiful books can be had in sets, put up in boxes, suitable for presents, as follows:

In three vols., cloth extra, . **7 00**

In five vols., cloth extra, . **9 00**

In five vols., cloth gilt, . **12 00**

In five vols. half calf, . **20 00**

In five vols full calf antique, **30 00**

The Pictorial Bible and Church History Stories, Abridged and Complete. 1 vol. With a view of Solomon's Temple, a bird's-eye view of Jerusalem, and upwards of one hundred beautiful Engravings. Crown 8vo, 300 pp. By Rev. Henry Formby. Cloth, extra, ... **1 50**

Cloth, gilt, ... **2 00**

Half-calf, ... **3 50**

Full-calf, ... **6 00**

This is an abridgment of the larger work described above.

The Book of the Holy Rosary. A Full, Popular, Doctrinal Exposition of its Fifteen Mysteries, and of their Corresponding Types in the Old Testament. Illustrated with thirty-six full-page engravings, printed in the best manner on toned paper, extra ornamental binding, and gilt edges. By Rev. H. Formby. 1 vol. quarto, full gilt, . . **4 00**

Life, Passion, Death, and Resurrection of Our Lord Jesus Christ. Being an Abridged Harmony of the Four Gospels in the Words of the Sacred Text. Edited by the Rev. Henry Formby. With over sixty engravings from original designs. 1 vol. 12mo, **1 00**

Cloth gilt, ... **1 50**

The Life of S. Catharine of Siena. 1 vol. 12mo, . . . **1 75**

An Epistle of Jesus Christ to the Faithful Soul that is devoutly affected toward Him. 1 vol. 16mo, . . **1 00**

History of the Church from its Establishment to the Reformation. By the late Rev. C. C. Pise, D.D. 5 vols. 8vo, . **7 50**

Another edition. 5 vols. 12mo, cloth, **5 00**

No. 9 Warren Street, New York.

The Catholic Publication Society.

The Illustrated Catholic Sunday-School Library. First Series. The following are the titles of the different volumes: Madeleine the Rosière. Crusade of the Children. Tales of the Affections. Adventures of Travel. Truth and Trust. Select Popular Tales. Handsomely bound and put up in a box. Cloth, extra, . . 3 00

Cloth, gilt, ... 4 00

The Illustrated Catholic Sunday-School Library. Second Series. The following are the titles of the different volumes: The Rivals. The Battle of Lepanto, etc. Scenes and Incidents at Sea. The Schoolboys, and the Boy and the Man. Beautiful Little Rose. Florestine. Handsomely bound, and put up in a box, cloth, extra, . 3 00

Cloth, gilt, ... 4 00

The Illustrated Catholic Sunday-School Library. Third Series. The following are the titles of the different volumes: Nettlethorpe the Miser. Tales of Naval and Military Life. Harry O'Brien, and Other Tales. The Hermit of Mount Atlas. Leo; or, The Choice of a Friend. Antonio; or, The Orphan of Florence. Handsomely bound, and put up in a box. Cloth, extra, 3 00

Cloth, gilt, ... 4 00

The Illustrated Catholic Sunday-School Library. Fourth Series. The following are the titles of the different volumes: Tales of the South of France. Stories of Other Lands. Emma's Cross, and Other Tales. Uncle Edward's Stories. Joe Baker. The Two Painters. Handsomely bound, and put up in a box. Cloth, extra, . 3 00

Cloth, gilt, ... 4 00

The Illustrated Catholic Sunday-School Library. Fifth Series. The following are the titles of the different volumes: Bad Example. May-Day, and Other Tales. James Chapman. The Young Astronomer, and Other Tales. Angel Dreams. Ellerton Priory. Handsomely bound, and put up in box. Cloth, extra, ... 3 00

Cloth, gilt, ... 4 00

The Illustrated Catholic Sunday-School Library. Sixth Series. The following are the titles of the different volumes: Idleness and Industry. The Hope of the Katzekopfs. St. Maurice. The Young Emigrants. Angels' Visits. Scrivener's Daughter, and Orange Girl. Handsomely bound, and put up in a box. Cloth, extra, . 3 00

Cloth, gilt, ... 4 00

The Illustrated Catholic Sunday-School Library. Seventh Series. The following are the titles of the different volumes: Tales of Catholic Artists. Honor O'More's Three Homes. Sir Ælfric, and Other Tales. Select Tales for the Young. Tales for the Many. Frederick Wilmot. In a box, illustrated. Cloth, extra, ... 3 00

Cloth, gilt, ... 4 00

The Illustrated Catholic Sunday-School Library. Eighth Series. The following are the titles of the different volumes: The Apprentice, and other Sketches. Mary Benedicta, and Other Stories. Faith and Loyalty, and The Chip Gatherers. Agnes, and Other Sketches. Lame Millie. The Chapel of the Angels. Handsomely bound, and put up in box. Cloth extra, . 3 00

Cloth gilt, ... 4 00

Dion and the Sibyls: A Classic, Christian Novel. By Miles Gerald Keon. One vol. 8vo, cloth, extra, ... 1 50

Illustrated Catholic Family Almanac for 1869, 1870, 1871, 1872, and 1873, each, 25 cts.

The Two Schools: A Moral Tale. By Mrs. Hughes. 12mo, cloth, . 1 00

Lives of the Fathers of the Desert, and of many Holy Men and Women who dwelt in Solitude. Translated from the French. Embellished with eighteen engravings. 18mo, cloth, . . . 60 cts.

Louisa; or, The Virtuous Villager. A Catholic Tale. New edition. 18mo, cloth, 60 cts.

Home of the Lost Child. This story is founded on fact, and records in a most interesting manner a singular instance of God's mercy. 18mo, cloth, . . . 60 cts.

Genevieve: A Tale of Antiquity, showing the Wonderful Ways of Providence in the Protection of Innocence. From the German of Schmid. 18mo, cloth, 60 cts.

Christine, and Other Poems. By George H. Miles. Cloth, . . . 2 00

Gilt, extra, ... 2 50

The "Old-Catholics" at Cologne. A Sketch in Three Scenes. By the author of "Comedy of Convocation." 1 vol. 18mo, 75 cts.

Father Rowland. A North American Tale. 18mo, cloth, . . . 60 cts.

The Reverse of the Medal. A Drama for Girls, ... 20 cts.

Ernscliff Hall. A Drama for Girls, 20 cts.

The Deaf-Mute. A Drama for Boys, 50 cts.

Elinor; or, Spain Fifty Years Ago. From the Spanish of Fernan Caballero. 1 vol. 12mo, ... 1 50

Eliza Despres; or, The Effects of Reading Bad Books, . . . 60 cts.

No. 9 Warren Street, New York.

The Catholic Publication Society.

Glimpses of Pleasant Homes. By the author of "The Life of Mother McCauley." Illustrated with four full-page Illustrations. 1 vol. 12mo, cloth extra, . . . **1 50**

Cloth, gilt, ... **2 00**

Books of Irish Martyrs. Memorials of those who Suffered for the Catholic Faith in Ireland during the Sixteenth, Seventeenth, and Eighteenth Centuries. Collected and edited by Myles O'Reilly, B.A., LL.D. 1 vol. crown 8vo, vellum cloth, . . **2 50**

Diary of a Sister of Mercy. Tales from the Diary of a Sister of Mercy. By C. M. Brame. 1 vol. 12mo, extra cloth, **1 50**

Extra gilt, ... **2 00**

Gropings After Truth. A Life-Journey from New England Congregationalism to the One Catholic Apostolic Church. By Joshua Huntington. One volume vellum cloth, ... **75** cts.

The Clergy and the Pulpit and their Relations to the People. By M. l'Abbé Isidore Mullois, Chaplain to Napoleon III. One vol. 12mo, extra cloth, . . **1 50**

Half-calf, extra, ... **3 50**

Symbolism; or, Exposition of the Doctrinal Differences between Catholics and Protestants, as evidenced by their Symbolic Writings. By John A. Moehler, D.D. Translated from the German, with a Memoir of the Author, preceded by an Historical Sketch of the State of Protestantism and Catholicism in Germany for the last Hundred Years. By J. B. Robertson, Esq., . . **4 00**

An Amicable Discussion on the Church of England, and on the Reformation in general, dedicated to the Clergy of every Protestant Communion, and reduced into the form of letters, by the Right Rev. J. F. M. Trevern, D.D., Bishop of Strasbourg. Translated by the Rev. William Richmond. 1 vol. 12mo, 580 pages, . . **2 00**

Anima Divota; or, Devout Soul. Translated from the Italian of Very Rev. J. H. Pagani, Provincial of the Order of Charity in England. This is one of the most instructive and useful books that enrich our spiritual literature. It is a series of excellent considerations relative to the Eucharist as a sacrifice and sacrament, and will be found by the pious Catholic to be a valuable manual in the preparation for Holy Communion. 24mo, cloth, ... **60** cts.

Bona Mors: A Pious Association of the Devout Servants of our Lord Jesus Christ, dying on the Cross, in order to obtain a good death. 24mo, cloth, . . **25** cts.

Why Men do not Believe; or, The Principal Causes of Infidelity. Translated from the French of Mgr. Laforet. Cloth, **1 00**

In Heaven we Know Our Own. Translated from the French of Père Blot. 1 vol. 18mo . . . . . **60** cts.

The See of Peter, the Rock of the Church, the Source of Jurisdiction, and the Centre of Unity. By Thomas William Allies. 1 vol., cloth, ... **75** cts.

Grounds of the Catholic Doctrine, contained in the Profession of Faith published by Pope Pius IV.; to which are added, Reasons why a Catholic cannot Conform to the Protestant Religion. 32mo, cloth, **20** cts.

The Gentle Skeptic; or, Essays and Conversations of a Country Justice on the Authenticity and Truthfulness of the Old Testament Records. Edited by the Rev. C. A. Walworth. 1 vol. 12mo, . . **1 50**

The Doctrine of Hell; ventilated in a Discussion between Rev. C. A. Walworth and Wm. Henry Burr. 1 vol. 18mo, **60** cts.

The Devout Communicant. By Rev. P. Baker. 24mo, ... **50** cts.

The Visible Unity of the Catholic Church maintained against Opposite Theories; with an Explanation of Certain Passages in Ecclesiastical History erroneously appealed to in their support. By M. J. Rhodes, M.A. 2 vols. in 1, 8vo, cloth extra, **5 00**

Letters to a Prebendary, Being an Answer to Reflections on Popery by Rev. J. Sturgis, LL.D. By Right Rev. J. Milner, D.D. 24mo, cloth, . . . **75** cts.

A Vindication of Italy and the Papal States, ... **40** cts.

The Government of the Papal States, ... **50** cts.

Fifty Reasons why the Catholic Religion ought to be Preferred, . . **40** cts.

The Holy Communion. Its Philosophy, Theology, and Practice. By John Bernard Dalgairns, Priest of the Oratory of St. Philip Neri. 1 vol. 12mo, . . **2 00**

Familiar Discourses to the Young, Preceded by an Address to Parents. By A Catholic Priest. 1 vol. 12mo, cloth, **75** cts.

Catechism of Council of Trent. Published by command of Pope Pius V. Translated by Rev. J. Donovan, Professor Royal College, Maynooth. 8vo, . **2 00**

Hornihold on the Commandments, etc. The Commandments and Sacraments explained in Fifty-two Discourses. By the Right Rev. Dr. Hornihold, author of "Real Principles of Catholics." 12mo, cloth, **2 00**

Spiritual Combat. To which is added, The Peace of the Soul and the Happiness of the Heart which Dies to Itself in order to Live to God. 32mo, ... **40** cts.

Practical Discourses on the Perfections and Works of God, and the Divinity and Works of Jesus Christ. By Rev. J. Reeve. 8vo, cloth, ... **2 50**

Triumph of Religion; or, A Choice Selection of Edifying Narratives. Compiled from various authors. 18mo, cloth, **60** cts.

No. 9 Warren Street, New York.

The Catholic Publication Society.

Stories on the Seven Virtues. By Agnes M. Stewart, authoress of "Festival of the Rosary." (This is a series of moral and interesting tales told with an elegant simplicity, each illustrating the triumph of one of the seven virtues.) 18mo, cloth, **60 cts.**

Spiritual Consoler; or, Instructions to Enlighten Pious Souls in their Doubts and allay their Fears. Written originally in Latin by Father Quadrupani. 18mo, . **50 cts.**

Oratory of the Faithful Soul; or, Devotions to the Most Holy Sacrament and to our Blessed Lady. Translated from the works of Venerable Abbot Blosius. By Robert Aston Coffin, Priest of the Oratory. 18mo, cloth, ... **50 cts.**

Nouet's Meditations on the Life and Passion of Our Lord Jesus Christ, for Every Day in the Year. By Rev. J. Nouet, S.J. To which are added, Meditations on the Sacred Heart of Jesus Christ, being those taken from a Novena in preparation for a Feast of the same. By Father C. Borgo, S.J. One vol. 12mo, 880 pages, . . . **2 50**

Familiar Instructions on Mental Prayer. By the Abbé Courbon. Translated from the French, and edited by Rev. W. T. Gordon, of the Oratory, London. 1 vol. 16 mo, cloth, ... **75 cts.**

Abridgment of the Christian Doctrine. By the Right Rev. Bishop Hay. 32mo, cloth, ... **30 cts.**

Confidence in the Mercy of God. Reflections on the Confidence in the Mercy of God. By the Right Rev. Joseph Languet. 18mo, cloth, . . . **50 cts.**

Sacred Heart of Jesus and the Sacred Heart of Mary. Translated from the Italian of Father Lanzi, author of "History of Painting," etc. With an introduction by Rev. C. P. Meehan. 24mo, cloth, **60 cts.**

Memorial of a Christian Life. Containing all that a soul newly converted to God ought to do that it may attain the perfection to which it ought to aspire. By Rev. Lewis de Granada. O.S.D. Revised and corrected by Rev. F. J. L'Estrange, O.S.D. 18mo, cloth, ... **75 cts.**

Month of Mary. Containing a Series of Meditations, etc., in Honor of the B. V. M. Arranged for each day of the Month. 32mo, cloth, ... **40 cts.**

Peter Claver; A Sketch of His Life and Labors in behalf of the African Slave. 1 vol. 16mo, ... **75 cts.**

Homilies on the Book of Tobias; or, A Familiar Explanation of the Practical Duties of Domestic Life. By Rev. T. Martyn. (Only a few copies of this book left.) 12mo, cloth, ... **1 00**

Counsels of a Christian Mother. 60 cts.

Shadows of the Rood. Eight Lenten Lectures, ... **1 00**

The Divinity of Christ. By Right Rev. S. H. Rosecrans, D.D., . . **60 cts.**

Legends of Holy Mary, . . **60 cts.**

Lenten Lectures. By the Rev. T. McGuire, ... **75 cts.**

Price of a Soul, . . . **50 cts.**

The Progress of the Age, . . **60 cts.**

A Treatise on the Catechism, 50 cts.

Marriage and Family Duties. By Archbishop Purcell, ... **25 cts.**

Galileo and Roman Inquisition, 30 cts.

Little Manual of Devotion to the Sacred Heart of Jesus, and Spiritual Bouquet, ... **50 cts.**

Imitation of Sacred Heart of Jesus. From the Latin of Arnoudt. . . **2 50**

The Hidden Treasure; or, The Value of Holy Mass, ... **50 cts.**

Imitation of the Blessed Virgin, in Four Books. 18mo, cloth, . **60 cts.**

Interior Christian, in Eight Books. with a Supplement. Extracted from the Writings of M. Bernier de Louvigny. 18mo, cloth, ... **60 cts.**

BOOKS BY THE PAULIST FATHERS.

Questions of the Soul. By Rev. I. T. Hecker. New edition, . . **1 50**
Cloth, gilt, ... **2 00**

Aspirations of Nature. By Rev. I. T. Hecker. Fourth Edition, revised, cloth, extra, ... **1 50**

Sermons of the Paulist Fathers, for 1864. New Edition. Cloth, extra, . **1 50**

Sermons of the Paulist Fathers, for 1865 and 1866. Cloth, extra, **1 50**

Sermons of the Paulist Fathers. Vol. VI. 12mo, 336 pages, cloth, . . **1 50**

Life of Father Baker. The Life and Sermons of the Rev. Francis A. Baker, Priest of the Congregation of St. Paul. Edited by Rev. A. F. Hewit. One vol. crown 8vo, pp. 504, . . . **2 50**
Half-calf or morocco extra, . . **4 00**

Guide to Catholic Young Women. Especially for those who earn their own living. By Rev. George Deshon, Missionary Priest. 1 vol. 12mo, . . . **1 00**

A New and Enlarged Edition of Father Young's
Catholic Hymns and Canticles. This edition contains twenty-one new Hymns; among which are five Christmas Carols, a charming carol for Easter, entitled "The Alleluia Bells"; several new and original Songs for Catechism; the popular Congregational Hymns sung in the Paulist Church by the Rosary and Christian Doctrine Societies, and at the Way of the Cross, etc., the whole forming the most complete Catholic Hymn-Book ever published. One vol. 12mo, **1 00**

No. 9 Warren Street, New York.

The Catholic Publication Society.

Problems of the Age. With Studies in St. Augustine on Kindred Subjects. By Rev. A. F. Hewit. 1 vol. 12mo, extra cloth, **2 00**

New and Enlarged Edition of

The Office of Vespers. Containing the order of the Vesper Service; the Gregorian Psalm Tones, harmonized, with the Psalms for all the Vespers during the year pointed for chanting. Common melodies for the Antiphons, and the Four Anthems of the B. V. Mary. By Rev. Alfred Young. With the Imprimatur of the Most Rev. Archbishop of New York. (The Gregorian Tones, and the words of the Psalms, by a new and original division, are so arranged that but one pointing of the Psalms, as given, is needed for all the Tones, with their various endings.) Single copies, . . . **75 cts.**
Per dozen, ... **6 00**

Hymns and Songs for Catholic Children. Containing the most popular Catholic Hymns for every season of the Christian Year, together with May Songs, Christmas and Easter Carols, for the use of Sunday-Schools, Sodalities, and Confraternities.
Paper covers, ... **15 cts.**
Cloth, flexible, ... **25 cts.**

Light in Darkness: A Treatise on the Obscure Night of the Soul. By Rev. A. F. Hewit. 16mo, cloth, extra, . **75 cts.**

The Invitation Heeded: Reasons for a Return to Catholic Unity. By James Kent Stone, late President of Kenyon and Hobart Colleges. 1 vol. 12mo, . . **1 50**

BOOKS IN PAPER COVERS.

The Catholic Christian Instructed. By Bishop Challoner. . . **20 cts.**

Bossuet's Exposition of the Doctrines of the Catholic Church on Matters of Controversy. With Notes. Large edition. **25 cts.**

Bossuet's Exposition of the Doctrines of the Catholic Church on Matters of Controversy. Without Notes. Small edition, **20 cts.**

The Poor Man's Catechism; or, The Christian Doctrine Explained. . **25 cts.**

The Poor Man's Controversy, 25 cts.

End of Religious Controversy, 50 cts.

Familiar Instructions to the Young, **30 cts.**

Gallitzin's Defence of Catholic Principles. . . . . . **25 cts.**

Gallitzin on the Holy Scriptures, **25 cts.**

Catholic Tracts. Vol. I., . . **60 cts.**

The Liquefaction of the Blood of St. Januarius. . . . . . **40 cts.**

Oakeley on the Mass, . . **25 cts.**

Oakeley on Catholic Worship, **25 cts.**

The Life of the Rev. Francis A. Baker. By Rev. A. F. Hewit, . . **50 cts.**

Lectures on Reason and Revelation. By Rev. T. S. Preston, . . **50 cts.**

Aspirations of Nature. By Rev. I. T. Hecker, ... **50 cts.**

Questions of the Soul. By Rev. I. T. Hecker, ... **50 cts.**

Paulist Sermons for 1864, . **50 cts.**

Paulist Sermons for 1866, . **50 cts.**

The Comedy of Convocation in the English Church, . . . **25 cts.**

Gropings after Truth. By Joshua Huntington, ... **25 cts.**

Not for the Fishers of Men. . **6 cts.**

FATHER FORMBY'S BOOKS.

The Parables of Our Lord Jesus Christ. With twenty-one illustrations, . **25 cts.**

Formby's School Songs. The Junior and Senior School Song-Book, complete in one. **20 cts.**

The Seven Sacraments. With Sixteen Illustrations, ... **25 cts.**

The Fifteen Mysteries of the Rosary. With Seventeen Illustrations, . **20 cts.**

The Seven Dolors of the Blessed Virgin Mary. With Seven Illustrations, **15 cts.**

The School Keepsake. With Four Illustrations, ... **12 cts.**

Life of Christ. Abridged. With several Illustrations, ... **25 cts.**

Historical Catechism. By M. l'Abbé Fleury. Continued down to the Present Day, by Father Formby. 18mo, paper cover, **10 cts.**

THE HOLY BIBLE.

Pocket edition, embossed, plain, . **$1 25**
Embossed, gilt, ... **1 75**
Calf, red or gilt edge, . . . **3 00**
Morocco, extra, red edges or gilt, . **4 50**
Morocco or calf, extra, full gilt, . **5 50**
Tooled edge, ... **6 50**
Morocco Turkey, bevelled, . **6 00**
12mo edition, embossed, plain, . **$1 50**
Embossed, gilt, ... **2 00**
Morocco, ... **4 00**
Morocco, extra, ... **5 00**
Full calf, ... **5 50**
" or morocco, tooled edge, . **7 50**
8vo edition printed on the finest quality of paper, with Illustrated Family Record, etc.
Arabesque, gilt, ... **$4 00**
Roan, gilt, ... **5 00**
Morocco, extra, bevelled, . . **7 50**
Full calf, bevelled, . . . **8 50**
" or morocco, tooled edge, . **9 50**

No. 9 Warren Street, New York.

The Catholic Publication Society.

NEW TESTAMENT.

12mo, cloth,	$0 75
Embossed, gilt,	1 25
Roan, gilt,	2 50
Morocco, extra, bevelled,	4 50
32mo cloth, embossed,	40
Arab, gilt,	75
Roan, full gilt,	1 00
Turkey morocco,	2 50
Full calf,	3 00

FOLLOWING OF CHRIST.

In Four Books. By Thomas à Kempis, with Reflections at the conclusion of each chapter. Translated from the French for this edition.

18mo, cloth,	$0 50
Arabesque, gilt,	1 00

Illustrated 12mo edition.

Roan,	$1 50
Turkey morocco, super extra,	4 00
Full calf,	5 00

Without the Reflections. 32mo, cloth,

flexible,	25
Cloth, extra,	40
Roan, gilt edge,	1 00
Turkey morocco, super extra,	2 50
Full calf,	3 00

OFFICE OF HOLY WEEK.

According to the Roman Missal and Breviary, in Latin and English. 18mo, cloth,

	$0 75
Arabesque, gilt,	1 50
Roan, gilt,	2 00
Morocco, gilt,	4 00

OFFICE OF HOLY WEEK.

According to the Roman Missal and Breviary, in Latin and English. 24mo, cloth, . $0 50

Arabesque, plain,	75
Arabesque, gilt,	1 00
Roan, full gilt,	2 00
Morocco, gilt,	3 00

PRAYER-BOOKS.

THE MISSION BOOK.

A Manual of Instructions and Prayers, adapted to preserve the FRUITS OF THE MISSION. Drawn chiefly from the Works of St. Alphonsus Liguori. NEW, IMPROVED, AND ENLARGED EDITION. *The handsomest Prayer-Book published.* Edited by the Paulist Fathers. 620 pages, illustrated with new Steel Engravings, got up expressly for this edition. It contains a complete Vesperal, with notes and other additions, making it 120 pages larger than former editions.

Fine Edition.—Arabesque plain,	$1 00
Arabesque, gilt,	1 50
Roan, embossed, gilt edges,	1 50
Roan, embossed, gilt edges, clasps,	1 75
Roan, full gilt,	1 75
Roan, full gilt, clasps,	2 00
Morocco, extra, bevelled,	4 00
Morocco, extra, bevelled, clasps,	4 50
Mor., extra, bev. tooled edges, etc.,	5 50
Morocco, rims and tooled edges,	7 00
Full calf,	4 50
Full calf, flexible,	5 00
Full calf, bevelled,	5 00
Full calf, tooled edges, etc.,	6 50
Full calf, rims and tooled edges,	7 50

Cheap Edition.—Arabesque, plain,	$0 75
Arabesque, embossed, gilt edges,	1 25
Arab., embossed, gilt edges and clps.	1 50
Roan, gilt,	1 50
Roan, gilt and clasps,	1 75
Morocco,	2 25
Morocco, full gilt,	2 50
Morocco, extra,	3 50
Morocco, extra, bevelled clasps,	4 50

This edition is printed on clear white paper, from the same type, and contains the same matter as the fine edition, making it the cheapest Prayer-Book ever published.

DAILY COMPANION.

Containing a Selection of Prayers and Devotional Exercises for the use of Children. Embellished with thirty-six very neat illustrative Engravings. 32mo, cloth, . $0 25

Arabesque, plain,	50
Arabesque, gilt,	60
Roan, gilt,	75
Roan, full gilt,	1 00
Morocco, gilt,	2 00
Full calf, antique, red edge,	2 50
Full calf, rimmed and clasp,	4 00

This book is printed on the finest quality of paper, and is a most appropriate present for children.

CHRISTIAN'S GUIDE TO HEAVEN.

32mo, arabesque,	$0 50
Arabesque, gilt,	75
Roan, full gilt,	1 25
Morocco, extra,	2 50
Full calf, antique, red edge,	3 00
Full calf, rimmed and clasp,	4 00

CATHOLIC MANUAL.

Containing a Selection of Prayers and Devotional Exercises. 18mo, cloth, . $0 75

Arabesque, plain,	1 00
Arabesque, gilt,	1 25
Am. mor. gilt,	2 50
Morocco, extra,	3 50
Full calf, antique, red edge,	4 50
Full calf, rimmed and clasp,	6 00

TRUE PIETY;

Or, The Day Well Spent. A Manual of Fervent Prayers, Pious Reflections, and Solid Instructions for Catholics. 18mo.

Arabesque and cloth,	$0 75
Arabesque gilt,	1 25
Roan, red edge,	2 00
American morocco, gilt,	2 25
American morocco, full gilt,	2 50
Morocco, gilt,	3 50
Full calf, antique, red edge,	4 50
Full calf, rimmed and clasp,	6 00

GARDEN OF THE SOUL;

Or, A Manual of Spiritual Exercises and Instructions for Christians who, living in the world, aspire to devotion. By Right Rev. Dr. CHALLONER. 24mo, cloth, . $0 50

Arabesque, gilt,	1 00
Roan, full gilt,	1 50
Morocco, gilt,	2 50
Full calf, antique, red edge,	3 00
Full calf, rimmed and clasp,	5 00

No. 9 Warren Street, New York.

The Catholic Publication Society.

THE KEY OF HEAVEN;

Or, Devout Christian's Daily Companion. To which is added, Daily Devotion; or, Profitable Manner of Hearing Mass. Illustrated.

24mo, cloth,	$0 50
Arabesque, gilt,	1 00
Roan, full gilt,	1 50
Morocco, gilt,	2 50
Full calf, antique, red edge,	3 00
Full calf, rimmed and clasp,	5 00

PIOUS GUIDE TO PRAYER AND DEVOTION.

Containing various Practices of Piety calculated to answer the demands of the devout members of the Catholic Church. 18mo.

cloth,	$0 75
Arabesque, gilt,	1 25
Am. mor., gilt edge,	2 25
Am. mor., full gilt,	2 50
Turkey mor., super extra, 8 plates,	3 50
Full calf, antique, red edge,	4 50
Full calf, rimmed and clasp,	6 00

This Prayer-Book contains the Profession of Faith, Bona Mors Festivals explained, as well as other important things not generally found in prayer-books.

PIOUS GUIDE.

24mo, cloth,	$0 50
Arabesque, gilt,	1 00
Roan, full gilt,	1 50
Morocco, gilt,	2 50
Full calf, antique, red edge,	3 00
Full calf, rimmed and clasp,	5 00

PATH TO PARADISE.

A Selection of Prayers and Devotions for Catholics. 48mo, cloth, $0 20

Arabesque, gilt,	40
Roan, full gilt,	75
Morocco, gilt,	1 25
Full calf, antique, red edge,	1 75
Full calf, rimmed and clasp,	3 00

THE MOST COMPLETE PRAYER-BOOK PUBLISHED.

THE CATHOLIC'S VADE MECUM.

A Select Manual of Prayers for Daily Use. Compiled from approved sources. New and improved edition, reprinted from the last London edition, containing Epistles and Gospels. 500 pages, 24mo.

Arabesque, plain,	$0 75
Arabesque, gilt,	1 00
Roan, full gilt,	1 50
Full morocco,	3 00
Full calf,	4 00

KEY OF PARADISE.

Opening the Gate to Eternal Salvation. 12mo,

cloth,	$0 75
Arabesque, gilt,	1 25
Am. mor., full gilt,	2 50
Morocco, gilt,	3 50
Full calf, antique, red edge,	4 50
Full calf, rimmed and clasp,	6 00

THE POCKET PRAYER-BOOK.

A Prayer-Book for Men. This book is printed from beautiful large type, on extra fine French paper, and, although containing 650 pages, is only ½ inch thick, 3¼ inches long, and 2¼ inches wide. It contains, besides Festival Days, etc., A Summary of Christian Doctrine—Morning and Evening Prayers—The Three Litanies—The Complete Mass, in Latin and English—Vespers—and the Epistles and Gospels.

Arabesque,	$0 50
Arabesque, gilt edge,	75
Roan, gilt,	1 25
Morocco, extra,	2 50
Full calf,	3 00
Morocco, tuck,	3 00

The Pocket Prayer-Book, *without* Epistles and Gospels. Suitable for the VEST POCKET.

Arabesque,	$0 40
Embossed, gilt,	60
Roan, gilt,	1 00
Morocco,	1 50
Full calf, limp,	2 00
Morocco, tuck,	2 00

The "Nonpareil" of Prayer-Books.

THE "RED LINE" POCKET PRAYER-BOOK FOR MEN.

Arabesque, gilt edge,	$1 00
Roan, full gilt,	2 00
Morocco, extra,	3 00
Full calf,	4 00

Large Type Prayer-Book.

MANUAL OF CATHOLIC DIVINITY.

WITH EPISTLES AND GOSPELS. 18mo.

Arabesque, plain,	$0 75
Arabesque, gilt,	1 00
Roan, full gilt,	1 50
Morocco, extra,	3 50
Full calf, extra,	4 00

The People's Pictorial Lives of the Saints, Scriptural and Historical. Abridged, for the most part, from those of the late Rev. Alban Butler. In packages of 12 each. One packet now ready, containing the lives of twelve different saints. Per packet, 25 cts. These are got up expressly for Sunday-school presents.

Packets of Scripture Illustrations. Containing Fifty Engravings of Subjects from the Old and New Testaments, after original designs by Elster. Price, loose packages of fifty, 75 cts.

Twenty Illustrations of the Holy Gospels. Done in colors after original designs. With appropriate texts, 25 cts.

Illuminated Sunday-School Cards. Ten Cards in each Packet.

First series, net,	30 cts.
Second series, net,	50 cts.
Third series, net,	30 cts.
Fourth series, net,	30 cts.

SUNDAY-SCHOOL CLASS-BOOKS.

The Catholic Teacher's Sunday-school Class Book. No. 1, paper, per dozen, 1 00
The Sunday-school Class-books. Cloth, No. 2, per doz. 2 00

Address

www.ingramcontent.com/pod-product-compliance
Lightning Source LLC
Chambersburg PA
CBHW051240300426
44114CB00011B/823